GEOMETRY FOR ART

Author and Creator - Steve Smith
Editor - Heath Burr
Art Director - Robert Voyvodic
Published by - Atum Media

For additional information contact HB@atum.tv

ISBN# 979-8-9890820-0-1

CONTENTS

OVERVIEW

Geometry for Art is designed to expose a number of methods that can be used in art creation. I show methods and techniques I have utilized. I would like to debug the perception that math and geometry are scary places for artists to tread. I like to have all the tools I can, at my beck and call. It is part of being efficient and getting the best results.

At an early stage I was intrigued by graph paper. I will be discussing grids as a structural device. There are a number of ways to create and use grids beyond graph paper.

Color By Numbers - an invention of ArtToyz Studios - is a method of "filling in" these grids. Counting with colors on grid is one of my main ways to use geometry. Tessellations will be covered as another method.

Sacred Geometry has been used by artists and craftsmen since ancient times. It is either rudimentary geometry or represents rudimentary concepts through geometry. Many define it as what can be created with a ruler and a compass. I will illustrate how it has influenced my work.

ArtToyz Studios has been creating fractals and fractal software since 1979. A fractal involves geometry that has been copied and modified with a set of rules. Natural geometry uses fractal concepts.

Isometric perspective has a relationship to optical illusions. My discussion involves hexagonal structured grids of triangles and in pseudo 3D, as it actually does not use "perspective" in the traditional sense. I will leave the subject of 1, 2 and 3 point perspective for other books on the subject as well as other forms of Optical Illusions.

Following my interest for simple rules of color and geometry to create art, I will cover Neo-Plasticism. Piet Mondrian is one of the designers of this art style, which actually dominates architecture and can be expanded into areas beyond the rectilinear.

The Realism section explores combinations of geometric art with figurative art. Software and compositing are discussed.

I will explore animation with 2 and 3D geometry. Temporal motion will lead us out of the book into online examples. I have animations that utilize grids and fractals. I will discuss some delivery options.

Throughout the book I will engage the reader with art techniques that can be implemented with traditional and digital methods. So get your pencils, rulers, and computers ready.

DRAWING BOARD

It seems a lot can be done with a ruler, pencil and paper.

I have read that sacred geometry can mostly be done with a ruler and compass. A ruler with holes in it is a form of a compass. Graph paper can be utilized in many ways. And you can invent your own "graph paper" of course.

Let's start with a piece of "sacred Geometry" studied by Leonardo DaVinci - Golden Rectangles.

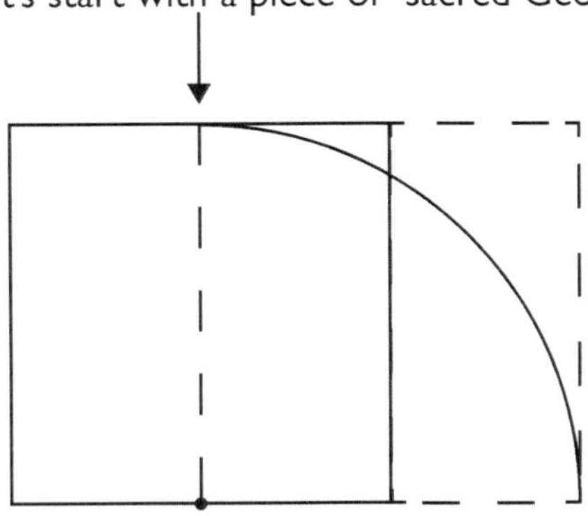

Start with a square. Four sides of equal length.

Find midpoint.
Try folding a strip of paper the length of one side in half.

Arc created from midpoint with compass.
Original square plus extra area is The Golden Mean, or Phi Ratio.

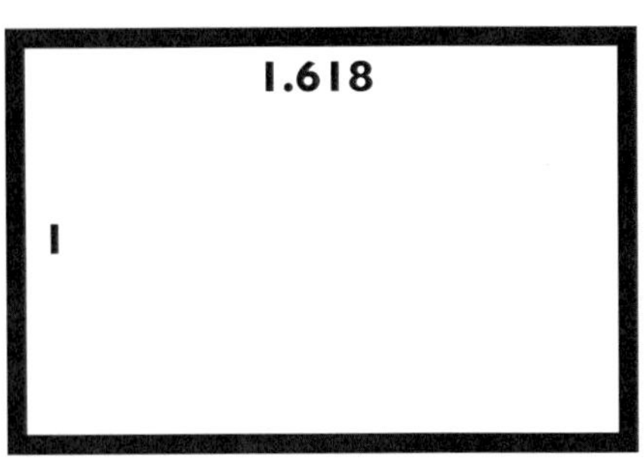

Golden Ratio: 1 x 1.618

Ratio can be used to extract either new dimension at any size. Just cross-multiply and divide to find a missing dimension. In this example I might only have a 12 inch" wide strip of canvas. I will solve for how long to cut the other dimension.

$$\frac{1}{1.618} \times \frac{12 \text{ inches}}{? \text{ inches}}$$

1.618 x 12 divided by 1= 19.416 inches

This can be applied to any missing dimension. Keep inches with inches, pixels with pixels, etc.

I have also created small Golden Ratio rectangles and used a diagonal through opposite corners to find larger proportional variations.

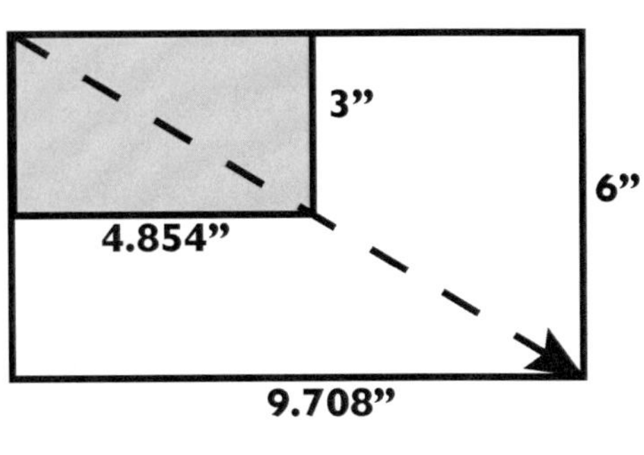

These proportional relationships are invaluable to artists working on rectangular surfaces. The technique illustrated on the left also allows for any proportions to be used to crop into other shapes and for scaling. If I want to use a rectangle projected over a photo or sketch to crop it, I can then use this technique again to upscale to any size canvas or surface, with proportions. I usually get out the calculator and cross-multiply and divide. I write the ratio out on paper with known measurements and X to solve for.

USING TOOLS TO DO THE MOST ACCURATE JOB

The computer is just another tool for artists. For some it is the only one. Many of the designs in this study would not be possible without computers (and programming). How you incorporate computing devices is up to you, based on accessibility, comfort level, and personal interest in streamlining art processes. In the Golden Ratio explanation above, a lot boils down to simple math done with a calculator (or yes - a piece of paper) to create custom dimensions within aspect ratios. Software (or programming) could be utilized.

Image processing software makes a good calculator for aspect ratio. Crop or create a 16 x 9 aspect image and then resize it to a dimension you were looking for with a lock on the dimensions. for a TV format. Truly simple.

There are lots of possibilities, but we want to work with files that can be modified and re-purposed easily. This is not the realm of pixels, paint and photos. AI will enhance this someday. The vector tools I am speaking of are a subset of 3D graphics and can be utilized in 3D programs at some point if desired. This object-oriented, vector software is preferable for designers because it can be scaled without degradation. It exists in a different category from computer paint and products such as GIMP and Photoshop. Vector graphics are quite small in data size compared to raster (pixel) graphics.

I will mention some software here. Adobe Illustrator is one of many vector graphics products that allows for quick, accurate design creation with this point by point (vector) approach. Microsoft Office and Corel Draw also have a good set of accurate image creation tools. Many 3D modeling and animation softwares have great 2D vector tools included. I make some of my designs in EscherSketch, ArtToyz Studios homemade solution.

One thing to look for in vector software are snaps. I want to quickly draw on grids and snap to vertices (points). Adobe Illustrator snaps to centers and edges as well. You may also need regular polygons, such as hexagons and octagons, in addition to squares and lines.

Computer Graphics takes patience, thought and skill, as well as knowledge of the software "ins" and "outs". You can use scanners, printers, and other devices effectively to size, transfer and save designs.

I often do quick sketches on small pieces of paper, then they are scanned or photographed so that I can place them and freeze them in the background (of Illustrator for instance). Then it is easy to do a cleanup layer with vector geometry with the sketch as a reference - an electronic light table. There are many other tools and techniques for this.

Once a design is ready, it can be sized for output. Adobe Illustrator has a print mode that allows an 8 X 10" design to be scaled across multiple 8.5 x 11" pages accurately. These can then be taped together for a large version of the original. When I create stained glass designs I use this a lot. I also make at least 2 copies in B&W of my design. For stained glass I cut on one and I assemble on the other. I also commonly have a color master, either as a .jpg file or as a color print.

All this just gets transferred to the next software for artworks that remain computer generated from this point on. Really simple, clerical practices can be utilized for efficiency and streamlining art processes. Save everything and document as much as you can. I often save variations of art in progress so that I can return to one point and take a different direction later. I also save mistakes and other alternative ideas for later research and fun.

If you are an artist and don't involve yourself with computers, consider this. Documentation should be digital. Photos of artworks should be digital. All artists should tap computers to organize their collections and work on promotions, entering exhibitions and a variety of other reasons.

OK, now we should look at some concepts.

GRIDS

RECTANGULAR GRIDS

Rectangles have a connection to human stability and order. They are the basis for a lot of architecture as well as wall art. They are our TV's and our windows in our buildings. Our book pages and our photos. Our containers and storage. Rectangular grids are the most straightforward of design guides. The most common rectangular grids are composed of square units (graph paper). This is a helpful way to design floor plans as well as other items. Grids help allow for accurate measurements and alternate views with matched scale.
They can easily extend into 3-dimensional space with cubic grid structures or as the topology of 3D models. They allude to and can directly imply infinity. The cells of a regular grid can be filled with anything. It is tempting to explore patterns. In fact, the majority of patterns repeat on 4-way grids.

Try using graph paper to make patterns. Get out the markers. Make a pattern, follow a rule to get there, go random, try something else, it's fun.

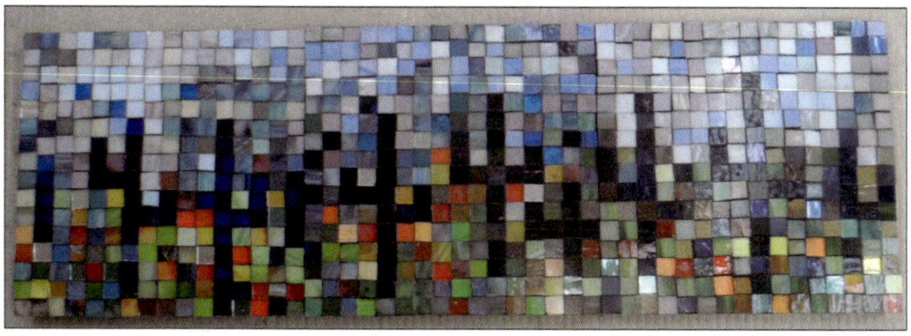

1.1a. Saguaros, Glass Mosaic, 12" x 36", 2003.

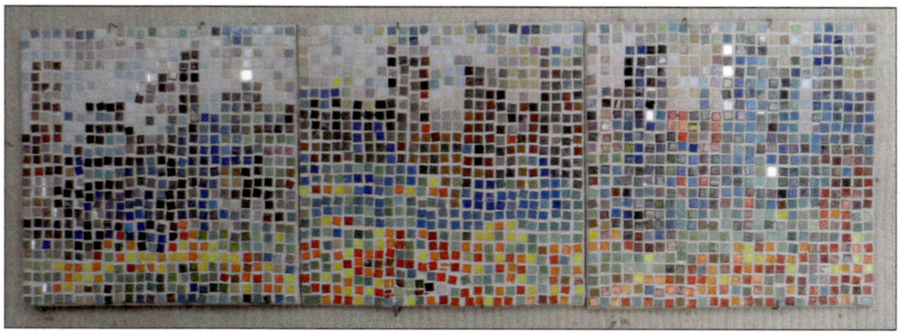

1.1b. Cityscape, Glass Mosaic, 12" X 36", 2003.

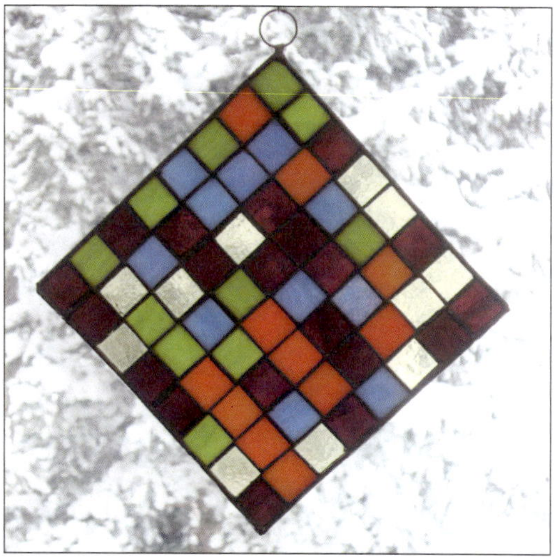

1.1c. Color By Numbers Liner Spiral, Stained Glass, 12" x 12", 2013.

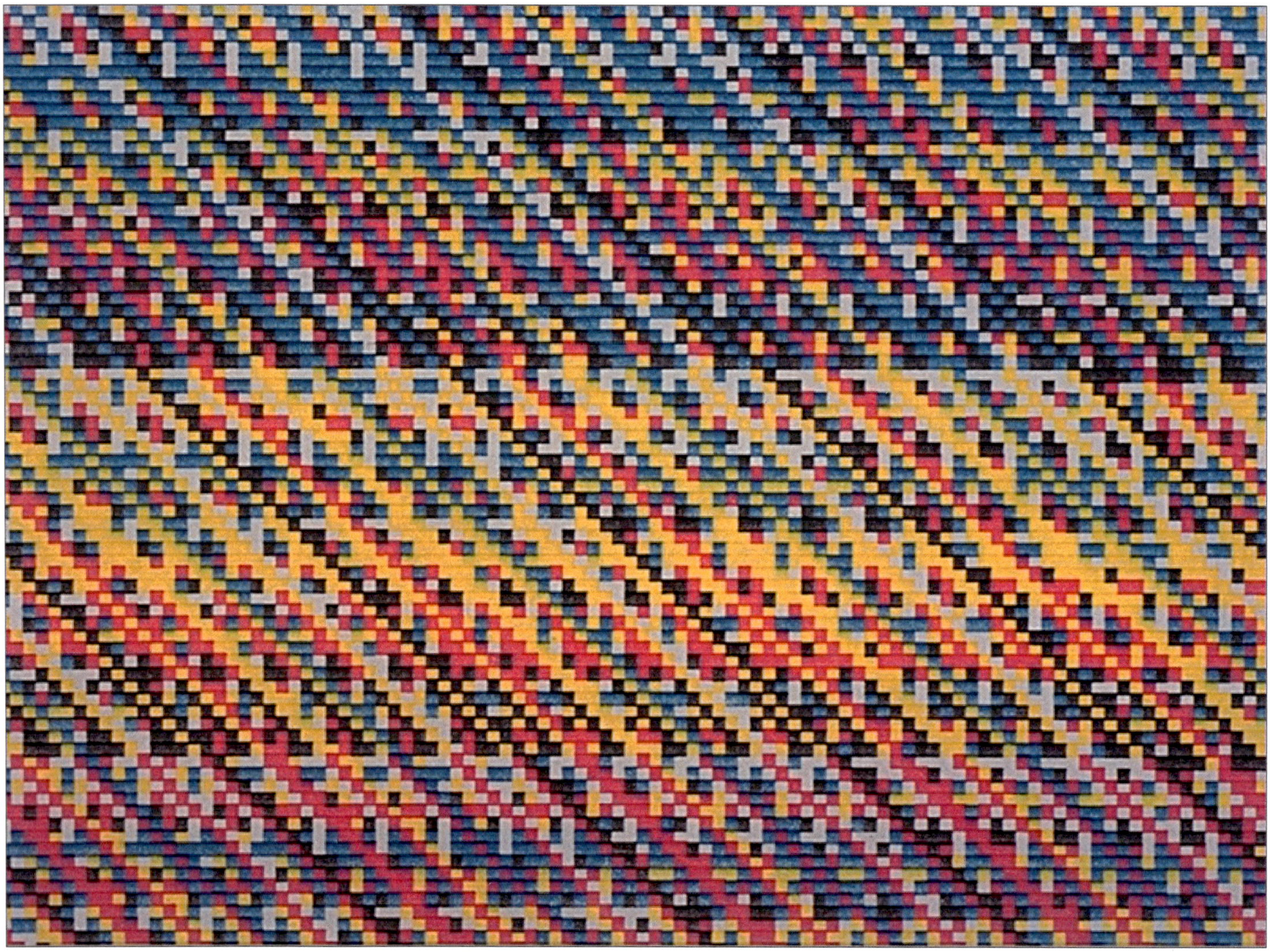

1.2. Color By Numbers Linear, A five color pen plot from my own computer program, 8.5" x 11", 1979.

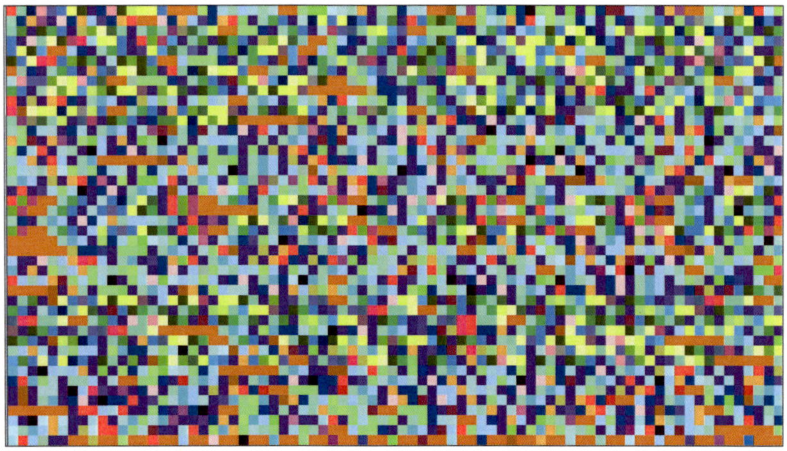

1.3. Excerpt from "The Tibetan Book of the Dead", Digital - Letters Encoded into Colors 783 x 442 Pixels, 2014.

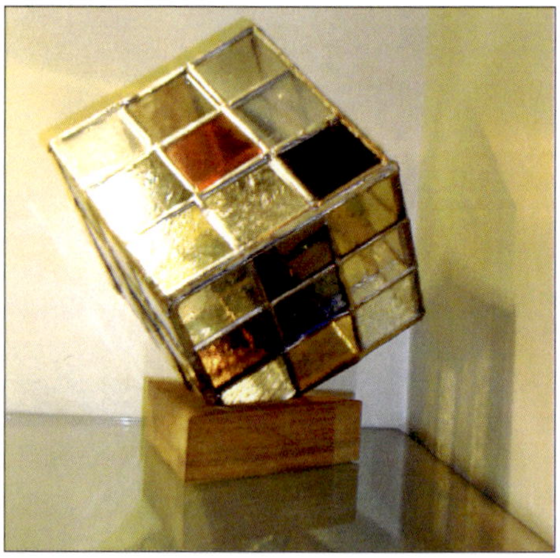

1.4. Cube Color By Numbers, Stained Glass, 9" x 9" x 9", 2018.

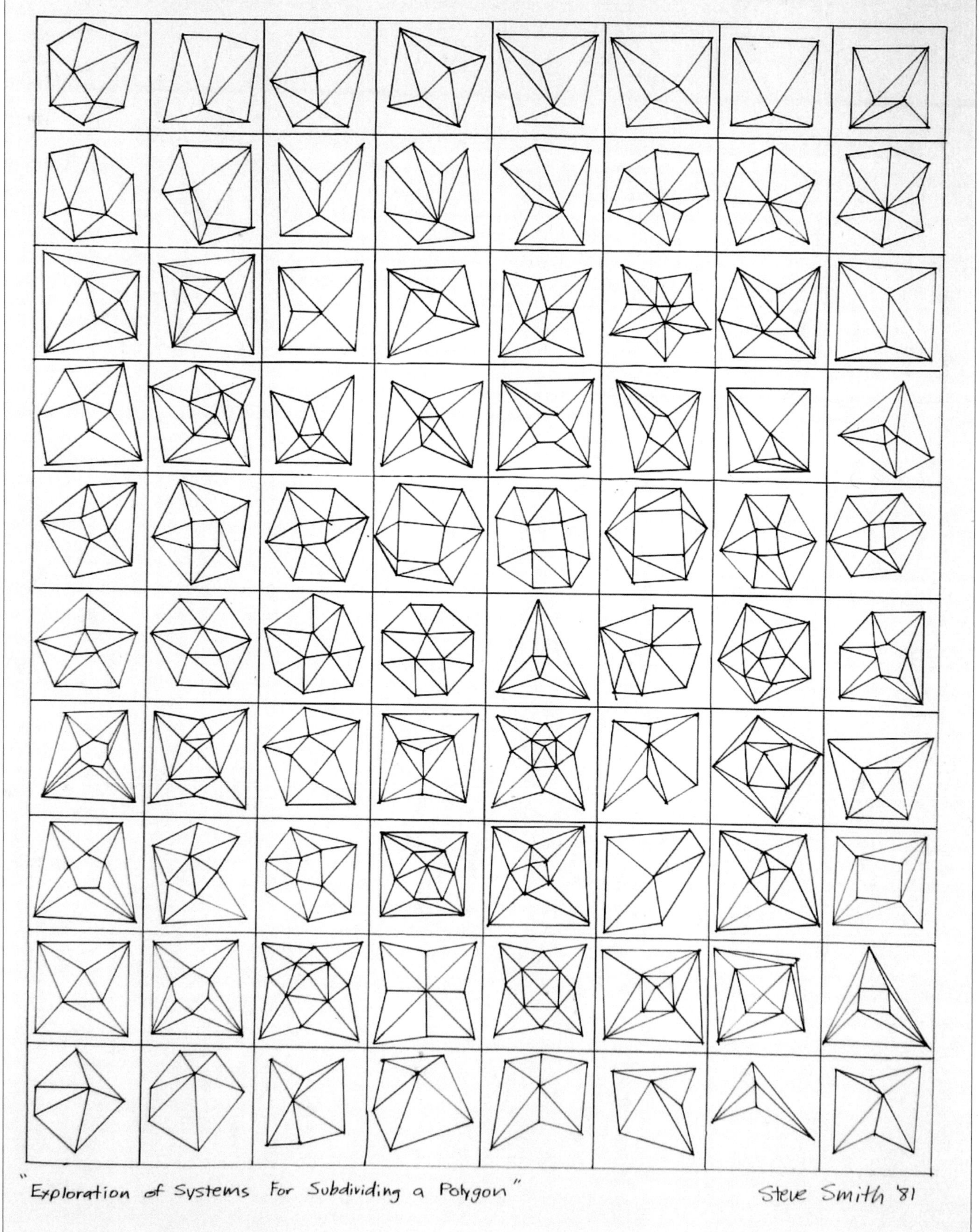

1.5. Exploration of Systems for Subdividing a Polygon,
Pen on Paper, 18" x 24", 1981.

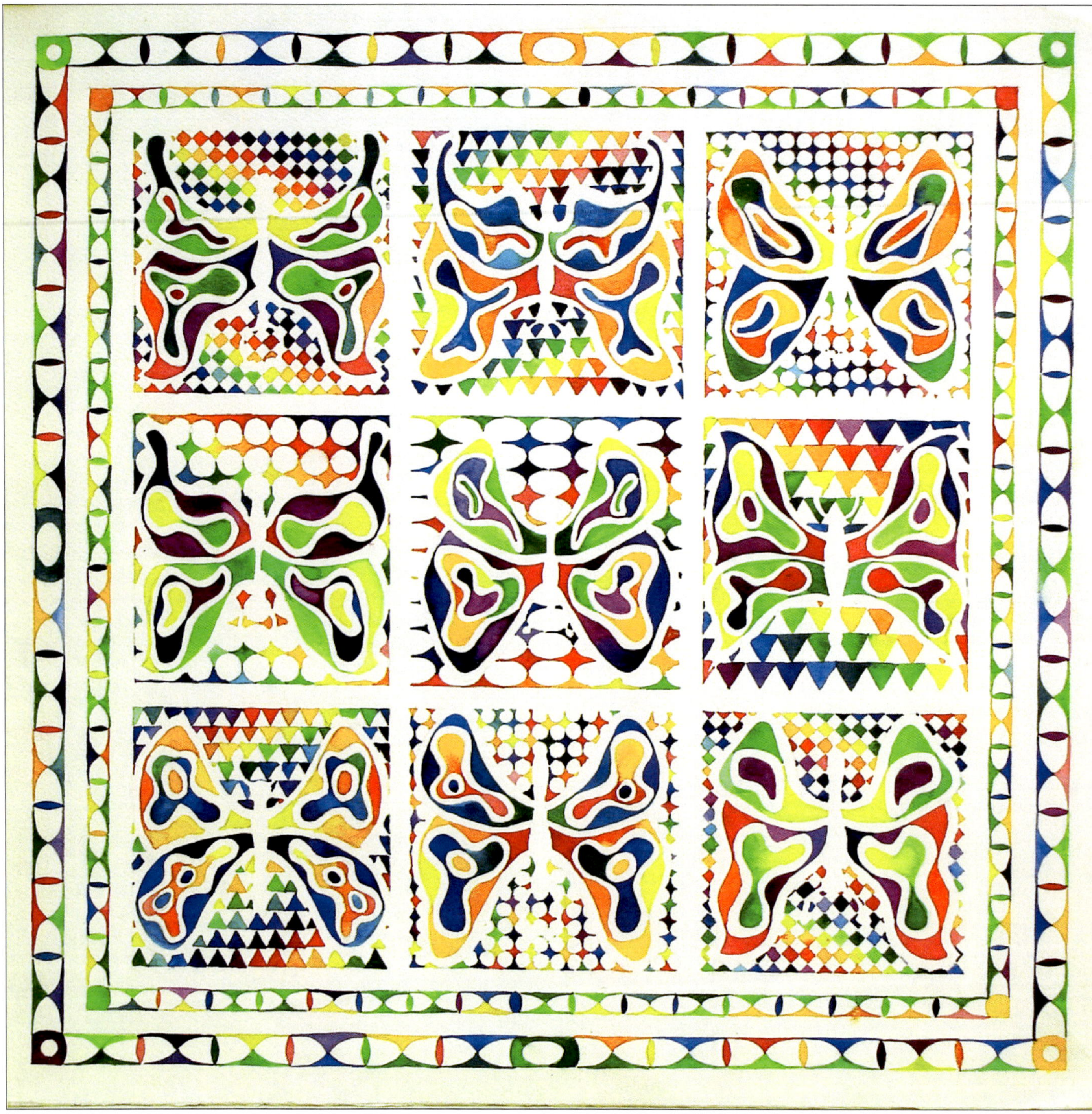

1.6.

Butterflies,
Watercolor,
24" x 24",
1978.

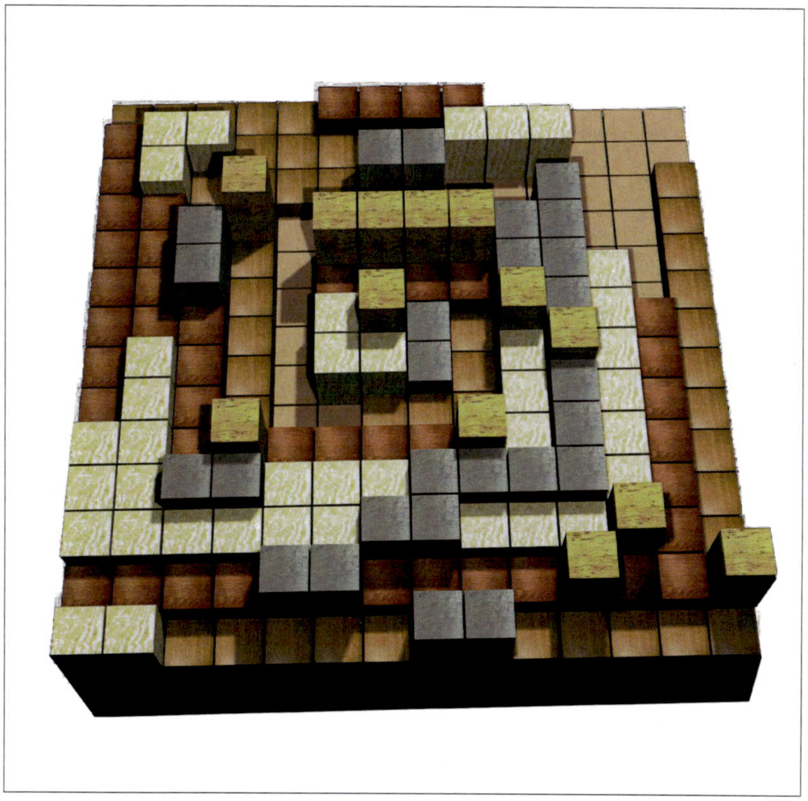

1.7.

A prototype of a Color By Numbers design executed on a 3D Cubic Grid, Digital, 2019.

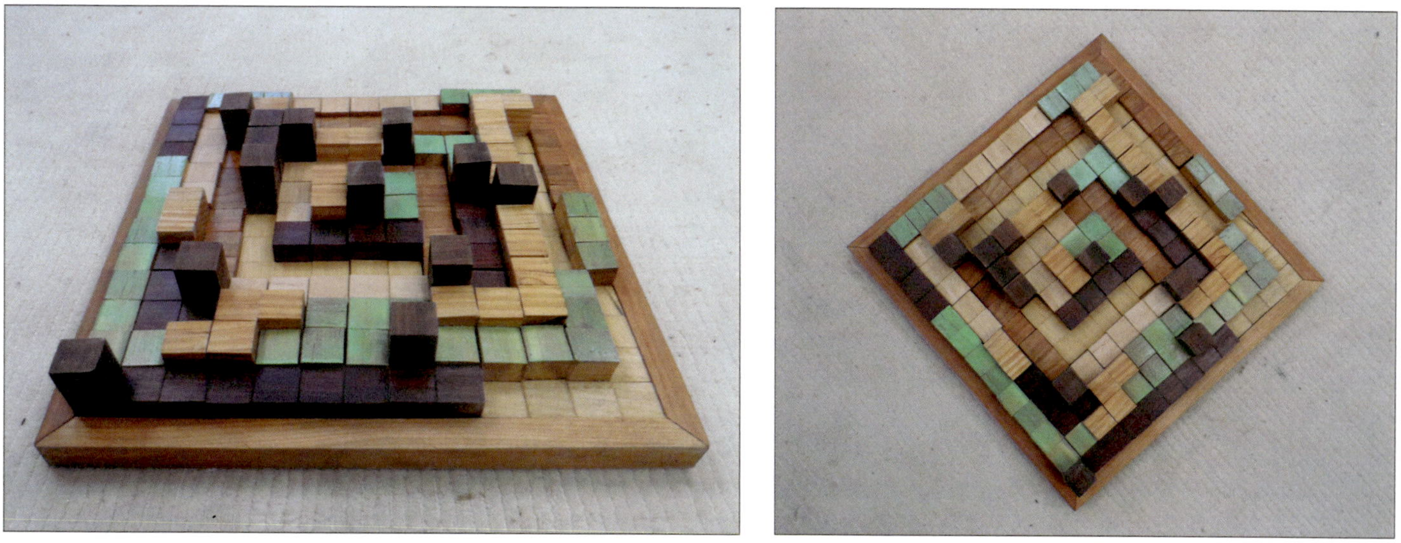

1.8. Two views of Color By Numbers Spiral, Various Types of Wood, 14" x 14", 2019.

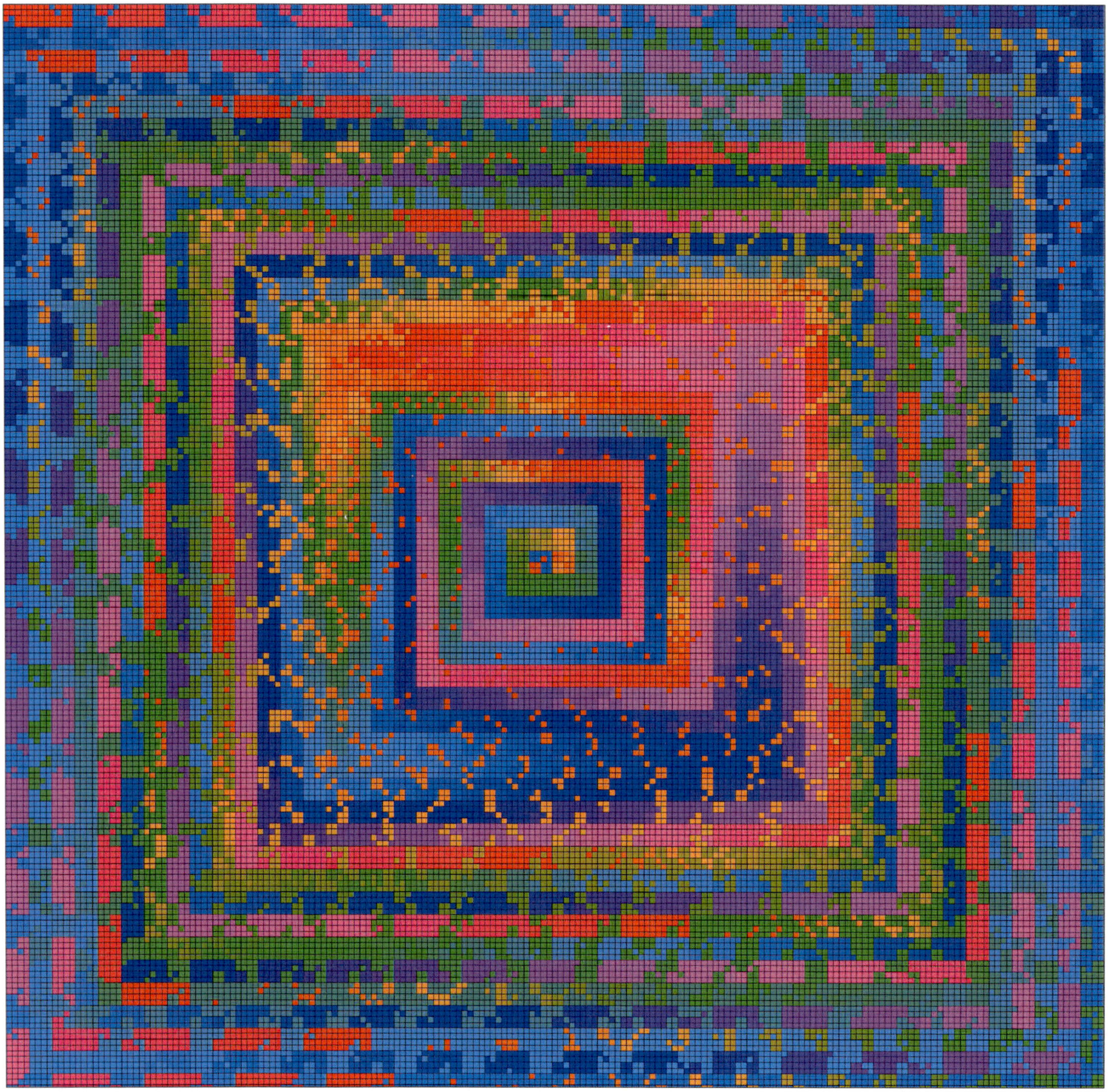

1.9. Color By Numbers Spiral, Digital, 4332 x 4332 Pixels, 2019.

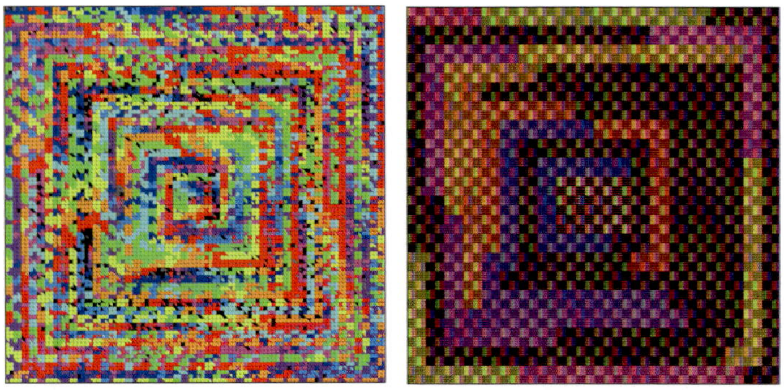

1.10a,b.

Color By Numbers Spirals, Digital, 2000 x 2000 Pixels, 2019.

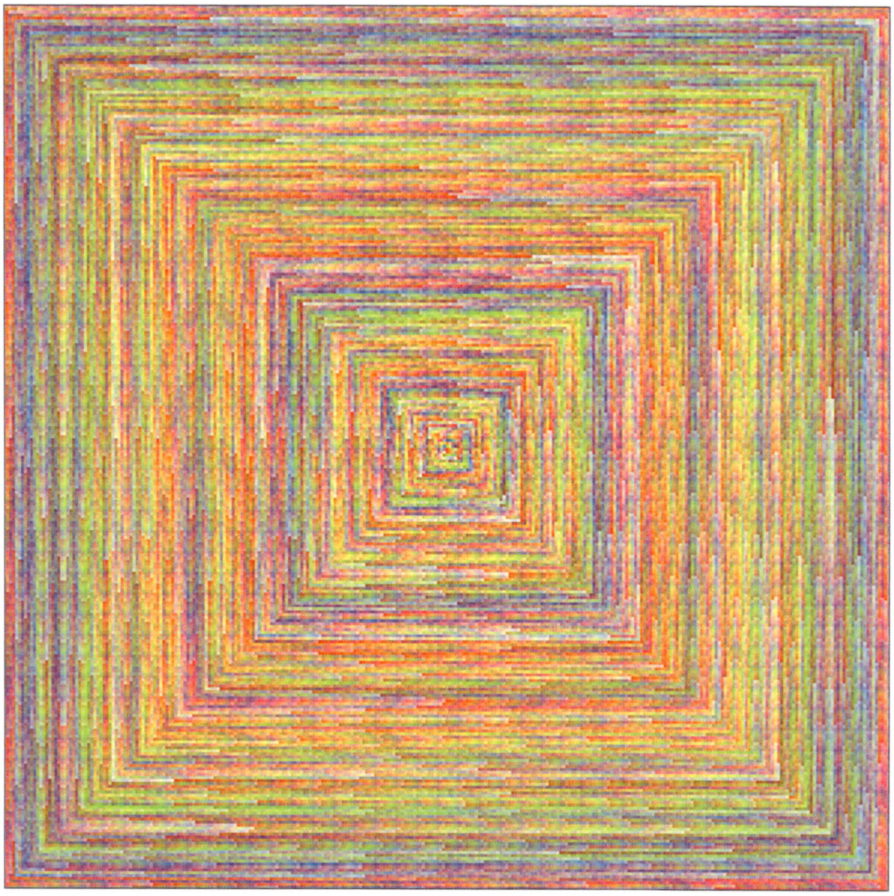

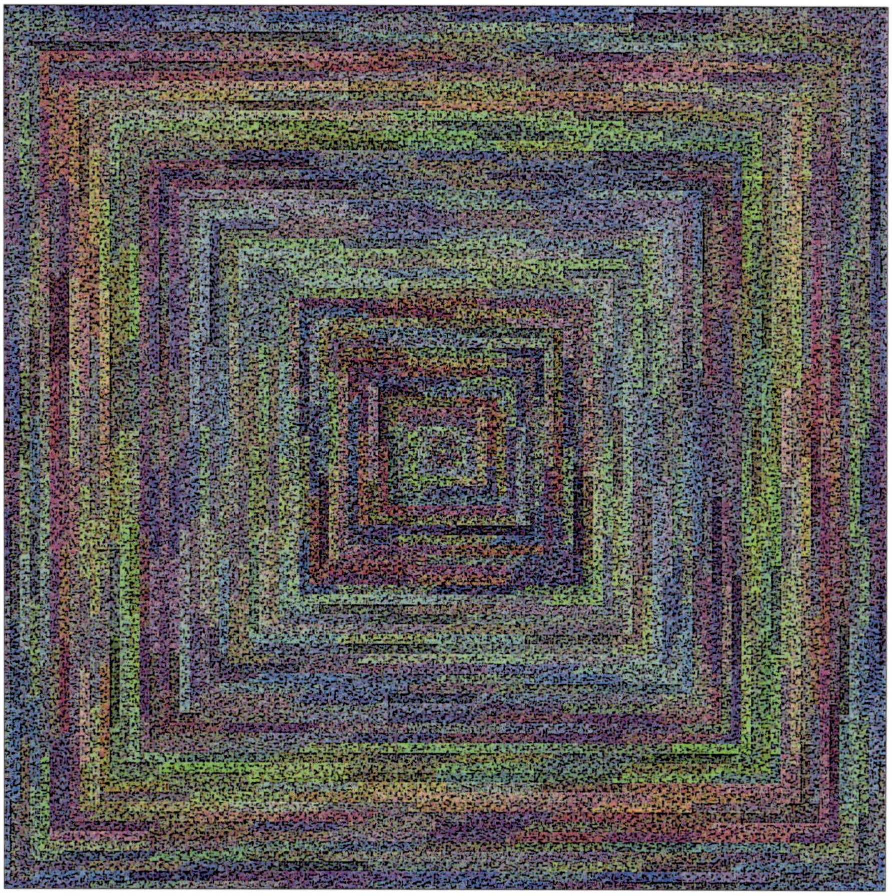

1.10.

Color By Numbers Spirals, Digital, 2000 x 2000 Pixels, 2019.

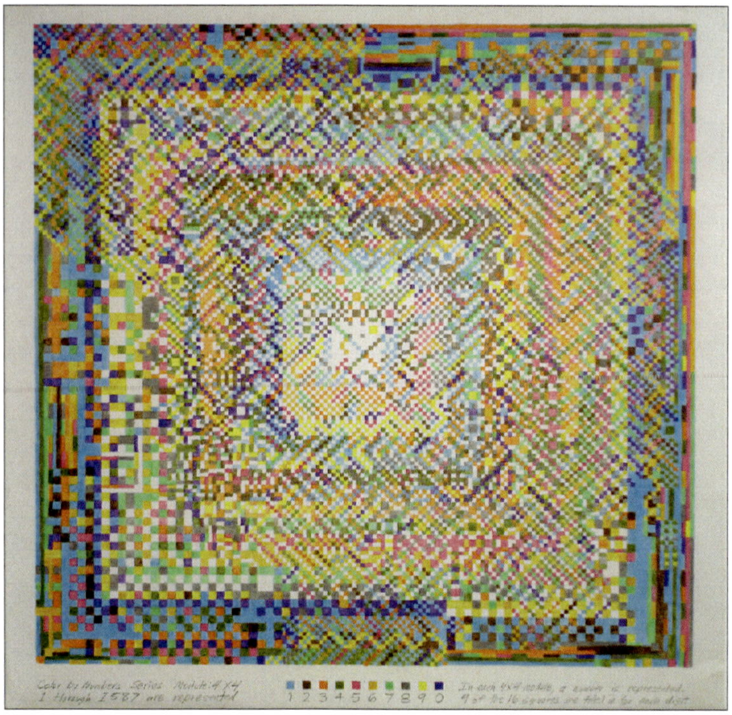

1.11. Color By Numbers Series Module: 4 x 4, 1 through 1587. Colored Pencil on Graph Paper, 18" x 18", 1980.

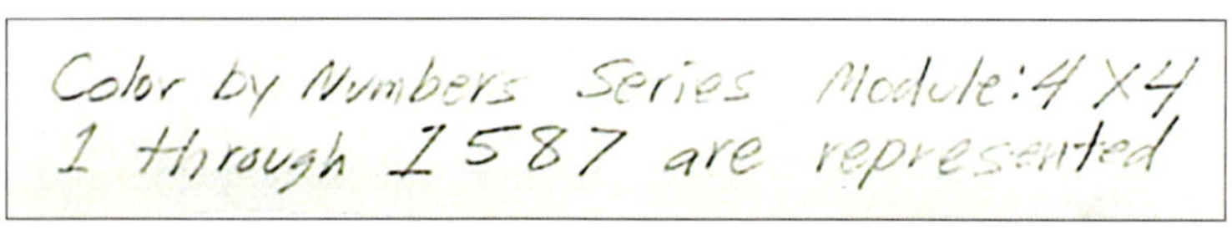

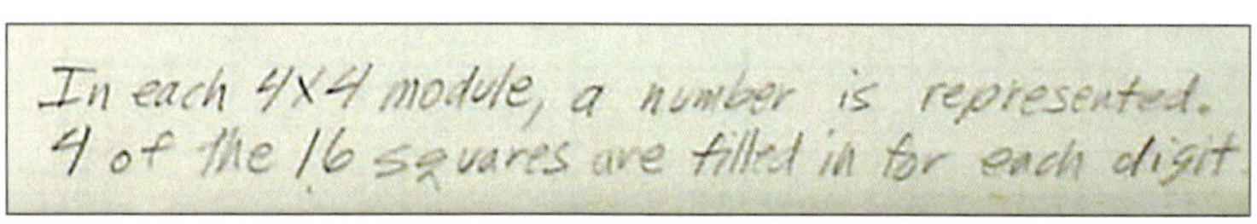

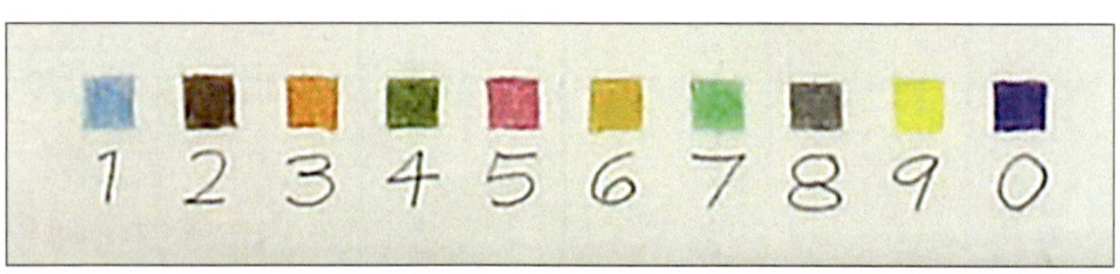

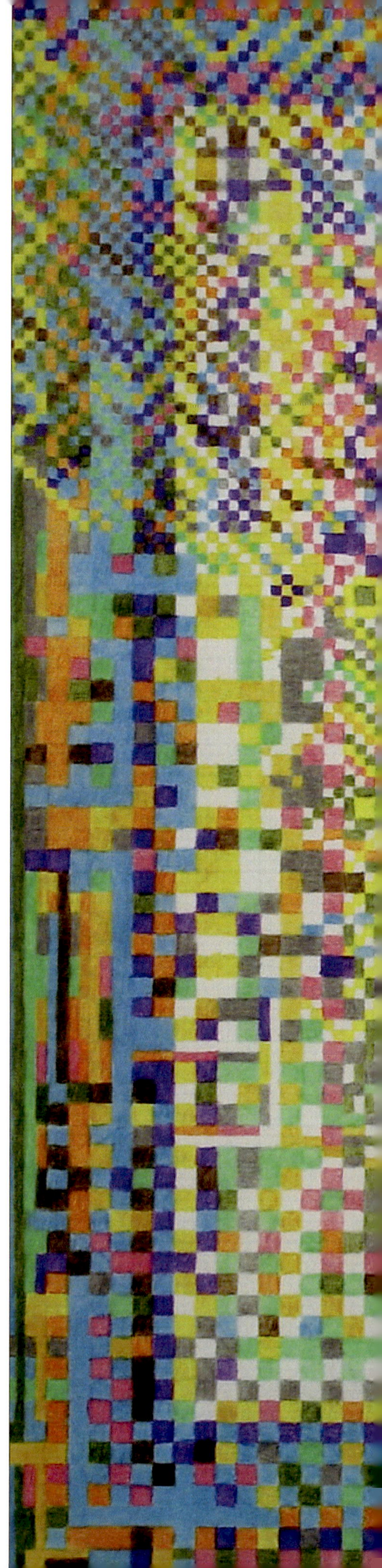

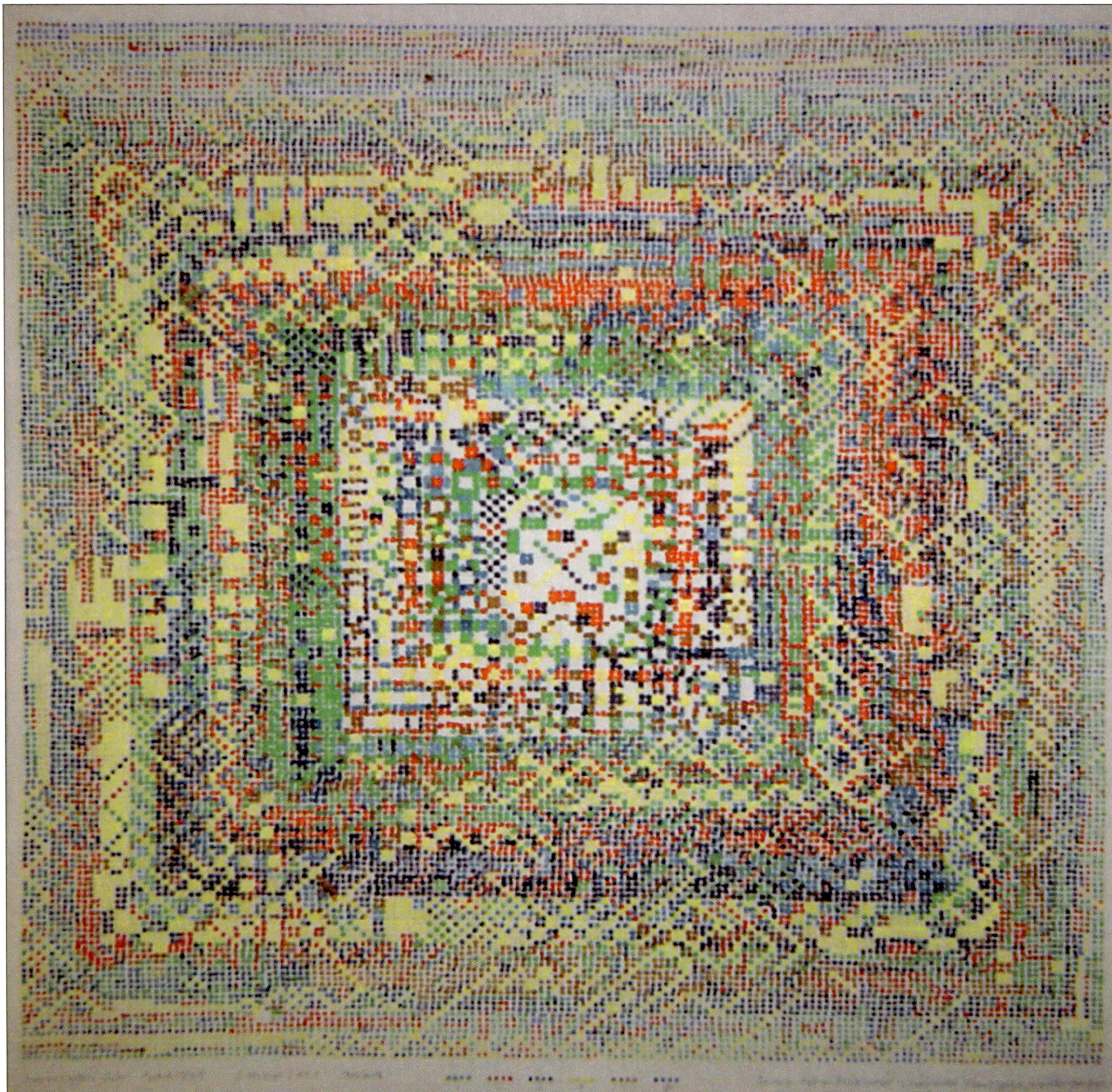

1.12.

Color AND Pattern By Numbers,
Acrylic on Canvas, applied through an industrial mesh, 3' x 3', 1990.

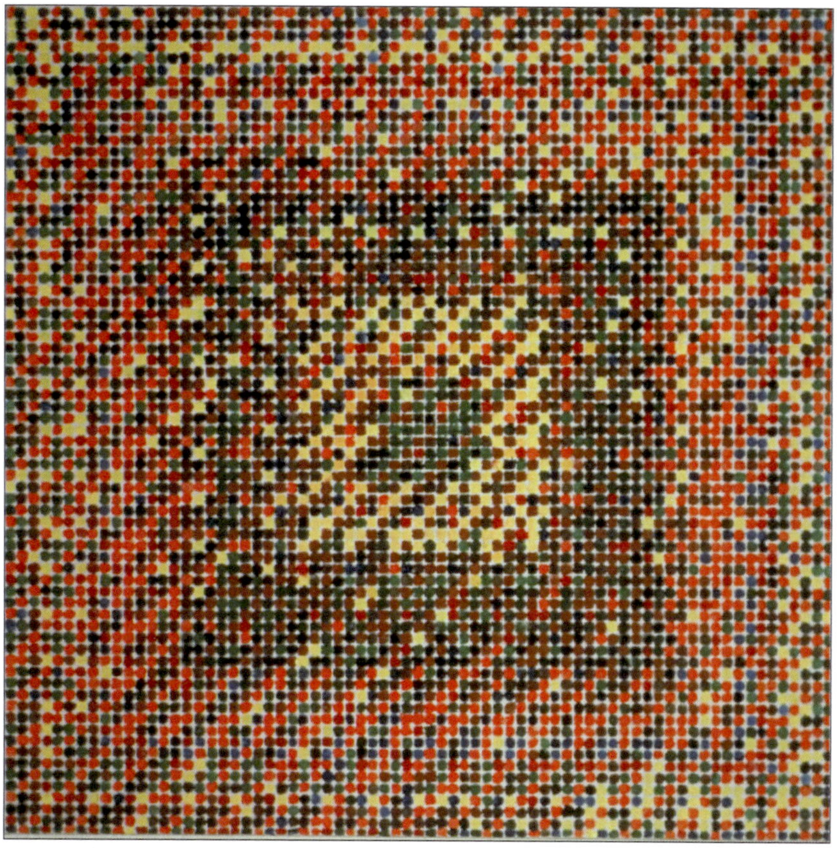

1.13.

Color By Numbers Spiral,
Acrylic on Canvas, 4' x 4',
1980.

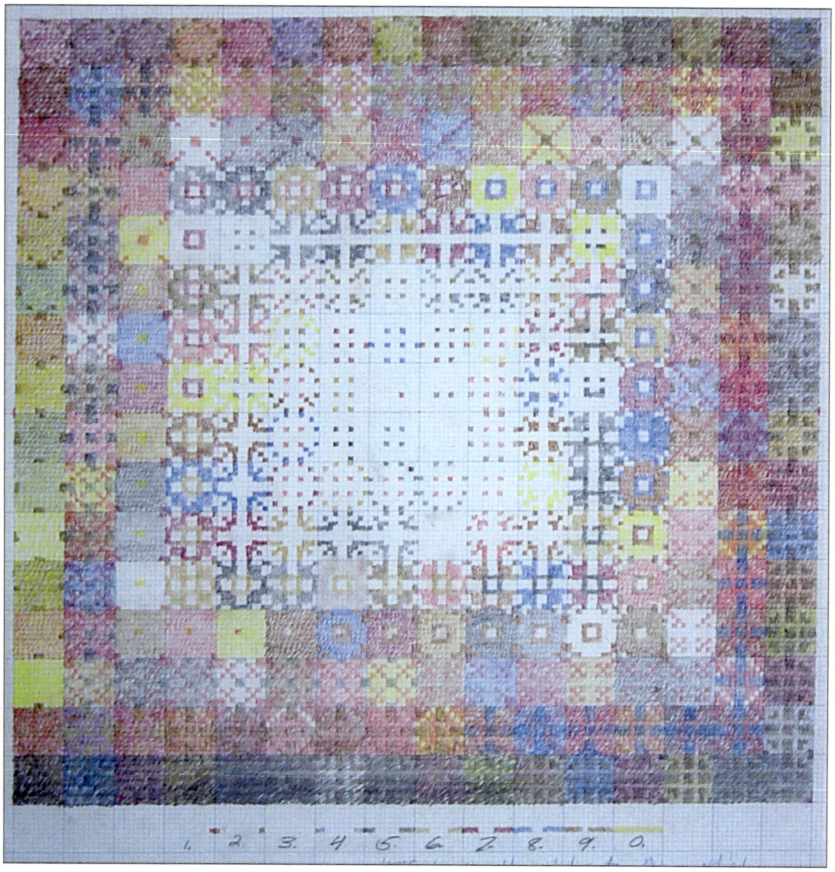

1.14.

Color By Numbers,
Pencil on Graph Paper, 22" x 24",
1979.

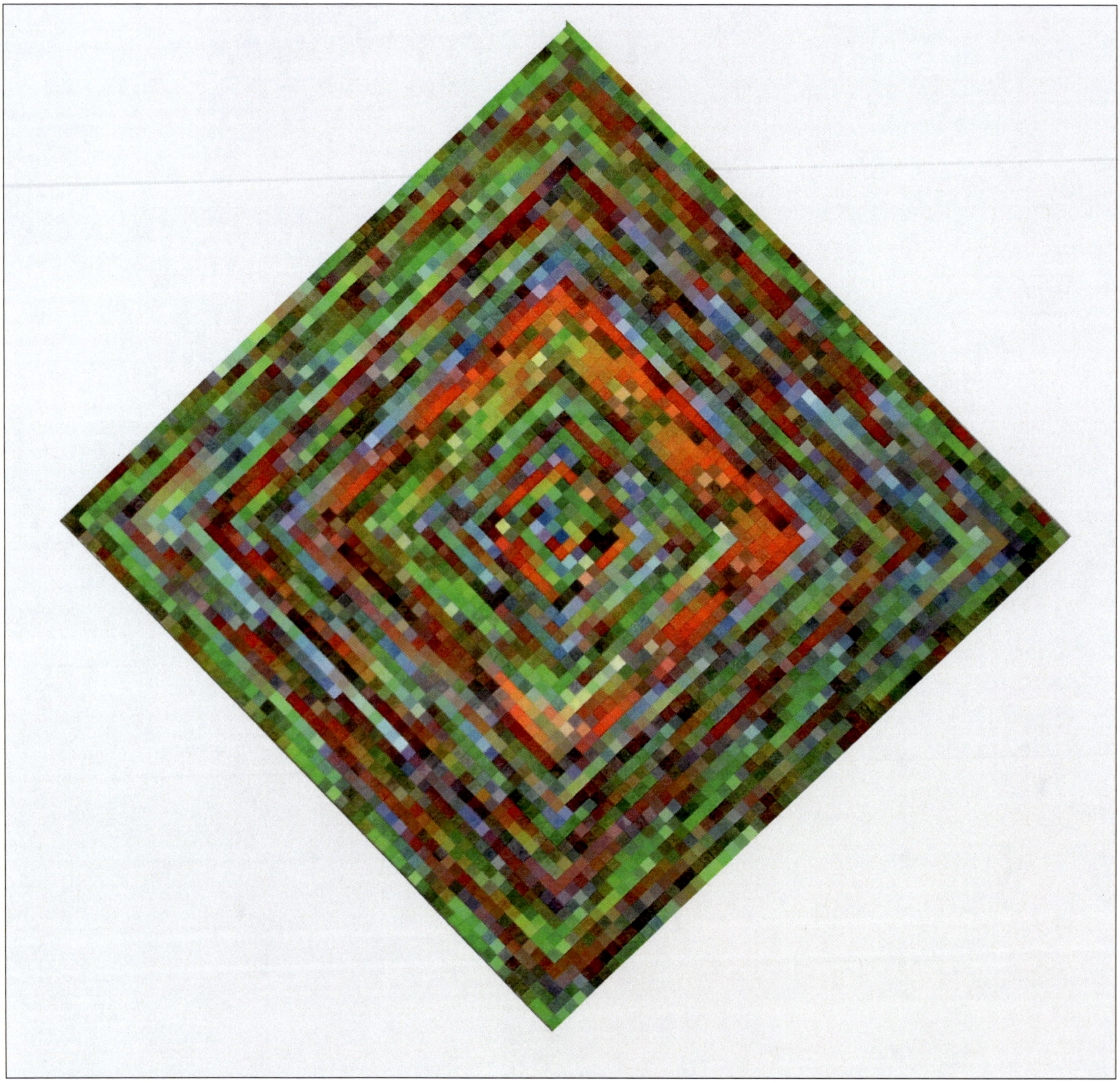

1.15. Color By Numbers Blended Spiral,
Acrylic on Canvas, 3' x 3' 1998.

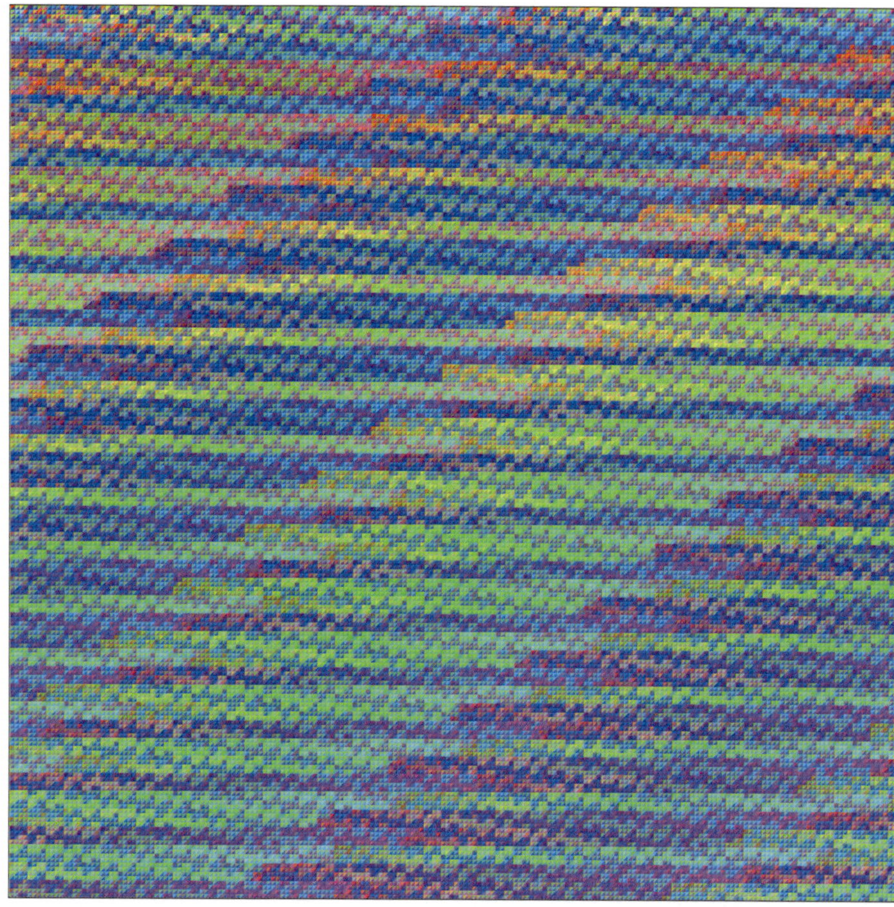

1.16.

Color By Numbers Linear on Sliced Square Grids, Digital, 2000 x 2000 Pixels, 2019.

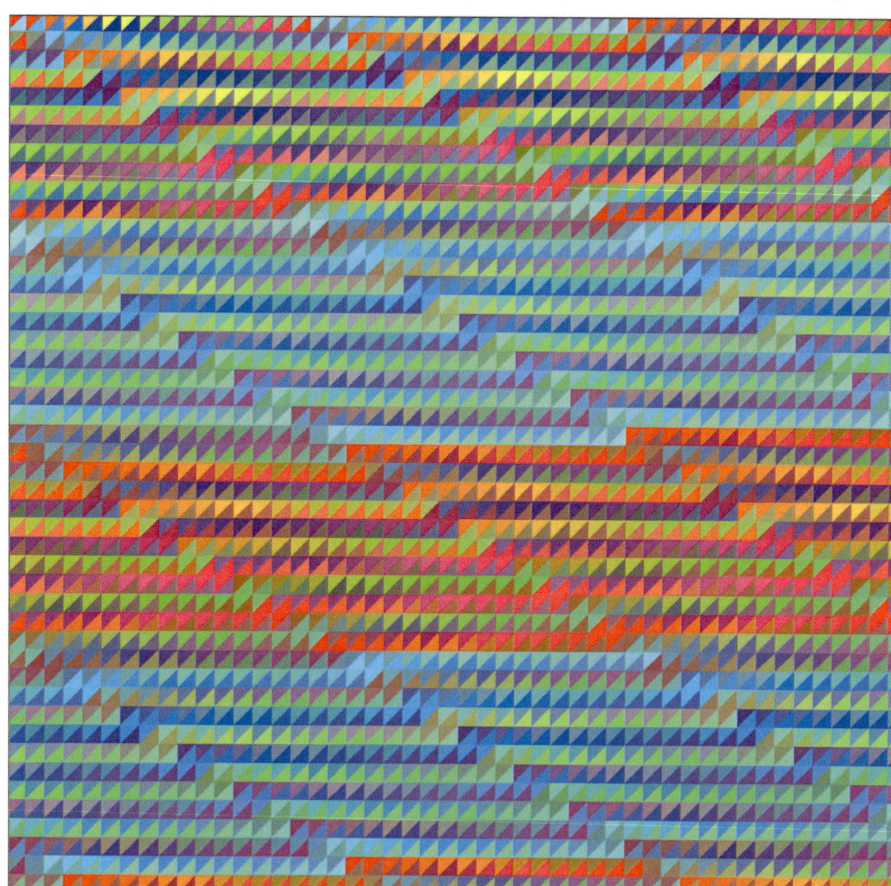

1.17.

Color By Numbers Linear on Sliced Square Grids, Digital, 2000 x 2000 Pixels, 2019.

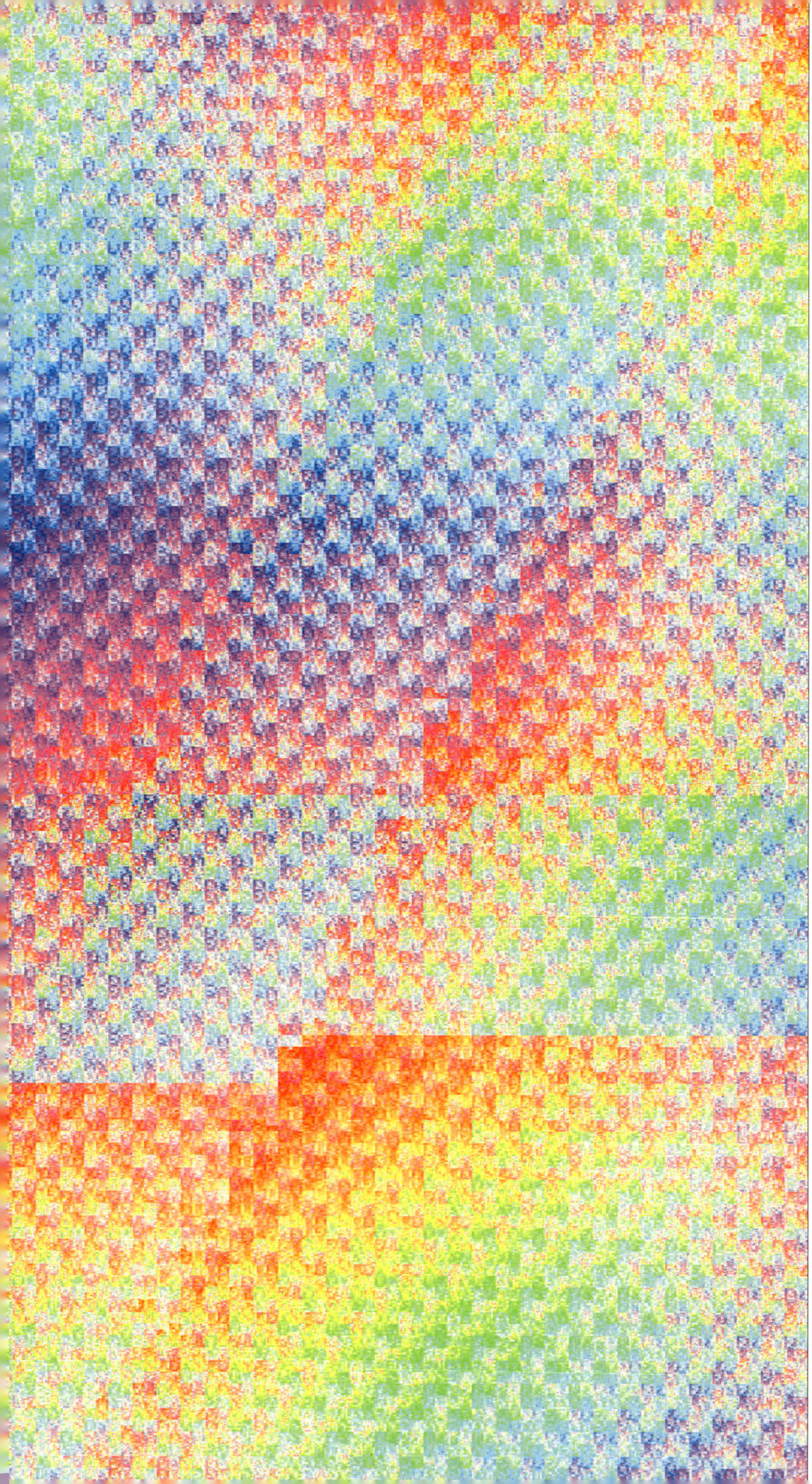

1.18.

Color By Numbers Linear, Digital, 2400 x 1600 Pixels, 2019.

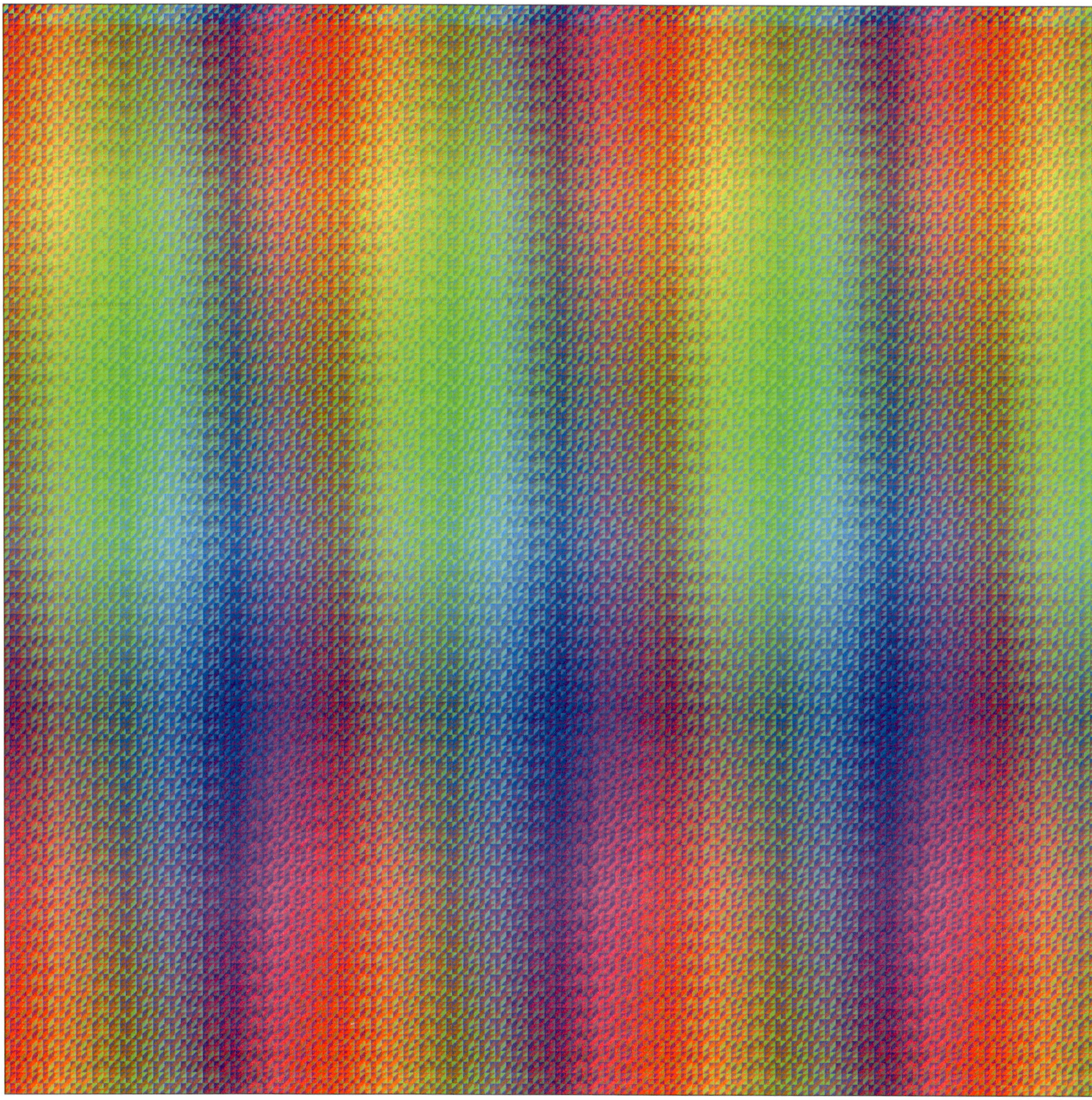

1.19.

Color By Numbers Linear, Digital, 2018 x 2018 Pixels, 2019.

1.20.

Color By Numbers Linear, Digital, 2018 x 2018 Pixels, 2019.

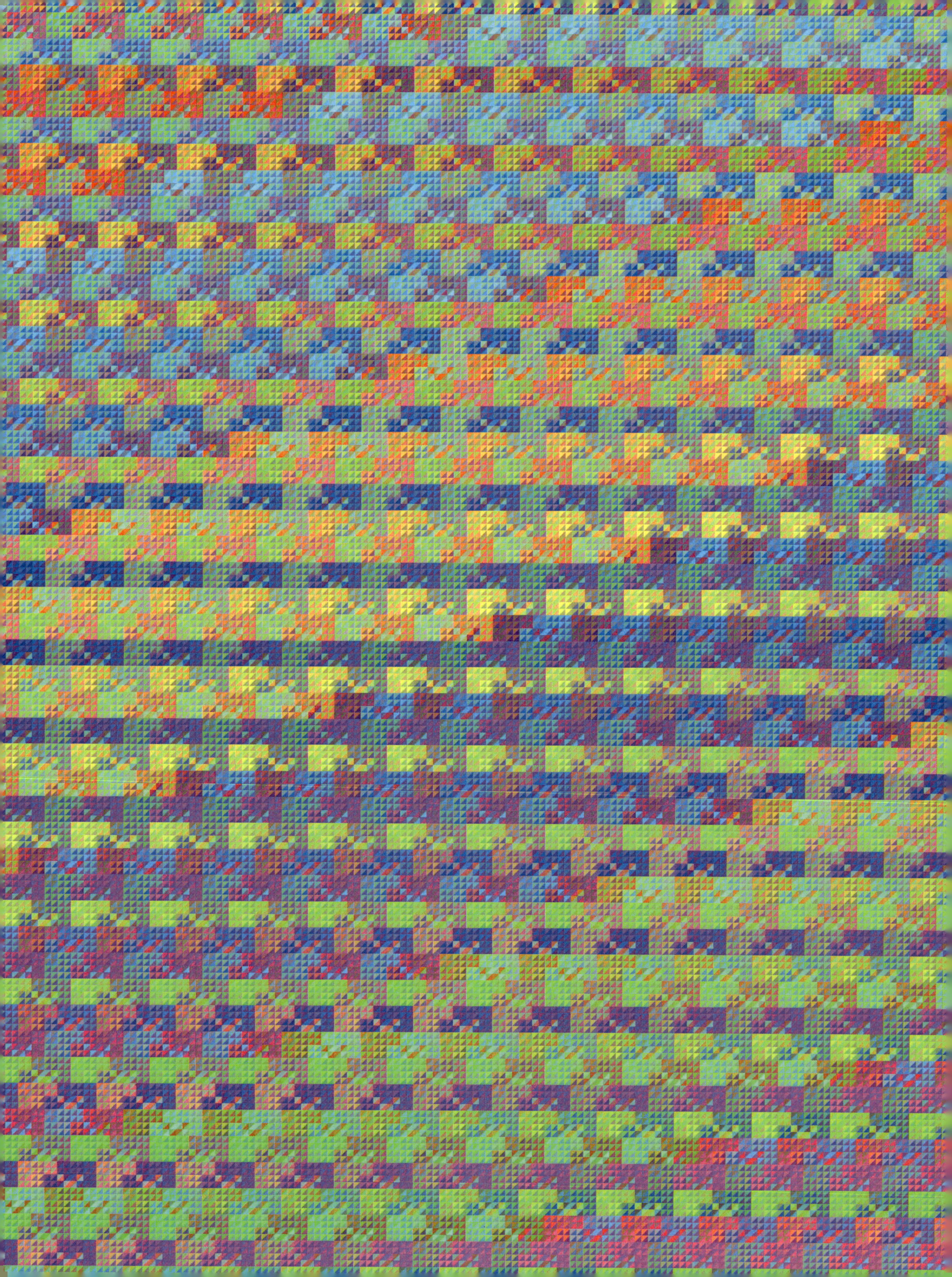

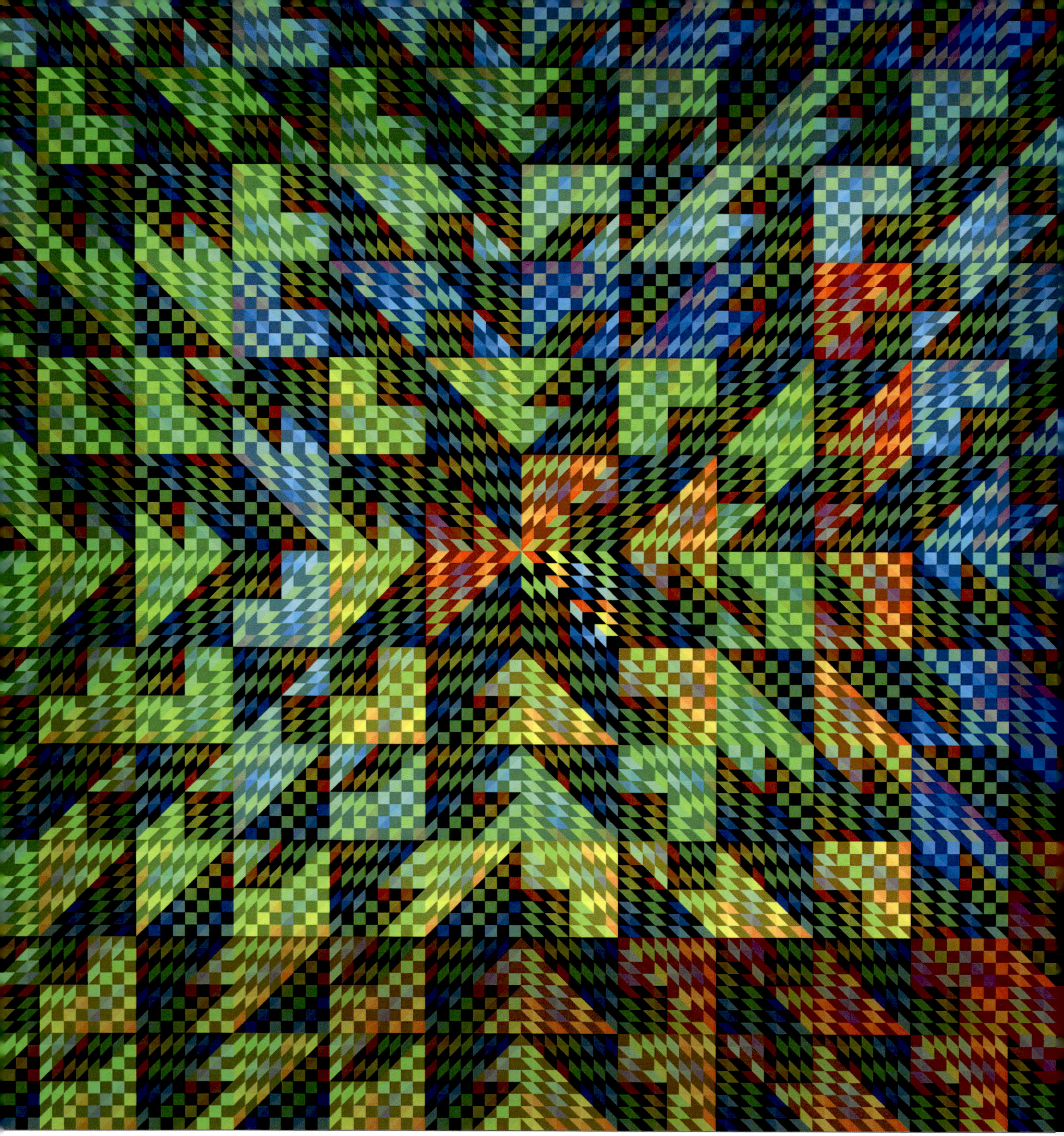

1.21.

Color By Numbers Spiral,
Digital, 3234 x 3234 Pixels,
2019.

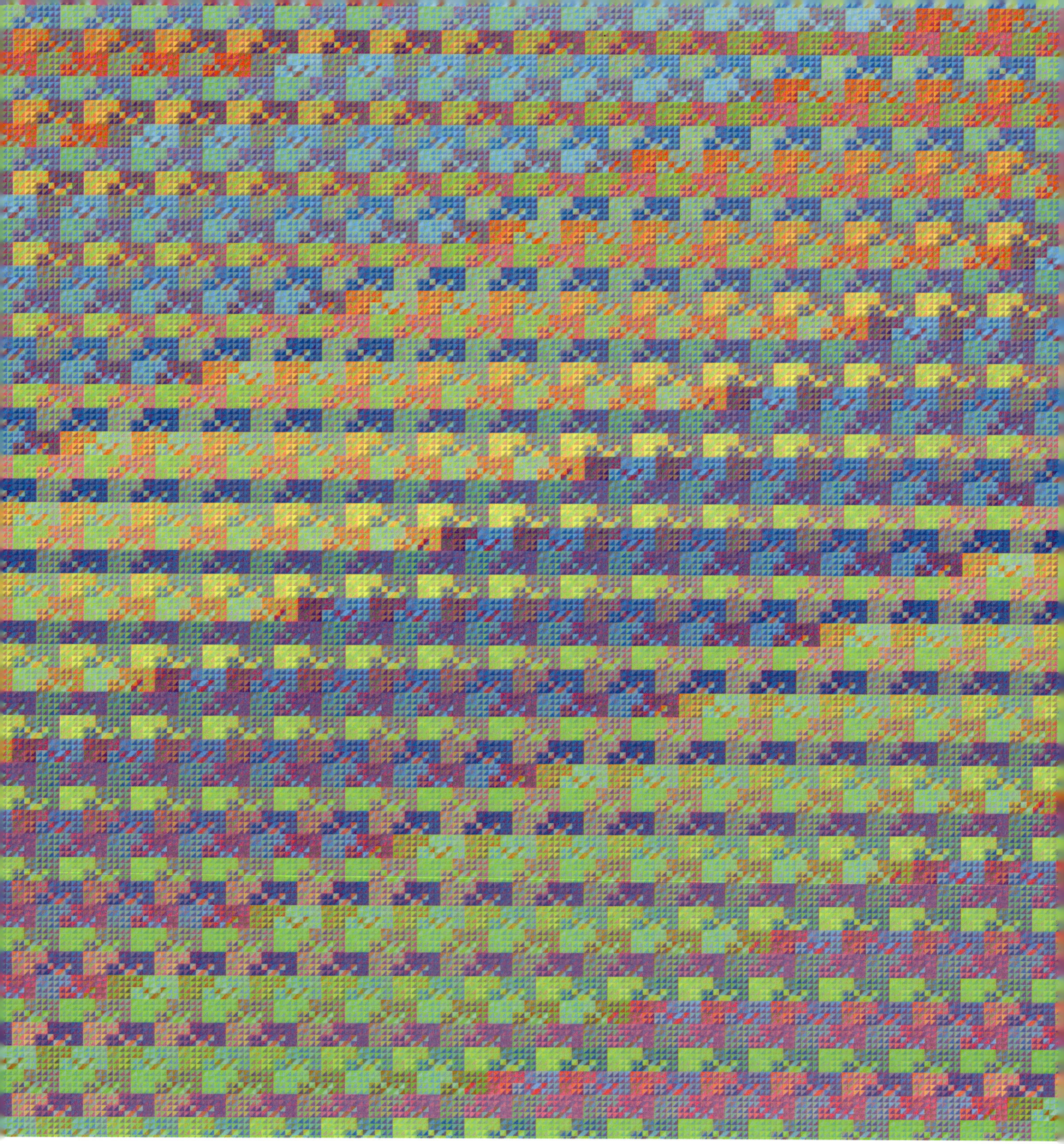

1.22.

Color By Numbers Spiral,
Digital, 3234 x 3234 Pixels,
2019.

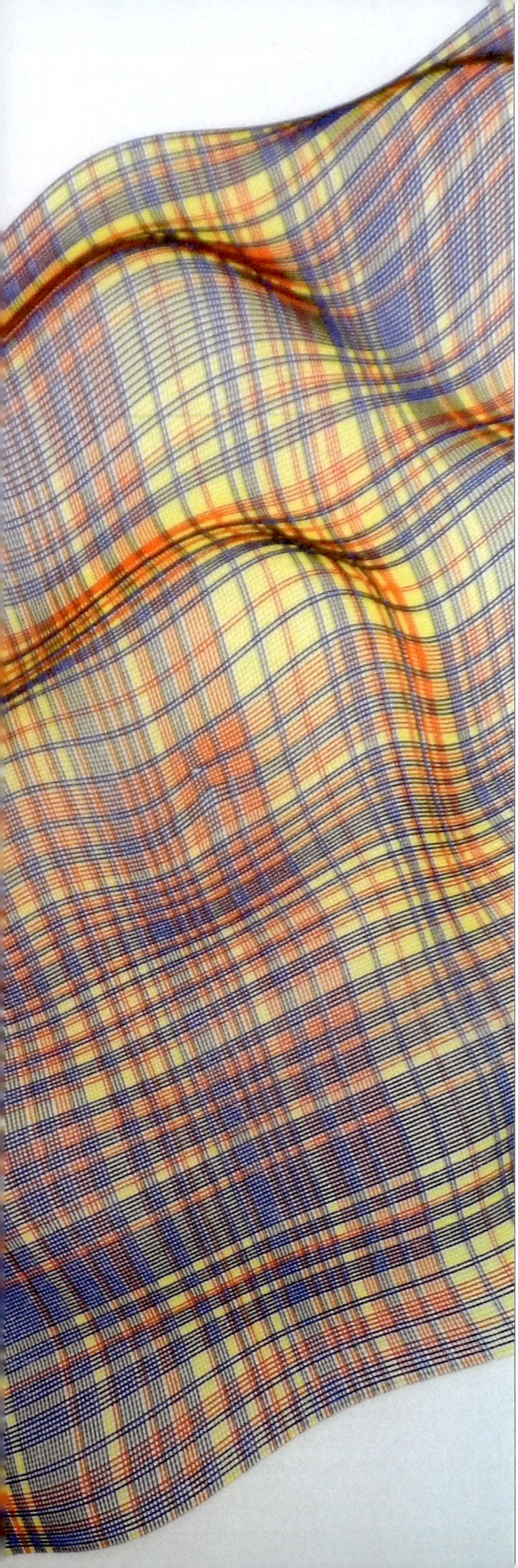

Rectangular grids are ready-made for plaids.

Plaids result when horizontal and vertical lines are intersected as in a weaving.

On the next page are illustrations using the Color By Numbers counting system with counting imposed on the horizontal and vertical lines to create plaids.

These computer graphics were created in 1980, before pixels and raster graphics were widespread. They are examples of the high accuracy and simple color related to vector graphics.

I could not draw these well by hand.

1.23.

Plaid Wave,
HP Pen Plot, 8.5" x 8.5",
1980.

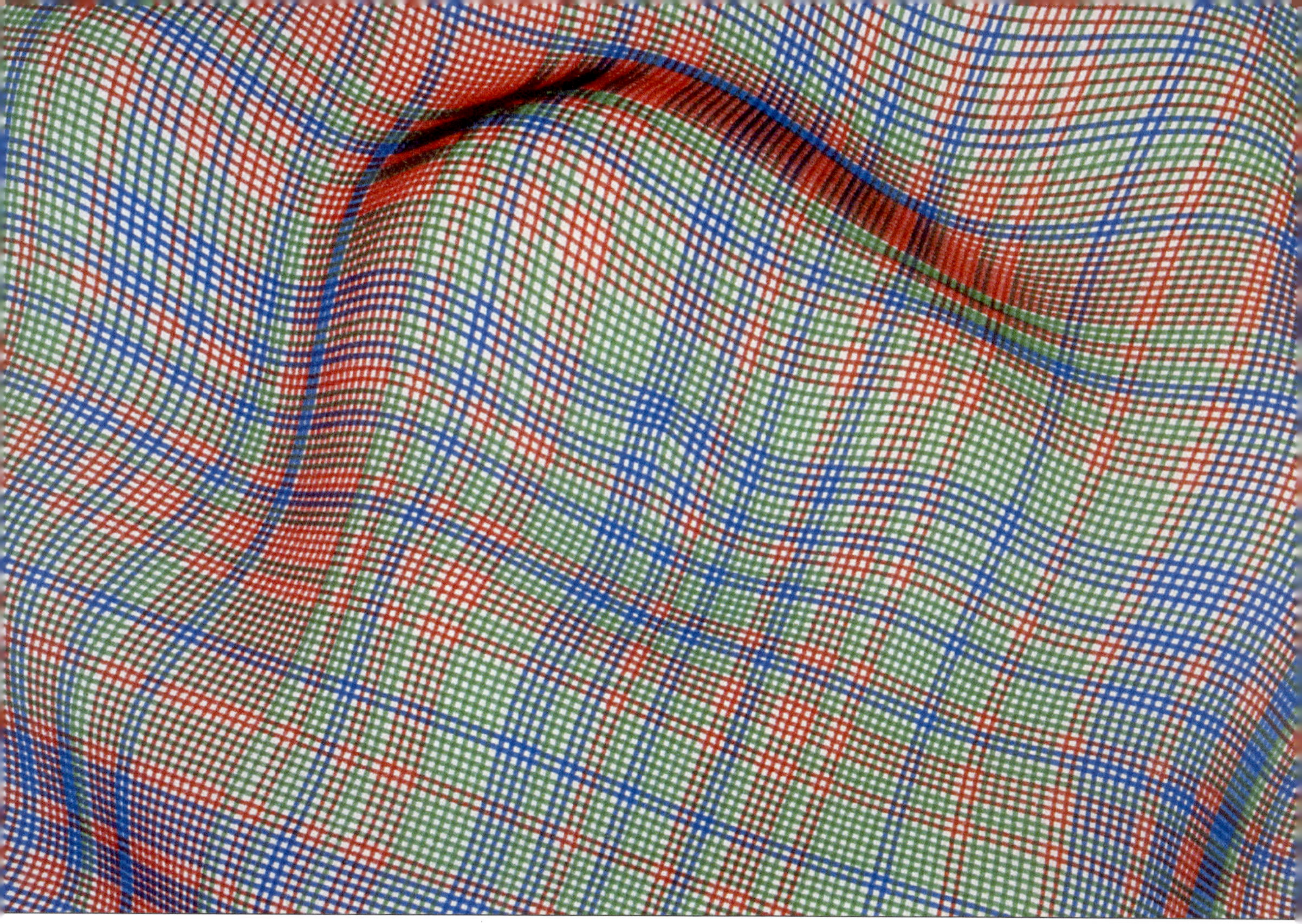

1.24. Cropped View of a Plaid Wave, HP Pen Plot, 8.5" x 8.5", 1980.

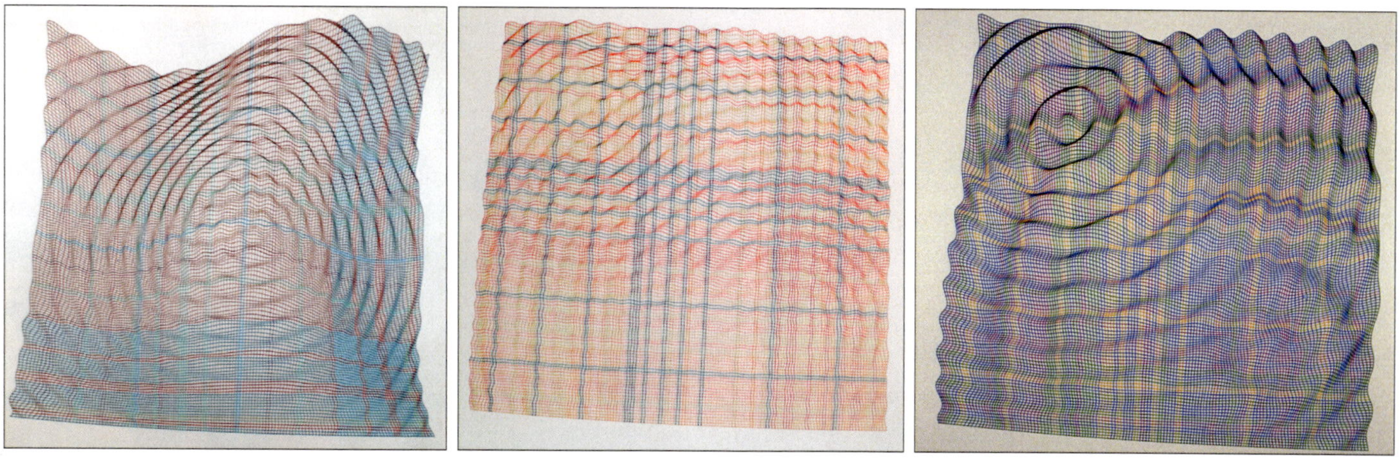

1.25. 3 examples from the Color By Numbers Plaid Splash Waves Series, HP Pen Plots, 8.5" x 8.5", 1980.

TRIANGULAR GRIDS

Triangular grids have similar properties to rectangular grids and are less often seen in designs. For instance if you look at the equilateral triangle grid to the right you can count 4 triangles along the bottom edge. There are 4 times 4 or 16 triangles in the grid. Just like there are 16 in the 4 x 4 square grid next to it. All grid lines are parallel with the outer edges and evenly spaced. Look for these triangle grids in the art design of science fiction shows.

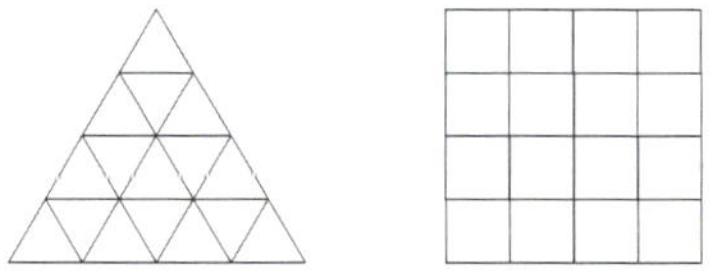

1.26 Simple grids above. Six triangle grids combined to create a polar grid below.

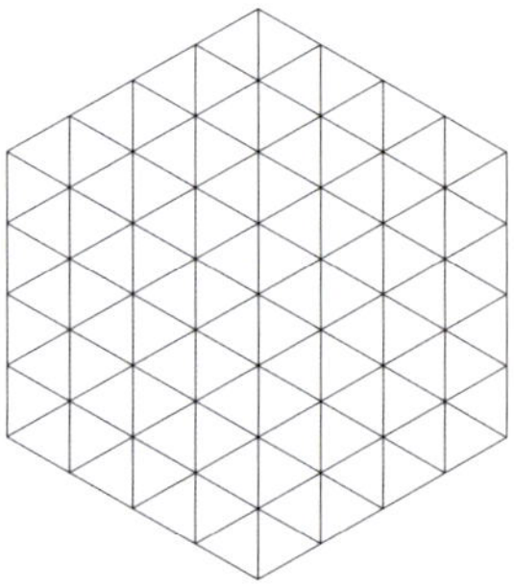

These structures have implied male and female polarity as well. Just like there are 4 solidly planted upwardly pointing triangles (male) in the above diagram, there are 3 downward pointing (female) triangles touching the bottom edge. The orientation of an equilateral triangle does matter!

As well, triangles are a very common logo treatment and have connections to the pyramids. Corporations, government agencies and military divisions quite commonly use the male form. Huh?
Something to look for perhaps.

It also turns out that triangle grids are the main way to create 3D mesh geometry. Though some systems also utilize 4-way (quad) grids for 3 dimensional forms. These grids "triangulate" space.

An architectural side-note is that the geodesic domes of Buckminster Fuller are highly successful in temperature stabilization as well as portability. All made of triangles - geodesics. So the simplest way to create a boundary or define a 2D space - a triangle - is quite a design tool. And its utility in 3D is extraordinary!

Triangle grids are a different coordinate system. Halfway to 3D. They can be used for isometric (non-perspective) 3D design and other approaches. 6 of these clustered around a central point make a hexagonal polar grid. These grids form a substructure that leads directly to hexagonal patterns and easily tessellate (see section on tessellations). They are the structural basis of much Islamic design and their pattern qualities are beautiful. You might research this online as well.

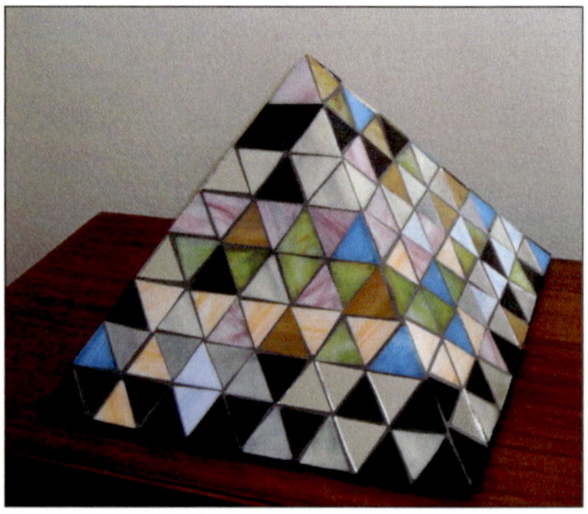

1.27 Color By Numbers Pyramid, Glass Mosaic, 10" x 10" x 8", 2017.

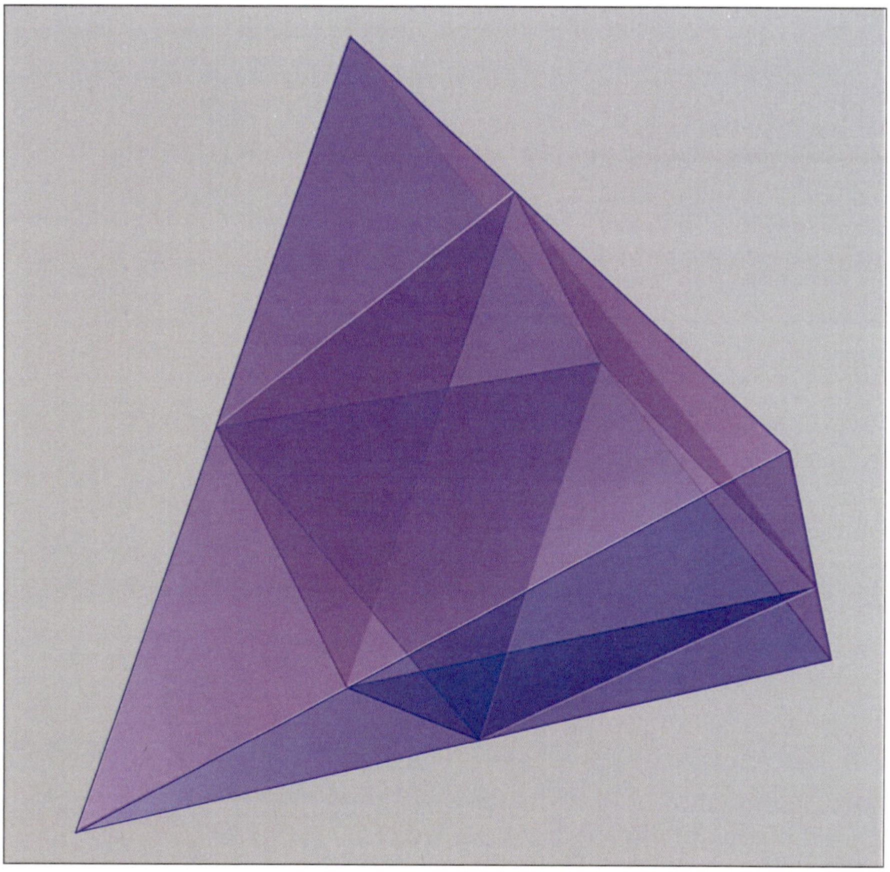

1.28

A computer generated Tetrahedron - the simplest 3D pyramid - with subdivided sides. Created from 4 equilateral triangles. One of the Platonic Solids.

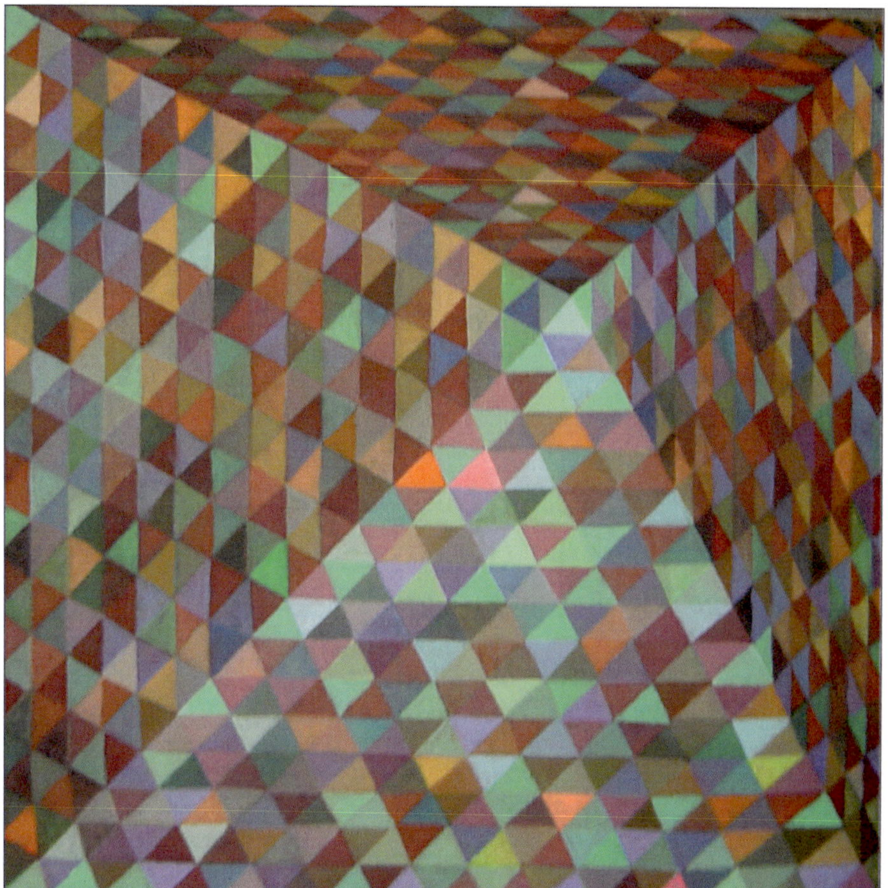

1.29

Pyramid, Oil on Canvas, 12" x 12", 2005.

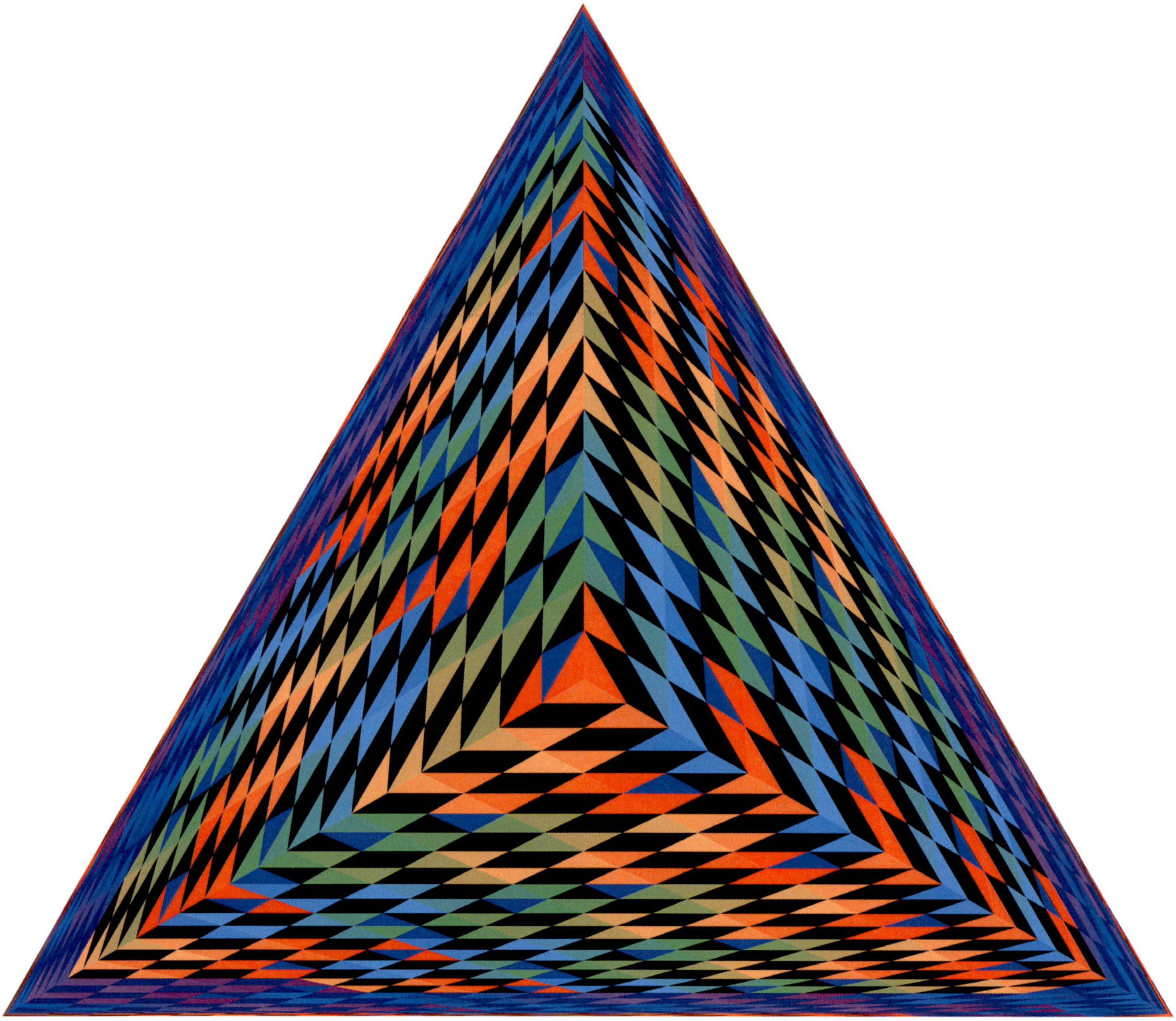

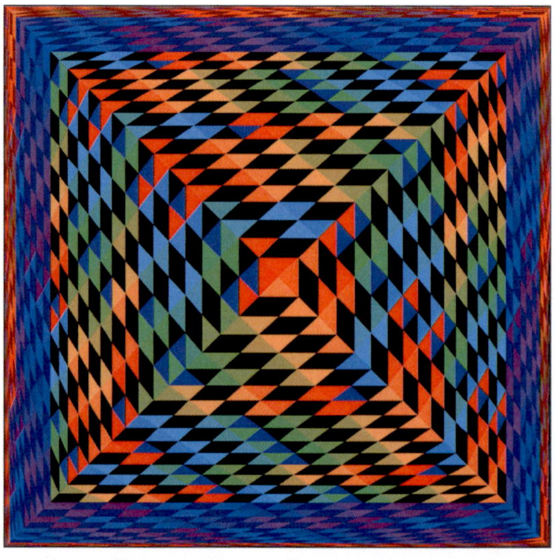

1.30.

2 examples from Color By Numbers software from ArtToyz Studios. The same color choices were used but placed on triangular and square base grids made of triangles.

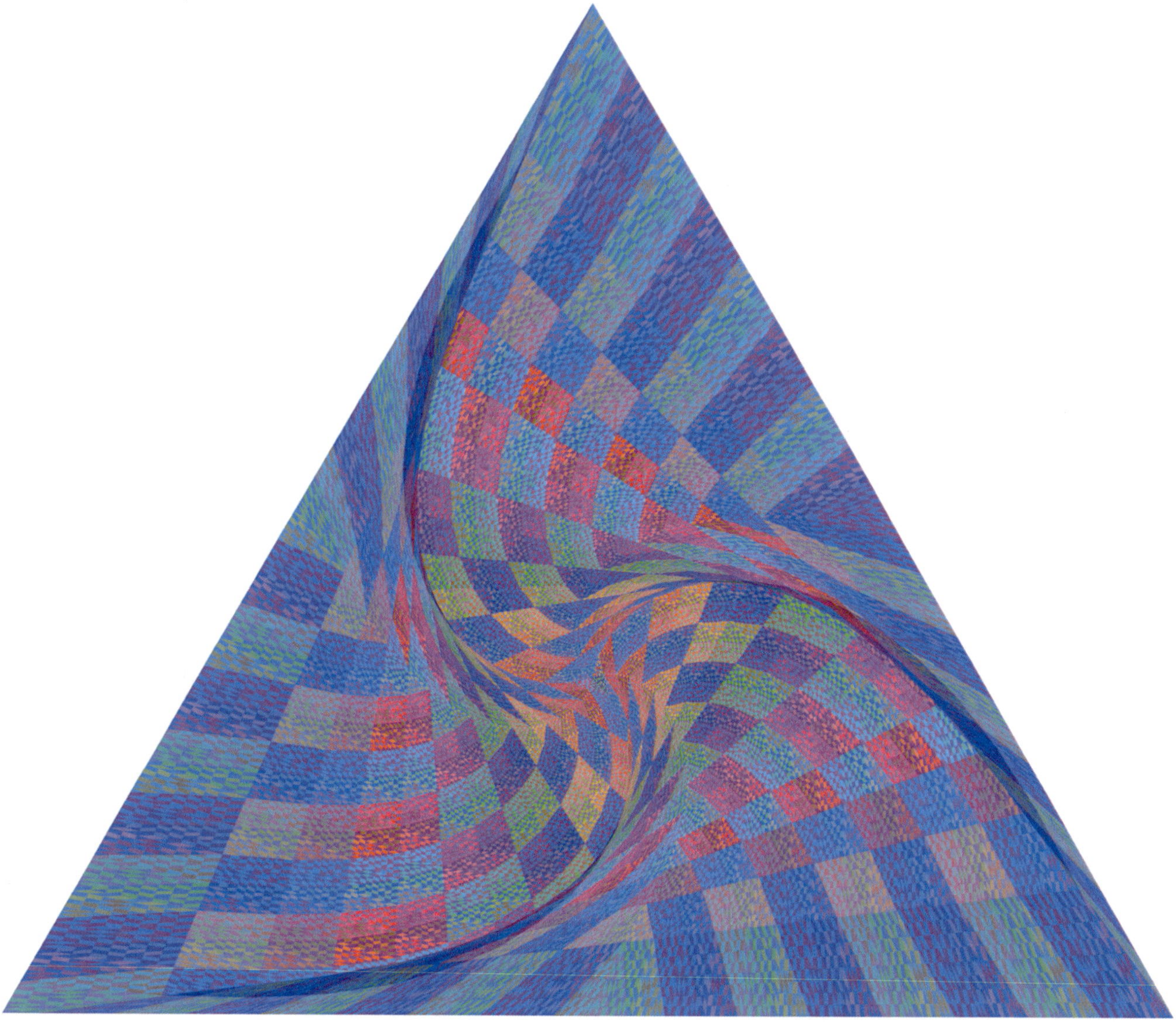

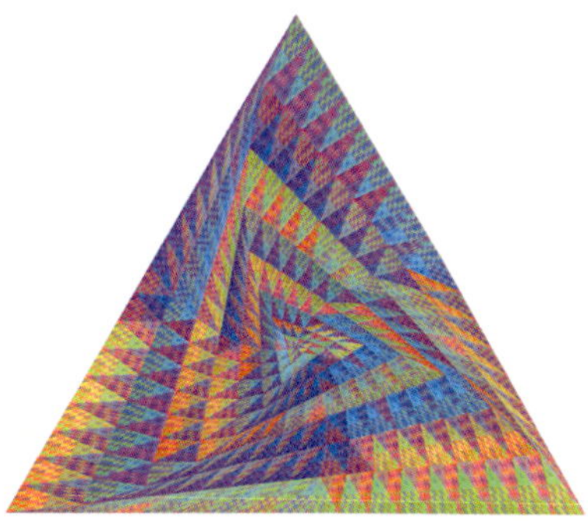

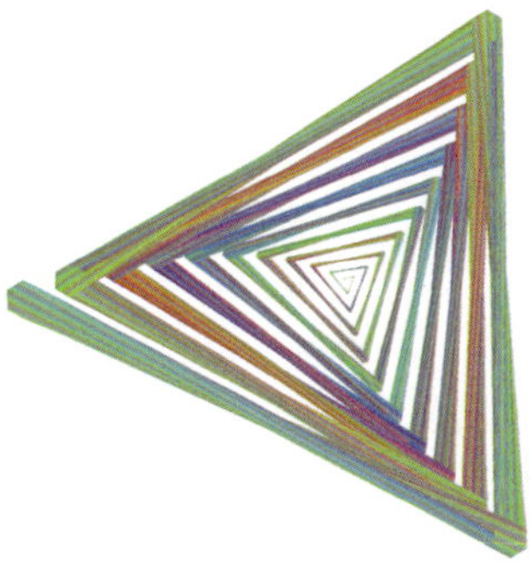

1.31.

3 more examples of triangular grid output from Color By Numbers software.
This software can spin elements of the grid as well as taper them to the edges. This illustrates some of the flexibility and potential of using grids.

Below are various examples of triangular-based grids using my coloring system, "Color by Numbers". See the next chapter for a thorough explanation. I have used this concept to explore many grid-based techniques and crafting methods.

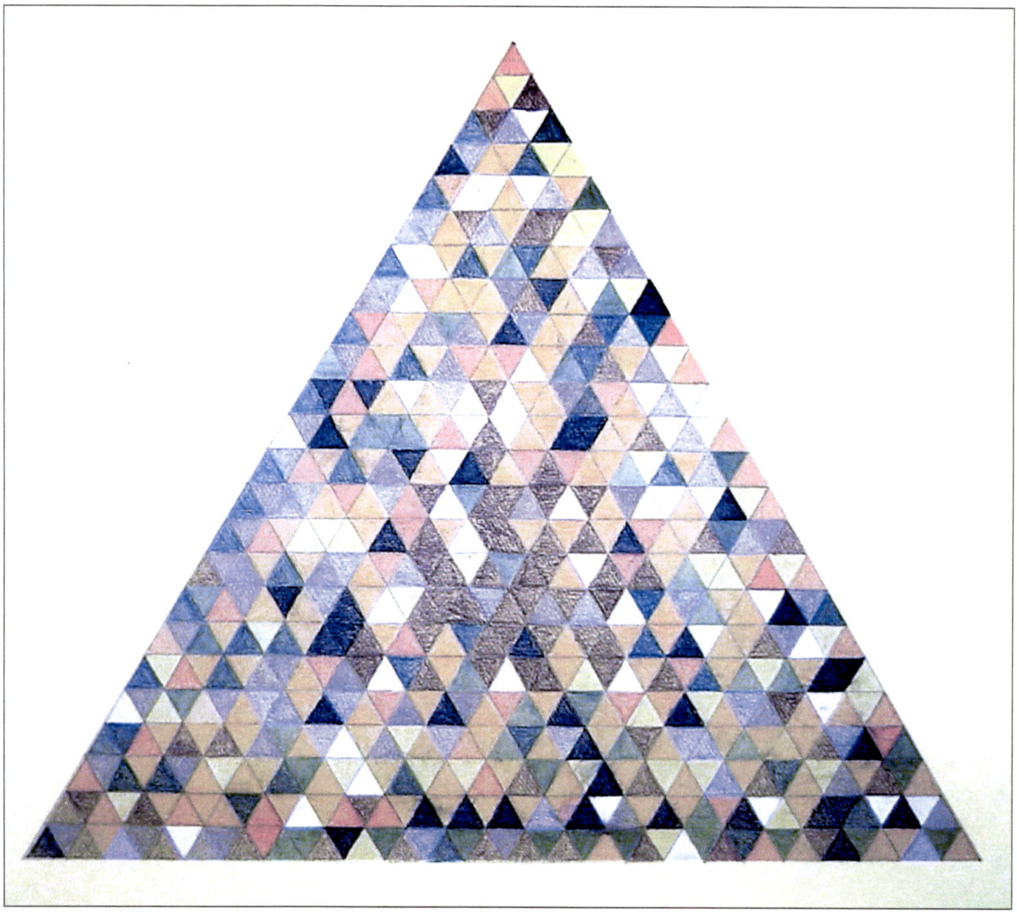

1.32.

Color By Numbers Spiral on Equilateral Triangle Grid, Colored Pencil on Paper, 18" x 18", 1982.

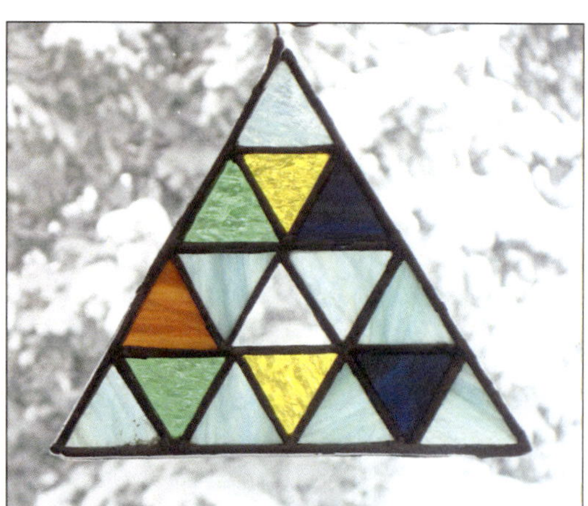

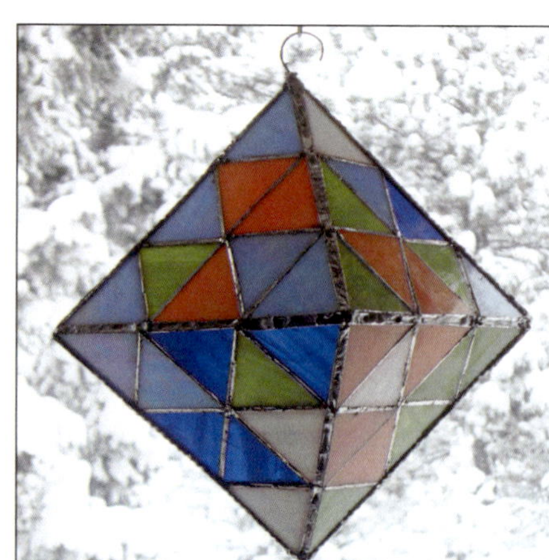

1.33a. Color By Numbers Triangle, Stained Glass, 6" x 6", 2014.

1.33b. Color By Numbers Pyramid, Stained Glass, 6" x 6" x 4", 2014.

It appears that rectangular, triangular and hexagonal (derived from triangles) grids are the only fully tessellating grids. Tessellations will be discussed further at the end of this chapter.

A fully tessellating grid cell repeats without yielding secondary spaces. It turns out that to get regular repetition of most regular shapes with 5, 7, 8, 9, etc sides, you end up with secondary shapes. An interesting note is that a grid of regular octagons (stop signs) creates a secondary grid of squares, a shape with 1/2 the number of sides.

Only recently have mathematicians figured out the possibilities of regular pentagonal (5-sided) mapping on grids. There are a number of solutions, but all will have secondary forms to pattern a space. Hexagonal grids made from triangles have special properties not available in other places. We will discuss them regarding optical illusion creation later.

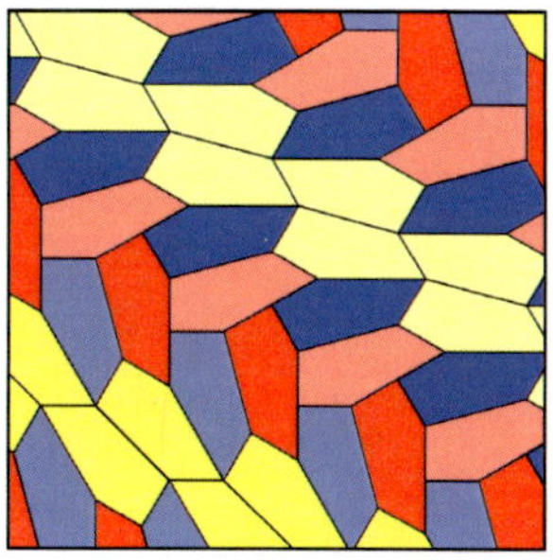

1.34a.

A tessellating pentagonal form that geometers discovered in 2015. This does not work with regular, symmetrical pentagonal forms.

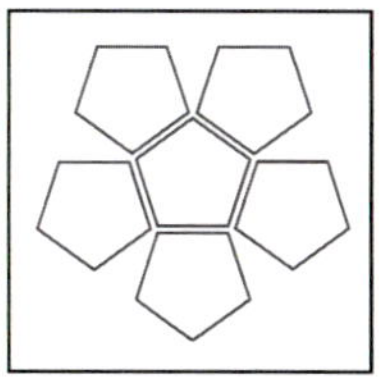

1.34b.

Regular, symmetrical pentagonal forms don't tessellate.

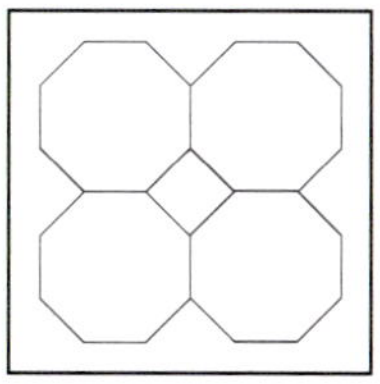

1.34c.

Patterned octagons create square "negative space".

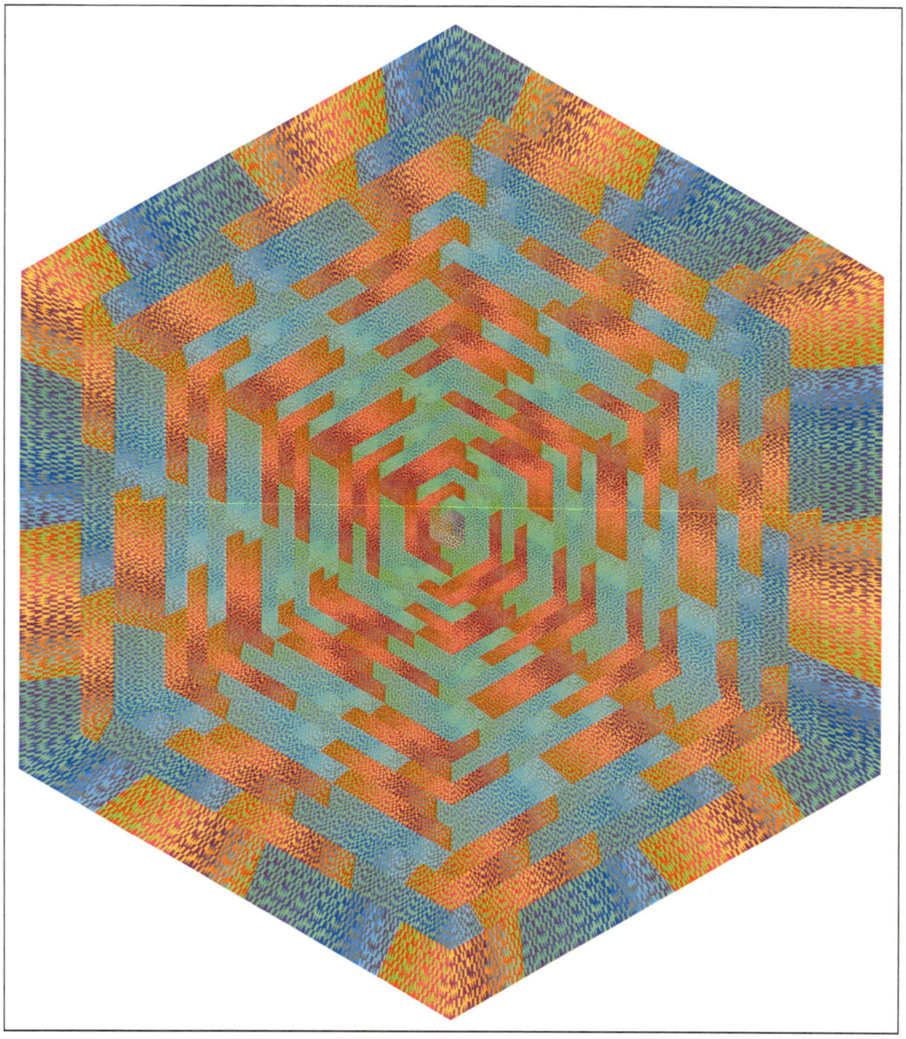

1.34d. Color By Numbers Spiral Blended, Digital, 2147 x 2147 Pixels, 2019

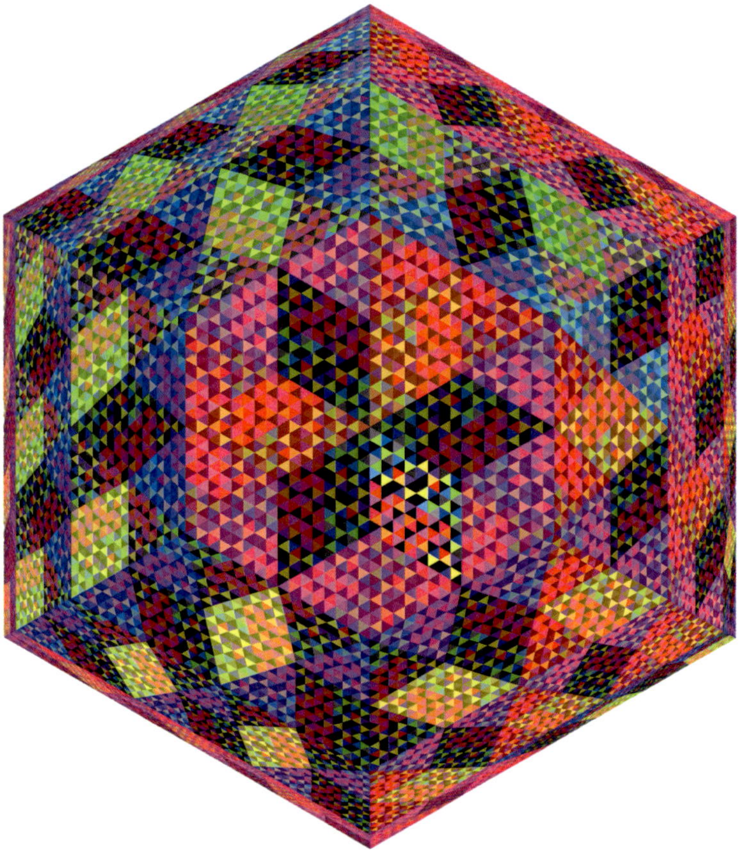

1.35a.

These grids have been logarithmically distorted to "bulge".

Color By Numbers
Blended Outie, Digital,
5000 x 4000 Pixels,
2019.

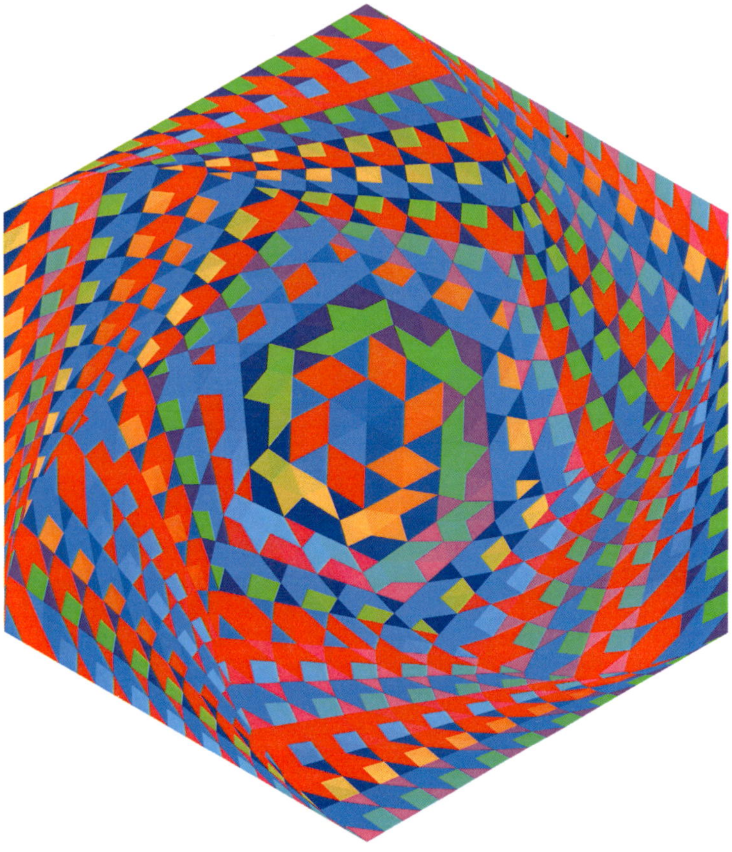

1.35b.

Color By Numbers
Blended Twisted Outie,
Digital, 2160 x 2160 Pixels,
2019.

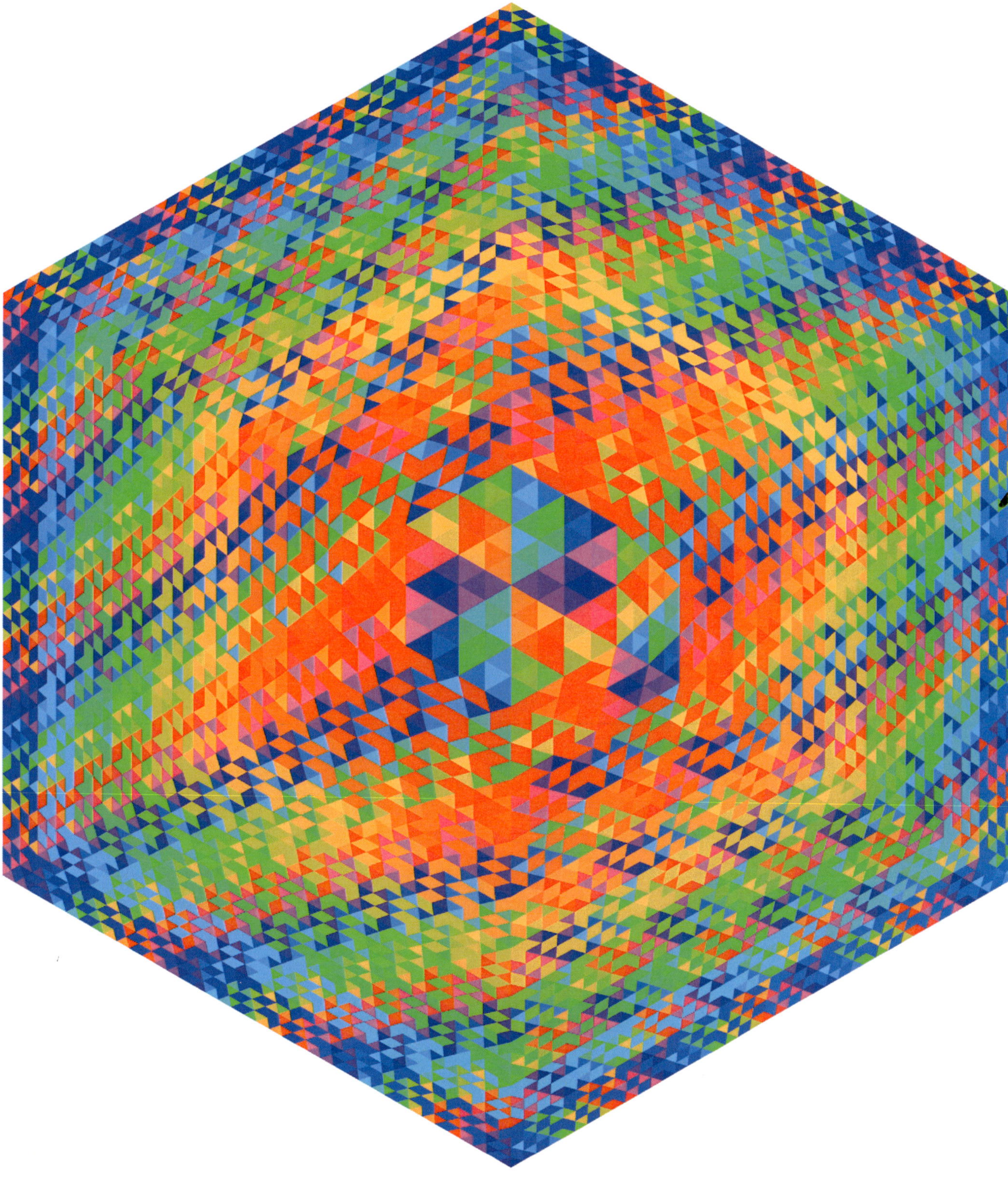

1.36. Color By Numbers Linear Outie,
Digital, 2160 x 2160 Pixels, 2019.

I developed "polar" triangle grids for Color By Numbers to spiral on. This is a color generating system I have been working with since 1979. These polygonal grids can be made with any number of sides radiating from a single point. That point does not have to be centered and can create dimensional effects. Their segments are subdivided into triangles. When working by hand I use equally subdivided segments. This can easily be accomplished by folding a strip of paper the length of a side multiple times and using the creases to mark the grid points on that edge. I also have developed these in the computer to be logarithmic or converging on the center or the edges. There are infinite permutations of course.

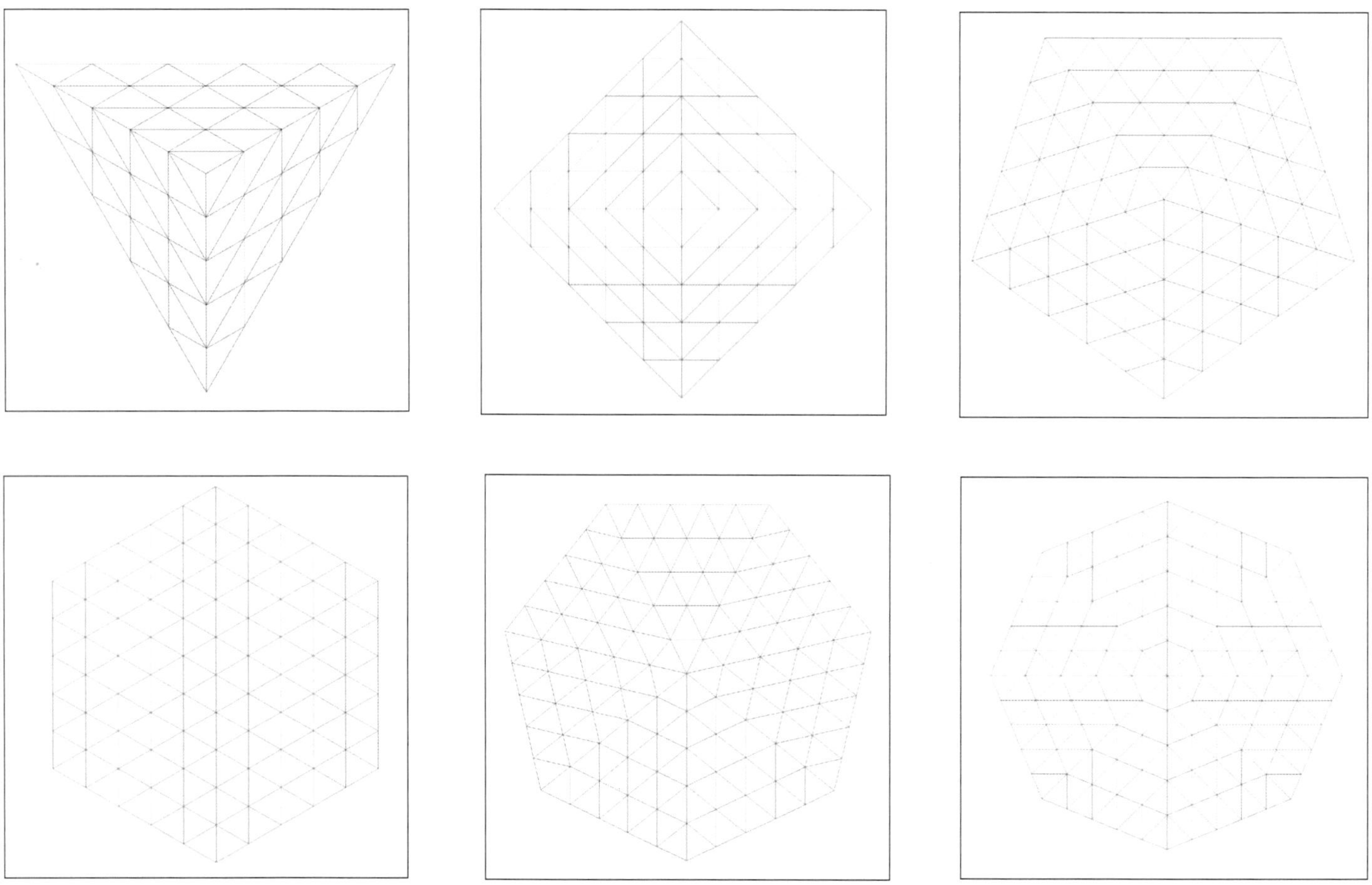

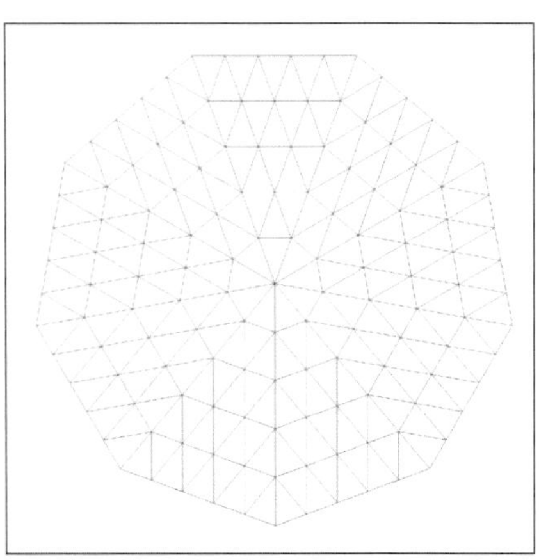

1.37.

Symmetrical polar grid structures.

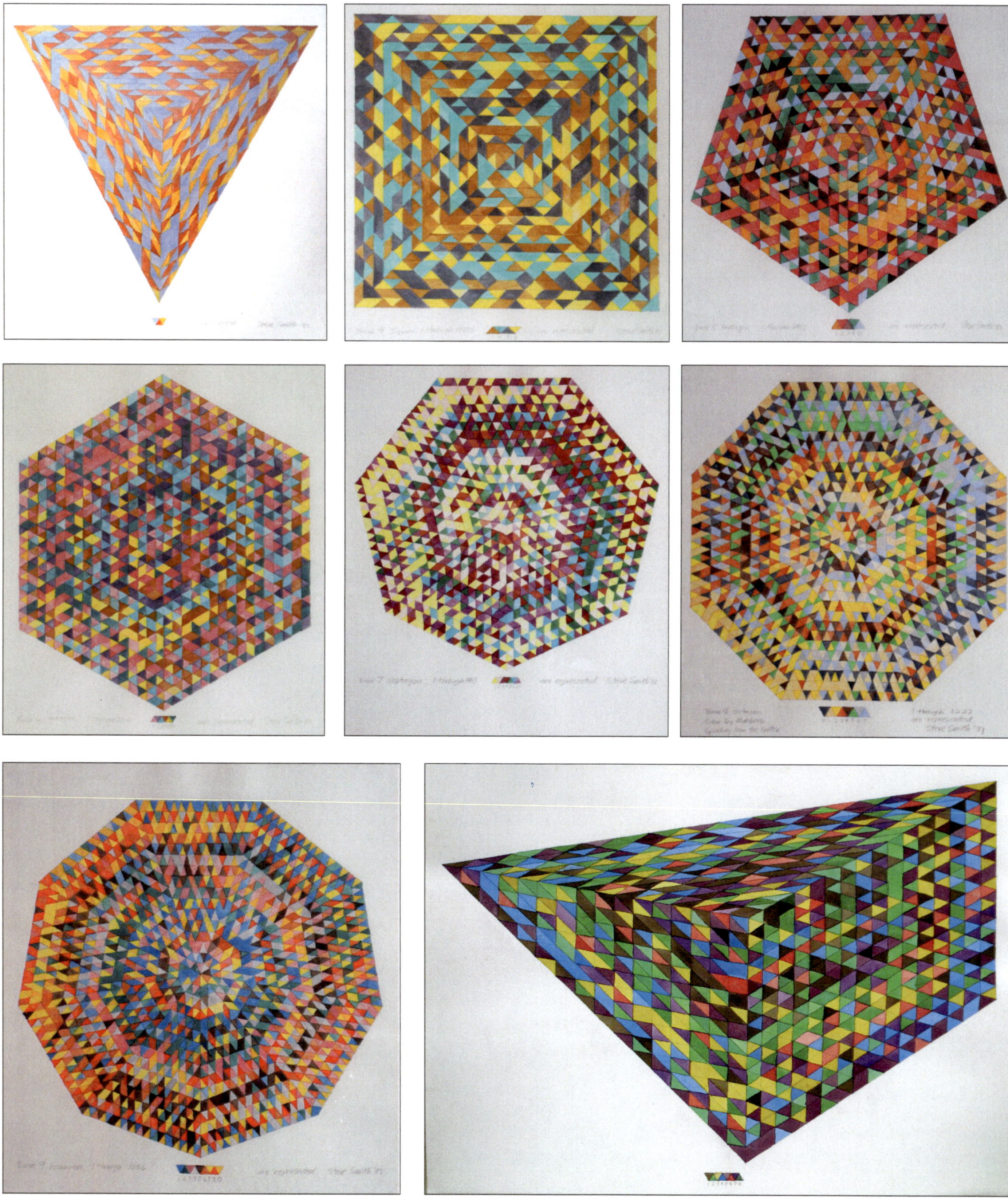

1.38. 8 watercolors I made in 1981 for my Master's Thesis.
These grids are derived from polar coordinate grids. These patterns are formed by counting with colors representing the digits of sequential numbers, and spiral from the centers of these grids. The bottom right illustrates non-symmetrical use of these grids.

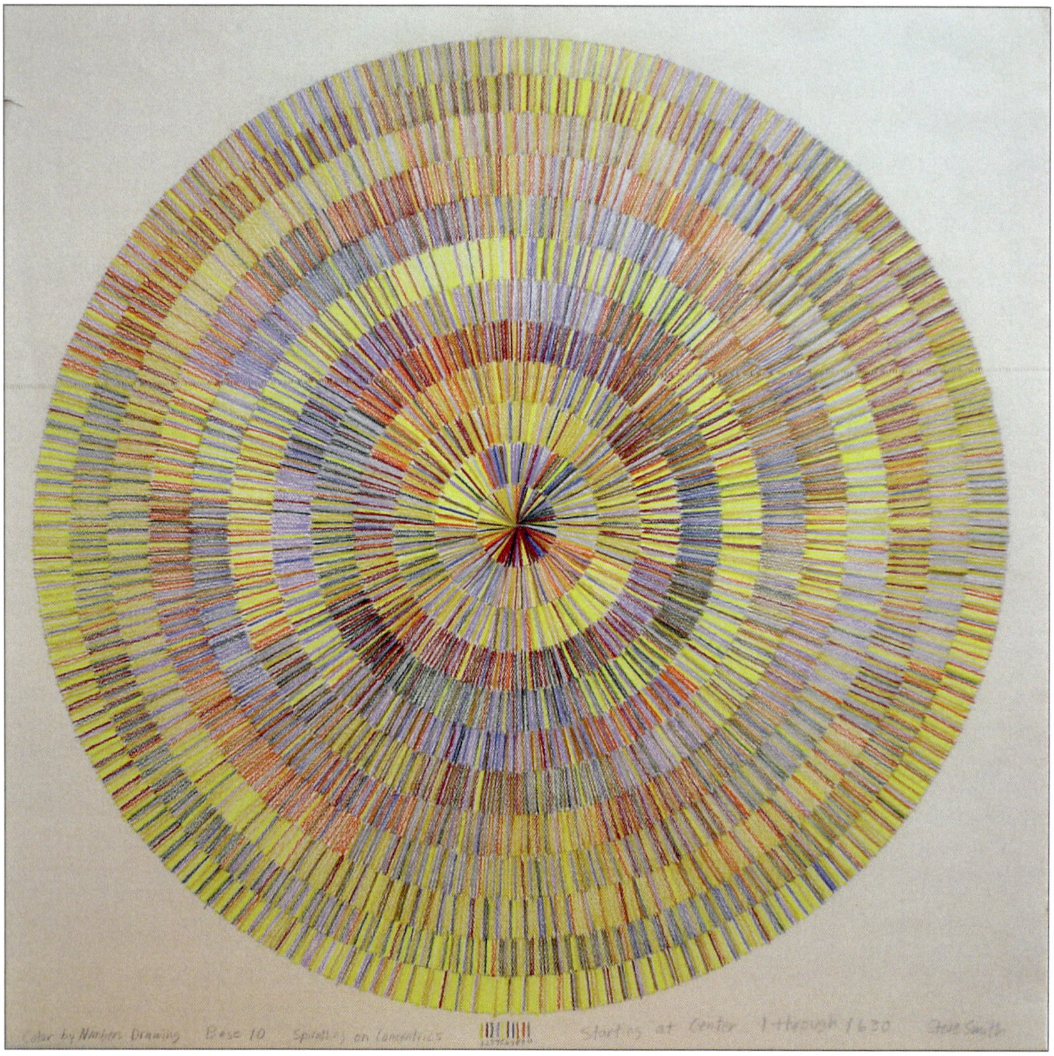

1.39.

Color By Numbers Radial Drawing, 1 through 1630, Colored Pencil on Paper, 18" x 18", 2019.

1.40.

Color By Numbers Linear Spiral On a Special Grid, Watercolor, 18" x 18", 1980. This triangular to octagonal grid successfully tests a theory that polar grids can be combined in simple ways.

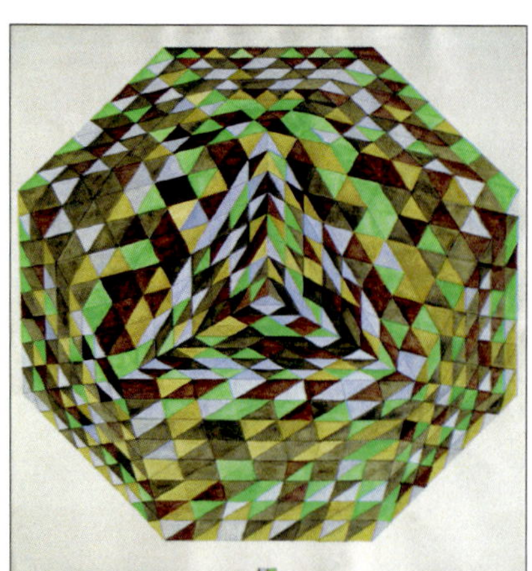

1.41.

Color By Numbers Linear Spiral Octagon, Stained Glass, 16" x 16", 2016.

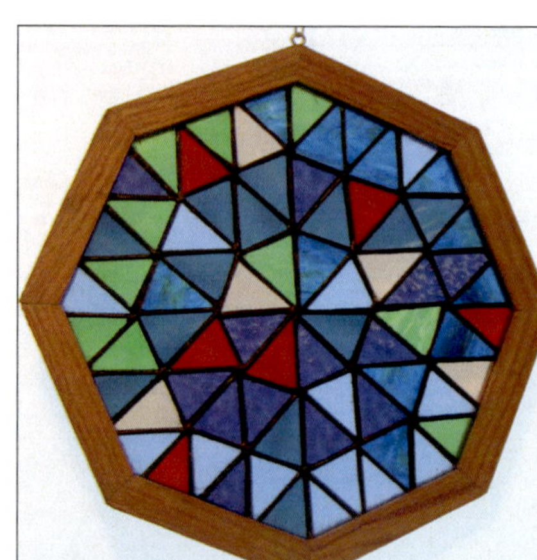

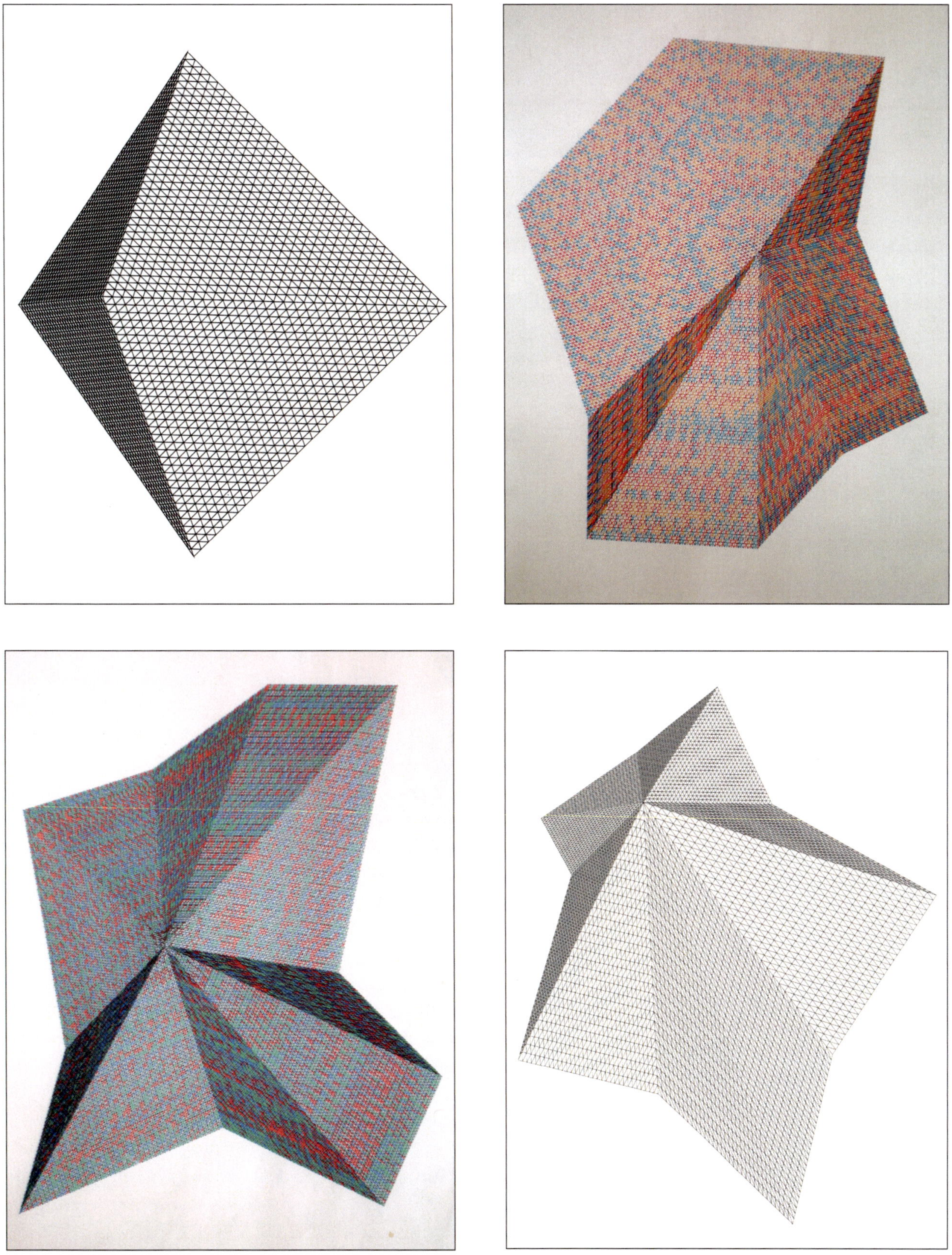

1.42.

Computer generated examples of non-symmetrical grids developed with this radial technique.

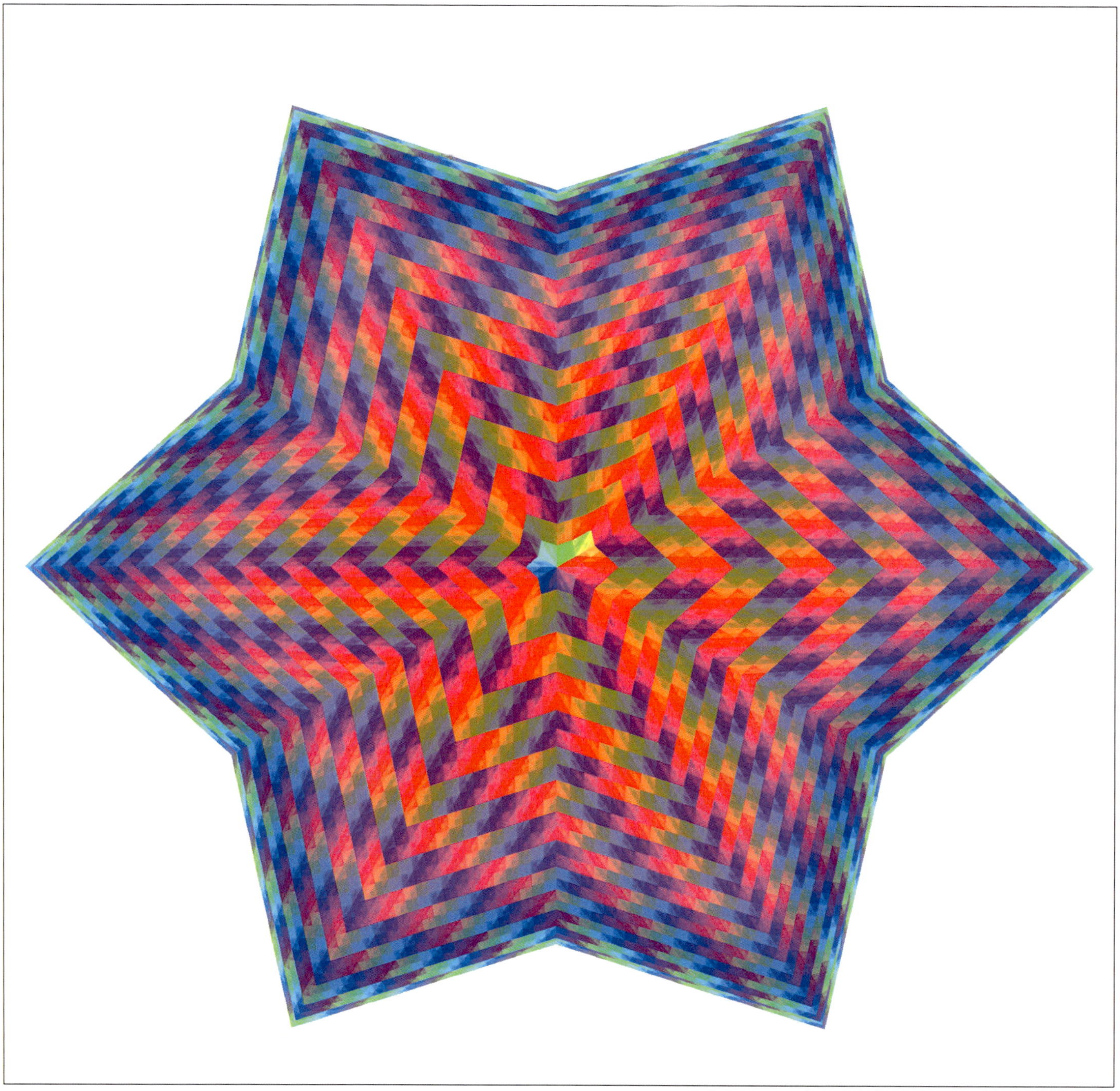

1.43.

Color By Numbers Spiral Blended on Hexagonal Star Outie, Digital, 2160 x 2160, 2019.

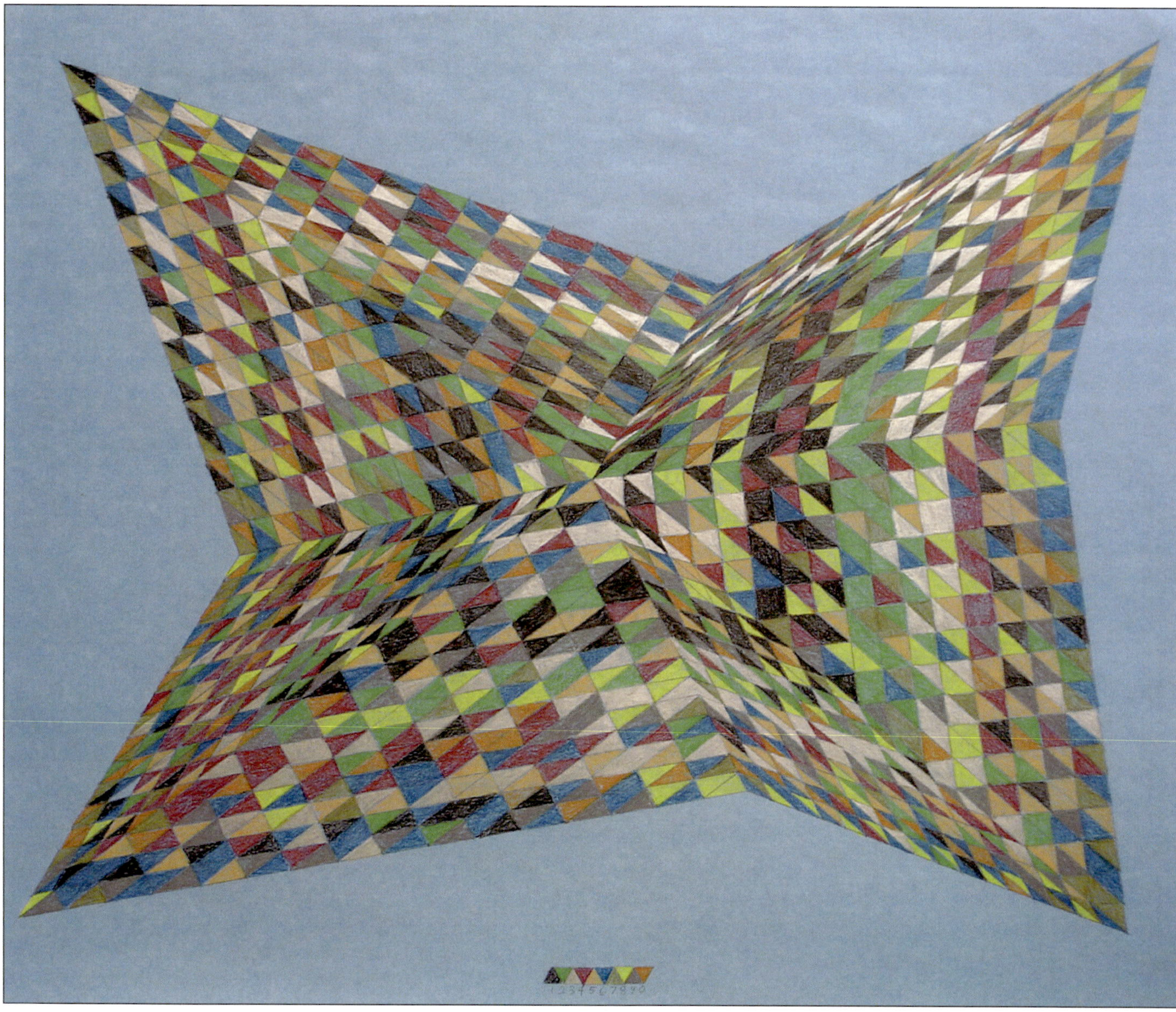

1.44.

Color By Numbers Linear Spiral on Polygonal Grid, Colored Pencil on Blue paper, 24" X 18", 1981.

TESSELLATIONS

Tessellations are forms of patterning that have been utilized for millennia. Examples of Roman mosaics have been uncovered dating back to the second century BC. Islamic art provides elaborate examples that cover floors, walls and ceilings. The Alhambra in Spain is an exquisite example. Apparently an aversion to realistic iconography helped develop Islamic patterning.

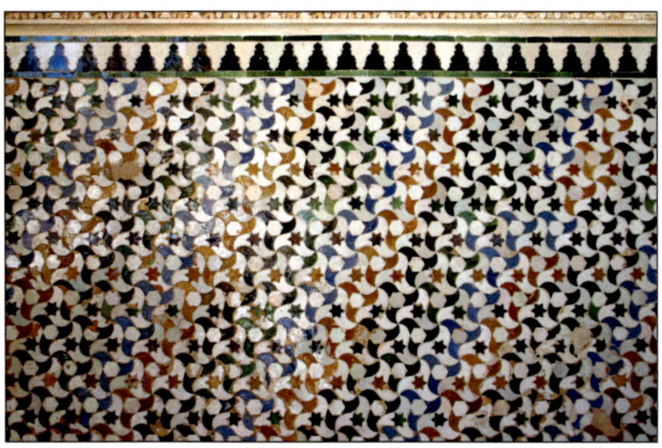

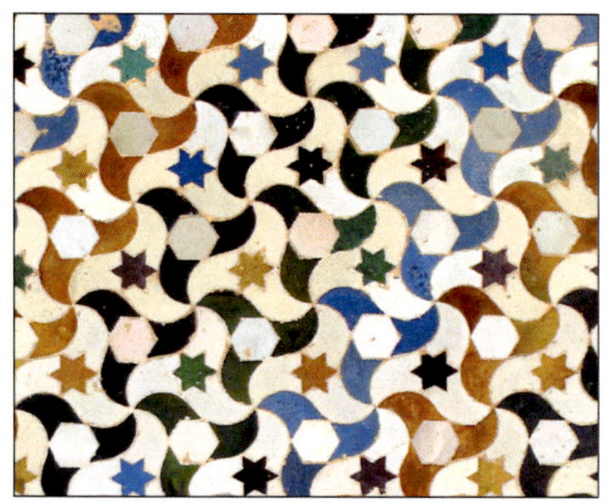

1.45. Alhambra in Spain, in full and in detail. Tessellations like these inspired M.C Escher's work. (*Image source: http://wikipedia.org*)

The Dutch artist M.C. Escher (1898-1972) was captivated at an early age by this art and he developed his own intriguing version of improbable tessellating creatures that are oriented in all directions and that fit together like puzzle pieces. Escher's methodology was, for the most part ruler and pencil. He was a master designer. The craftsmanship shown in his prints is exquisite His art deserves to be studied. He used a lot of triangular grids, but he developed square grid versions as well.

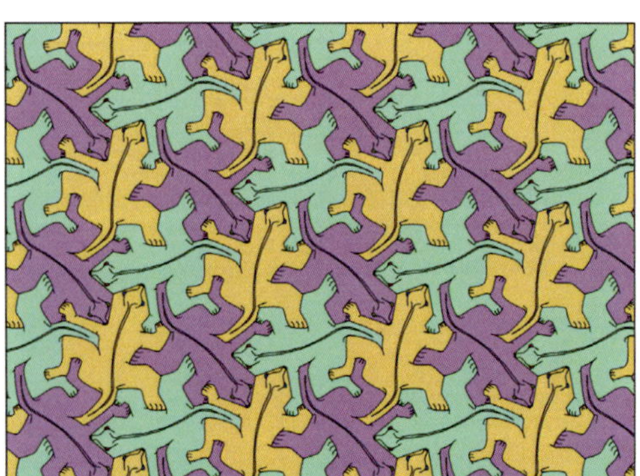

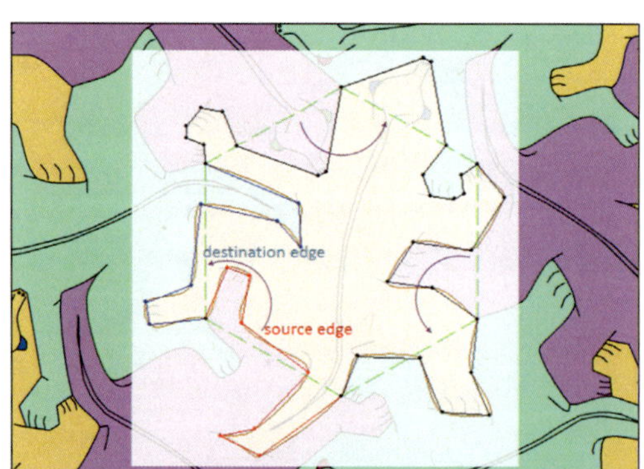

1.46. A re-creation of a pattern originally developed by M.C Escher. The image on the right illustrates some of the logic behind these grid-based patterns.

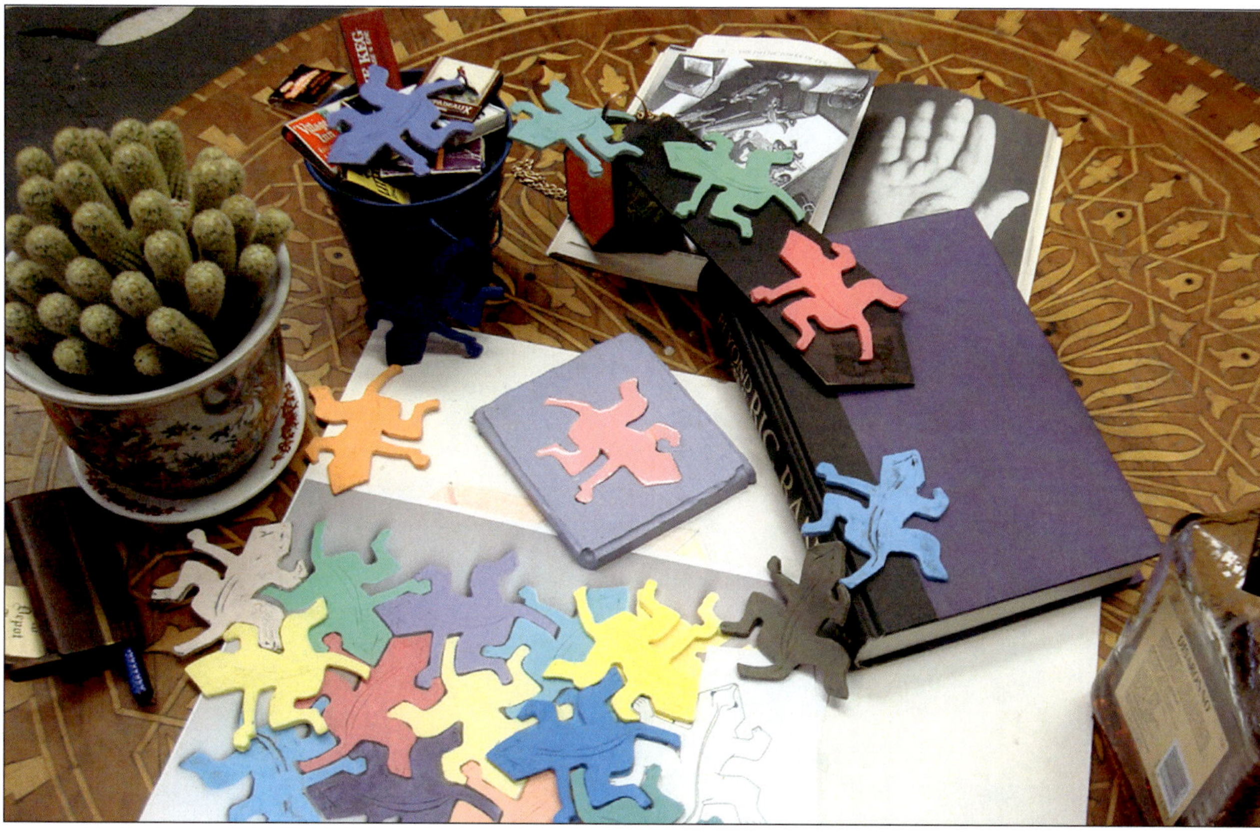

1.47. A re-creation of a famous lithograph by M.C. Escher. This one is in color and uses tessellating 3D forms made with a 3D printer and a mold in various colors. Created at ArtToyz Studios, Golden, Colorado, 2015.

The tiles are created to fit together with precision. Escher used a variety of techniques to guarantee these fit. They include reflection (mirroring), rotation, and cloning, usually applied to opposite edges. This process is a bit mind-boggling to perform and computers can help. Grid patterns tessellate fully if they fit together without any "secondary" shapes. Escher exploited these secondary tessellations with his birds vs. fish and his "Metamorphosis" series. This is another good topic worthy of research, if you are interested.

One of his areas of exploration was to represent a "portion" of eternity through pattern. Wow - leave it to artists to define the undefinable. Tessellating fields within a rectangle imply a crop to a larger undefined space Bending the edges a bit sends it towards infinity. He worked with mathematicians using parametric distortion and developed ways of sending grids to convergence on the edges or the center. It appears some of his ideas came from staring into a chrome globe. This is one of the techniques for creating Virtual Reality displays with full dimensional viewing in the 21st century, by the way. Here again, a computer is very helpful. Without one, Escher was a technical genius and a pioneer!

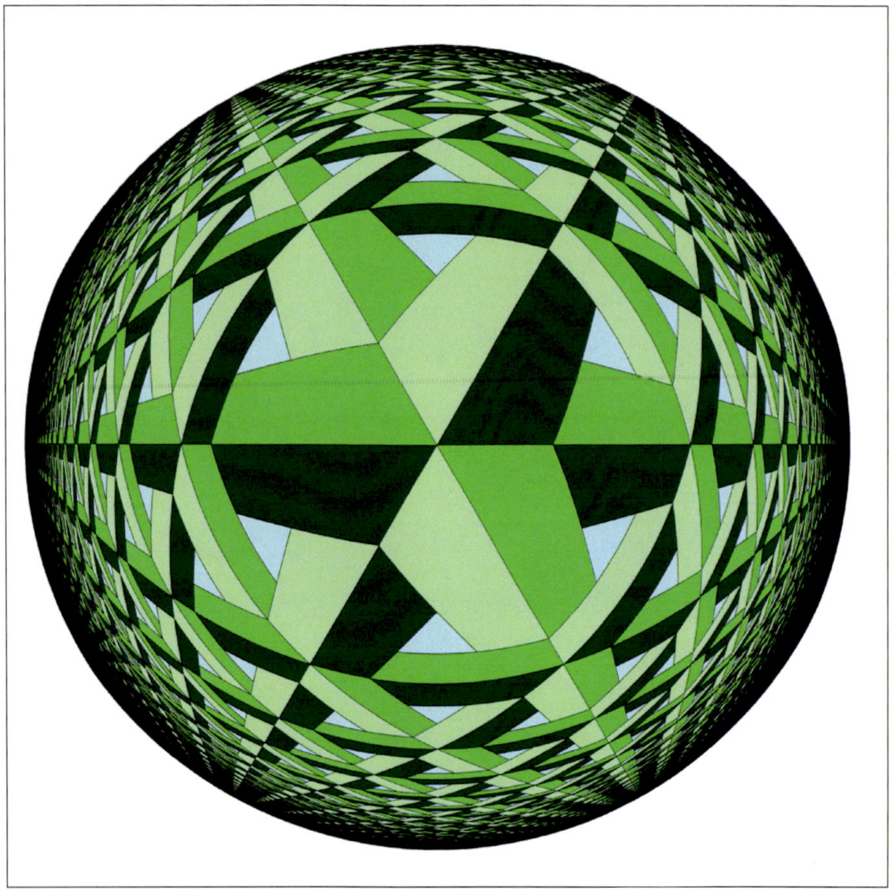

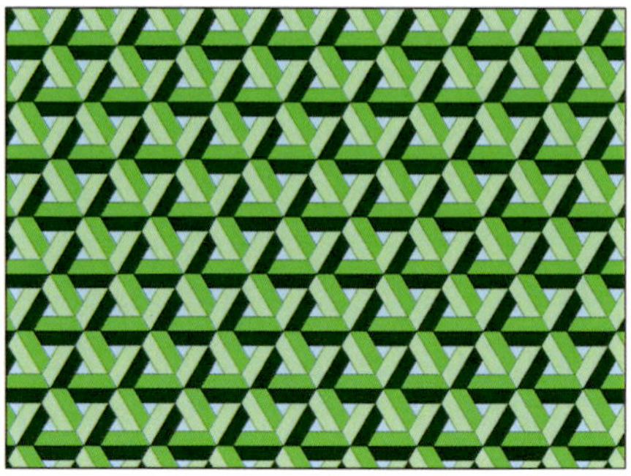

1.48.

A nice triangular tessellation - an isometric grid illusion made in EscherSketch (an ArtToyz Studio Software) plus an outie and an innie as ways to converge the grid towards infinity.

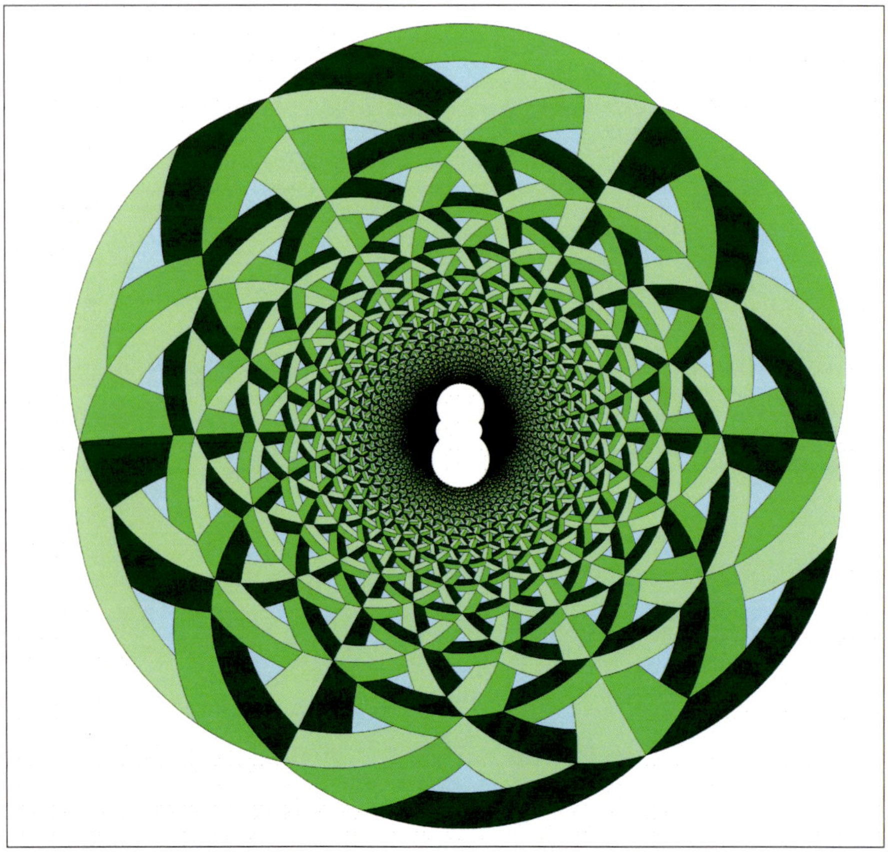

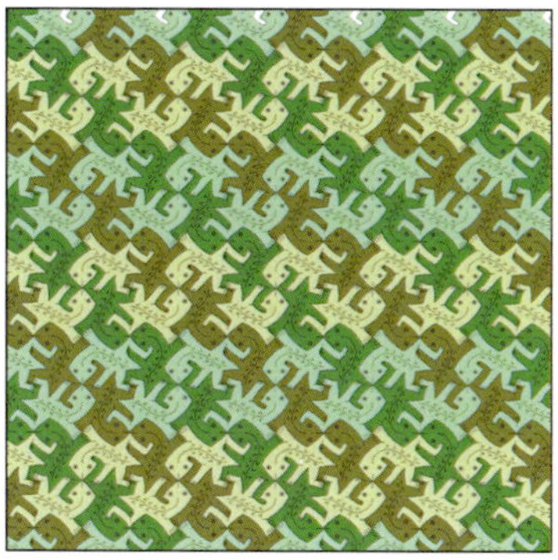

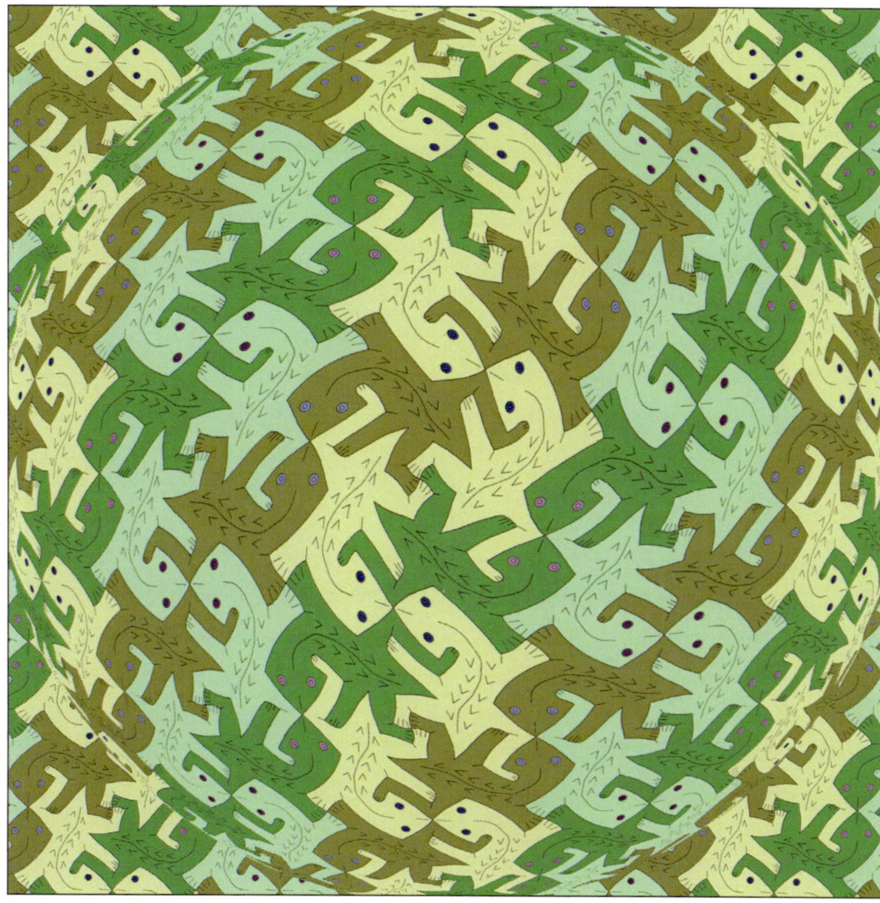

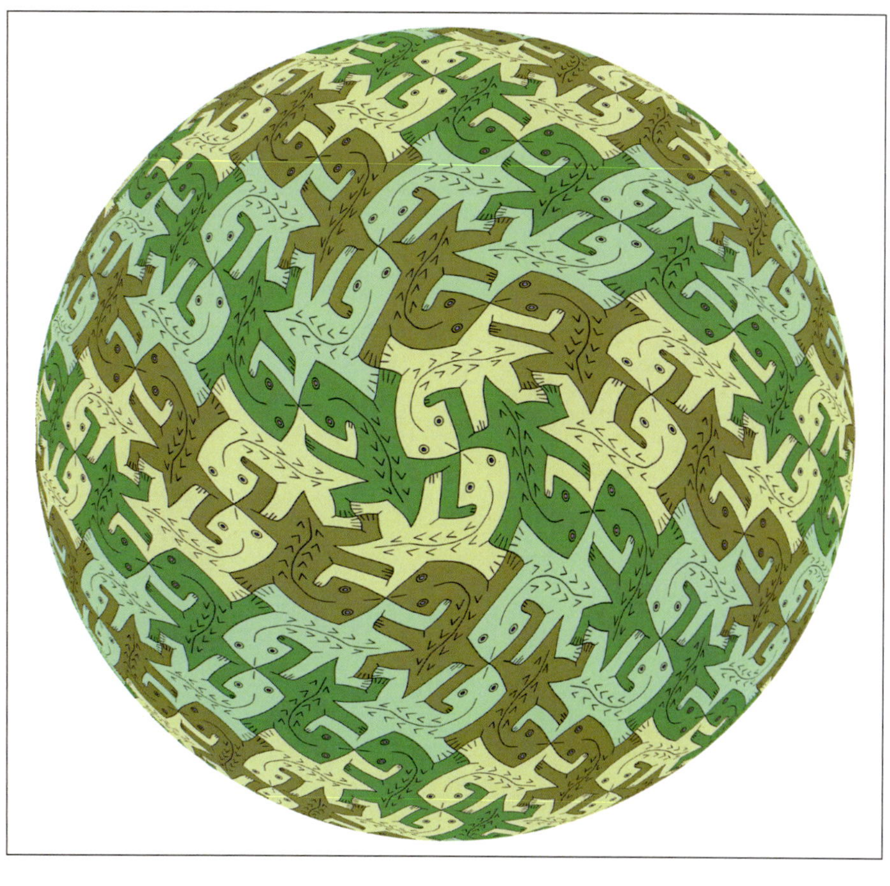

1.49.

Lizard tessellations and explorations of transformations for bending towards infinity.

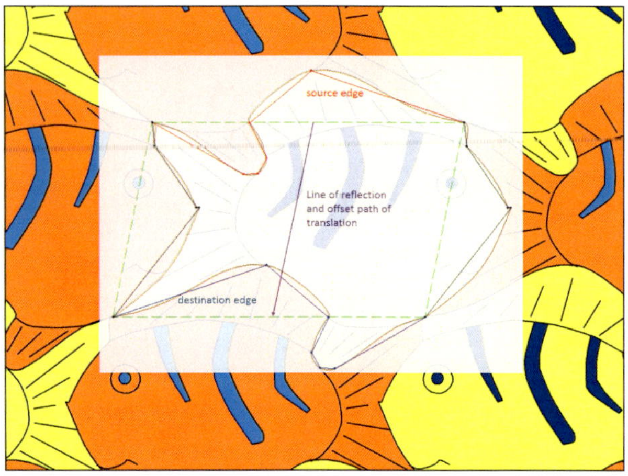

1.50a. A fish tessellation from EschersSketch by ArtToyz Studios with notes on techniques

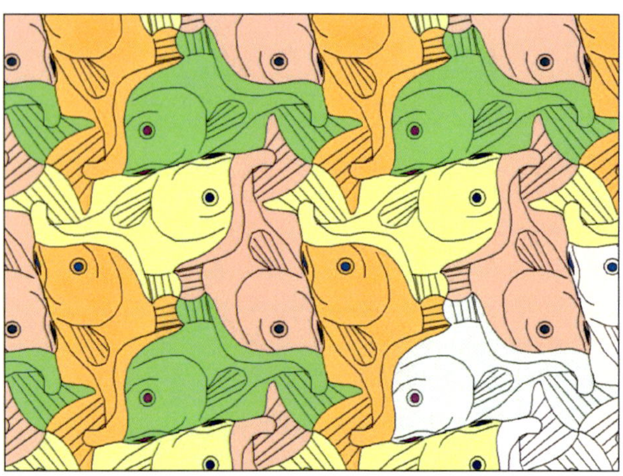

1.50b. Another fish tessellation from ArtToyz Studios Eschersketch Software.

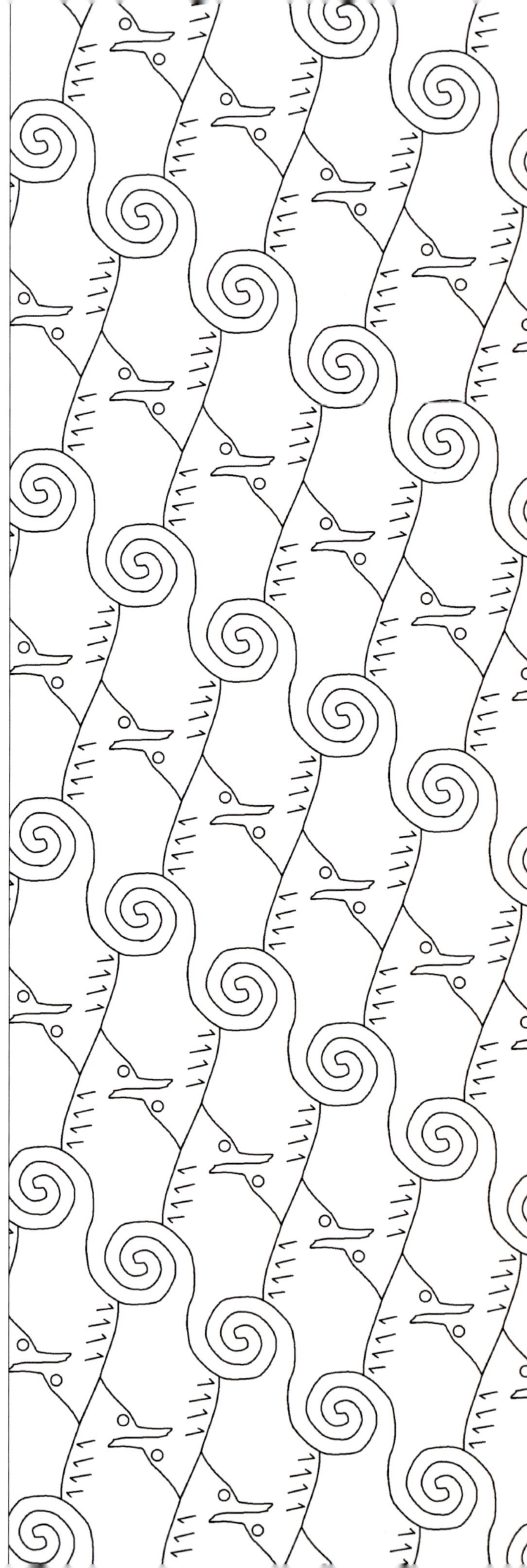

1.50c.

Another aquatic themed tessellation from ArtToyz Studios Eschersketch Software.

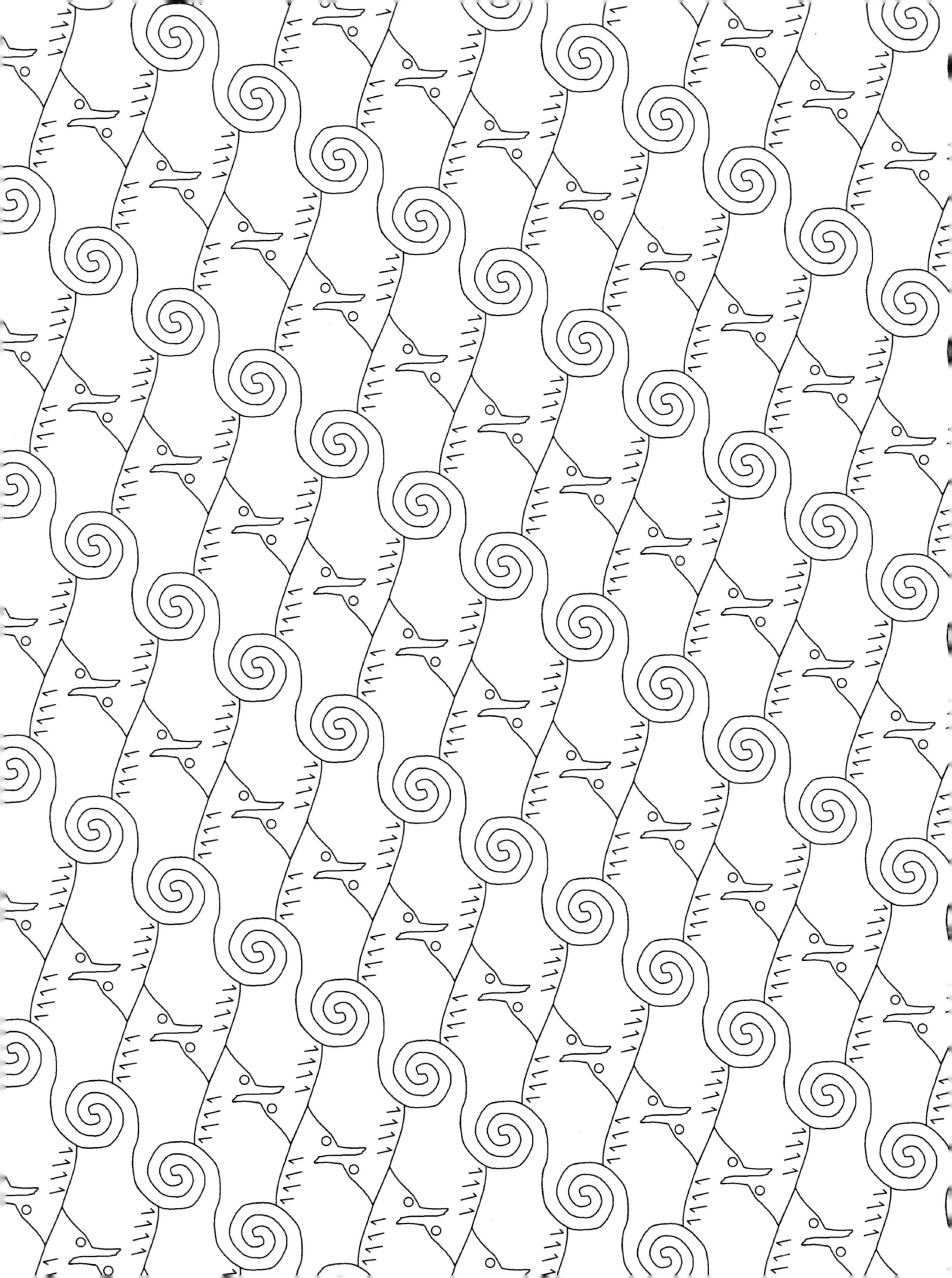

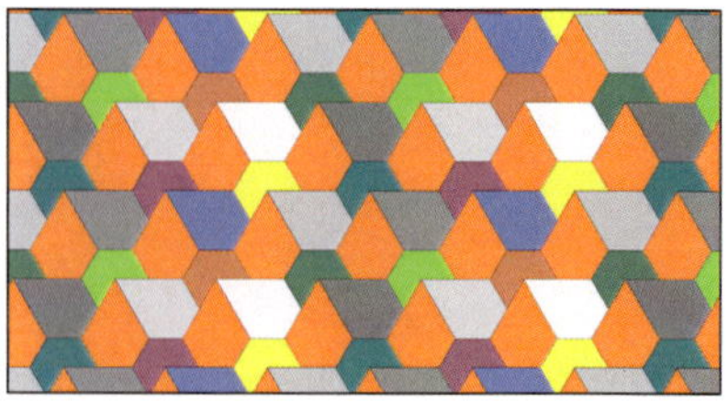

1.51a. A tessellating design that resembles cubes, created by the author.

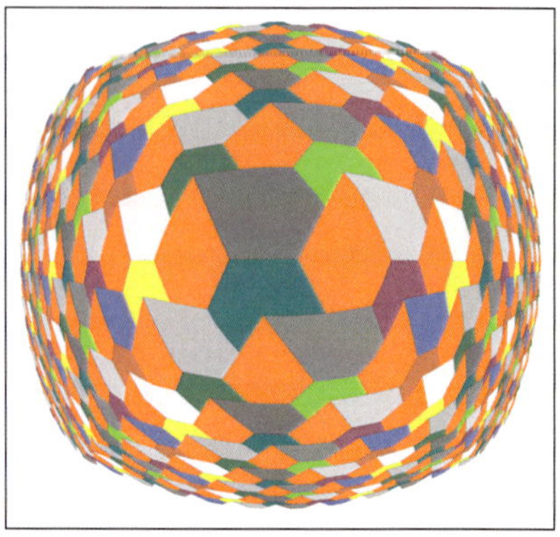

1.51b. The same pattern distorted by non-Cartesian geometry to indicate blending towards infinity.

In the appendix we describe in detail this software drawing tool (EscherSketch) that assists artists and designers who aspire to create these images on their own, but with a level of automation that was unavailable to Escher.

The methodology for creating such tiles, along with the assisting capabilities provided by the application is described in detail. A brief discussion of non-Cartesian tessellations and animated transformation is described.

Emphasis is placed on tessellations of the type developed by M.C. Escher in which complex tiles resembling objects and creatures can be created and assembled in a tessellating plane. He had even more genius devising 2 opposing creatures to morph across the page.

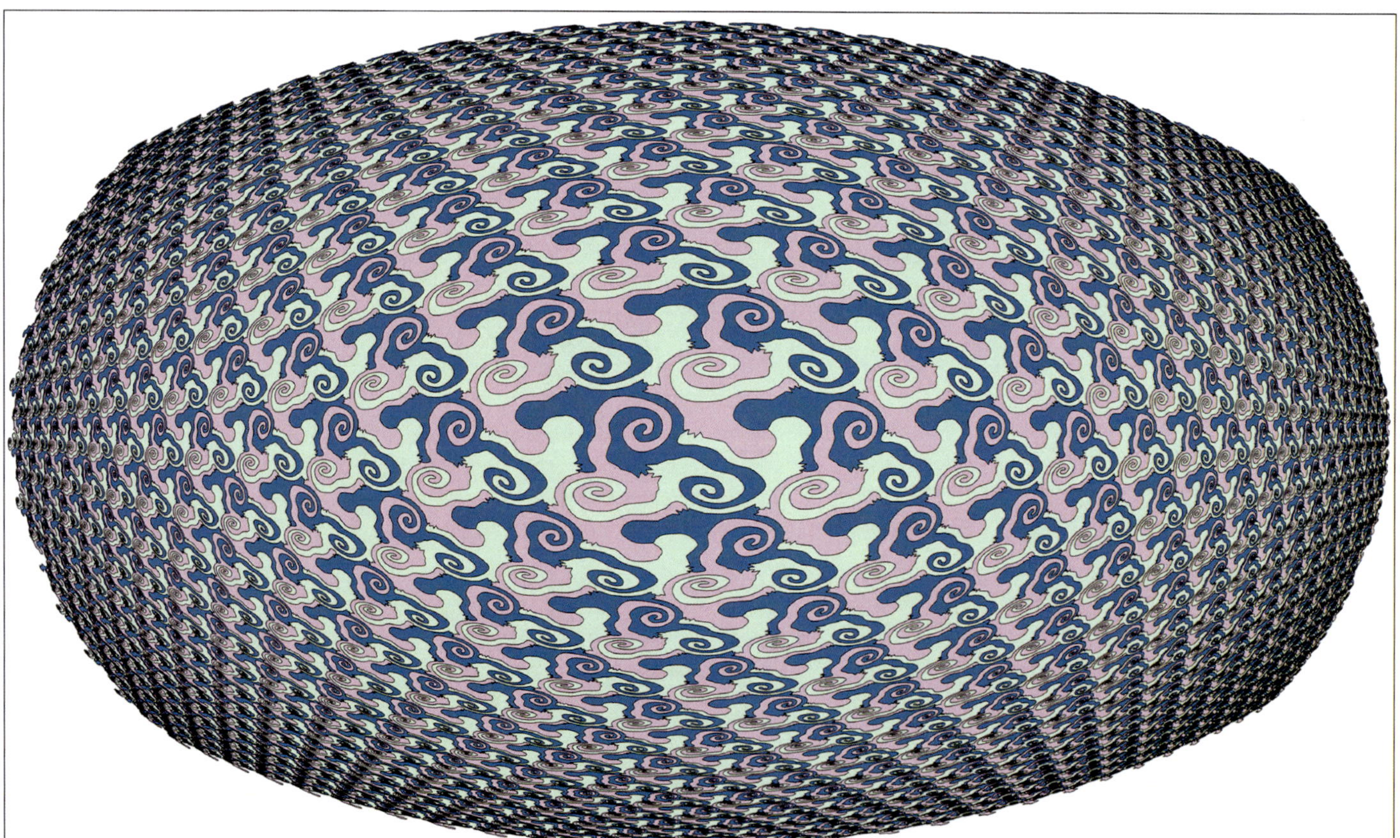

1.52. A tessellation derived from lizards with geometric distortion applied in EsherSketch software to create an "outie". M.C. Escher was acquainted with the advance mathematics of Henri Poincaré and others to create distortions like this. The effect is like bending around a 3D object and is used as an artistic device to show how pattens can imply infinity.

POLAR GRIDS & OTHER VARIATIONS

Poincaré transformations that stretch grids towards circles have various parameters in EscherSketch software. These grids are similar to looking at earth meridians and latitudes from above the North Pole. An outie is somewhat like a fish-eye view.

Below I distorted a Color By Numbers digital image in EscherSketch Software.

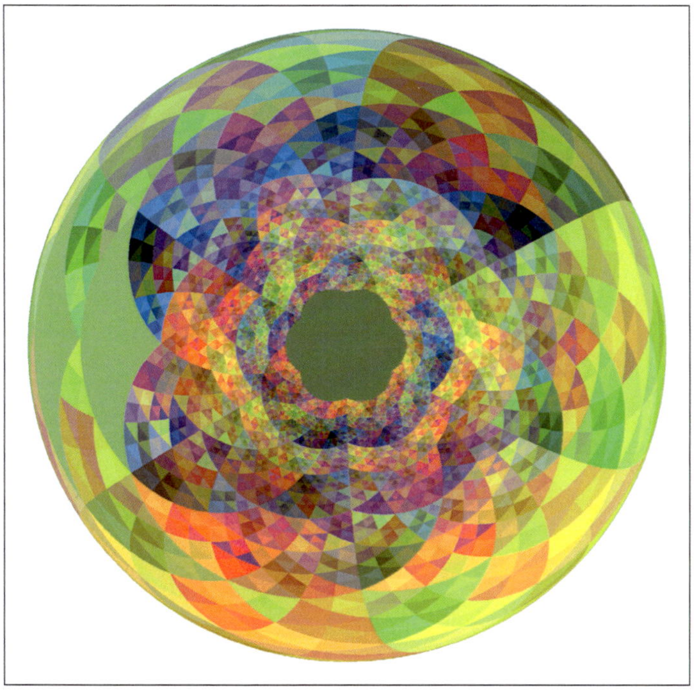

1.53a. An "Innie" wraps around an inner center point like a donut.

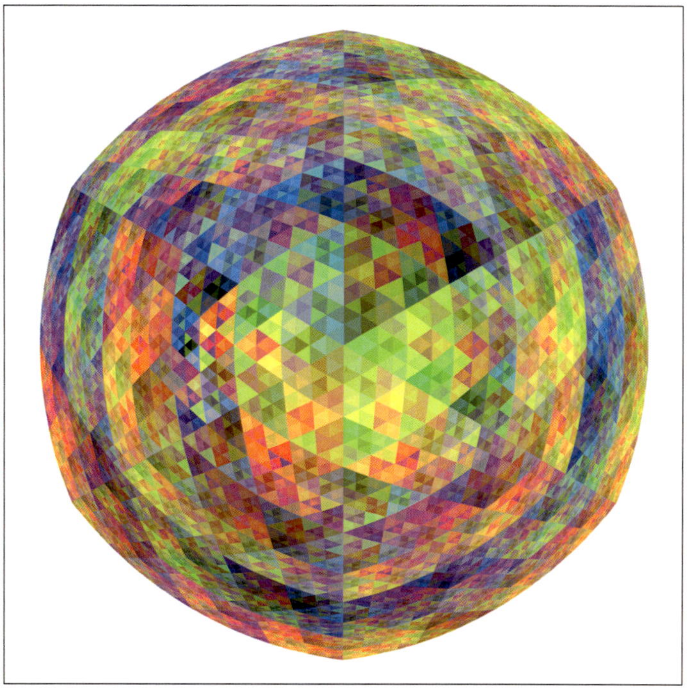

1.53b. An "outie" converges more and more as you move to the outer edge of a circle.

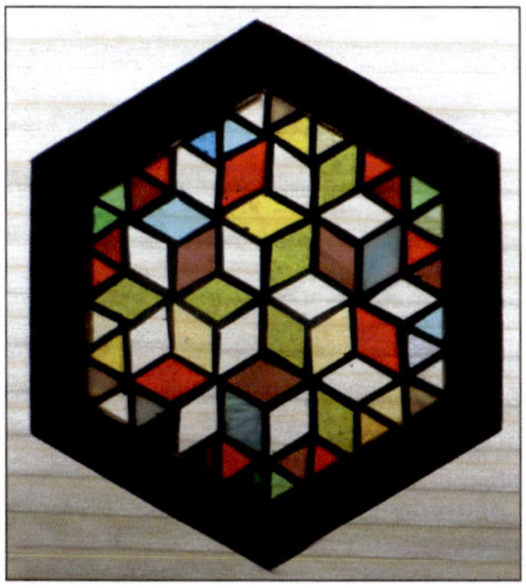

1.54a.

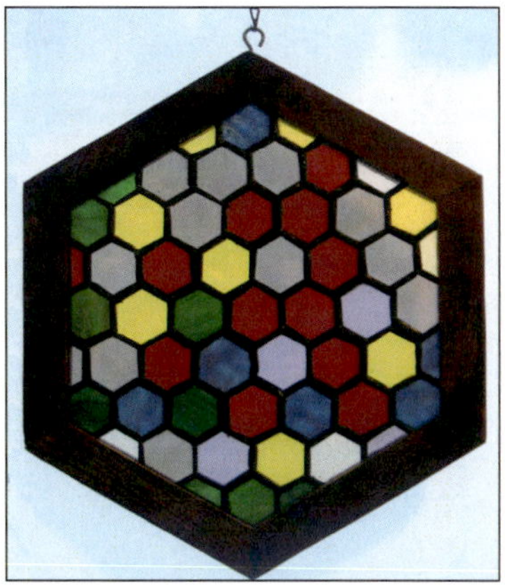

1.54b.

1.54a. Some examples (stained glass) on an hexagonal grid. This is actually a distinct grid type of it's own. The glass chips had to be truncated to fit into a frame. This cropping to the frame forces the implication of the grid being extended past the frame towards infinity, or at least towards a larger view.

1.54b. A Color By Numbers linear pattern spirals on a purely hexagonal grid. Both Stained Glass pieces are 8" in diameter and were created in 2018.

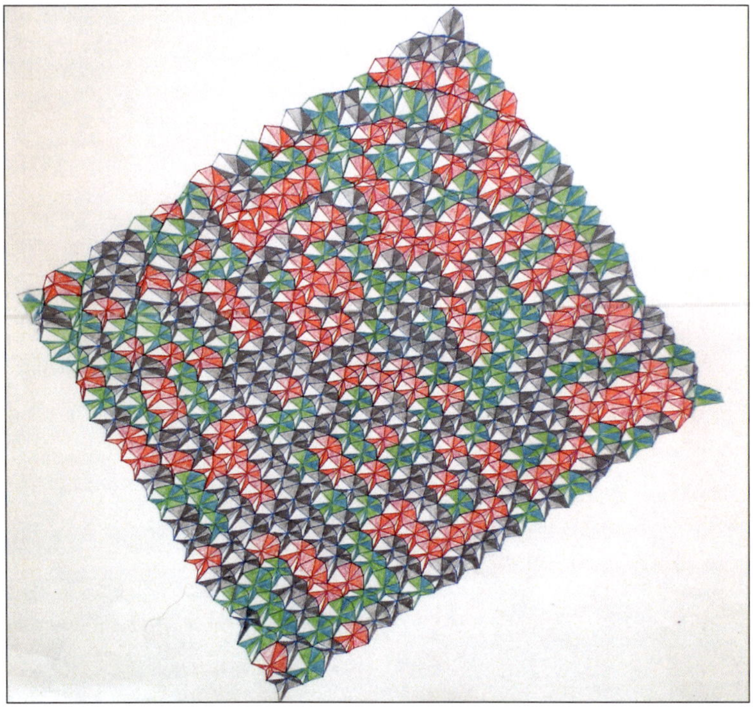

1.55.

A Color By Numbers Base 3 pen plot from 1980, colored pencil added in 1990, photographed in 2000.... or so.
It is a 3 dimensionally distorted tessellating grid with color by numbers patterning imposed, originally drawn in 3 pen colors. It crosses media, time, and techniques. The tessellating form is an optical illusion made from a polygon grid. It tessellates on a rectangular grid, which is mildly distorted with a splash wave.

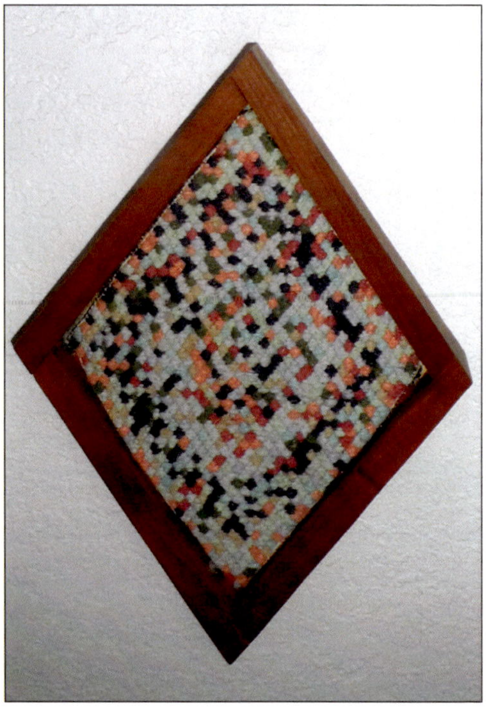

1.56.

A parallelogram skewed from a naturally stretched needlepoint. A nice variation on a rectangular grid.

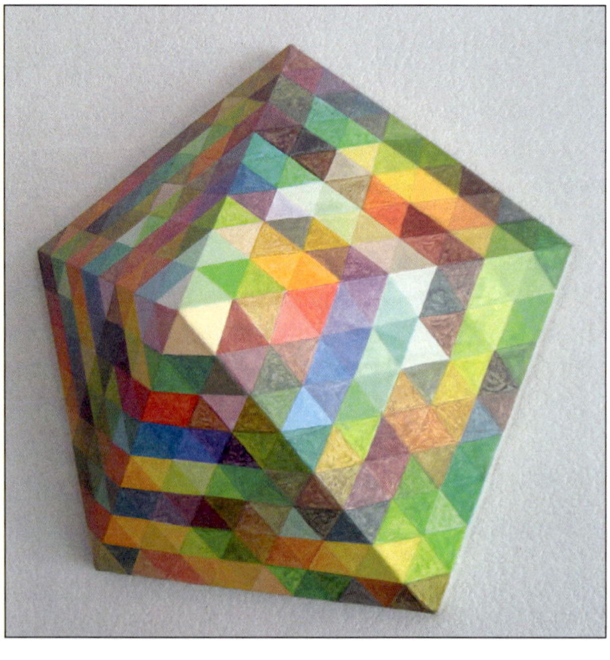

1.57.

A pentagonal 3D "shaped" pyramid canvas with a Color By Numbers pattern mapped on it. Spiraling from the center, with color blending. Utilizing dayglo colors, it looks a bit different in person (as these colors are hard to photograph), as well as in a blacklight. 12" diameter, acrylic on shaped canvas, 2007.

COLORING BY NUMBERS

"The universality of Number can be seen in another, more physical context. We learn from modern physics that from gravity to electromagnetism, light, heat, and even in what we think of as solid matter itself, the entire perceptible universe is composed of vibrations, perceived by us as wave phenomena. Waves are pure temporal patterns, that is dynamic configurations composed of amplitude, interval and frequency, and they can be defined and understood by us only through Number. Thus our whole universe is reducible to Number."

- Robert Lawlor, *Philosophy and Practice Sacred Geometry*

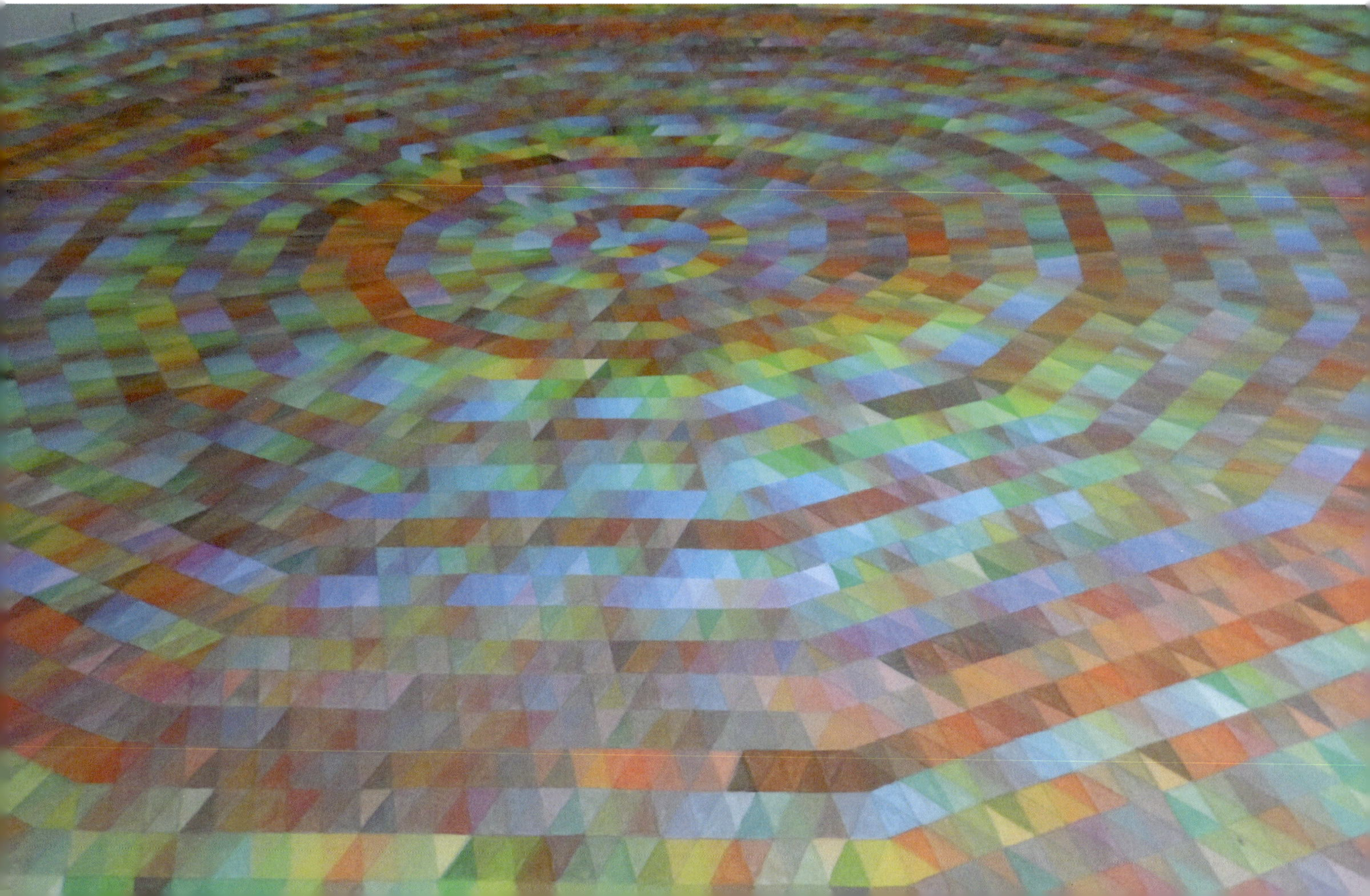

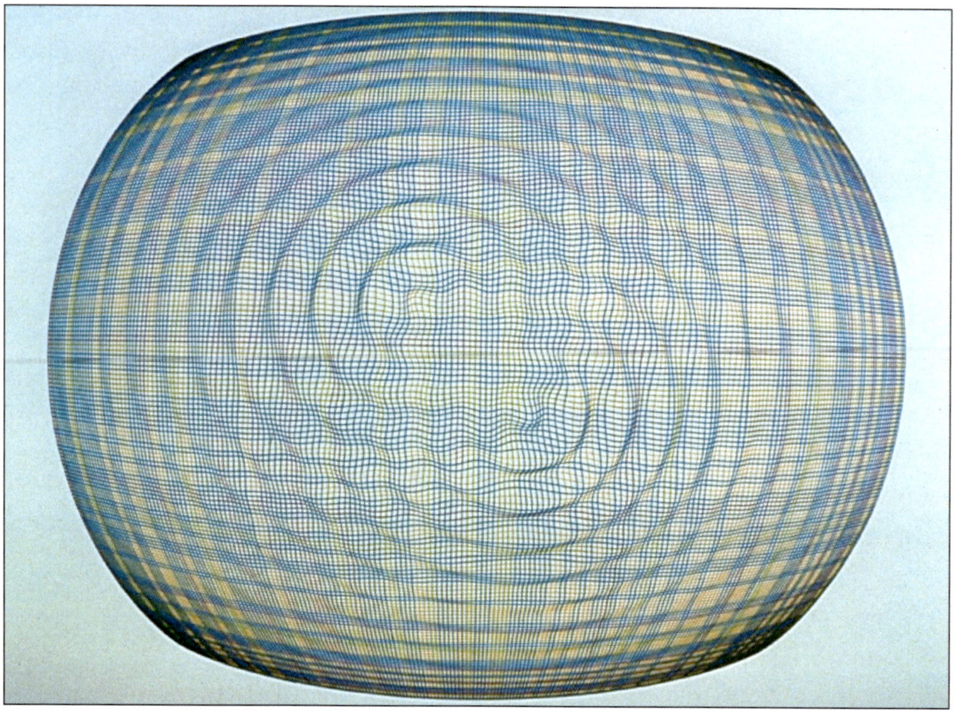

2.1.

(Previous page)
Color by Numbers blended spiral, large acrylic painting on pinned canvas. 7' diameter, 1983

This one took 12 months to paint. Counting 1 to ~12,000, with color blending of the digits on each grid element. In other words, each triangle's color is a color mix of equal values of the colors representing that number. For instance 12,000 would have equal values of color 1, color 2 and 3 times color Zero.

2.2.

Color By Numbers Plaid Wave, Pen Plot, 8.5" x 11", 1980.
This one always reminded me of waves on a TV screen.

The universe is built from vibration - sound, light and geometry. They are the elements of art and music. It appears there are certain universal principles regarding form. Spiraling invisible energy, Platonic solids, octaves of color and sound, mathematics and numbers.

Geometry has a power to gather energy in ways we can explore. Architecture is one area that has explored this through the ages – the pyramids, the renaissance cathedrals, geodesic and domed structures. Some of these ways are inextricably tied to religion. Some are tied to sacred art – the mandala, the cross, archetypes. Many of these powerful elements are being discovered through science on a way to understanding the power and structure of the universe.

Numbers are the basis of mathematics and counting. They are universal, being used by humans (and likely by aliens) in their daily lives. By visualizing number systems, I turn the abstract idea of counting into an image of patterning. I materialize a predefined arrangement. The grids and patterns in Color By Numbers systemic structures are innate to math and geometry and both have fractal principles. The art of this is conceptual as well physical or digital.

I have realized that counting itself is a fractal principal. It has repetition, self-similarity, iteration, and infinity. Counting may be the earliest fractal man ever invented. It has been latent in the face of mathematicians and scientists for ages. I feel it is time to explore counting's multi- dimensional ramifications. I am not particularly interested in numerology, but that could also be used to create number patterns using these systemic approaches.

Counting can be expressed through color (and other variables as well). Simply assign a variable to a number and count to get periodic, infinitely variable arrays, with a certain amount of control. When imposed on grid surfaces, these structures can be expressed as static visuals. By assigning color to number, I have been exploring and searching for new dimensions of patterning. I am also pursuing the beauty, synchronicity and coherence of number systems in these structures.

COLOR BY NUMBERS SYSTEMS (CBN)

Color By Numbers mixes fundamental mathematics with fundamental geometry as it manifests color fractals. More on fractals later. CBN is a methodology for patterning regular geometric structures with counting. Colors are mapped to numbers which array linear pattern sequences on grids. It encodes a counting algorithm on grids.

Counting is a numeric fractal which iterates and scales to infinity, but can be viewed within limits. Patterns are created through repetition and scaling as counting evolves and adds to itself. We can count by "x" or in reverse, starting from any number. I'm pretty sure Nikolai Tesla would count by 3's. Numeric sequences could also be manifested in temporal arrangements to create audio and video. A door opens to a plethora of possibilities. I got started on graph paper.

We can program computers to graph the resulting patterns. We can also do this directly with physical media, turning a canvas (or other media) into a sort of handmade computer for patterns.

The results are predetermined after the initial choice of colors and arrangement. There is a broad freedom in choosing the colors, the number base (which is also the number of colors), the way they are arranged, on what surface structure they are arrayed upon, and the media used to express this patterning. A set of rules combines the way color is used with the way grids are used. The resulting pattern spreads magically on the surface and inundates it with a visual effect.

NUMBER BASES

You can count (colorize) in various number bases depending on how many elements you would like to work with. Base 10 uses 10 colors, Base 2 uses 2 colors, etc.

Below is an example of a base 2 array of counting presented as if reading a book (left to right, jumping to the next line down vertically). This is one of my earliest computer graphics. I had successfully seen this on a Black and White Monitor before making a pen plot.

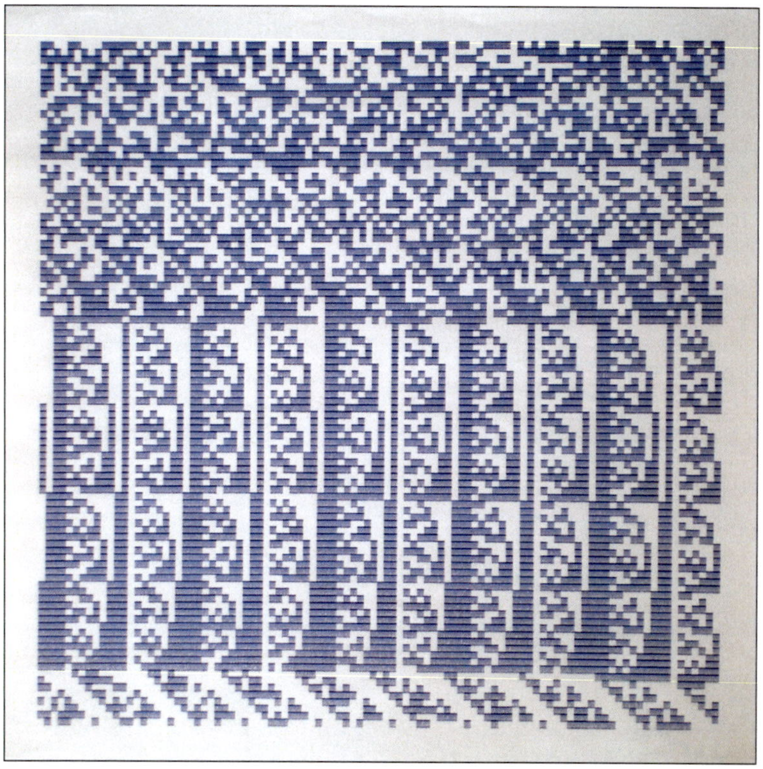

2.3.

Base 2 Sequential Digits, Pen Plot, 11" x 11", 1979. This is one of the very first Color By Numbers ever generated on a computer.

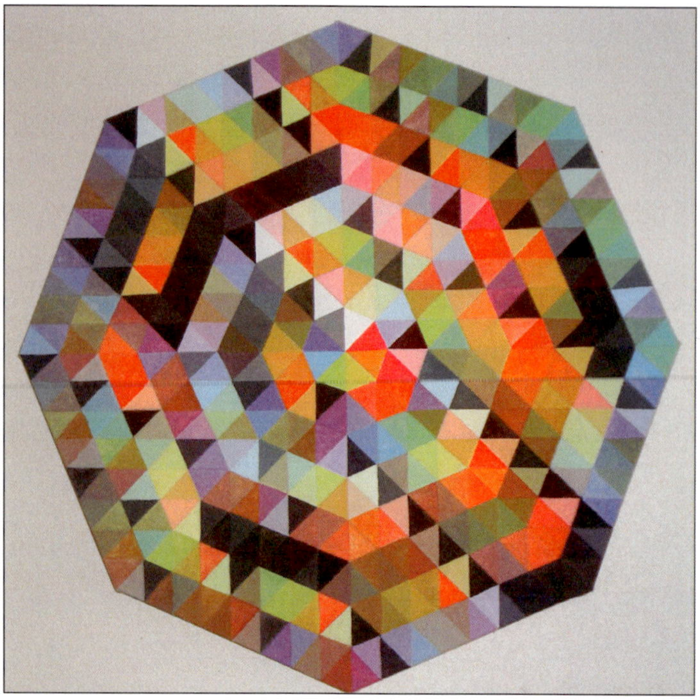

2.4a. Color By Numbers Painting in Base 8, manually blended colors, acrylic on octagonal canvas, 18" diameter, 2011.

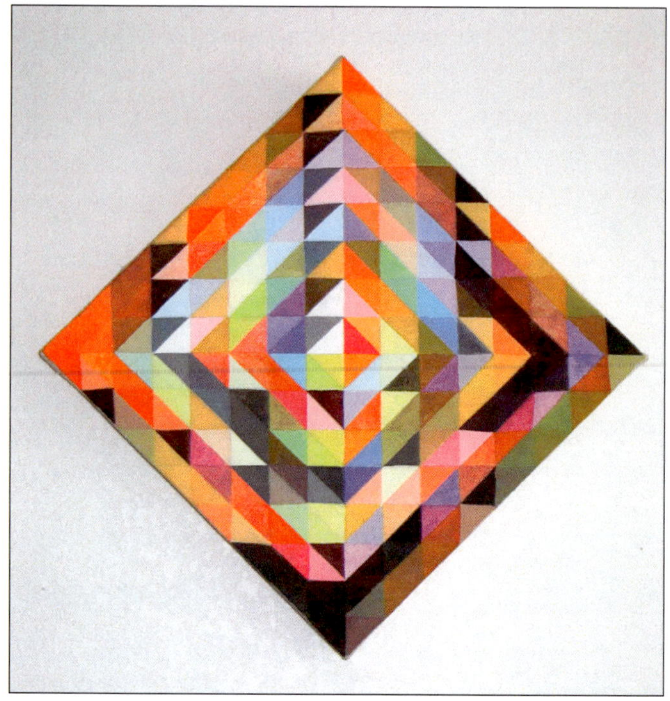

2.4b. Color By Numbers Painting in Base 8, manually blended colors, acrylic on square canvas, 12" x 12", 2011.

Note that counting thresholds (ie. hitting 1,000) are abrupt (quantum) and can form into columns depending on the width of the structure and the number of digits involved in displaying each numeral. Number bases can be utilized to limit the palette and therefore expand the creative possibilities. Grid elements can easily include other structures than just color.

I have created patterns from counting with alphabet letters in base 26. Perhaps of interest, this uses z for zero. This encodes letters to numbers. The resulting array includes all possible words (as well as all unused letter combinations) from our alphabet. This creates a word database that is comprehensive, organized and searchable for mild deviations.

For clarity, I am talking about counting in other number bases than our familiar base 10.

Binary - base 2 is an obvious example. In Color By Numbers software you can count in base 2048 - a bit of a preposterous idea, but why not?

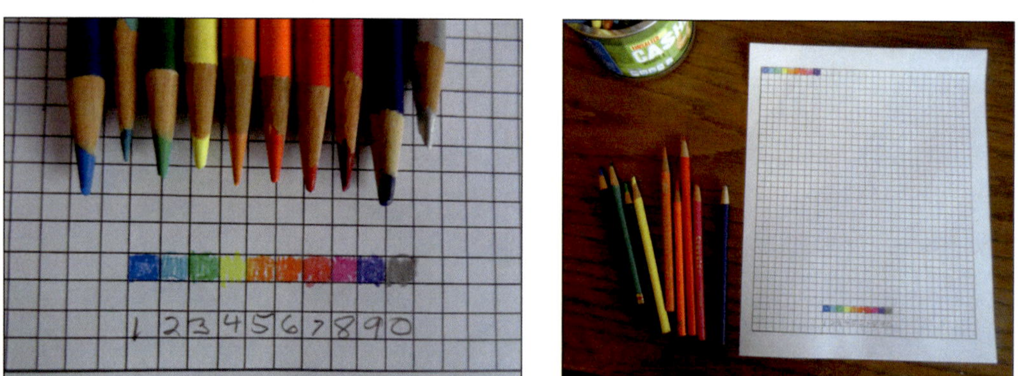

2.5. A brief photographic explanation of how I created my first Color By Numbers drawings on graph paper with colored pencils.

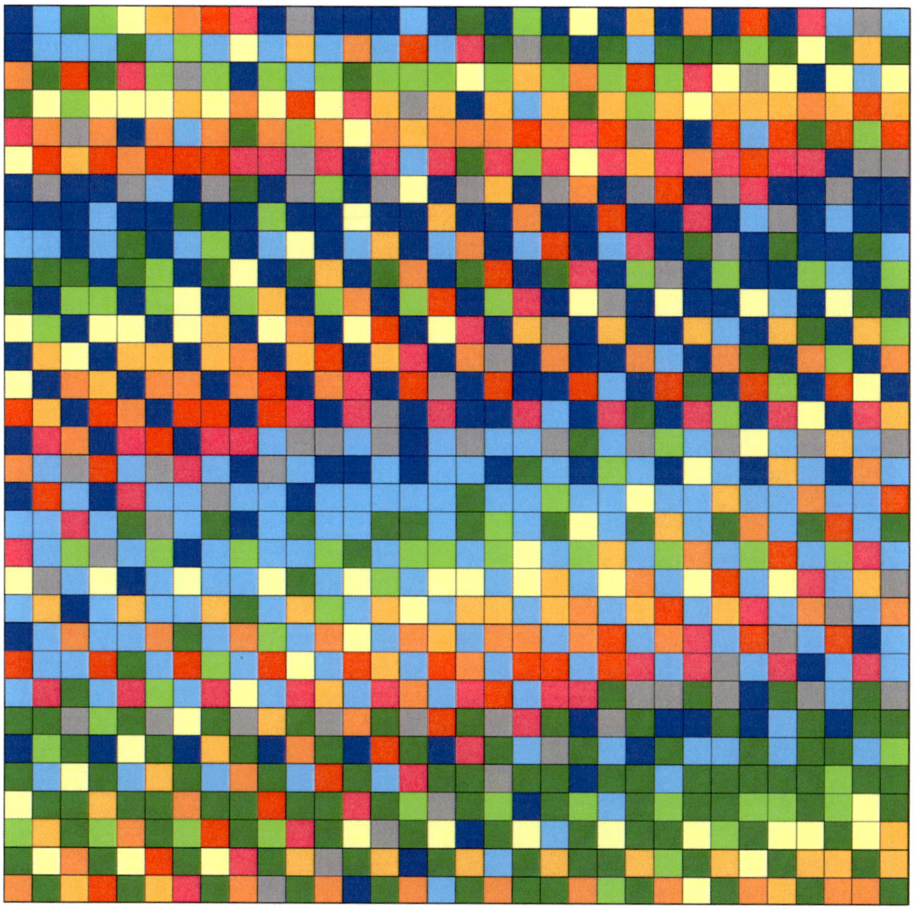

2.6a.

Base 10 Color By Numbers reading like a book. - "linear". Each digit of each number is represented by a square on the grid. The first 961 digits and It looks like it just clears 1 to 377 in counting.

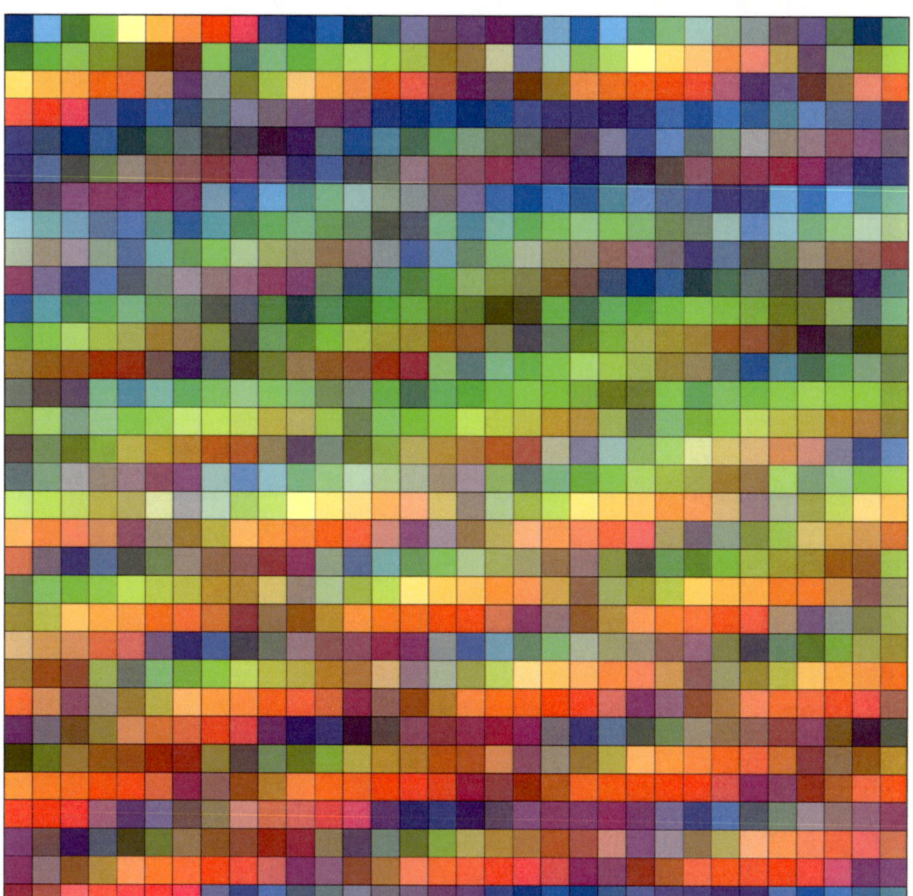

2.6b.

Base 10 Color By Numbers "blended" reading like a book. Each number is represented by a square on the grid. Each cell has all of the colors from all of the digits blended. Counting is from 1 to 961.

My first explorations with Coloring by Numbers and an interest in computers quickly led to a partnership with Jeff Yetter from Hewlett Packard who assisted me in programming early HP machines to create counting patterns in 1979. I had created numerous hand drawings and had been using a limited number of colors in base 10. We used sequential counting that represented the digits in a linear array in these explorations. This was an excellent match for a pen plotter; which accommodated only a handful of colors and was the only available high resolution output at the time. Raster graphics was in its infancy in 1980 (mostly black and white). The number of colors was influenced by the number of working pens we had. The sequence counted in a number base that matched the number of pens. See next page for an example.

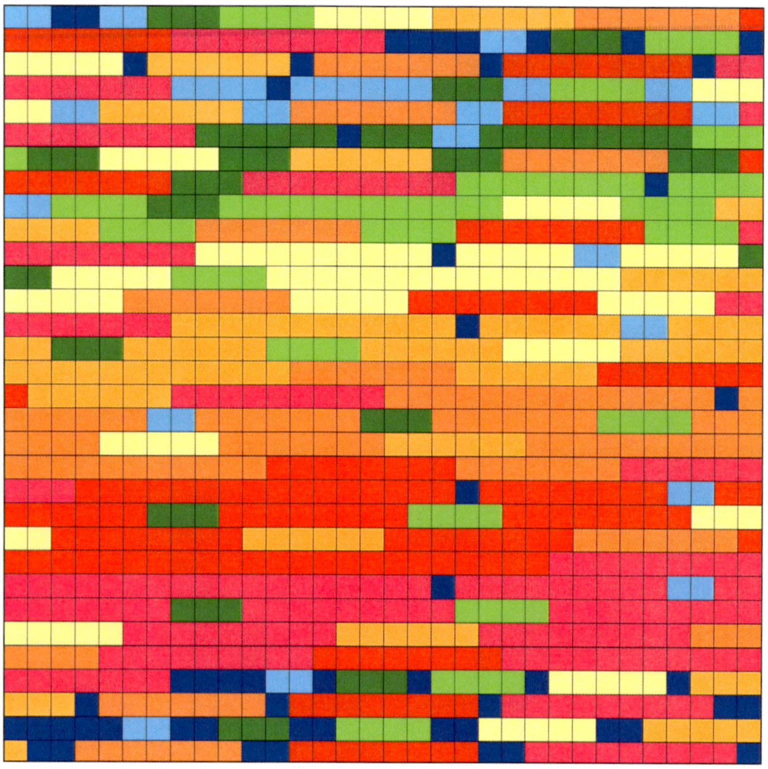

2.7a.

An attempt to use quantity. Each digit of each number is represented by that quantity of squares. Zeros are skipped. Linear and no blending. The first 961 digits counting to 119. The sequence begins after 3 gray squares (my glitch).

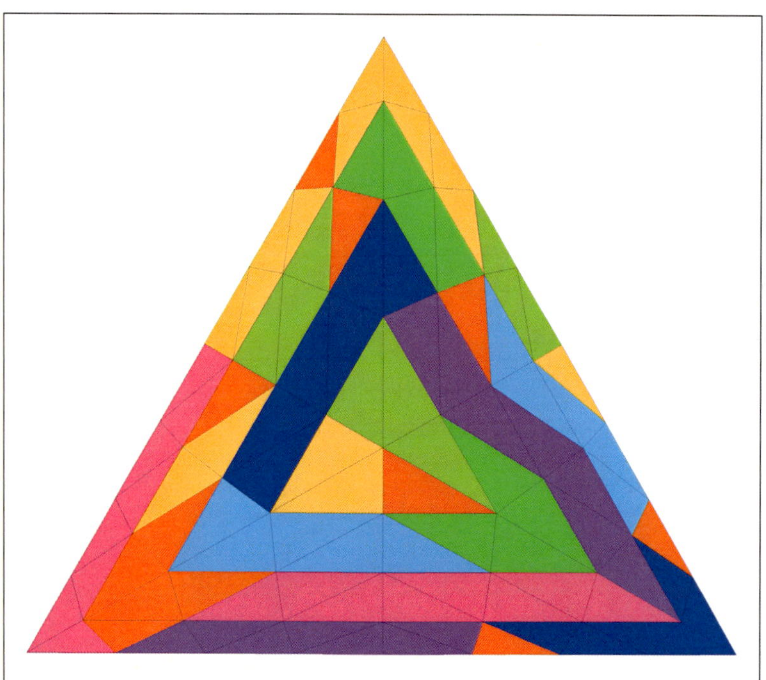

2.7b.

An example of quantity fill arrayed in a spiral on a triangular grid.

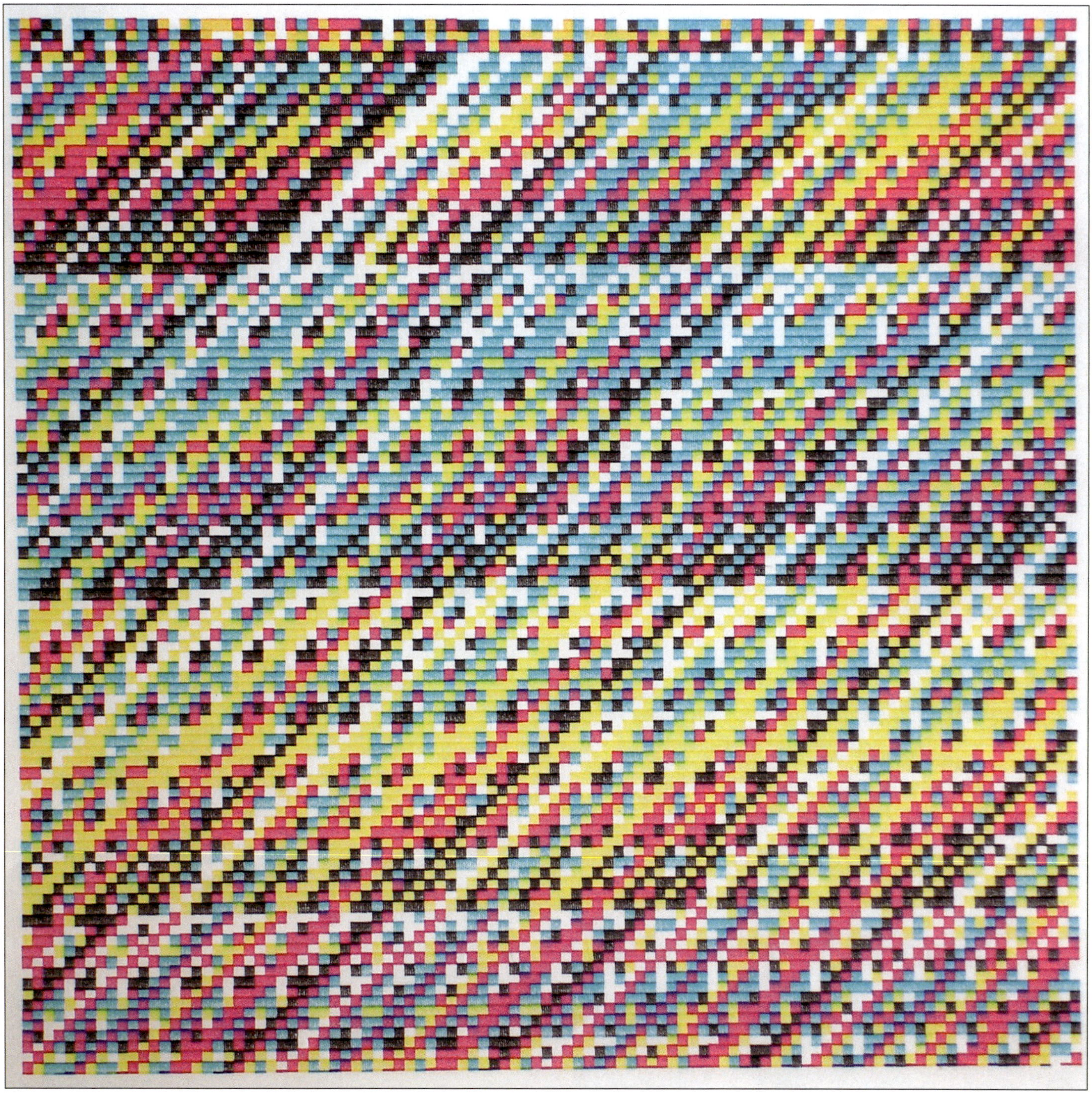

2.8. Color By Numbers Base 5 made with 4 pens and a blank space in a pen plot on paper from 1980, 11" x 11".

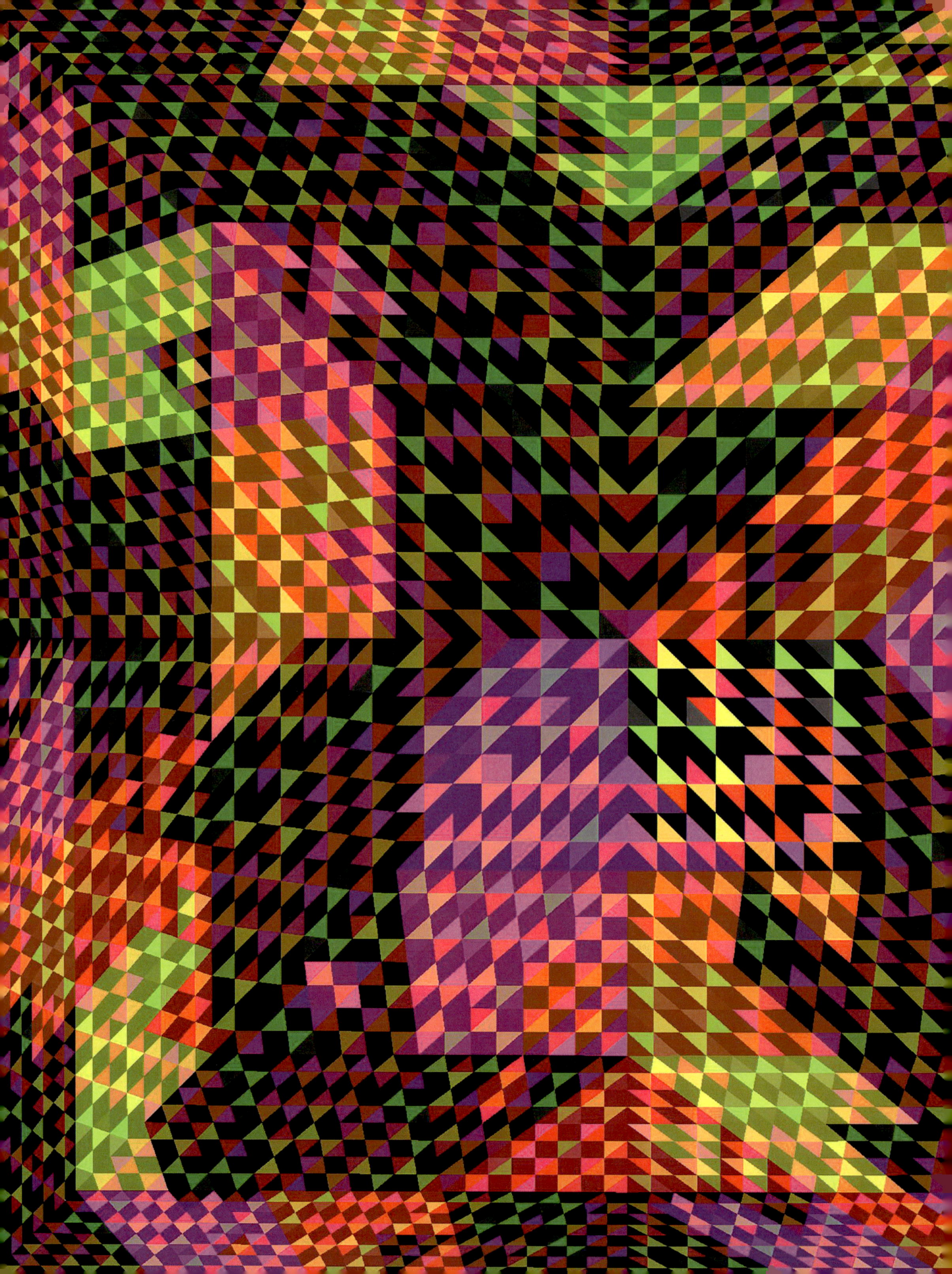

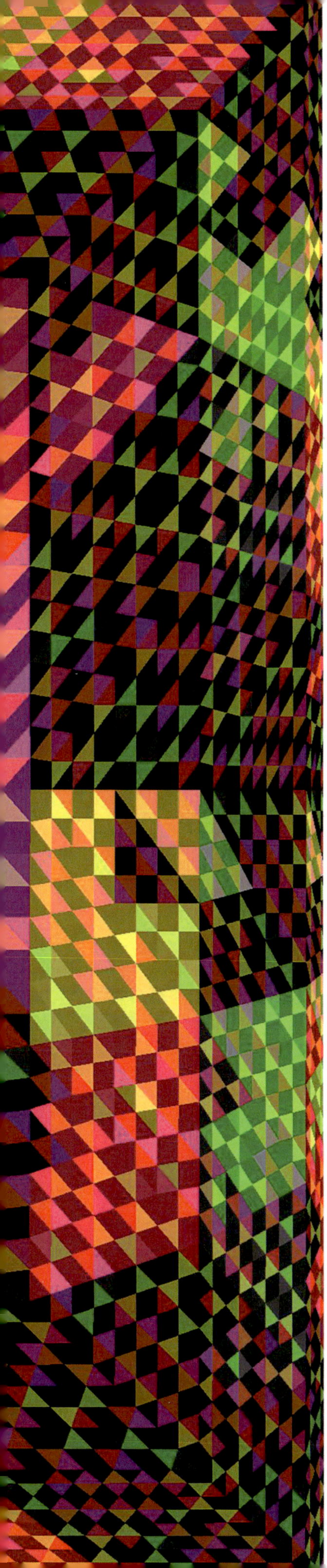

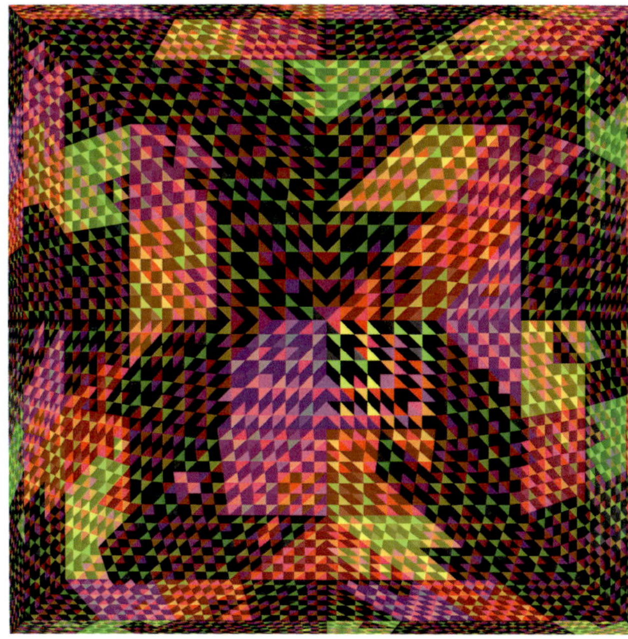

2.9.

Color By Numbers on a bulge grid,
Digital, 2160 x 2160 Pixels, 2021.

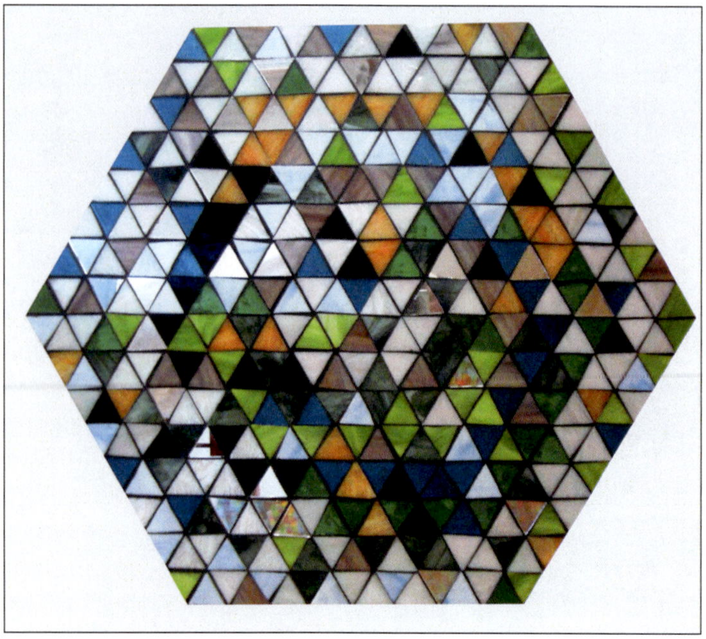

2.10. Color By Numbers Linear Spiral, Glass Mosaic, 18" Diameter, 2014.

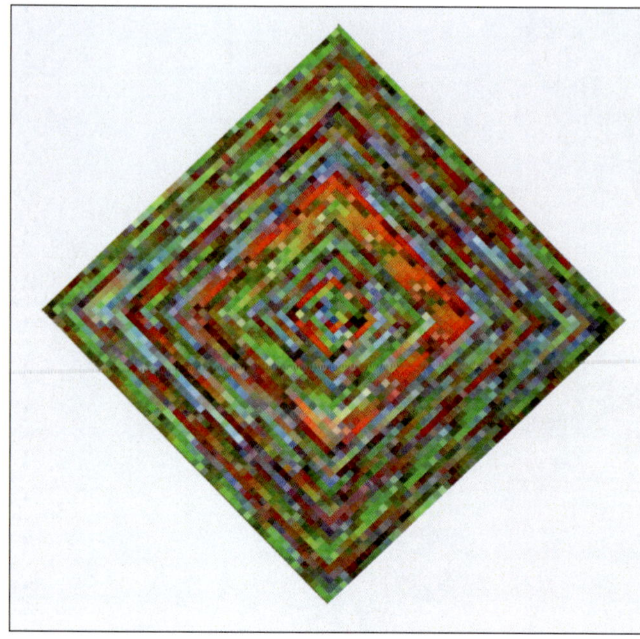

2.11. Color By Number Blended Spiral, Acrylic on Canvas, 3' x 3', 2007.

GRID STRUCTURES AND ARRANGEMENT ON GRID SURFACE

I am launched into an exploration of grids by necessity when creating a static image representation of counting patterns. Temporal exploration without grids is, of course, another possibility. An experiment with just counting with a colored light source had some interest.

Visual representation on grids has physical limits. Therefore grids can give birth to larger, conceptual grids as they imply an expansion towards infinity, but cropped by limits in space. CBN allows the co-creation of divine patterns. We can explore the pre-conceived by birthing our own arrangements and color choices on grids.

Regarding organization on the grid, linear number sequences could read like a book, wrap around themselves in spirals, read left to right, right to left, array in plaid form or move through 3D space (or whatever we decide that works).

SQUARE GRIDS

Square grids are the most common grids. They are implicit in two dimensional coordinate systems. They were the first I explored. I quickly decided to spiral from the center as it easily implied the continuity on the grid towards infinity.

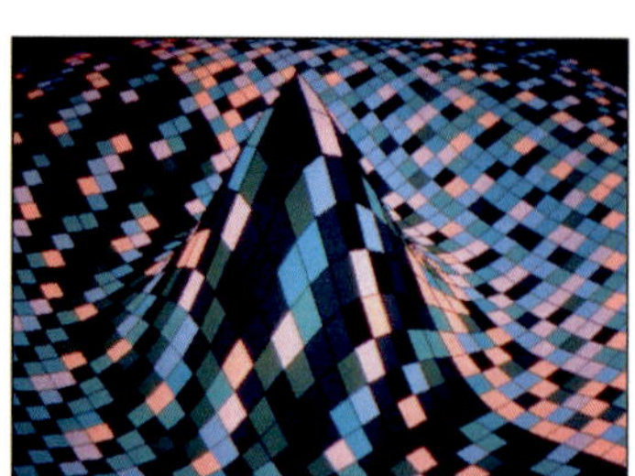

2.12.

Color By Numbers, Screen Photograph.
Early Raster Graphics, 1982.

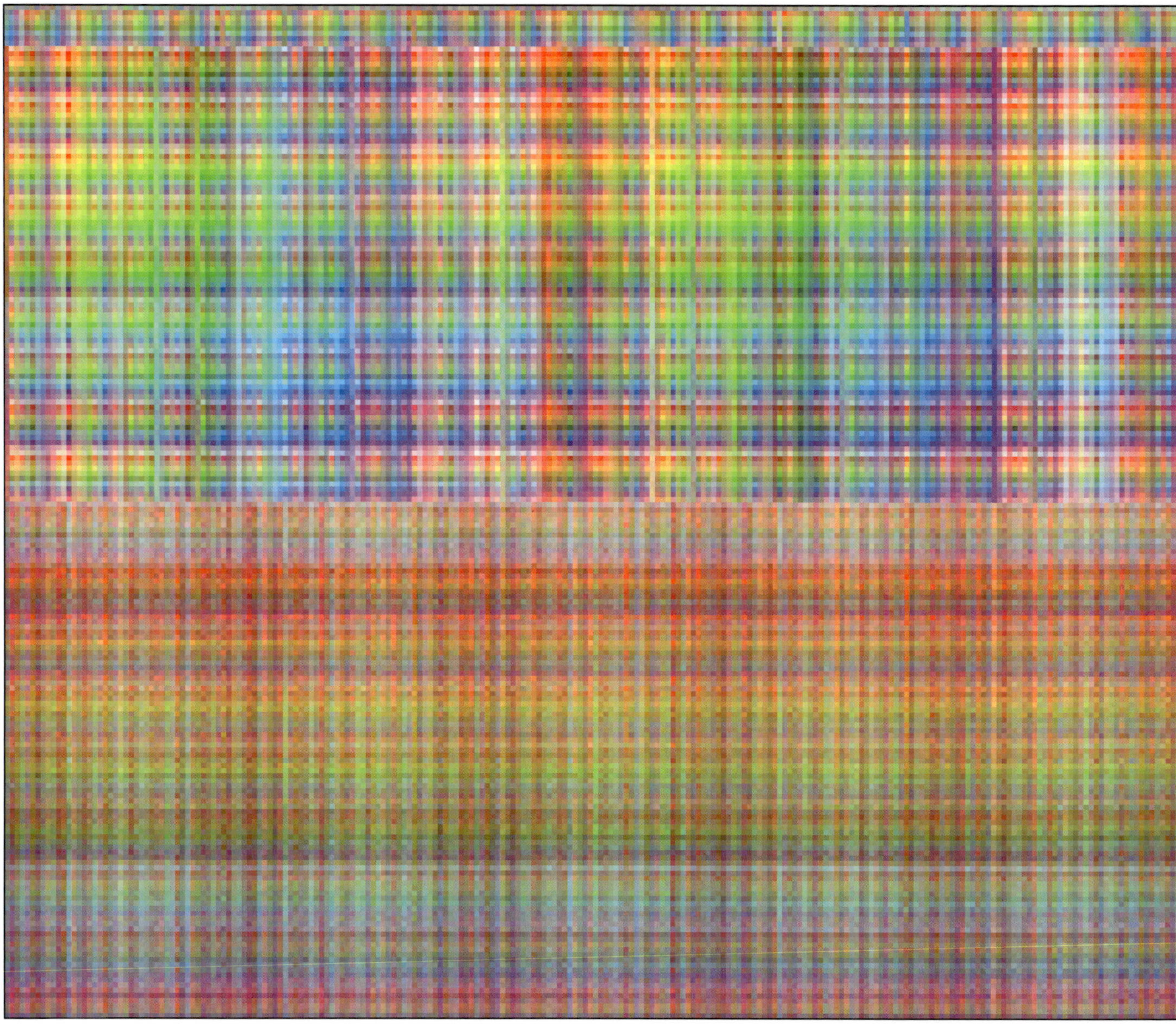

2.13.

The first one million numbers of base 10, blended and arrayed like a book. 2013 from "CBN Blaster" an auto generating pattern routine. Plaids are formed with a fortuitous alignment of numbers and columns. This screen saver was made with a very early software version of Color By Numbers that only uses regular rectangular grids. To watch CBN Blaster in action, visit the support page for Geometry for Art, by scanning the QR code.

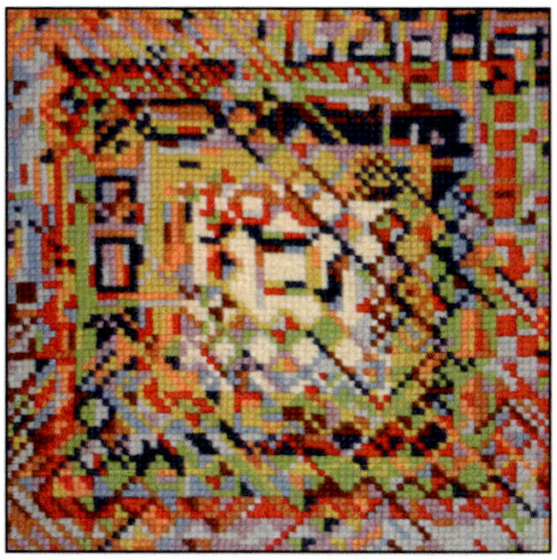

2.14.

Color And Pattern By Numbers Spiral, Needlepoint, Base 10, 1985.

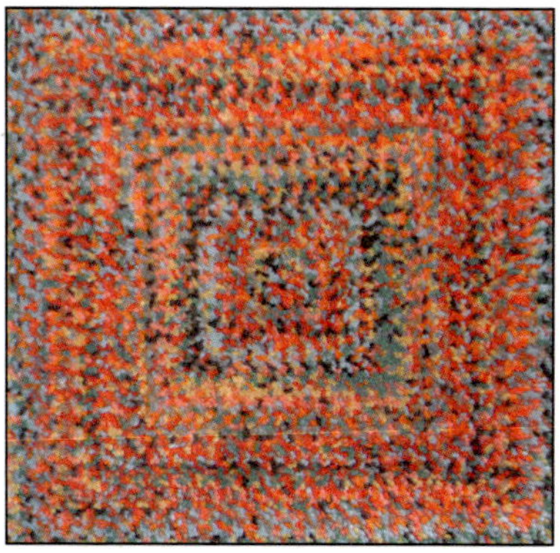

2.15.

Color By Numbers Linear Spiral, Hook Rug, Base 10, 10 Colors of Yarn, 2011.

PATTERN BY NUMBERS

Rather than just a color, a pattern and a color can be applied to the grid. There are infinite possibilities here as well.

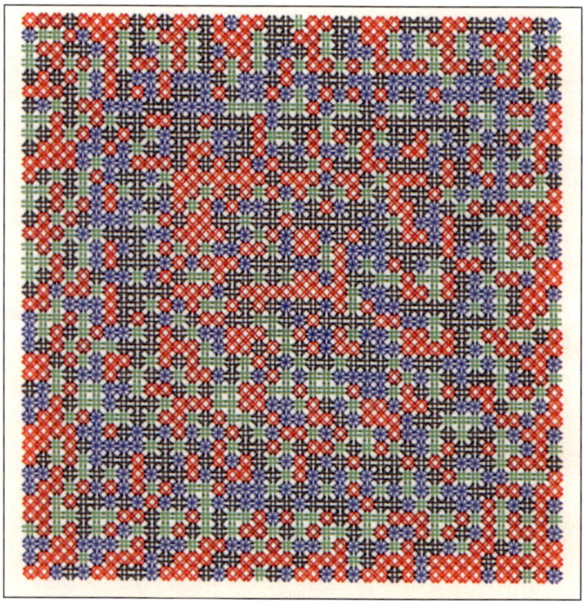

2.16.

Color and Pattern By Numbers Linear Spiral, Pen Plot,
11" x 11", 1980.

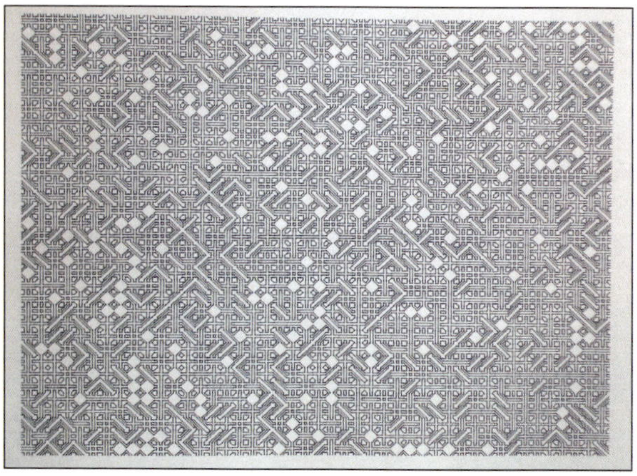

2.17.

Pattern By Numbers Linear, Pen Plot, 11" x 14", 1980.

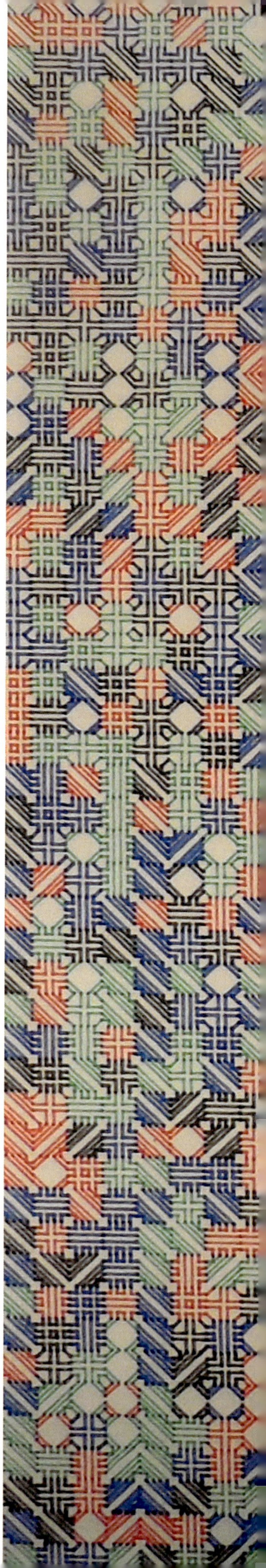

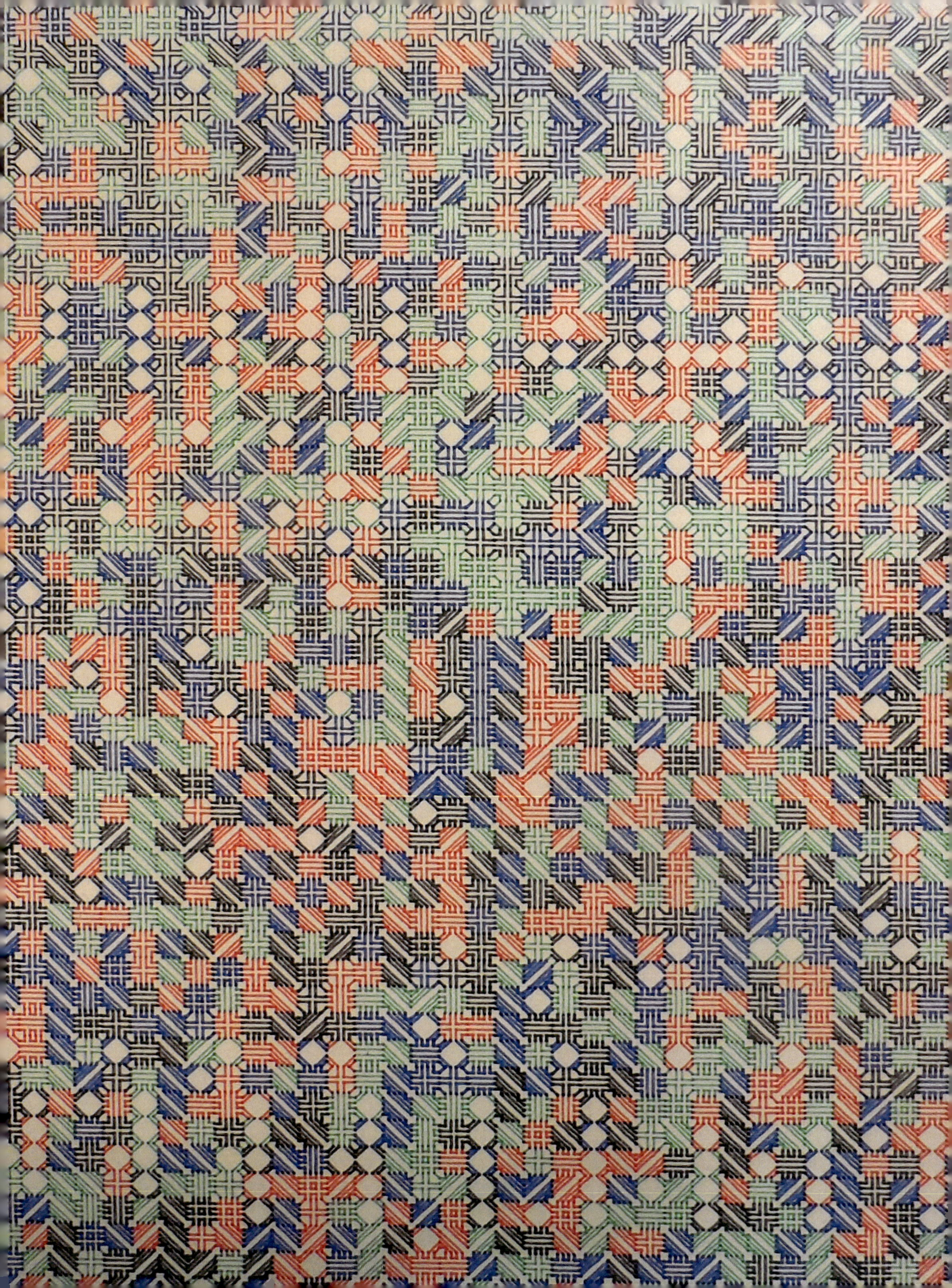

LINES AND PLAIDS

Sequences of lines can be used in counting. This has worked well for weaving and simple drawings. There are infinite variations on this theme alone, considering the variables of color choice, number bases, and range of counting activity (what number you start and end with).

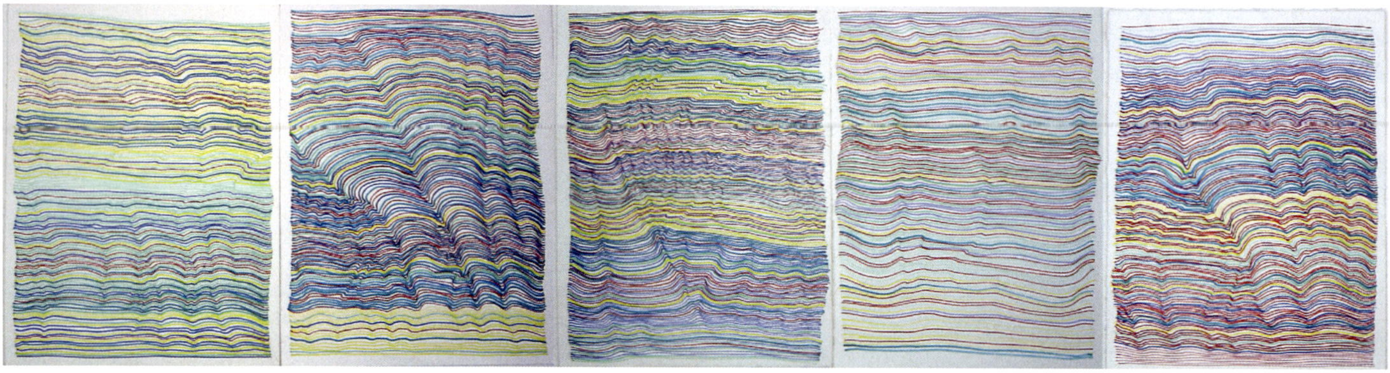

2.19. 5 Color By Numbers Line Drawings, 8.5" x 11" each, Colored Markers on Paper, 1985.

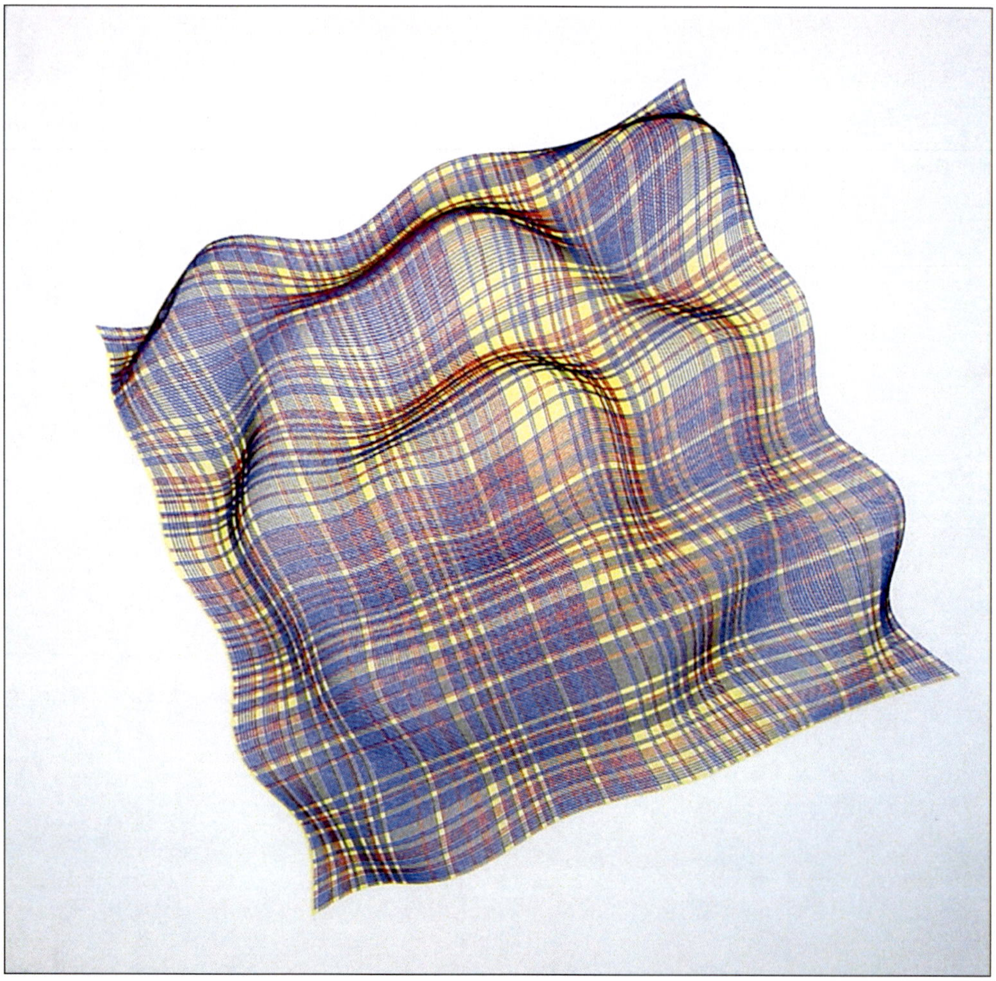

2.20.

Color By Numbers Plaid Wave, Hand-pulled, 3 Color Lithograph on Paper, 17" x 17", 1981.

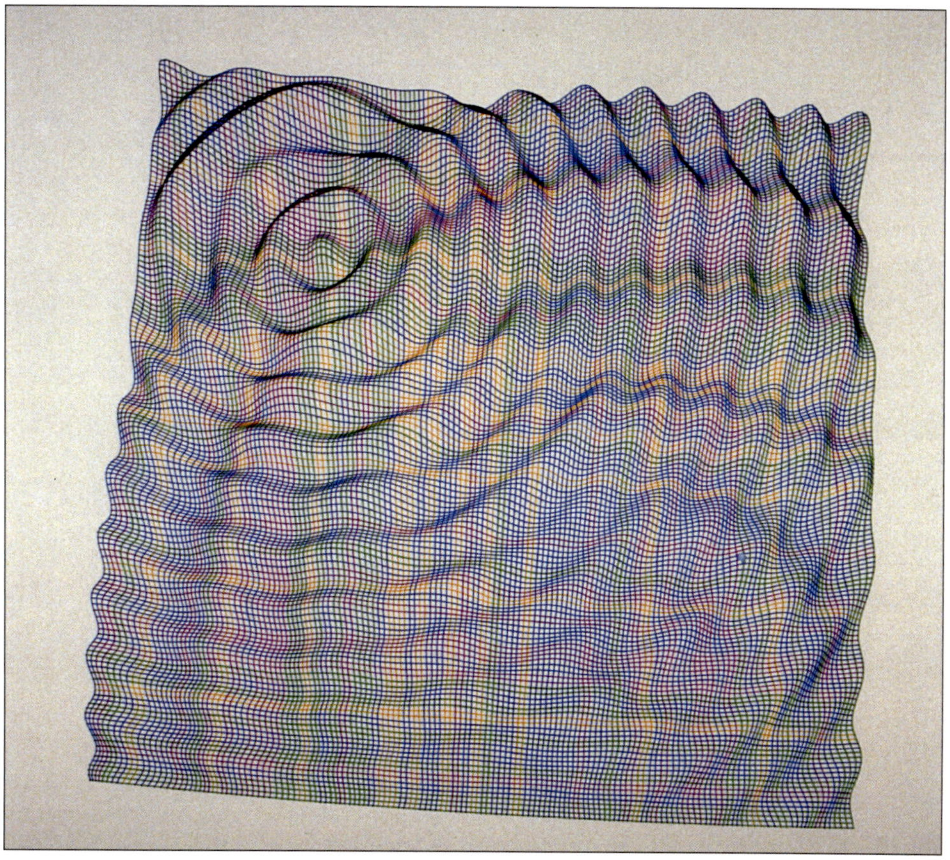

2.21.

Color By Numbers
Plaid Wave,
Pen Plot on Paper,
11" x 11", 1980.

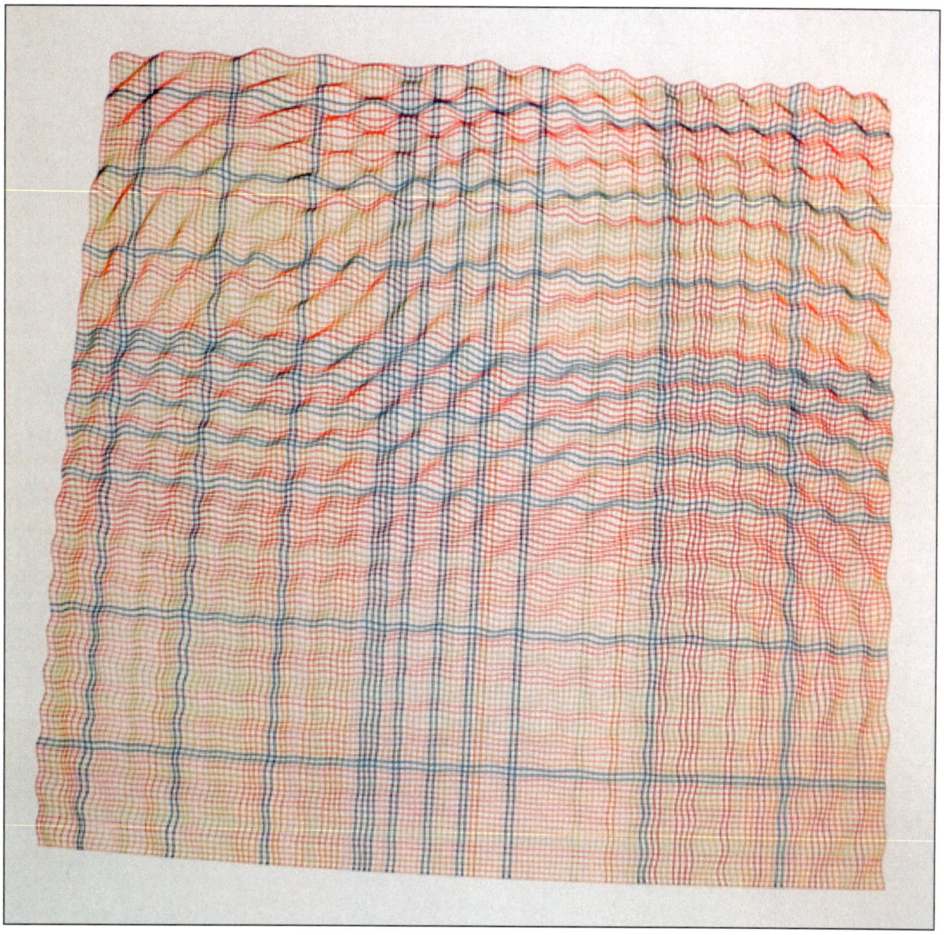

2.22.

Color By Numbers
Plaid Wave,
Pen Plot on Paper,
11" x 11", 1980.

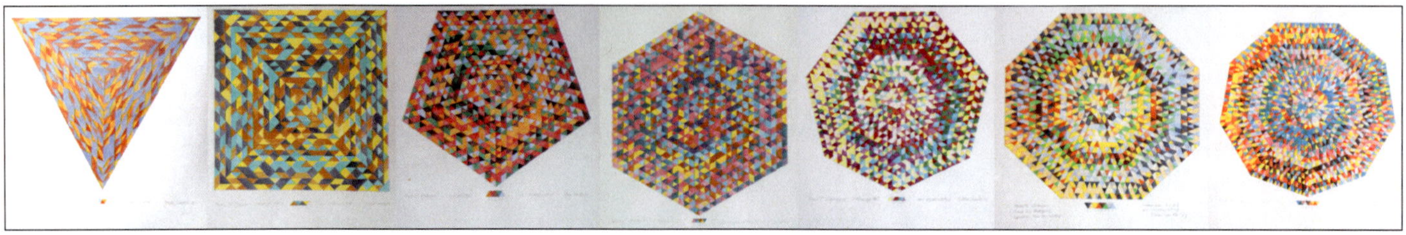

2.23. Color By Numbers on 7 Regular Polygons, Watercolors on Paper, 18" x 24" each, 1982.

POLYGONAL GRIDS

My polygonal grids were inspired by tessellation geometry and optical illusions. Beyond the viewing surface, the viewer can mentally continue the pattern (with some effort). This implied continuation infers and compels the infinite expansion that is possible. To say this another way, Color By Number spirals represent the inception of an infinite field of patterned colors (radiating outward) limited by the edge and size of the grid.

Polygonal grids can subdivide most any polygon. That is another realm to explore. These grids are fractals themselves since they are comprised of grid triangles self-similar to the "facet" of the polygon. Most of my CBN explorations involve grids wherein I begin from the center and spiral outward, usually clockwise.

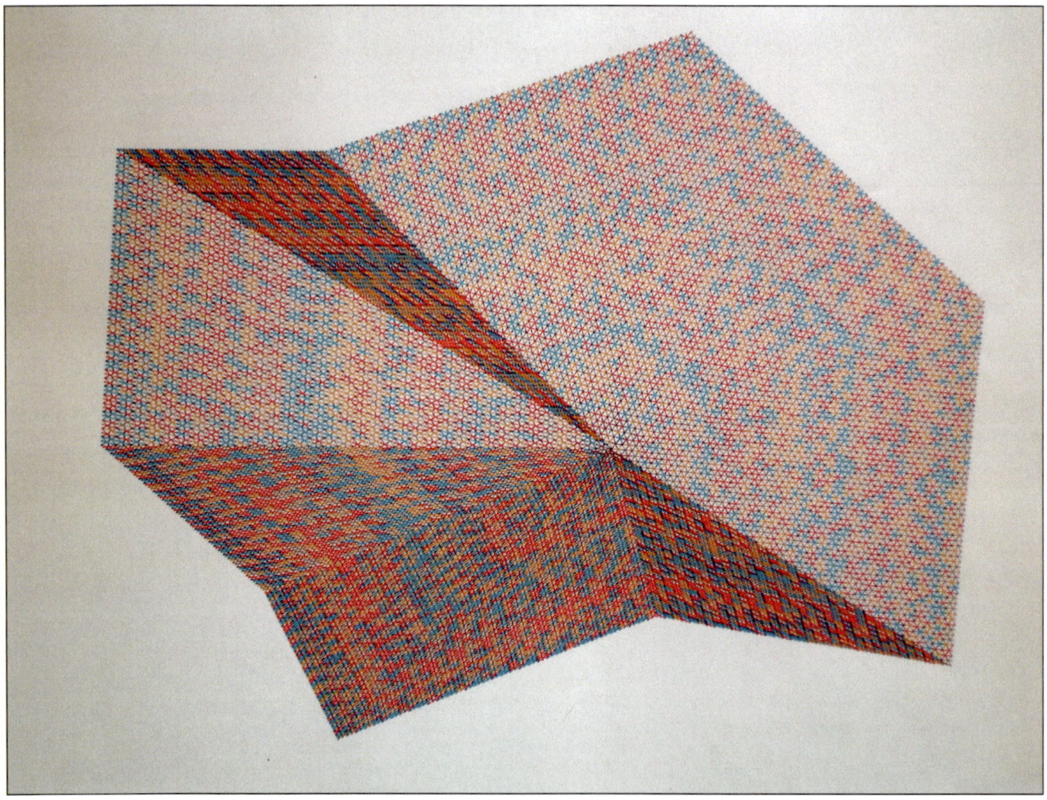

2.24. Color By Numbers Linear Spiral on Subdivided Polygon, Pen Plot on Paper, 11" x 14", 1980.

"To assert that computer assisted art is not art is as absurd as saying that computer assisted music is not music."

COMPUTER GRAPHICS

Utilizing simple mathematics, I can program a Color By Numbers pattern into traditional media. The color choices act as a seed to the overall design and, pre-ordained, dictate the final outcome. These ideas can add meaning to abstract art. Natural counting structures can be analyzed and appreciated.

Objectifying art into systems (systemic art) can minimize spontaneity and expression. A certain diligence is required to execute drawings of systemic structures. One factor for me is keeping count. So I have looked at a computer to execute the final drawing for assurance of accuracy. Computers are precise, consistent, versatile, accurate and tireless. They cannot be ignored as valid tools for visual artists. With their use comes a certain loss of individuality and a denial of hand craftsmanship, but computer graphics has the potential to map realities that go beyond human capability (by hand).

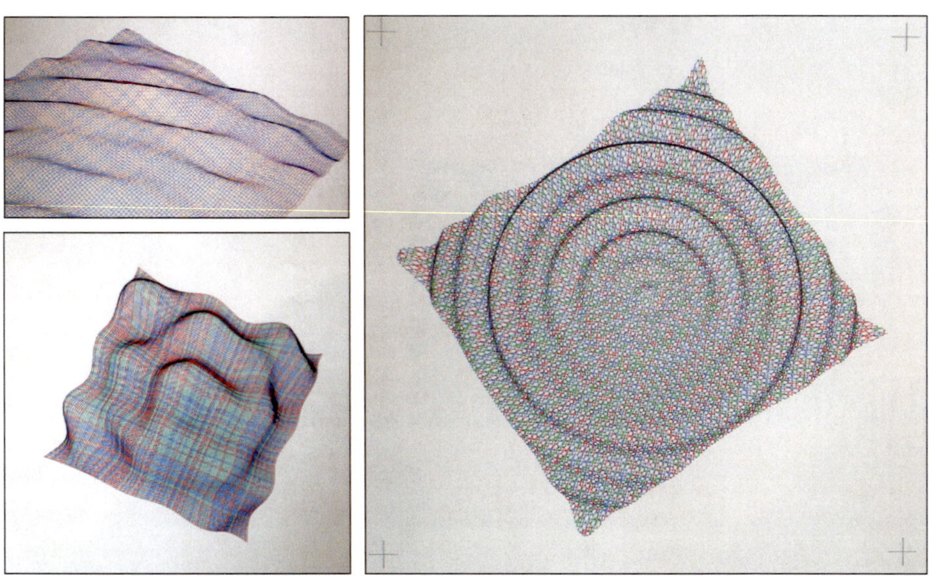

2.25.

Color By Numbers Plaid Waves.

Top Left is a Pen Plot, 11" x 14",
Bottom Left is a Pen Plot, 17" x 17",
On the Right is a Hand-Pulled Lithograph on Paper, 15" x 15",

All from the Early 1980s.

This work with pen plotters using 3D grids in perspective is an illustration of an impossible task for the human hand to execute. Even the best draftsman could not execute these drawings without error, I believe. The computer can output this work with a speed and perfection which is alarming. Zoom in close to witness this impeccable draftsmanship.

Perfection becomes the norm. Human skill is evident, not in execution or expression, but in the structure, concept and color choices. One program can be used to create endless variations on one idea or arrangement, with minimal time and effort. They are output as "files", and therefore are easily archived and reproduced in various media. Computer Graphics is like print - except the plates don't wear out and can be stored in a really minute digital storage space.

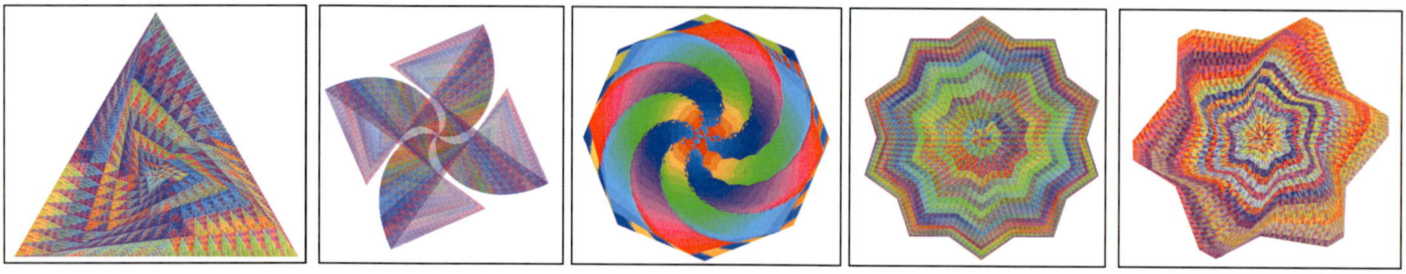

2.26. Assorted Digital Output from Color By Numbers Software by ArtToyz Studios.

3D graphics and animation are areas I have dedicated a lot of time to exploring. I can assign animateable and static parameters to numbers to create geometry that represents the counting and have some fun while I make it change over time.

These numeric sequences could also be presented in temporal arrangements to create audio and video. We can make our own rules and use numbers however we want. Maybe the Fibonacci sequence, maybe primes, primes backward...

Note: there is no requirement to count forwards (or to start with 1).

Please help me explore these realms of pattern structures. Visit ArtToyz Studios website at http://www.arttoyz.com. The website has software and images that are free of charge and of copyright restrictions. Collaboration and creative use of CBN are welcomed.

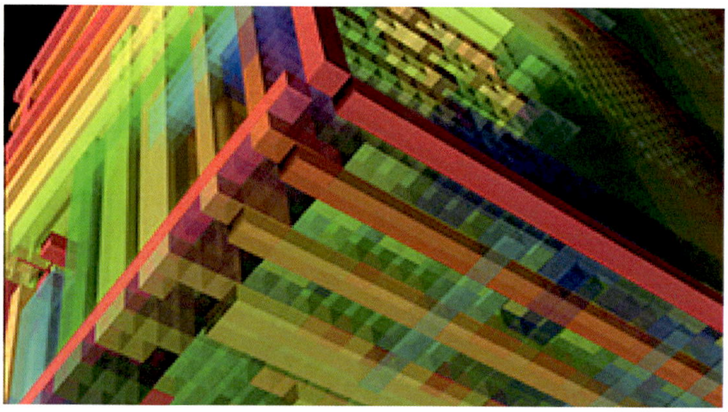

2.27a. Still from "Cube Counter" CBN 3D Animation.

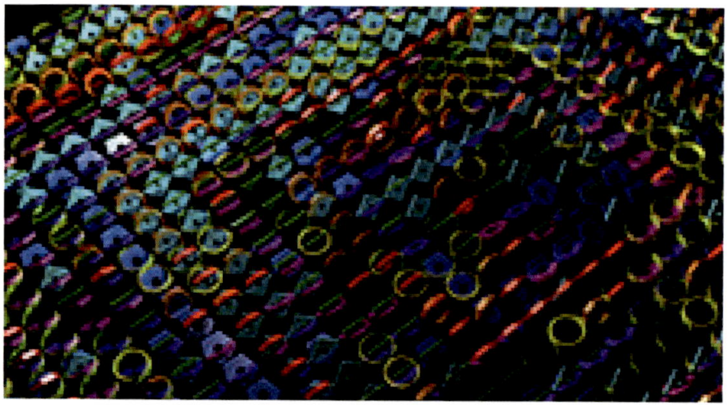

2.27b. Still from "Cube Counter" CBN 3D Animation. Visit the support page for Geometry for Art by scanning the QR code.

CHOICE OF MEDIA

Media choice adds another arena of variables for CBN. Colors, patterns, images, audio or video bits can represent the digits of the numbers or can be mixed to represent complete integers. Animation allows geometry to form before your eyes.

Many modular systems and tessellations are ripe for this kind of patterning. One of the reasons I wanted to develop computer software for this is because I was making errors in the execution, meaning the resulting patters were questionable as valid.

However, I developed ways of staying on track and maintaining accuracy while working by hand. Though using a computer is fully accurate, pleasing patterns can be created with colored pencils on graph paper or with grid-based media such as mosaic tile, weaving, hook rugs, and needlepoint.

Over the years, I have rendered Color By Numbers designs in a lot of various media. Some are shown here. Others include drawing, wood relief, watercolor, needlepoint, collage, LED lighting, and many forms of computer graphics output, including audio, video and animation.

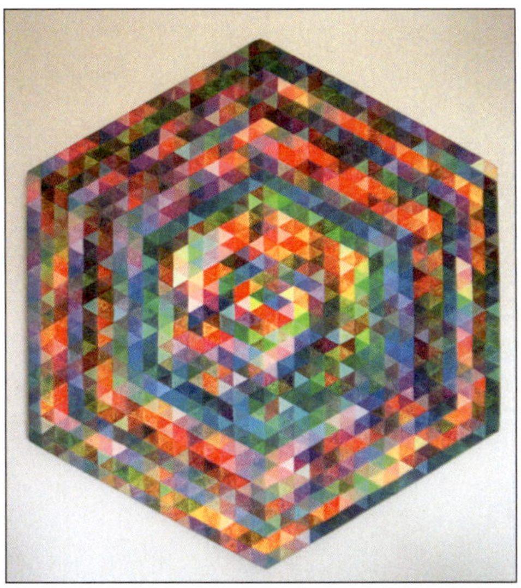

2.28a. Acrylic Painting on Canvas, with Dayglo Colors, 15" Diameter, 2011.

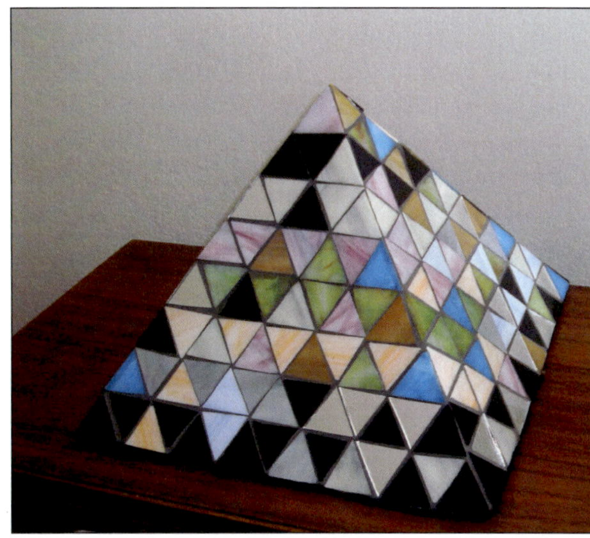

2.28b. Glass mosaic Color By Numbers Pyramid, Wood and Glass, 12" x 12" x 10", 2011.

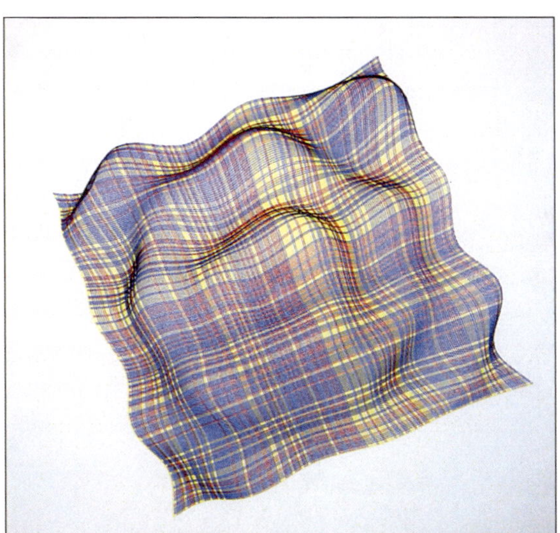

2.28c. Plaid Wave, Hand-pulled color lithograph, 18" x 18", 1982.

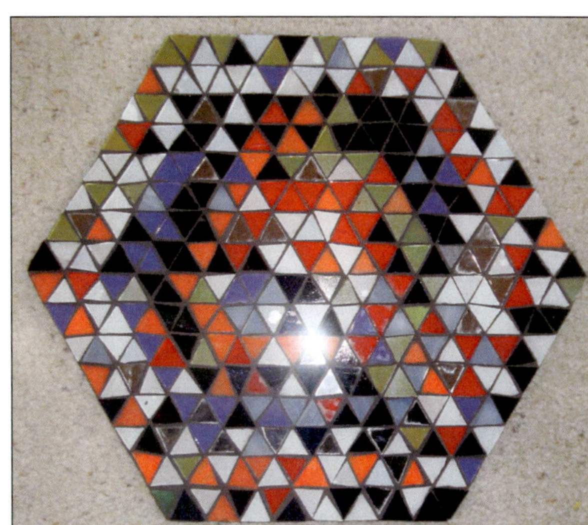

2.28d. Color by Numbers Linear Spiral, Glass and Mirror Mosaic, 16" Diameter, 2010.

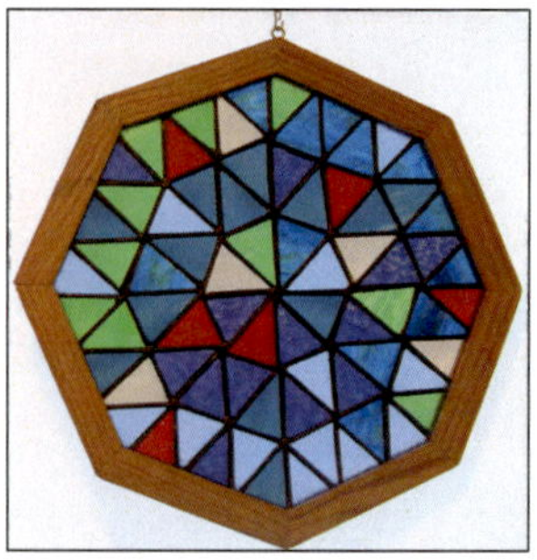

2.28e.

Stained glass, 1982.

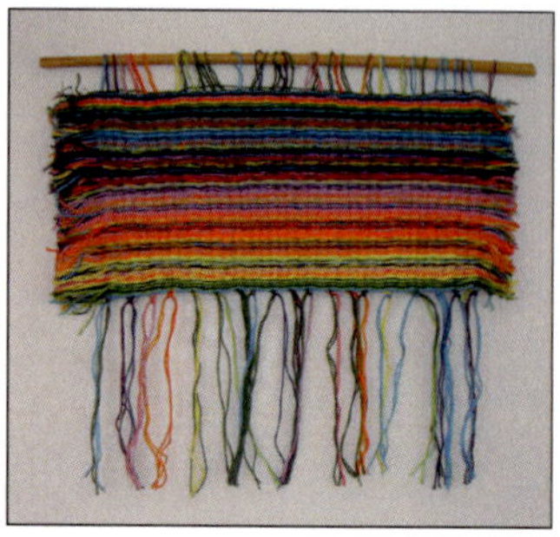

2.28f.

Weaving, 2008.

CBN FOR SCIENCE

CBN is a regulated, but seemingly random, way of mixing colors. This can be used to chart subtle variations in color mixing, including all (actually this is infinite) possible mixing of any set of colors. Out towards infinity, any subtle layer can be analyzed by zooming in on that numeric section of the counting pattern. An application for color matching and paint mixing is one possibility. Existing colors can be matched with only a certain, limited number of source colors. An example would be a paint store that is out of a certain base pigment. Perhaps there is an available substitute – the exact proportions of the existing pigments just need to be determined.

CBN allows user controls at many levels. Numbers can be charted and displayed with a seeming randomness. This could have many scientific and other useful ramifications. It could augment or replace a scientific dependence on random number generation and add a stable, chartable substructure. This could track a set number of variables (or constants) in a database that charts all possible combinations of those variables (or constants). Trends would highlight themselves in color.

Color By Numbers might also make a nice color design generator for Computer Graphics and 3D applications.

QR (Quick Response) Codes are a new phenomenon. It is encoded data, just like CBN. Perhaps CBN could yield color variations with multiple levels of information concurrently. This idea was aroused by the fact that QR codes remind me of my early CBN explorations.

There are perhaps unrealized applications to science and other fields. I invite readers to pursue any ideas along these lines and I would be glad to assist in such undertakings.

I am currently exploring octaves and harmonic structures. I have started using rainbows (octaves) of colors. Vibrational relationships and scales of colors are being explored with subtle filtration and mixture. My goal is to seek coherence in the patterning I am generating.

The potential is endless. Color By Numbers is multi-dimensional. Perhaps we can materialize harmonic structures and scales – just as music utilizes. Color vibration is just like tones in music – but faster.

Many of the paintings I have done in the last few years mix blacklight pigment with regular pigments to create gradations of blacklight effects. This expands beyond the traditional colors that can be reproduced through printing, computer graphics or photography as they are outside the gamut of RGB or CMYK. It also means the paintings look completely different in a blacklight. A blacklight could sort out certain data.

2.29a.

QR code for ArtToyz.com, 2011 (Yeah, Go There).

2.29a.

CBN base 2 from Visual basic program, 1999.

ARTISTIC INFLUENCE BEHIND COLOR BY NUMBERS SYSTEMS

Color By Numbers influences include a mixture of science, art and religion. One influential area for the development of CBN includes elements of Tibetan Art – Yantra and Mandala. M.C. Escher's grid studies from the Alhambra were a major influence on my conception of periodic, triangular grid structures (Islamic). The 60's spawned many ideas: Conceptual Art (Sol LeWitt), Op Art (Victor Vasarely) and Blacklight (Dayglo) Art. I started making "Op Art" in high school and making mandalas in college.

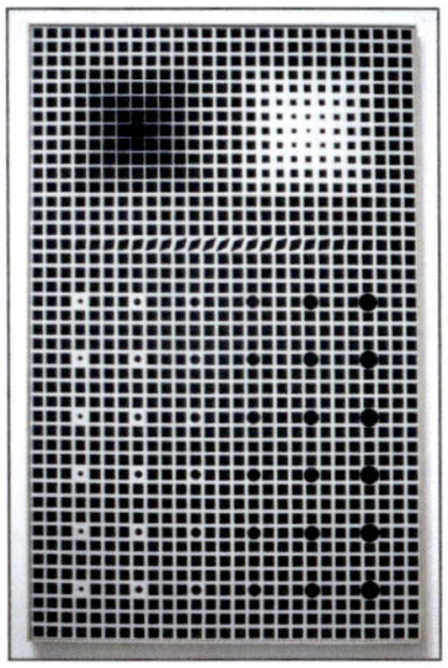

2.30a.

Supernovae. Victor Vasarely, Circa 1960.

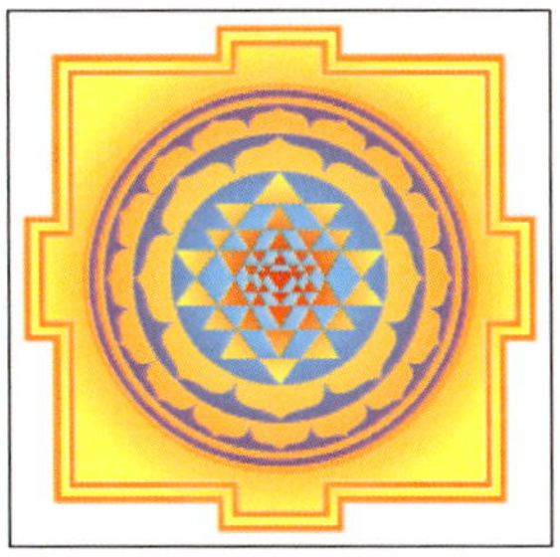

2.30b.

Sri Yantra. Tantric art and mandalas were an early attraction for me.

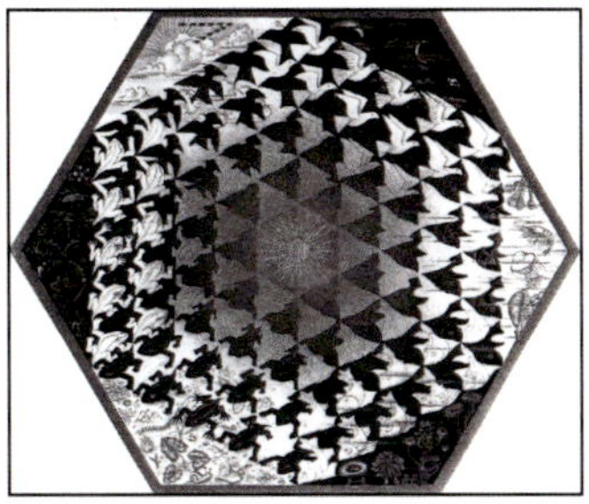

2.30c.

M.C. Escher's metamorphosis series. Part of his magic here is to vary the interacting tessellations across the space.

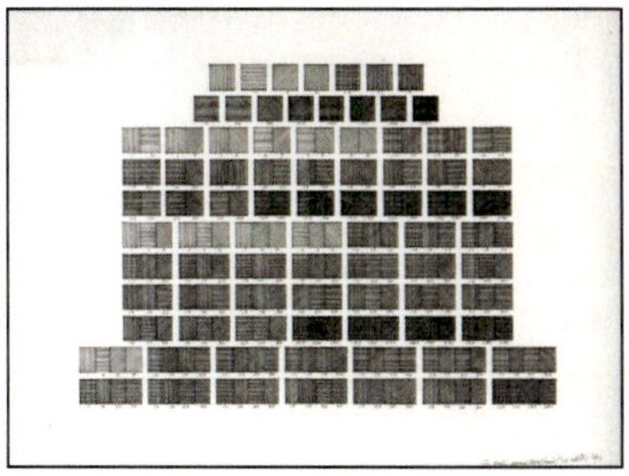

2.30d.

Sol LeWitt, All Single, Double, Triple, and Quadruple Combinations of Lines in Four Directions One-, Two-, Three- and Four-Part Combinations (for Center Spread/Art and Project), 1969. I love his conceptual art.

These highlight a few of my influences. I also want to include Benoit Mandelbrot and Drumvalo Melchizedek. More on them later. I have also been influenced by the numerous softwares over the years that programmers have offered us artists as a platform to create on. The realism section lets on that I have also been influenced by Surrealism and Psychedelic art. Here I have always looked to Rene Magritte, Salvador Dali, Alex Grey and others. Without influences and reworked ideas, art would be static and die with the artists.

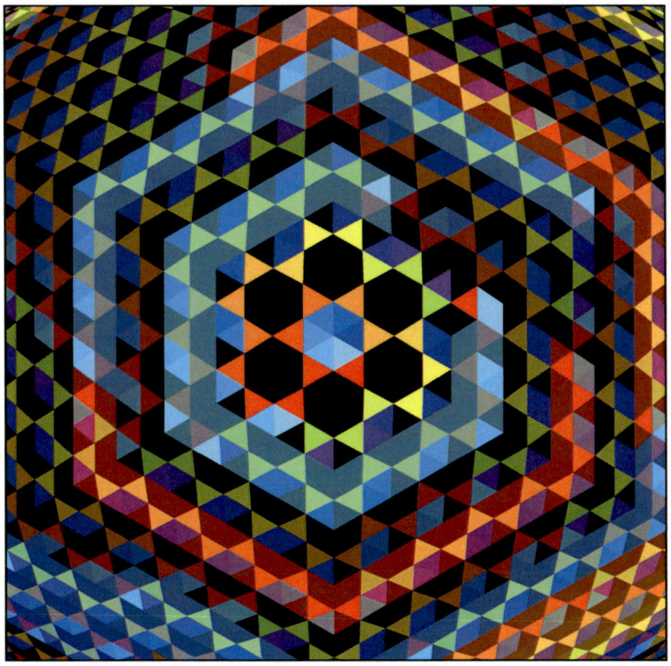

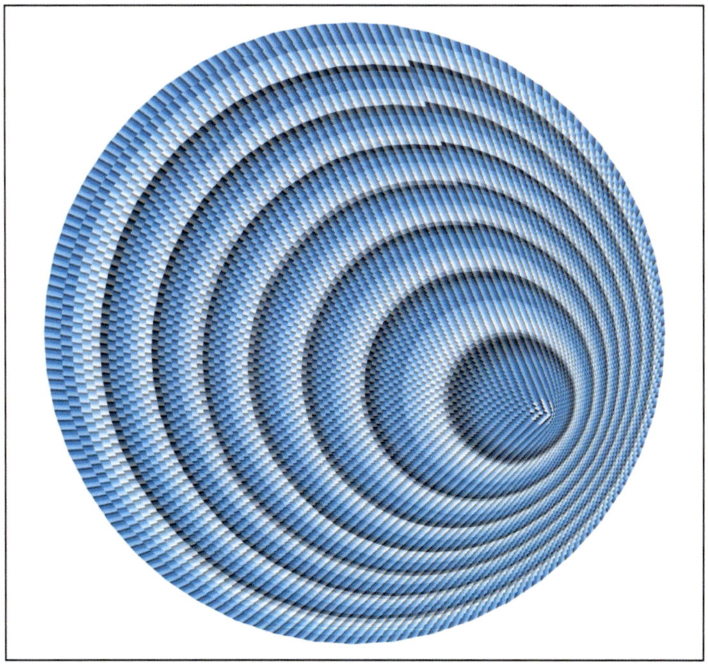

2.31a,b. A couple examples of Color By Numbers that look like Op Art, created with ArtToyz Studios Color By Numbers homegrown software.

To crop or not to crop?

Color by Numbers look quite a bit different when they explore alternate grids versus being locked into a rectangular "window".

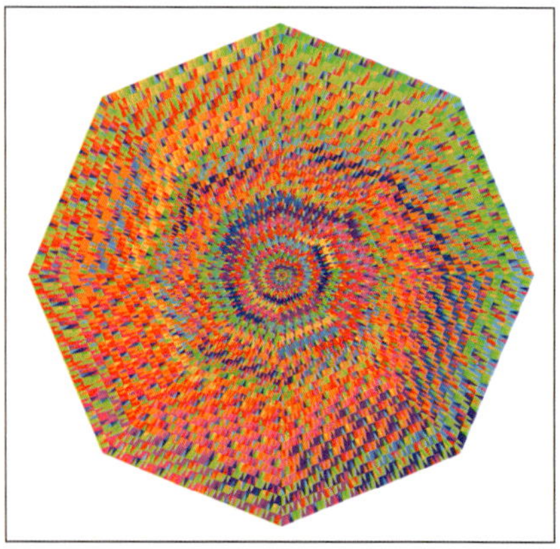

2.32.

Color By Numbers Blended Spiral on an Octagon, Digital, 4800 x 4800 Pixels, 2019.

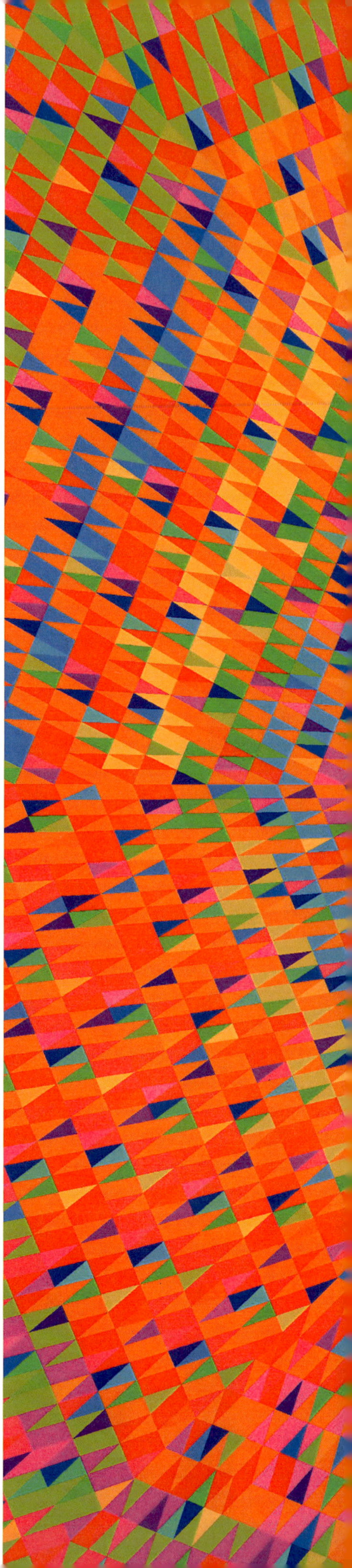

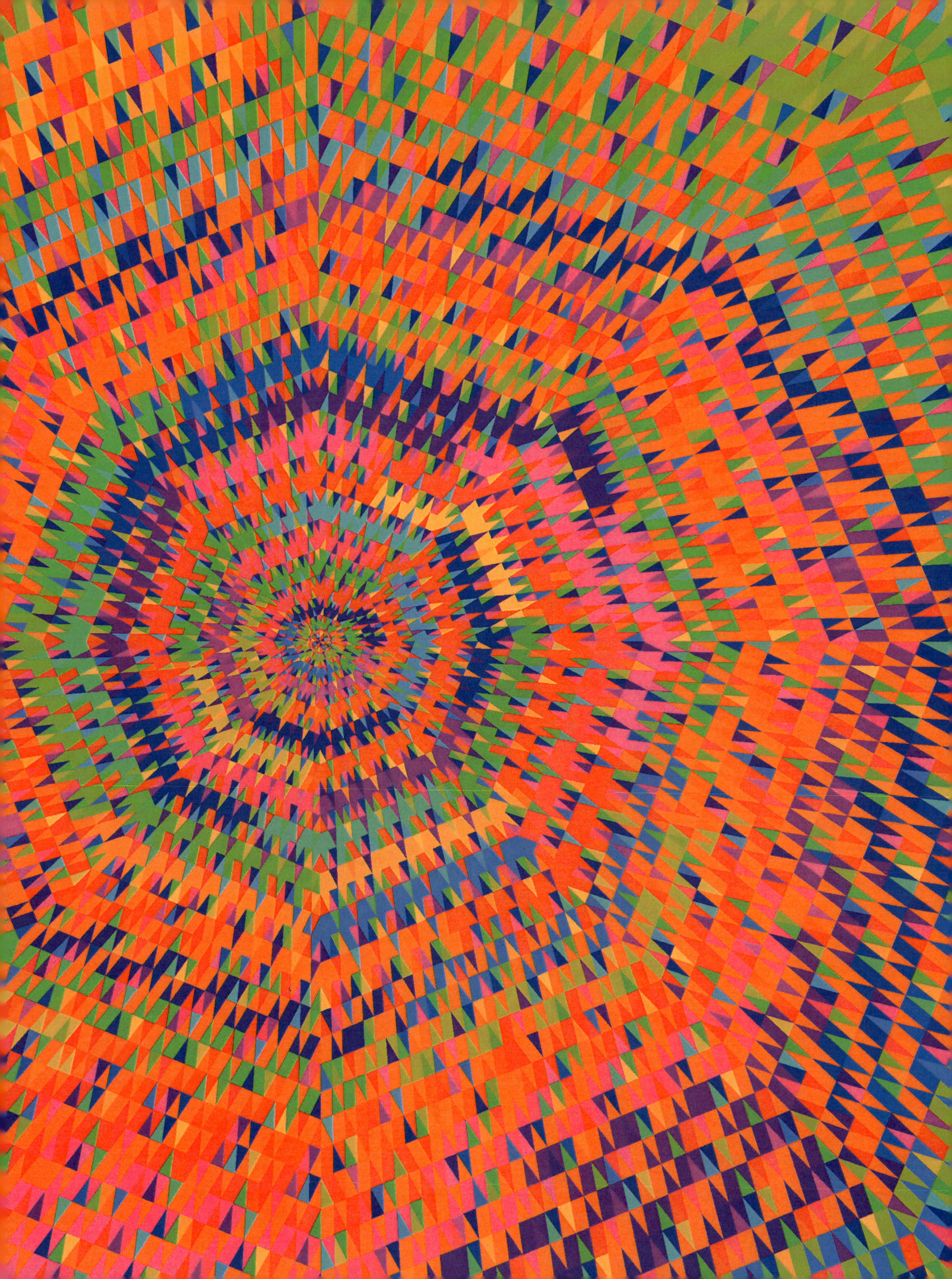

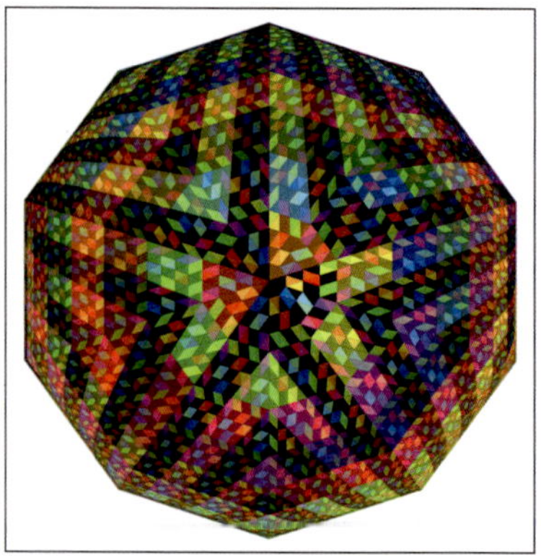

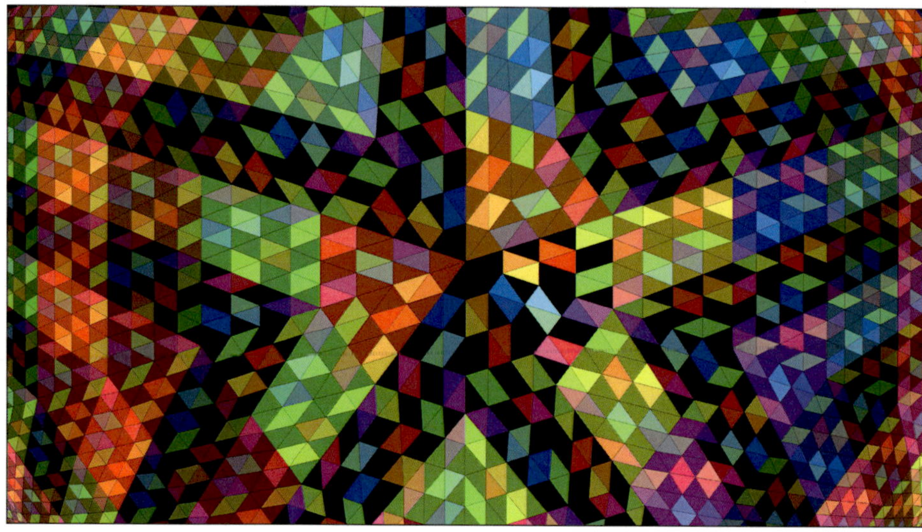

2.33.

Color By Numbers Blended Spiral, Digital, 4800 x 4800 Pixels, 2019.

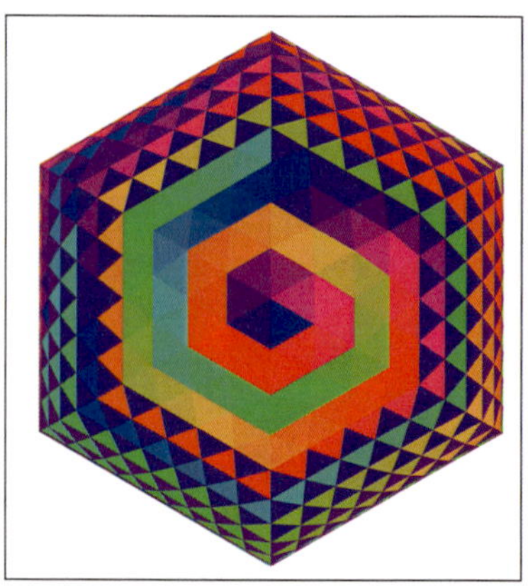

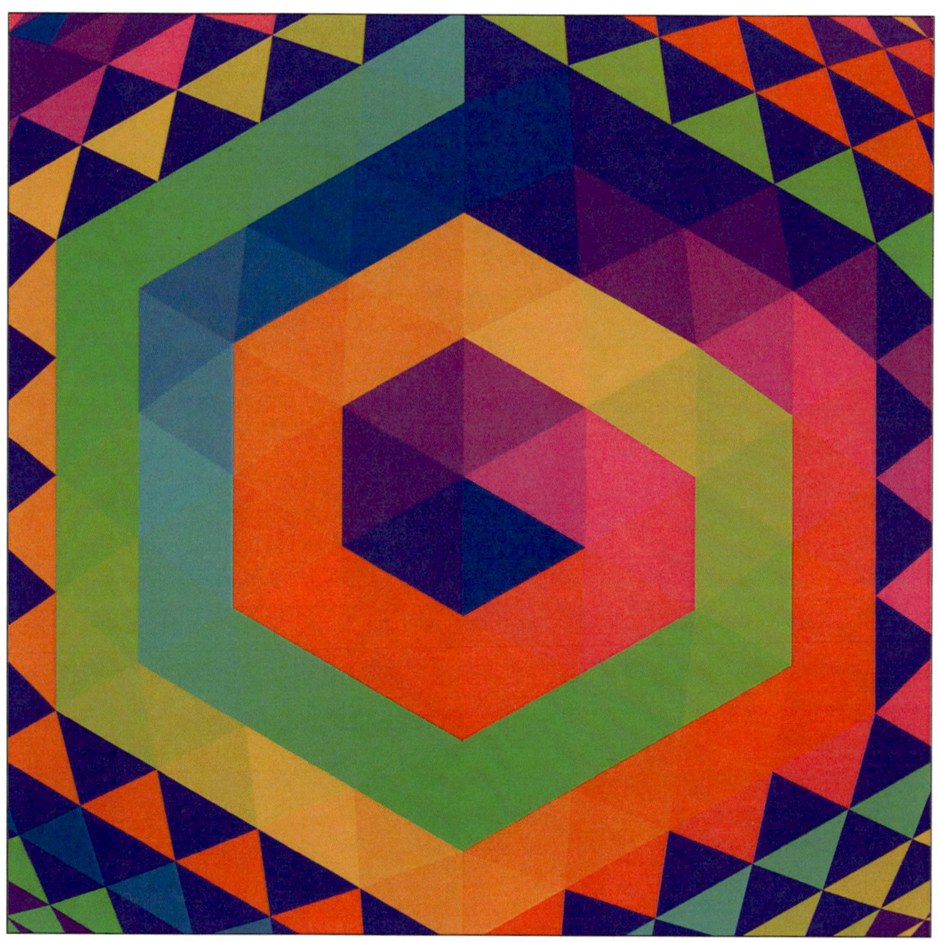

2.34.

Color By Numbers Blended Spiral, Digital, 4800 x 4800 Pixels, 2019.

These digital files are just waiting to be output to large print formats. New technologies such as Computer Etching, Laser Cutting, Embroidery and a host of new output possibilities await exploration.

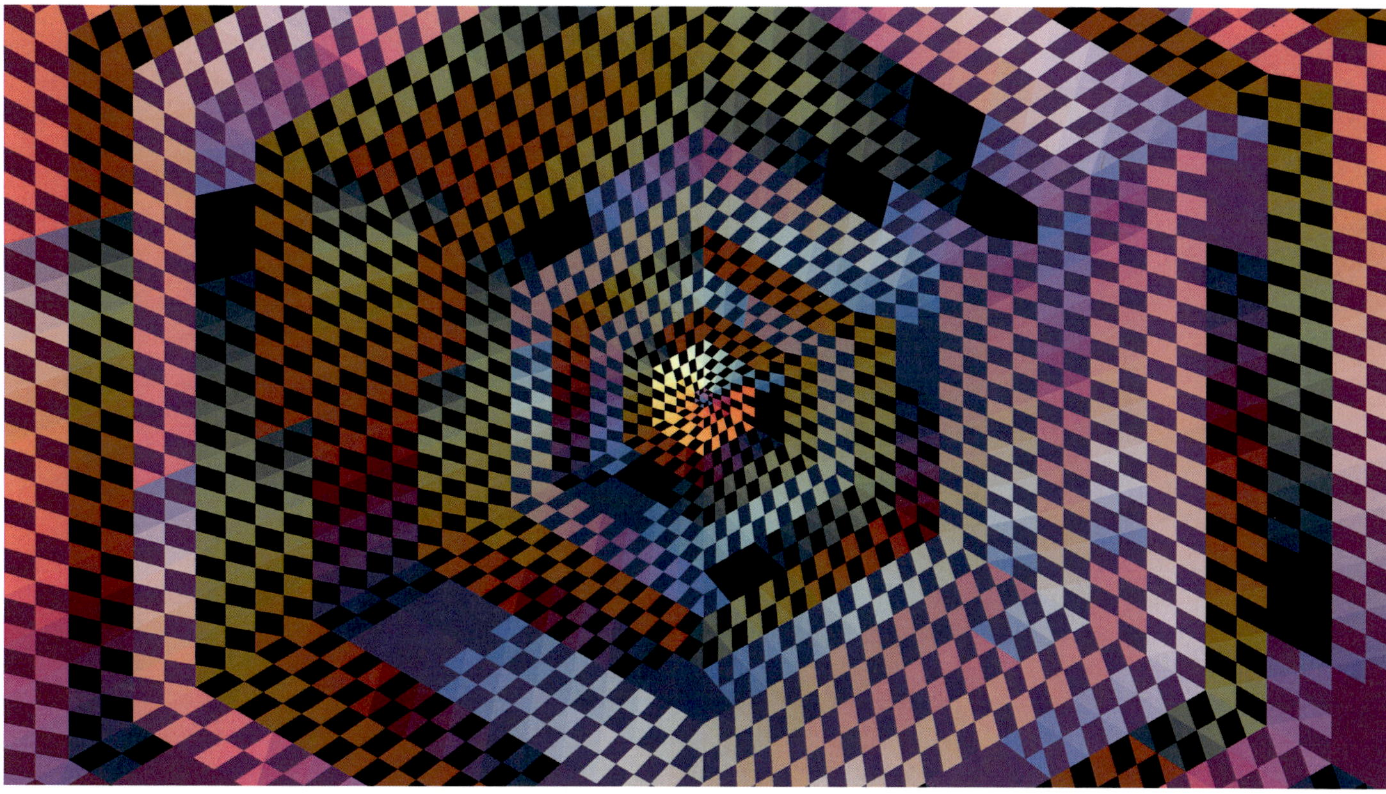

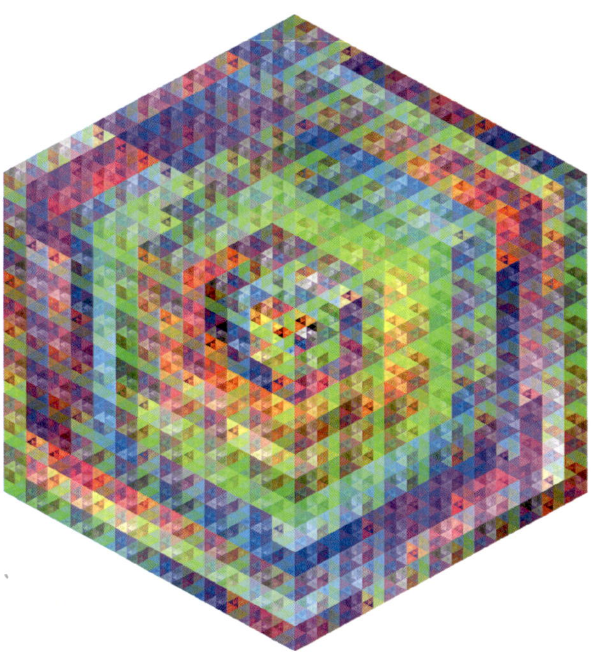

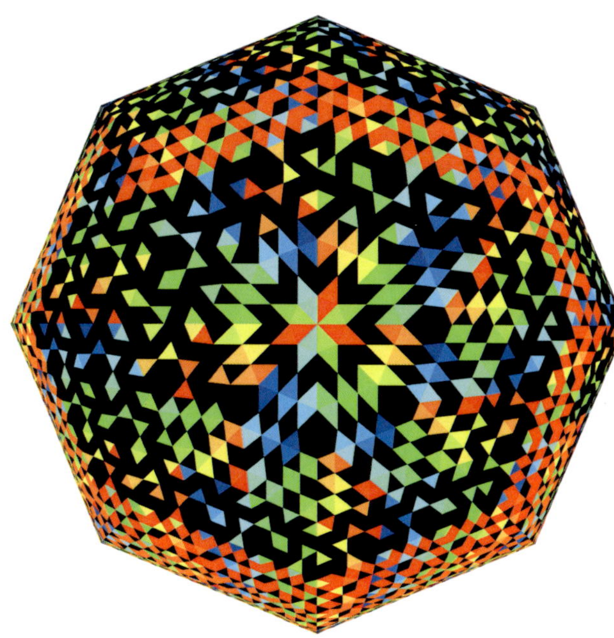

2.35a-c. Various output from ArtToys Studios software.

Through these objects we are in touch with the finite. Infinity is implied in these structures as the continuity and fulfillment of what is predefined. The earth and its wonders are finite, but we are constantly teased with infinity. The number of trees in a forest – all forests; the number of grains of sand at a beach – all beaches; the number of rocks – all rocks on earth – all in the universe. They are all finite pieces of an implied infinity.

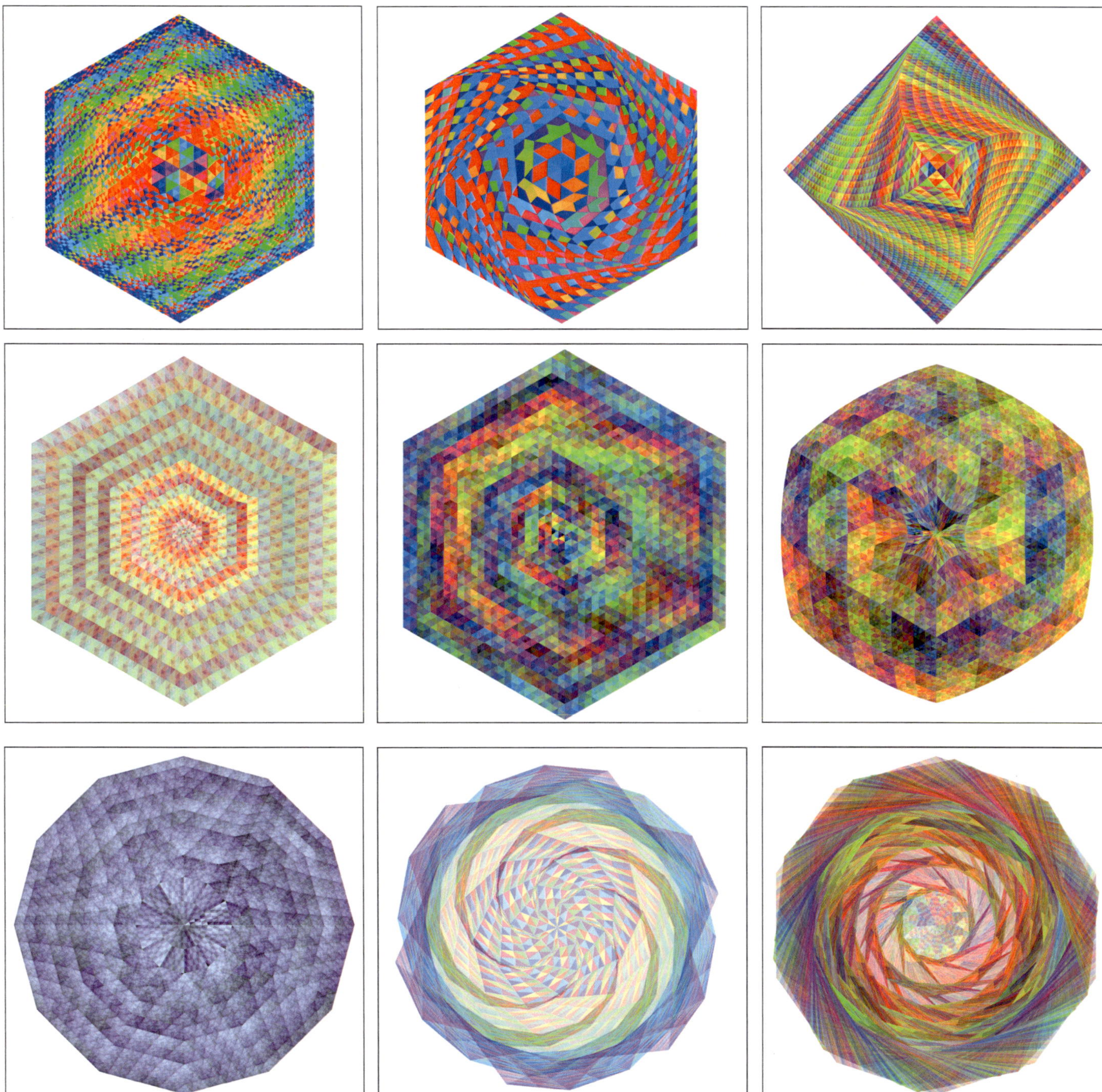

2.36a-c.

Various output from ArtToys Studios software.

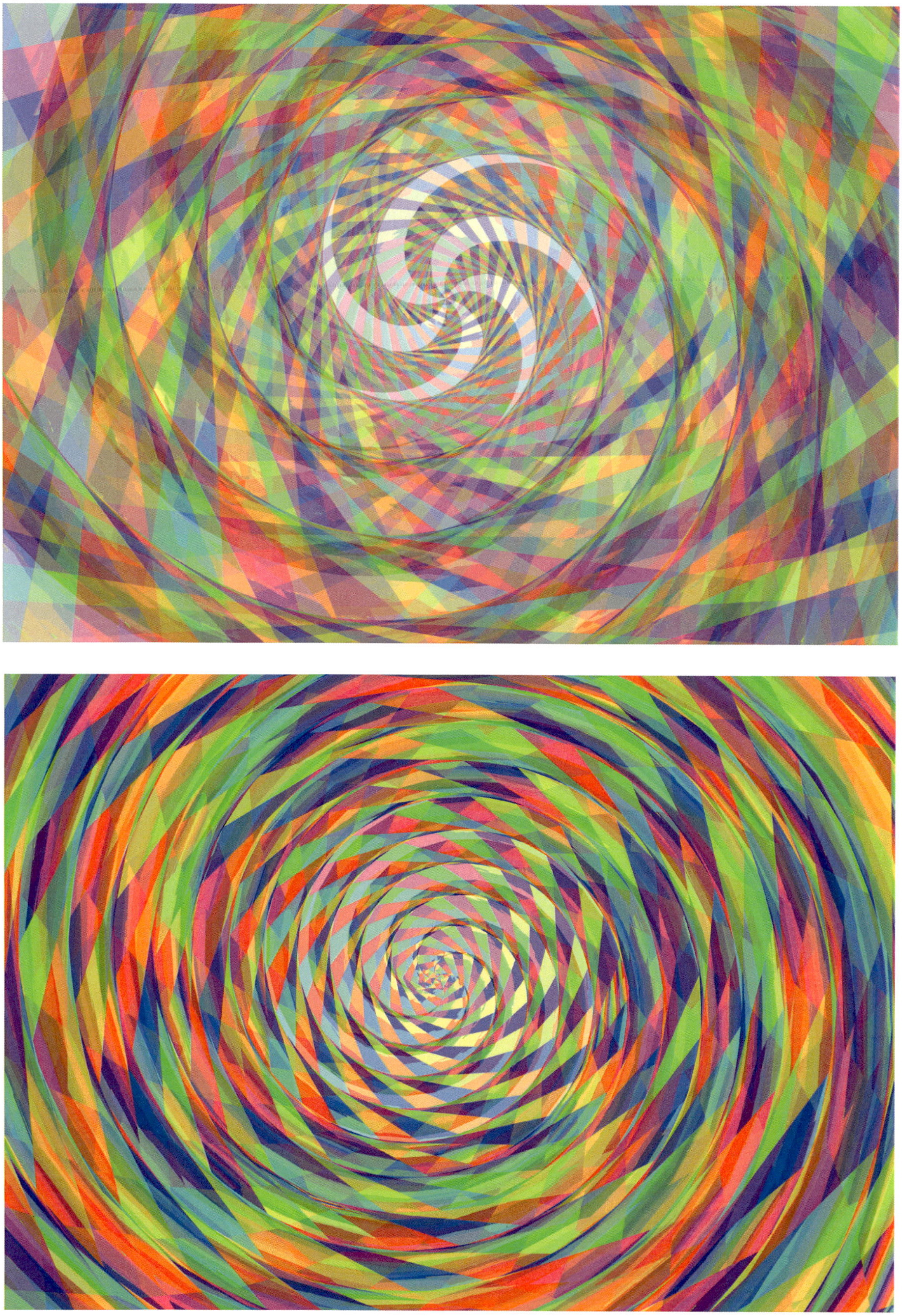

2.37a.b. Color By Numbers pattern spun with geometry distortions involving incremental grid divisions and rotation of certain vertices. Transparent layering allows for a more coherent overlap of spinning forms.

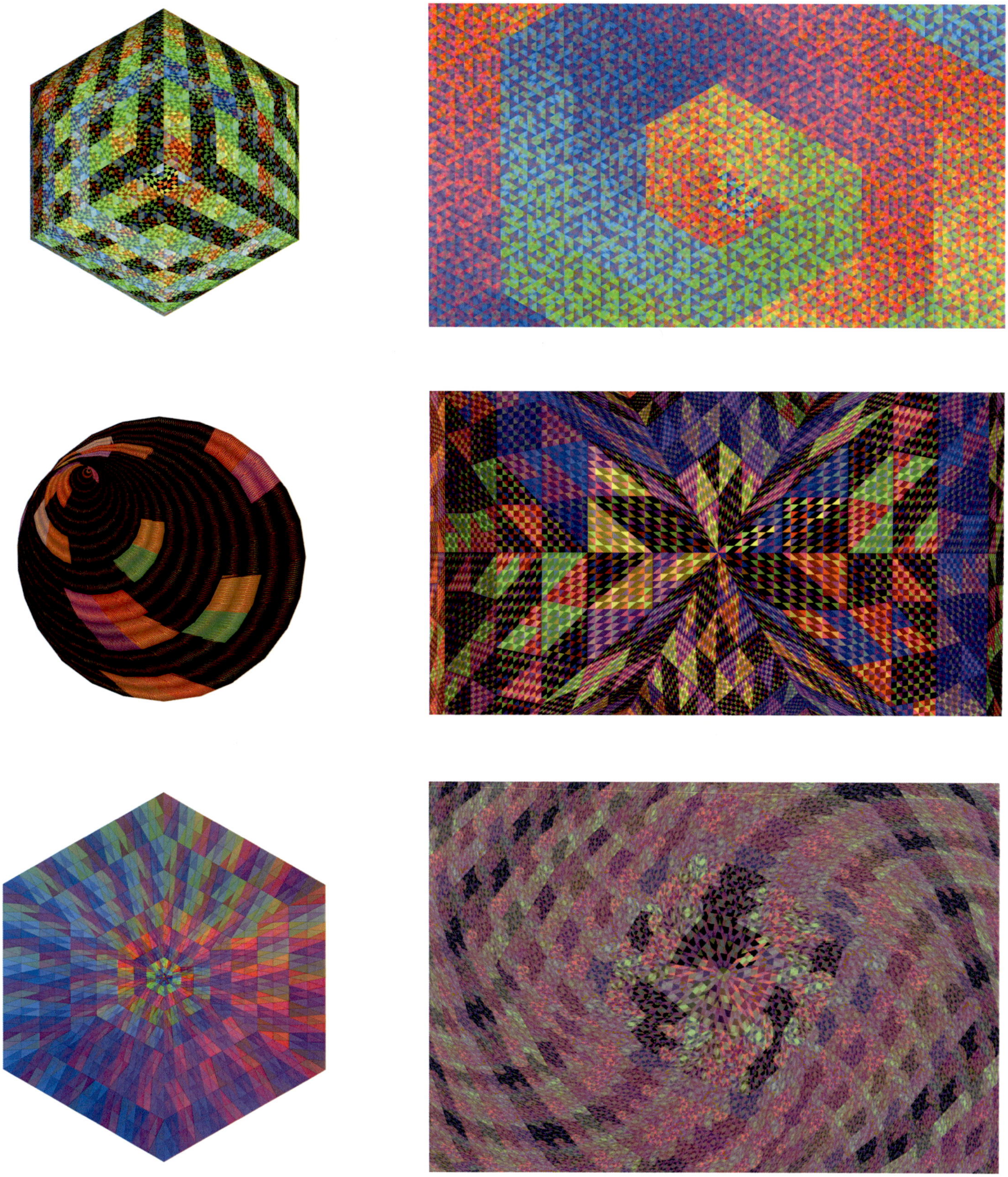

2.38a-f. Output from my Color By Numbers pattern generation software with various settings dialed in. Obvious influences from Op Art.

SACRED GEOMETRY

The Flower of Life - depicted here as a stained glass piece, with my coloration - has gained great notoriety recently as a prime example of sacred geometry. But there are the Platonic solids, mandalas and many other ways to create something "sacred". Fundamental principles and symbols are communicated with this method. Multiple sources claim that most of this special use of geometry is within the reach of a ruler and a compass.

This Flower of Life symbol, made from repeating circles, was found in ancient Egypt, Rome and other places around the world. Leonardo DaVinci studied it during the Renaissance. Science has found it in unexpected places such as DNA cross sections and molecular and cellular formations. A beautiful enigma.

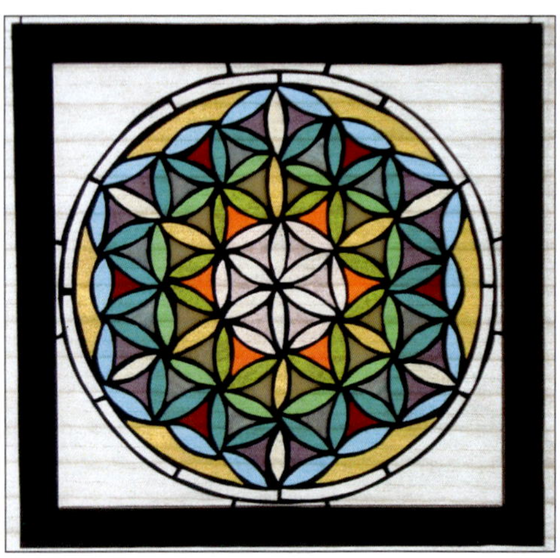

3.1. Flower of Life (My color choice), Stained Glass, 16" x 16", 2019.

Sacred geometry practitioners spend time looking for coherent, special arrangements with subsets of the flower of life. The center rings make the "seed of life," there is a"tree of life", and there is a thing in there called Metatron's Cube. You can look these topics up online if you want some more info.

Wilkipedia describes the Flower of life like this:
"An overlapping circles grid is a geometric pattern of repeating, overlapping circles of an equal radius in two-dimensional space. Commonly, designs are based on circles centered on triangles (with the simple, two circle form named vesica piscis) or on the square lattice pattern of points."

"... Patterns of seven overlapping circles appear in historical artifacts from the 7th century BC onwards; they become a frequently used ornament in the Roman Empire period, and survive into medieval artistic traditions both in Islamic art (girih decorations) and in Gothic art ... The name "Flower of Life" is given to the overlapping circles pattern in New Age publications".

A vesica piscis is a"petal" in the flower of life and has its own sacred meaning. It is commonly seen in the "fish" designs for Christianity. Not shown here. Drumvalo Melchizedek is given credit for naming the Flower of Life and discusses it extensively in his books, "The Ancient Secret of the Flower of Life, Volumes 1 and 2", from 1999. One of the ideas he projects is that the Flower of Life represents an initial core of cells that a human carries with him for life, the first 64 cells. This can be visualized in 3 dimensions, using 64 tetrahedrons or in 2 dimensions as seen on the next page. Color is used to distinguish the separate, but integrated cells.

Drumvalo also speaks extensively about the merkaba, a form that looks like a Star of David in 2 dimensions, but is a star dodecahedron in 3 Dimensional geometry. These books are full of great stories. We will just have to trust Drumvalo on their authenticity. This is a must read book for those interested in sacred geometry.

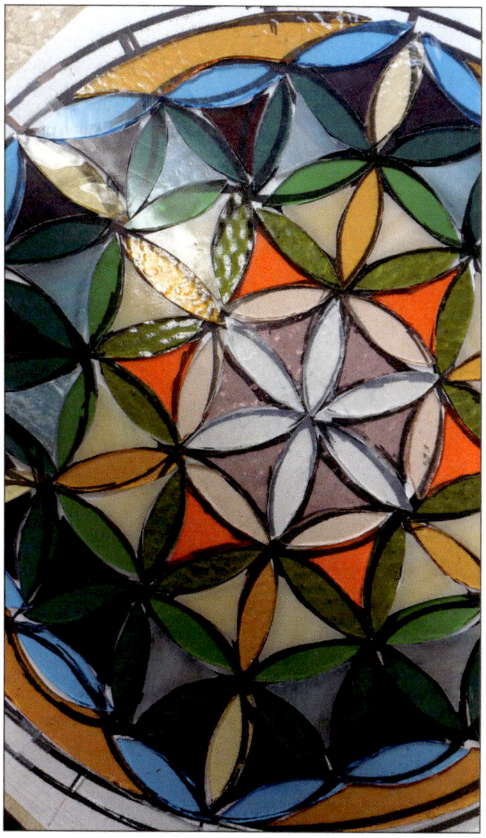

3.2. Closeup of the Flower of Life stained glass from the previous page being created. The glass is laid out on the original computer printout, waiting to be foiled.

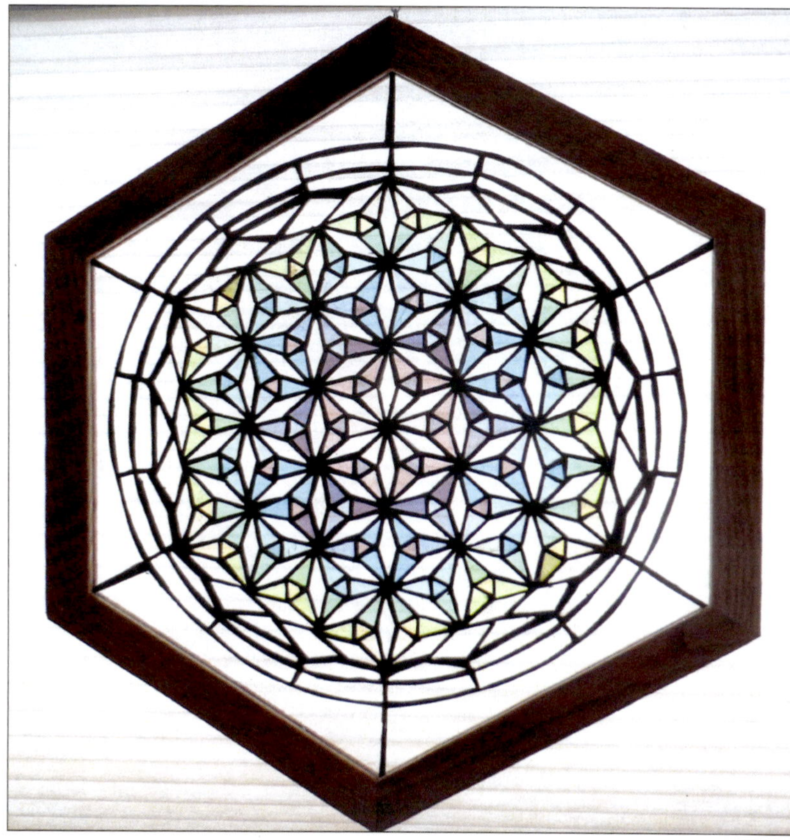

3.3. My version of the flower of life made with no circles. This uses triangles and my choice of color. Created in ArtToyz Studios EscherSketch software. Stained Glass, 18" Diameter, 2020.

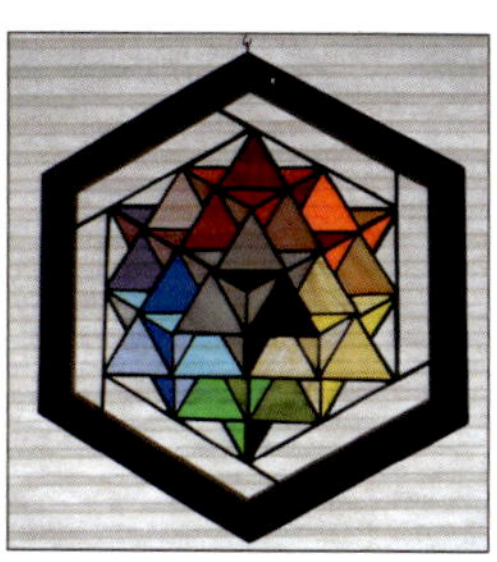

3.4a.

Inspired by Drumvalo, the initial core of 64 cells represented as tetrahedrons in Isometric Perspective. Stained Glass, 15" in diameter, 2018.

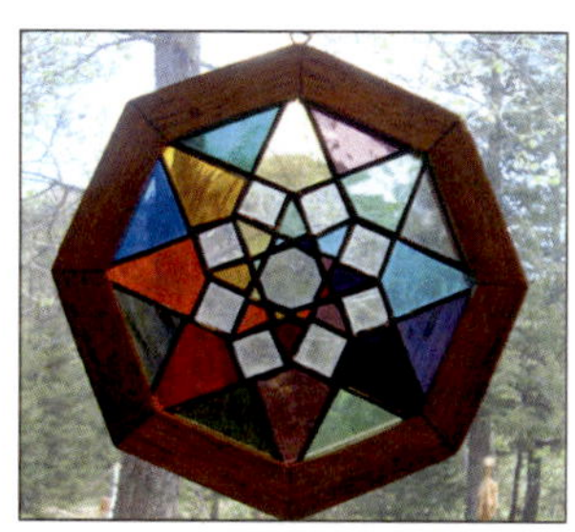

3.4b.

Octagonal Star, Stained Glass, 12" in diameter, 2018.

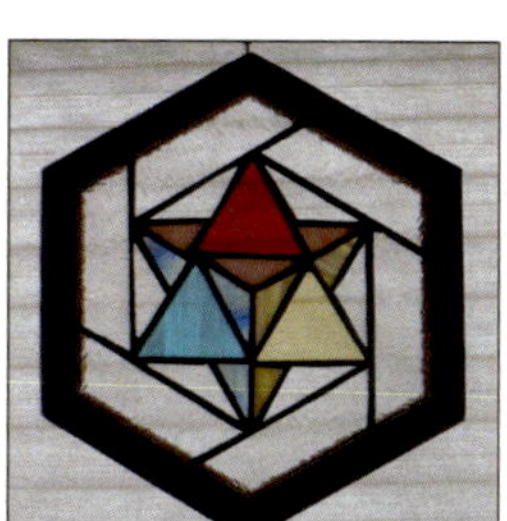

3.4c.

"Merkaba" created from intersecting Tetrahedrons, Stained Glass, 10" in diameter, 2018.

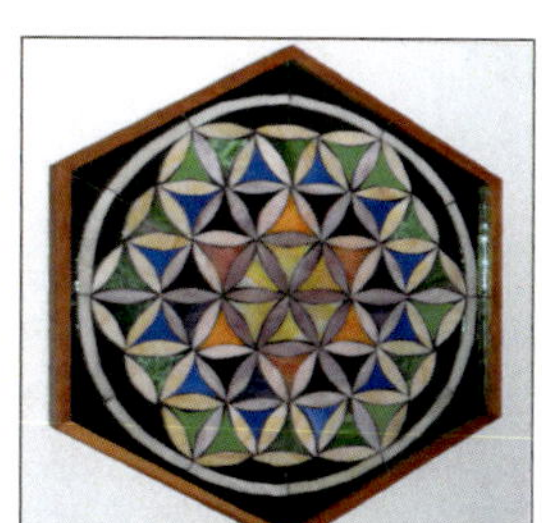

3.4d.

Flower of Life, Glass Mosaic, 18" in diameter, 2018.

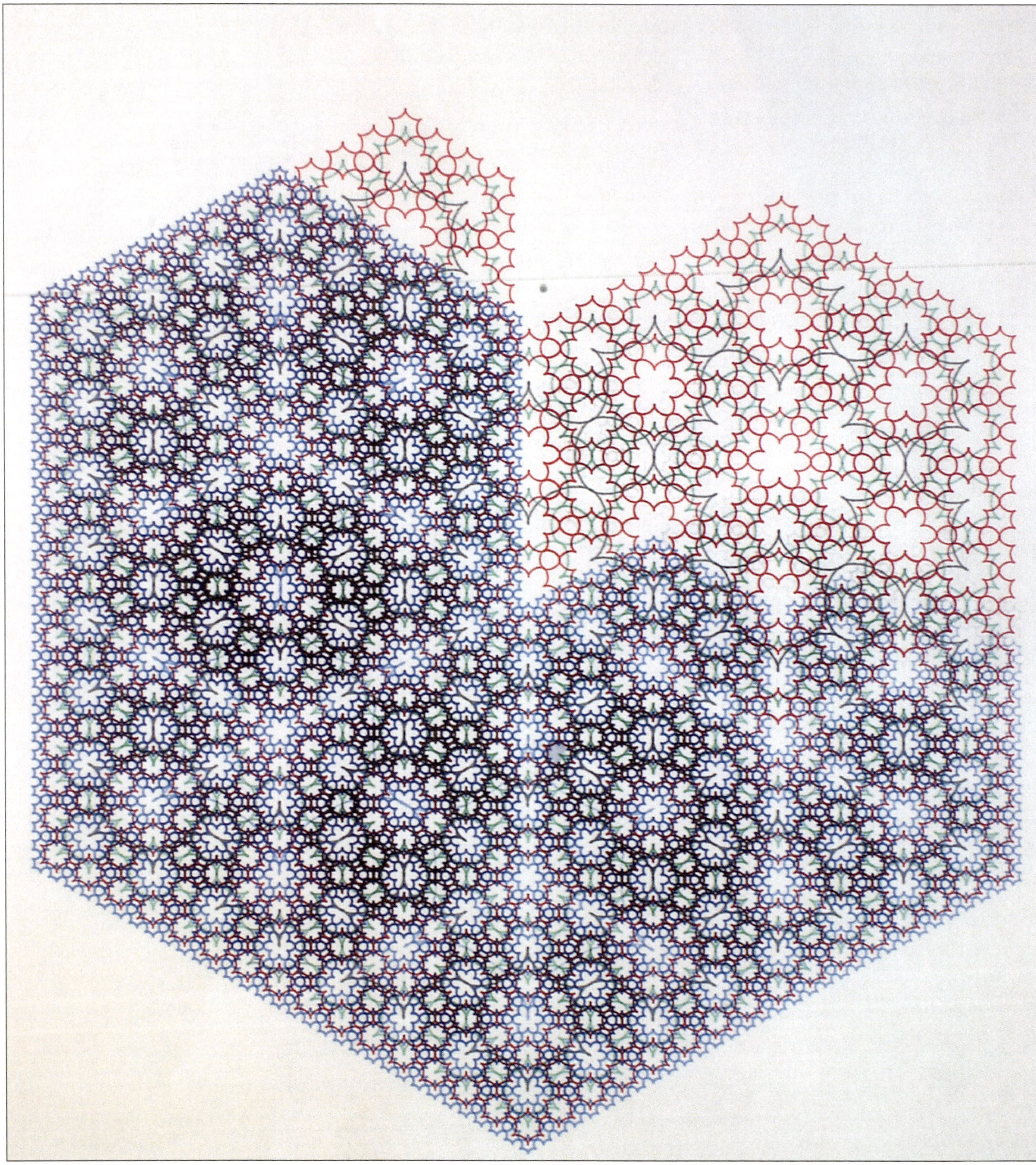

3.5a.

In 1980 I wasn't aware of the Flower of Life. I created this fractal pen plot and it ran out of ink. Only recently did I realize that the geometry is related to the Flower of Life. More on fractals in the next chapter.

Pen Plot, 11" x 11", 1980.

Full spectrum color and radial symmetry are part of my design repertoire.

Mirroring in many directions is a unique concept. I have long been intrigued with images using this radial symmetry approach. Early on in my art career I began to explore mandalas. They are fun to make and can integrate a wide variety of approaches.

I see a relationship to kaleidoscopes and Tibetan Mandalas, which are a sort of 4-way kaleidoscope.

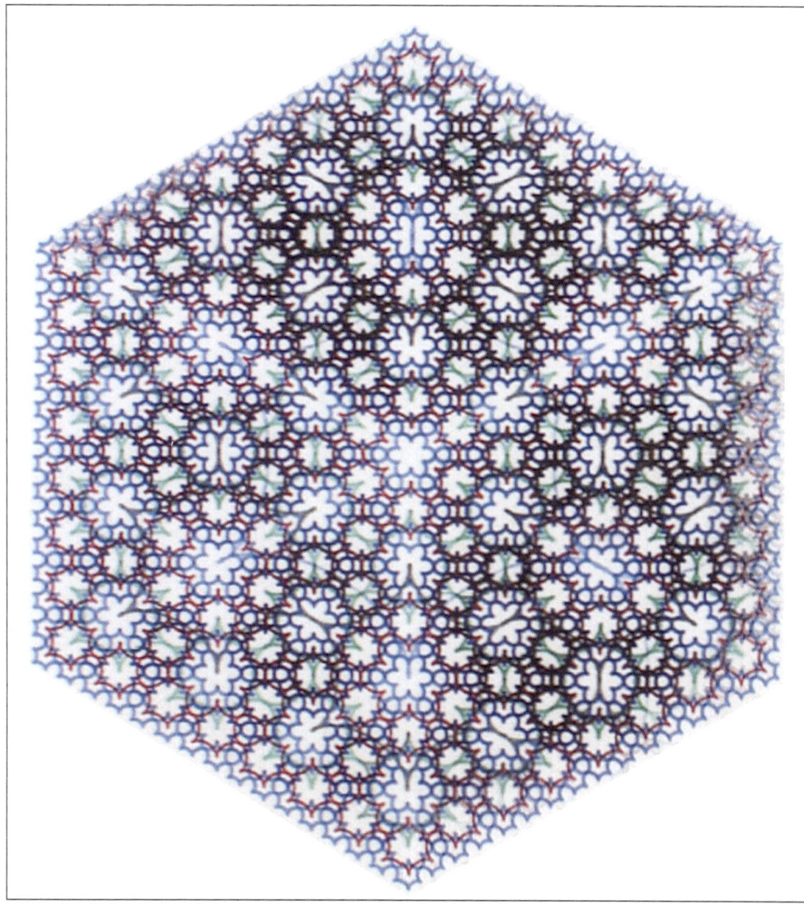

3.5b. I decided to use Photoshop to salvage a portion of Figure 3.5a. The seed for this fractal is a hexagonal star made with 6 arcs.

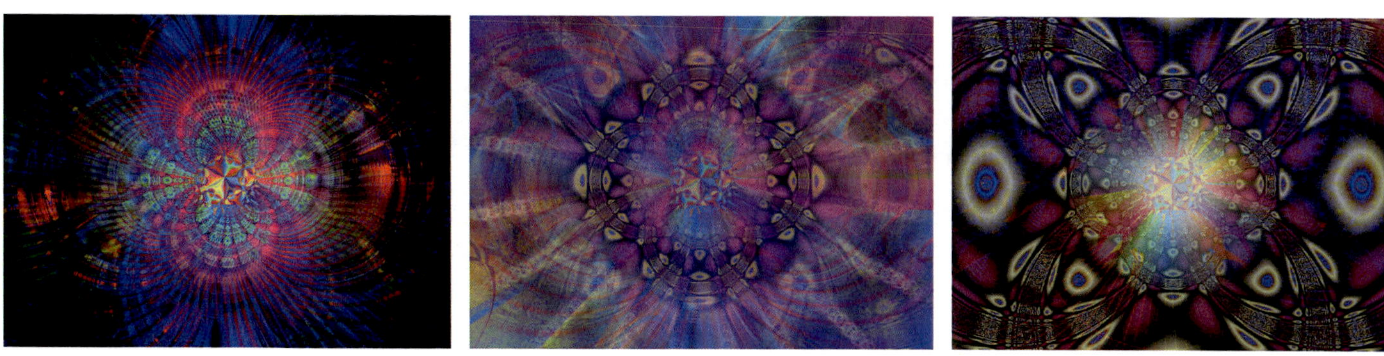

3.6. Some graphics from my desktop designs in the 1990s. They utilize mirrored symmetry and fractals.

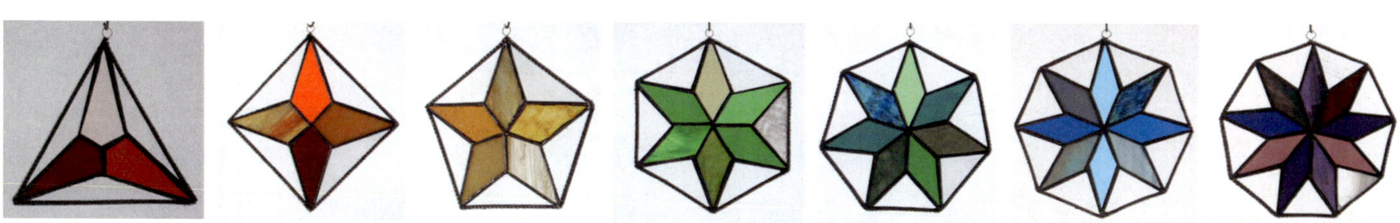

3.7. Star forms inside 7 regular polygons with sides 3 - 9 with colors derived from the chakras, Stained Glass, Approximately 6" in diameter each.

The "Polar Coordinates" we looked at in the grids section can be utilized to create kaleidoscopes. In the early 1980s ArtToyz Studios designed this software from the original concept of "String Art", done with yarn on boards with nails. At the time it was concurrent with a rather innocuous screen saver. Pen plotters limited us to 4 colors.

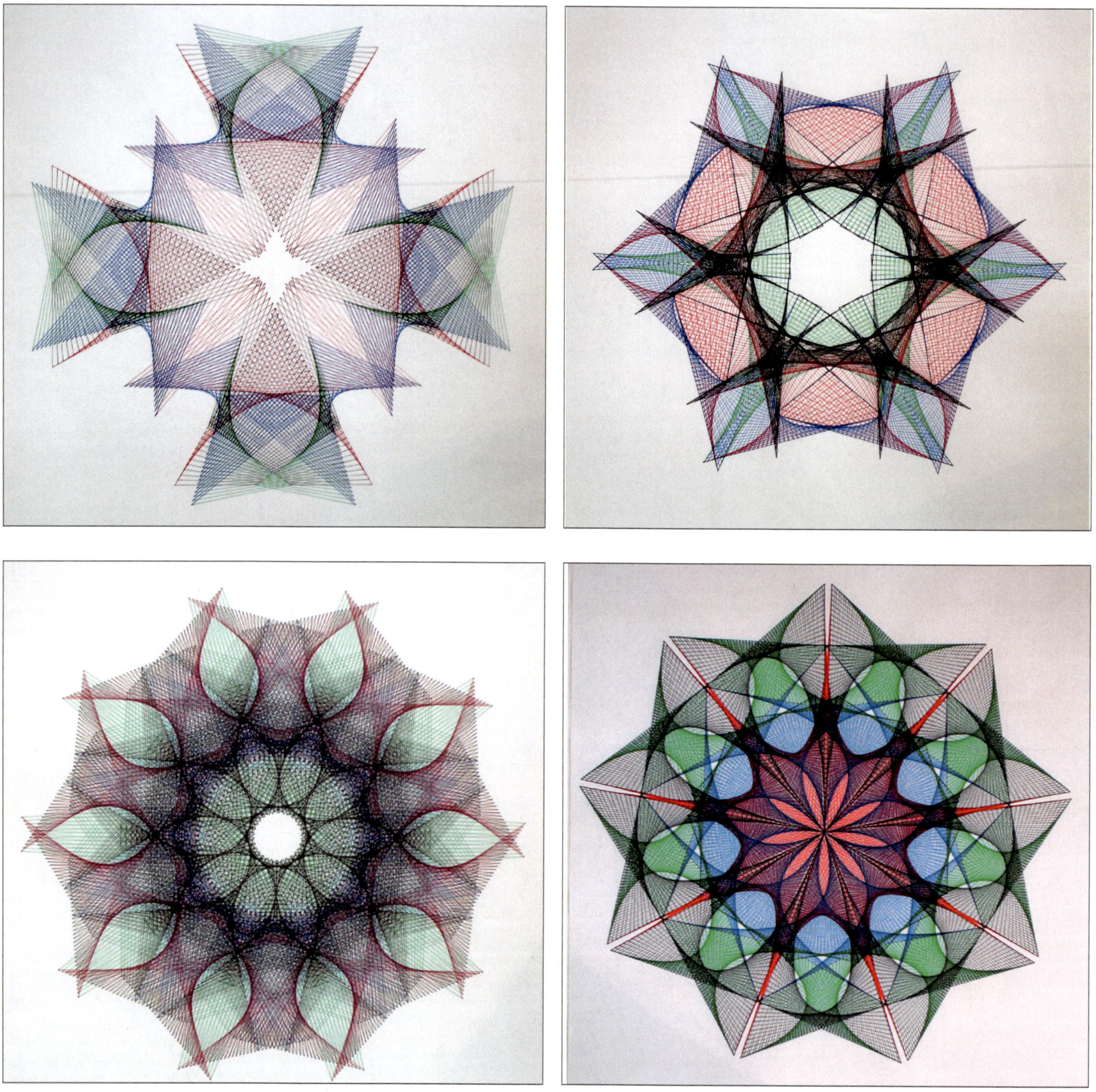

3.8.

Kaleidoscopic String Art Pen plots, 11" x 11", 1979.

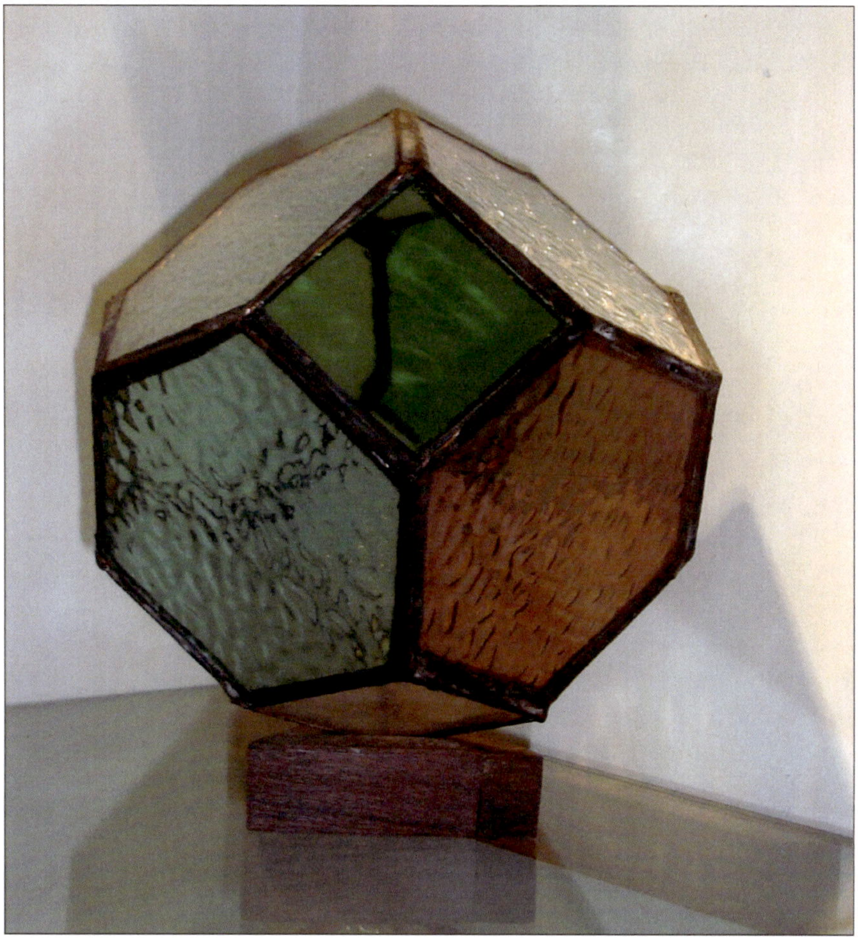

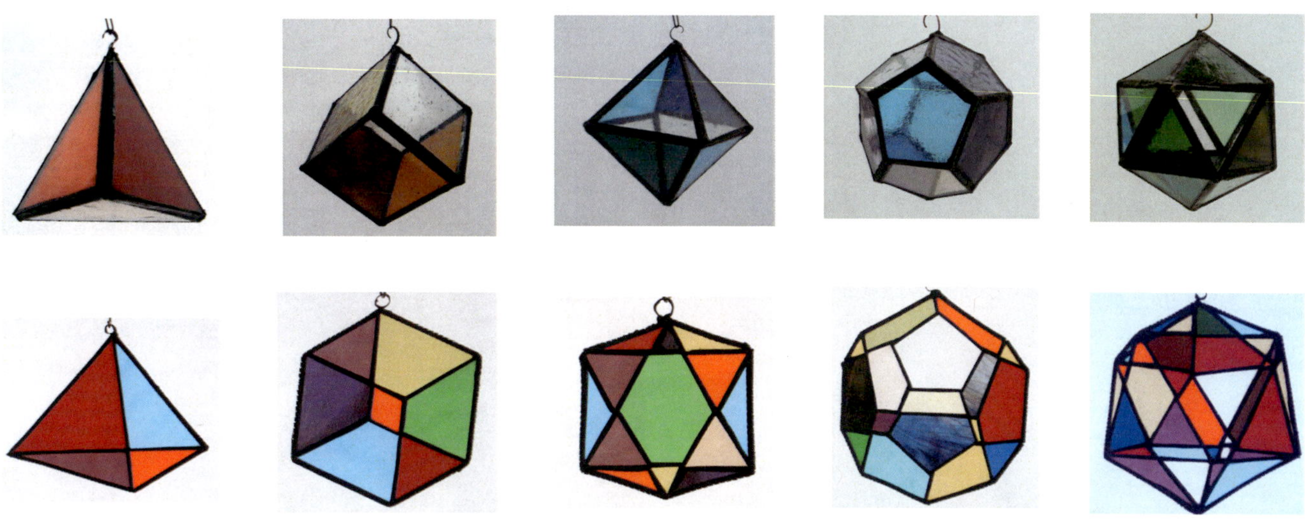

3.9.

Here are some stained glass pieces. The 2D ones on the bottom row are flat, isometric perspective projections of Platonic forms and pyramids. Above those are sculpted physical 3D Solids.
All Platonic Solids are created from the same-length segments and their outer points are inscribed in a sphere. The edges converge with the same angles. Wow. Only 5. Tetrahedron, Cube, Octahedron, Dodecahedron, Icosahedron. Do you know which is which?
The Greeks also discovered Archimedean solids in geometry, which have less rules. Many are "truncated" as shown in the large photo above. Pyramids with polygonal bases plus crystal forms are similar areas to explore.

The Platonic Solids and other symbols aside, there are also "knots". Celtic designs take advantage of this depth trick. Our eyes follow lines through other shapes. This and similar colors allows the look of overlapping ribbons or knots. These ideas will be further explored in the chapter on Optical Illusions. This motif is also used a lot in Islamic art and will continue to be of interest for my explorations.

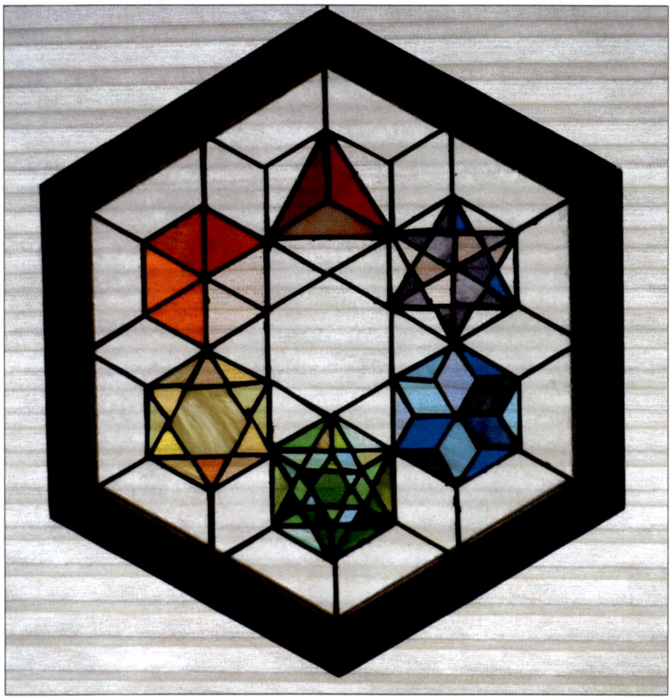

3.10a. An array of symbols in 2D, starting with the 5 Platonic Solids, Stained Glass, 15" diameter, 2018.

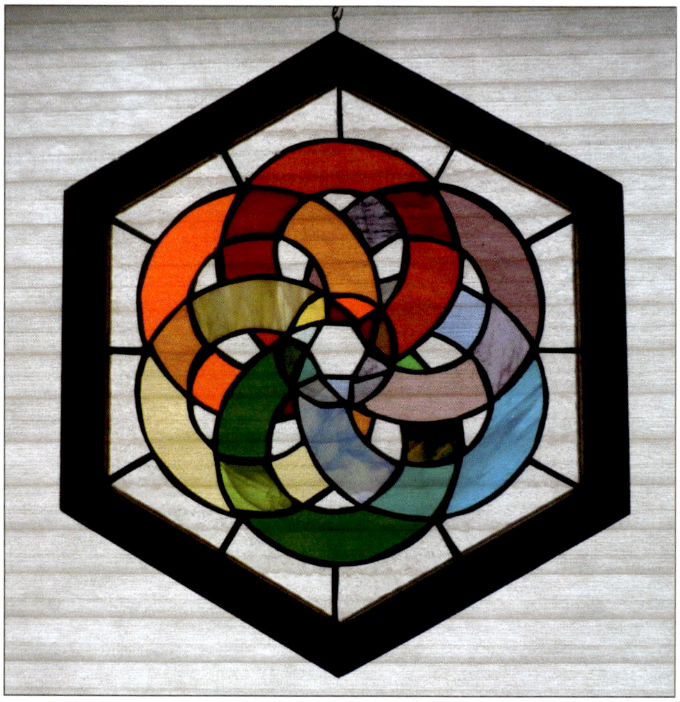

3.10b. An overlapping set of rings, Stained Glass, 15" diameter, 2018.

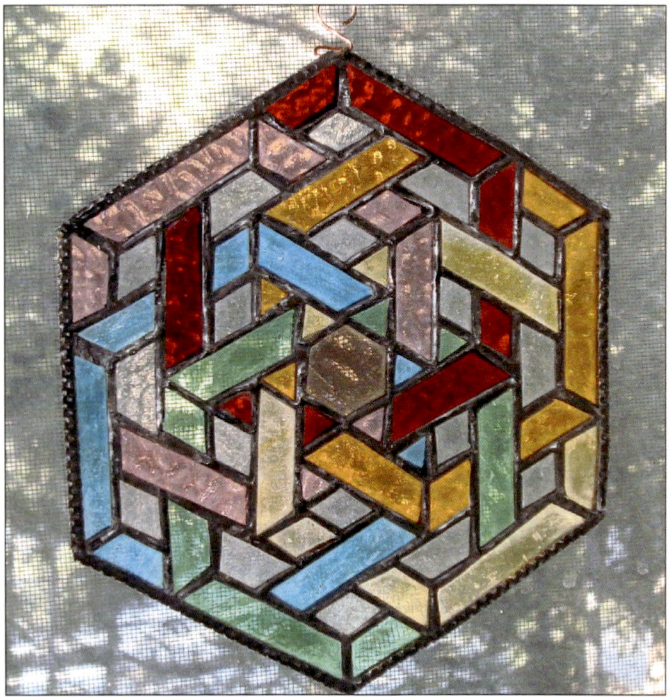

3.10c. An example of layering with ribbon forms, Stained Glass, 12" diameter, 2018.

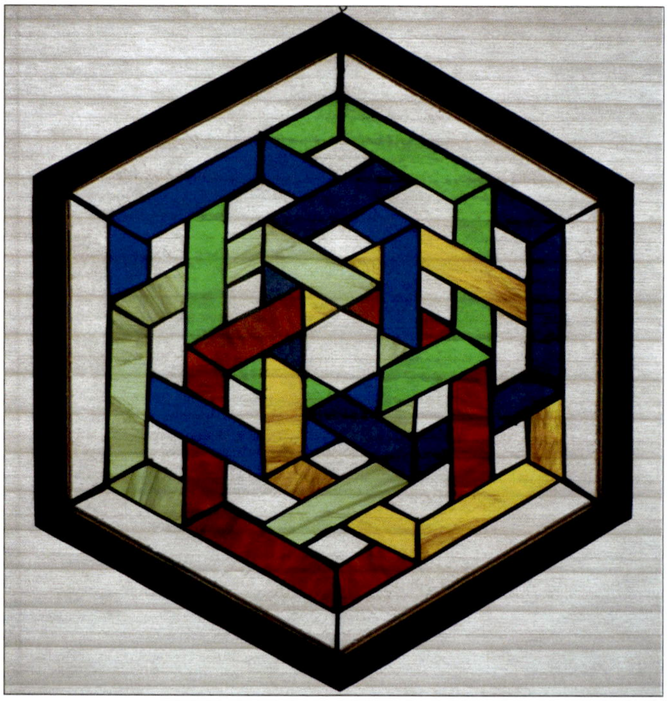

3.10d. More ribbon layering based on Islamic patterns, Stained Glass, 17" diameter, 2018.

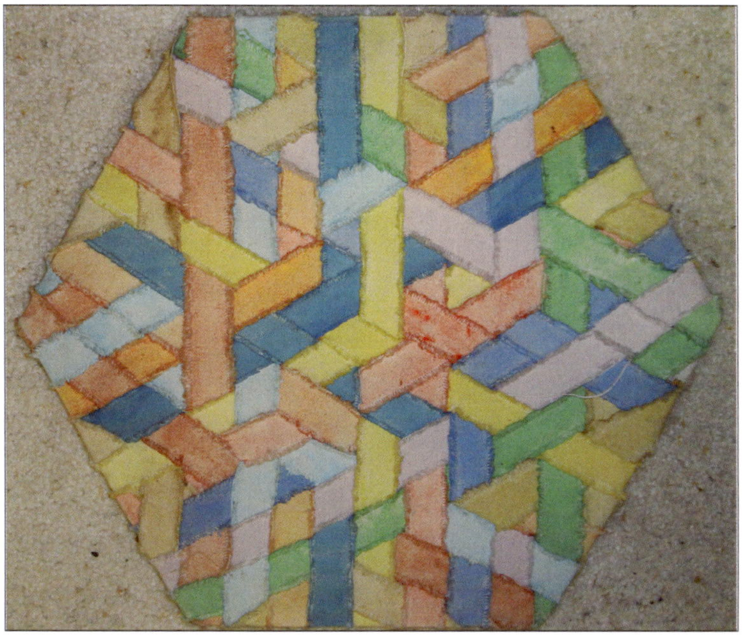

3.11.

A weaving I made in the 1970s. It is made from strips of torn, hand-dyed canvas and I am still perplexed by how this was even possible, to some extent.

It does create a regular triangular grid, three layers thick, years before I developed them for the computer.

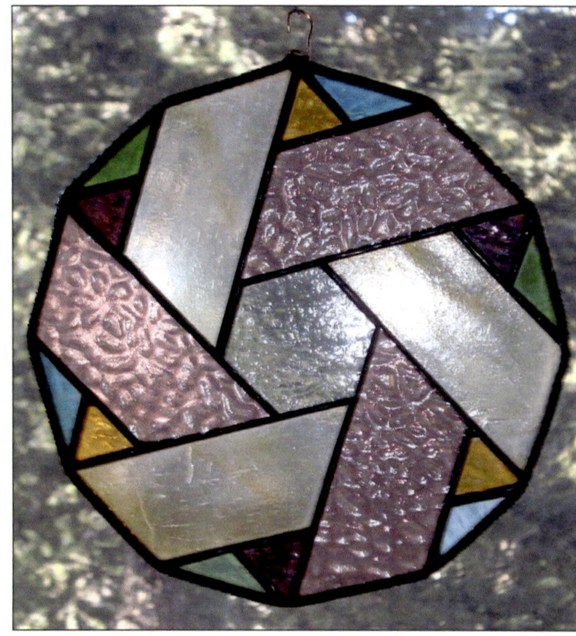

3.12.

Some Mobius Ribbons, Stained Glass, 10" diameter, 2018.

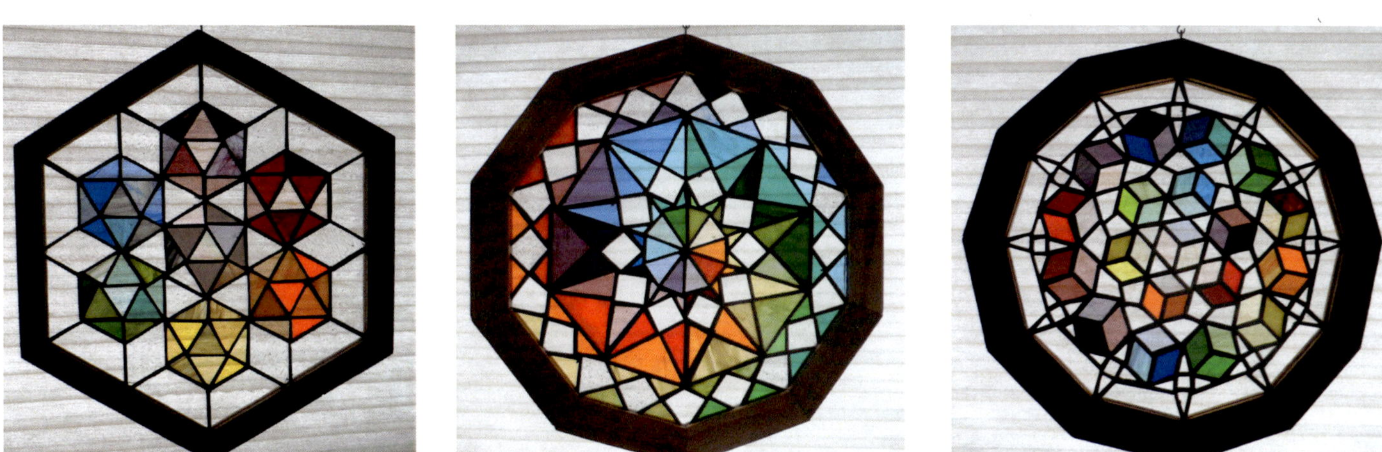

3.13.

Explorations of geometric and crystalline forms, Stained Glass, 15" diameter, 2018.

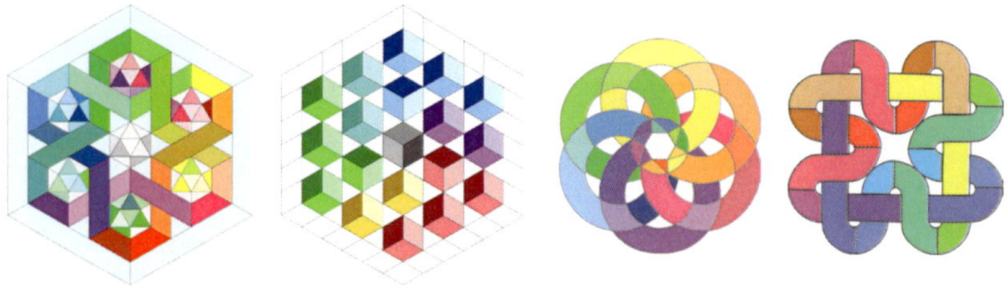

3.14.

Some designs made with EscherSketch Software and Adobe Illustrator.

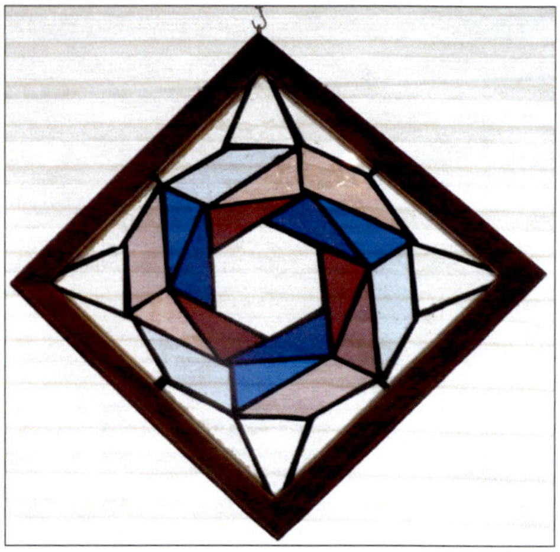

3.15.

12 sided form inscribed in a square, Stained Glass, 12" x 12", 2013.

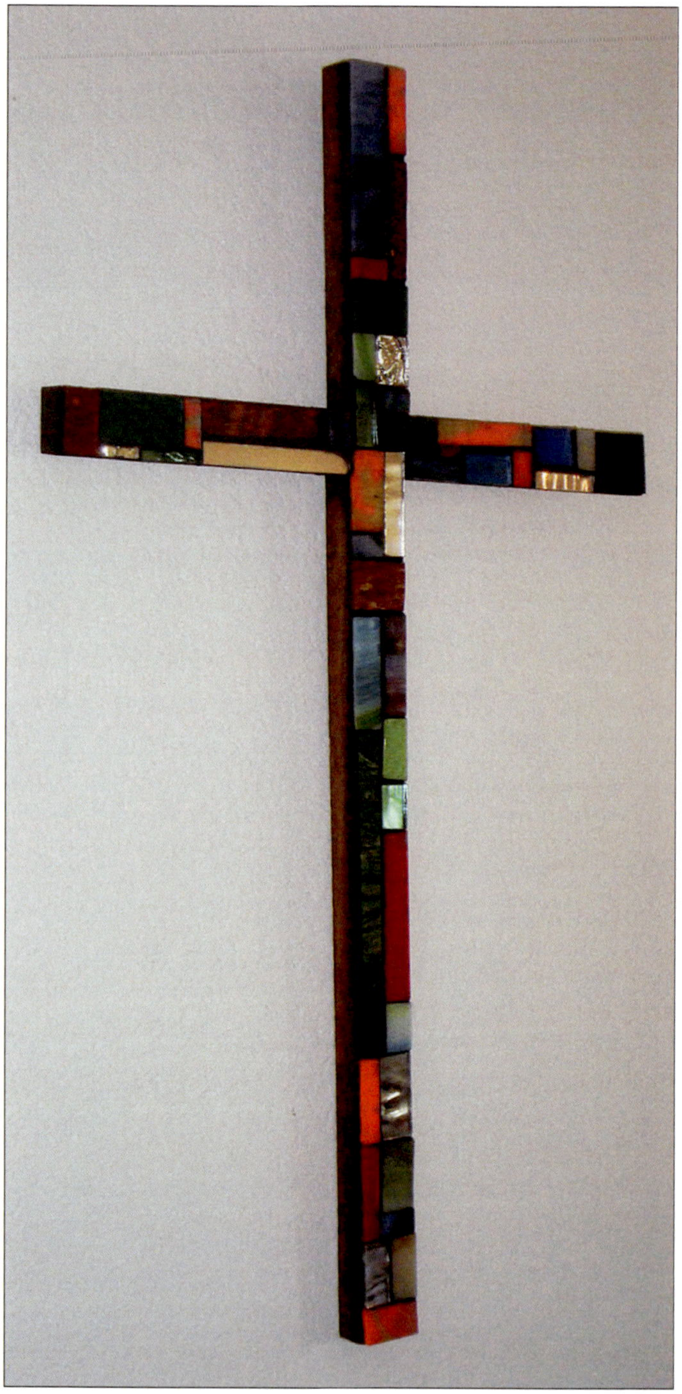

3.16. A Cross, Glass Mosaic on Wood with Neoplastic Design, 8" x 14", 2011.

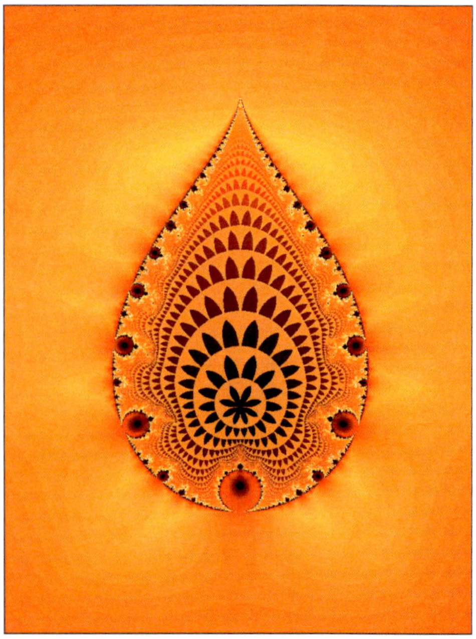

3.17.

A fractal from the early days of Computer Graphics. Made with Fractint Software, Digital, 1983.

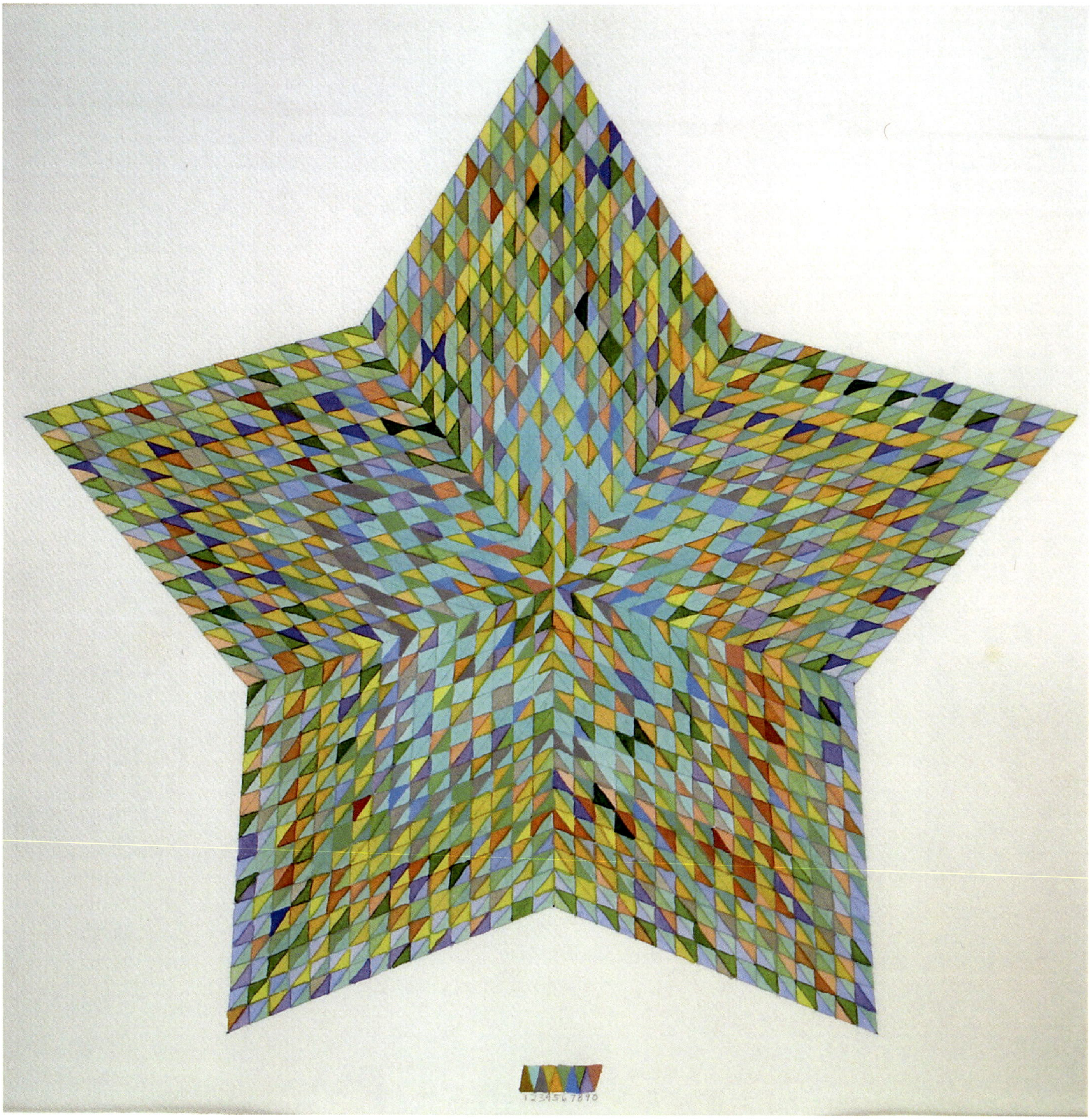

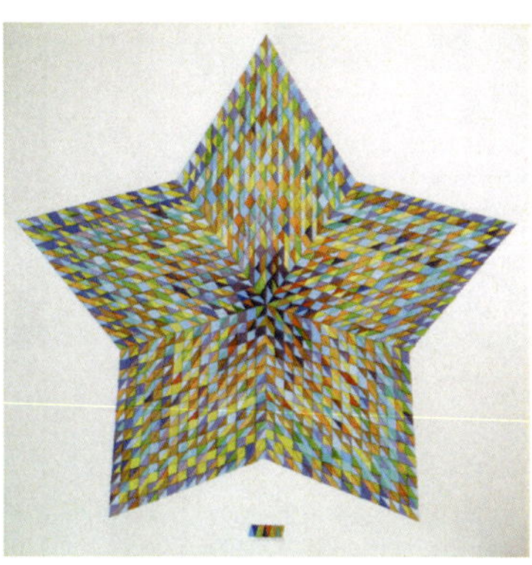

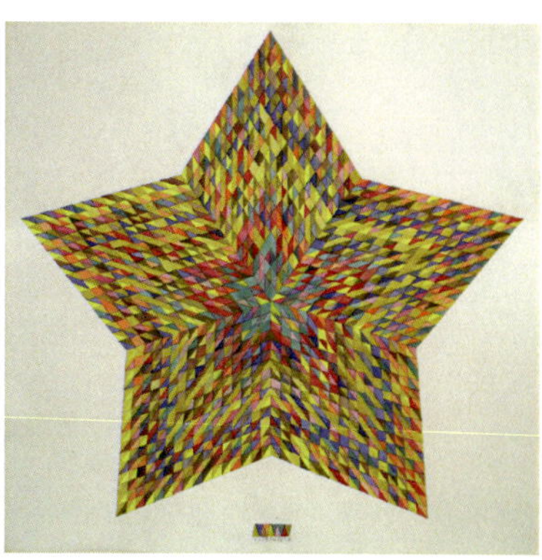

3.18.

Color By Numbers Stars made with altered 10 sided regular polygons and arranged to spiral outward, Note the Legends at the bottom, indicating my seed color choices in base 10. Watercolors on Paper, 18" x 18", 1980.

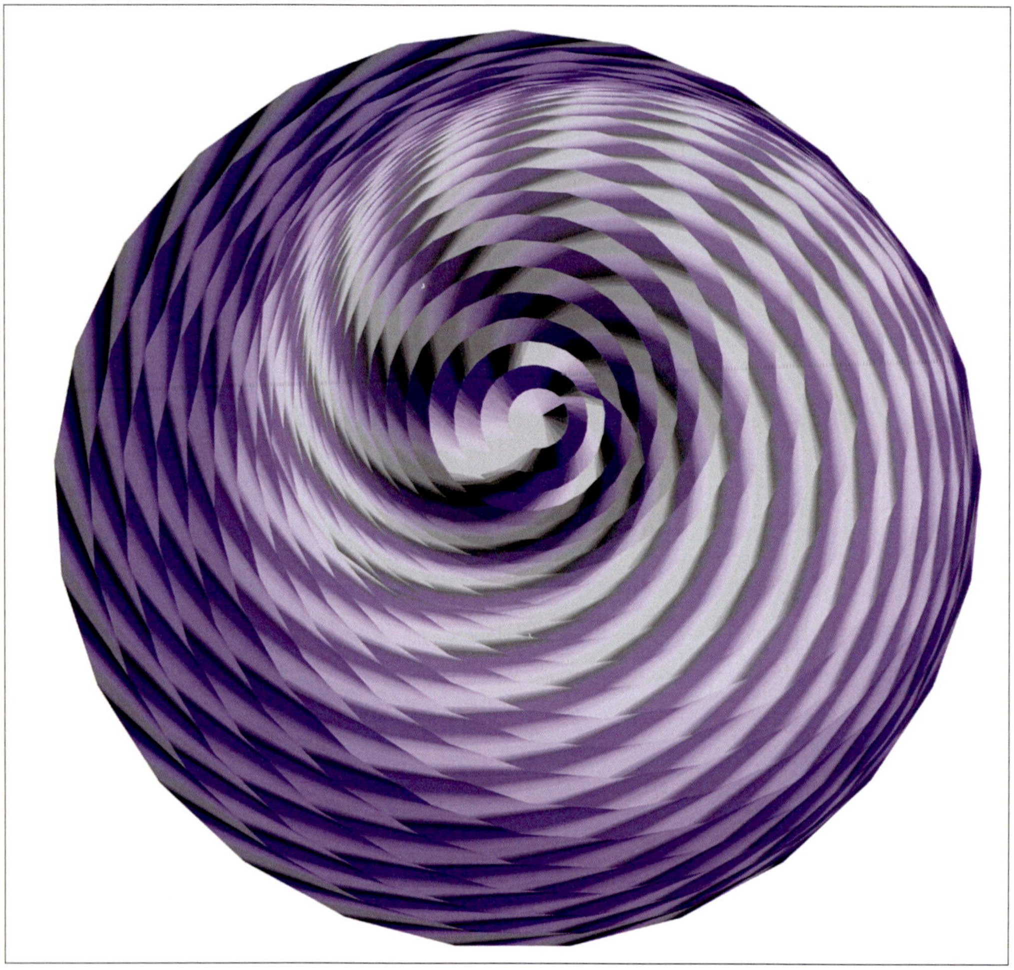

3.19a.

Some examples of output from Color By Numbers software. The images on this page are digital, from 2019.

Geometric points can be rotated and a spiral is born. If the center point is offset a bit, the spiral changes properties.

Spirals represent infinity, they have golden proportions (the Phi Ratio) and they are found in many places in nature, both visible and invisible. I am including them with sacred geometry.

Torus energy field structures have a major role to play in physics. These structures spiral, are self repetitive and allude to infinity. They appear in black holes and lots of other places. They represent energy in motion and are part of nature's geometric building blocks as seen in pine cones, sunflowers and many other forms from nature.

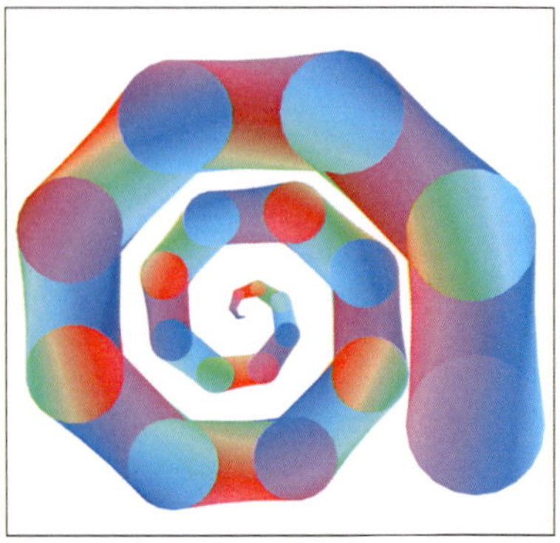

3.19b.

A spiral whose geometry stacked up at intersecting nodes to create circles.

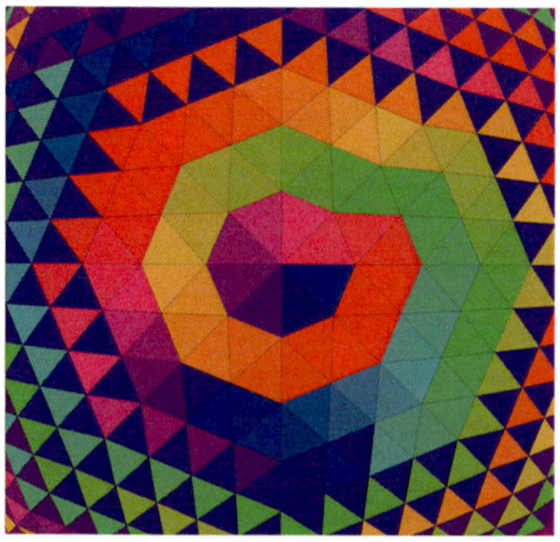

3.19c.

A spiral made with color only, as it progresses in a linear sequence.

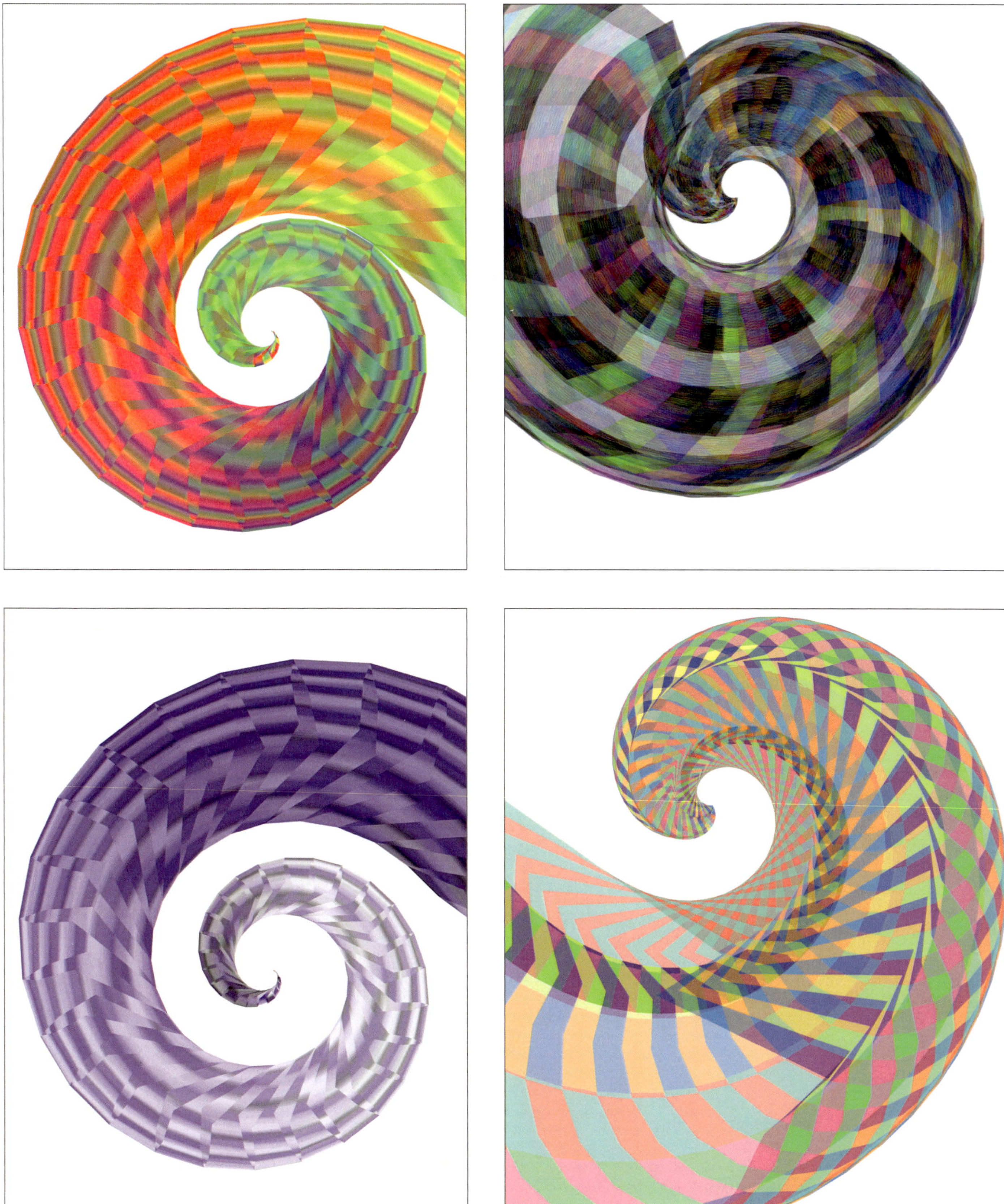

3.20. Some more examples of spiral output from Color By Numbers software. Notice the variance as the center point is located in different spots. These 4 images are digital, from 2019.

FRACTALS

So how hard is it to create a fractal?

My friend Jeff Yetter taught me the principles of fractals. He learned about them in a math class in college in the 1970s. For the most part fractals are about geometric iteration and recursion. This is a fancy way of saying that forms repeat, but can be altered as they repeat.

Let's create a fractal from scratch on paper.

Below I have created a star in Adobe Illustrator. When Jeff explained this to me in 1979, he used paper and pencil. Next (to the right) are 5 stars located near the centers of the radial points of the original star. I have scaled them to 50% and rotated them 36 degrees. I now have a "rule" to follow. It is an algorithm. This step can be repeated and the numbers of copies will grow quickly.

I made a group of this single iteration in Illustrator. I then scaled and rotated this group to create the one with 2 iterations. Below is the version with 2 iterations. Adobe Illustrator has wonderful new tools for patterning, including kaleidoscopic repetition with parameters. The standard old tools were used here and are available in most drawing software. I used snaps and I typed in the values for rotation and scaling.

It wouldn't have been much more difficult to create stencils and do this manually.

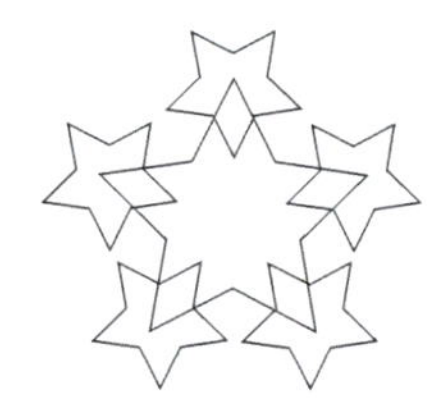

1 iteration = "a rule"

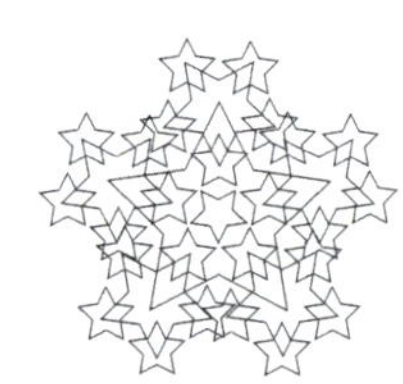

2 iterations

4.1. At this point I made a .jpg file and went to Photoshop for coloring. This was done because coloring in Illustrator would be a lot of tedious edits. So I rendered it to a .jpg file for use in PhotoShop.

We would have to make separately fillable forms. With pixels in Photoshop, I can use the fill bucket with tolerance levels to quickly add color.

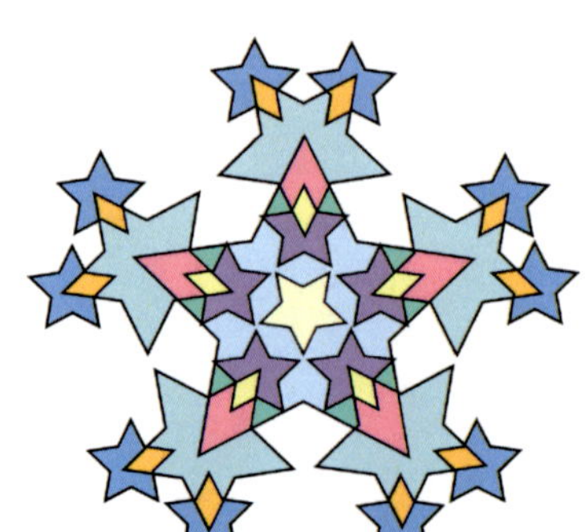

Wikipedia says "Recursion... occurs when a thing is defined in terms of itself or of its type. ... The most common application of recursion is in mathematics and computer science, where a function being defined is applied within its own definition. While this apparently defines an infinite number of instances (function values), it is often done in such a way that no infinite loop or infinite chain of references can occur."

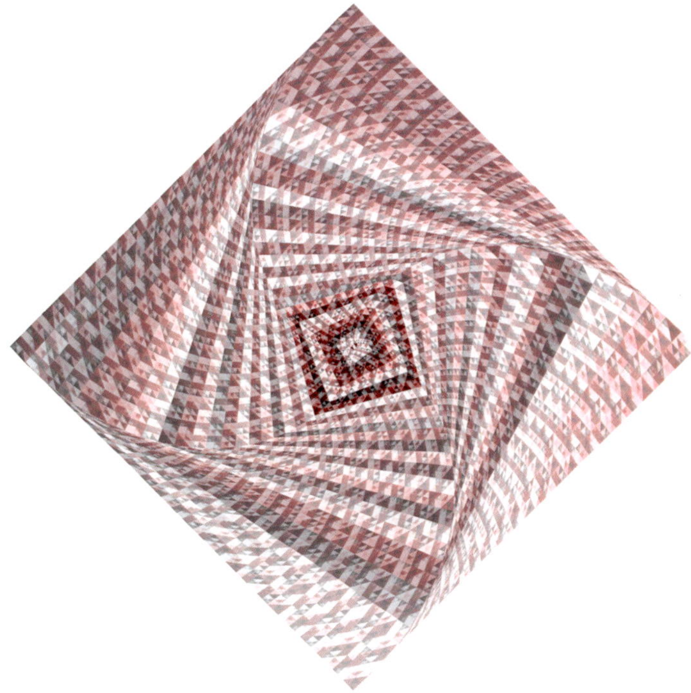

4.22. A simple, spiraling Color By Numbers pattern. The levels repeat and are scaled smaller towards the center.

Usually iteration is driven by such factors as scaling, rotation, translation, or a combination of any of them. A simple fractal can be generated by reference points, scaling and orientation. Wikipedia again says "Iteration is the repetition of a process in order to generate an outcome. The sequence will approach some end point or end value. Each repetition of the process is a single iteration, and the outcome of each iteration is then the starting point of the next iteration."

In other words iteration defines how many times you repeat the process. It usually ends with the resolution of your output or your pencil width. It turns into pixel mush or blobs of drawing lines and you lose your iterative cycles in the detail. Once you can't see it the drawing or rendering you have reached a physical limit.

Fractals have infinity built into them. You just have to realize there are limits in our reality. As you zoom in to finer details on a fractal you see self-similar details. However we have to view this through an isolated, relative "frame" that limits us from the rest. The resolution we view the fractal at also is a limited piece of the full mathematical infinity. Most fractals have infinite detail (or the potential thereof). Limits are imposed by physical materials.

> *"The beautiful is a manifestation of the secret laws of nature... When nature begins to reveal her open secret to a person, he feels an irresistible longing for her most worthy interpreter, art."*
> *- Johann Wolfgang Von Goethe, early color theorist*

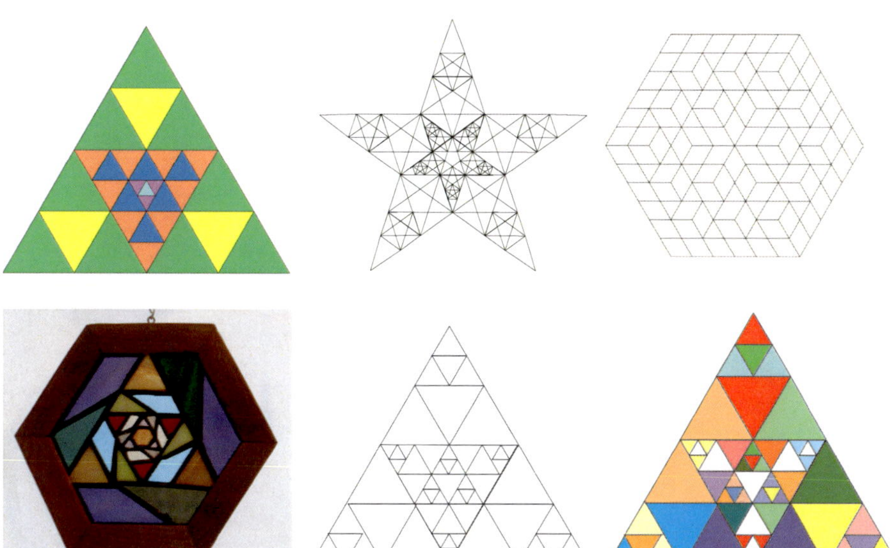

4.22.

Some examples of fractal concepts used in designs.

All digital from 2020, except for the lower left which is a Stained Glass, 8" diameter, 2018.

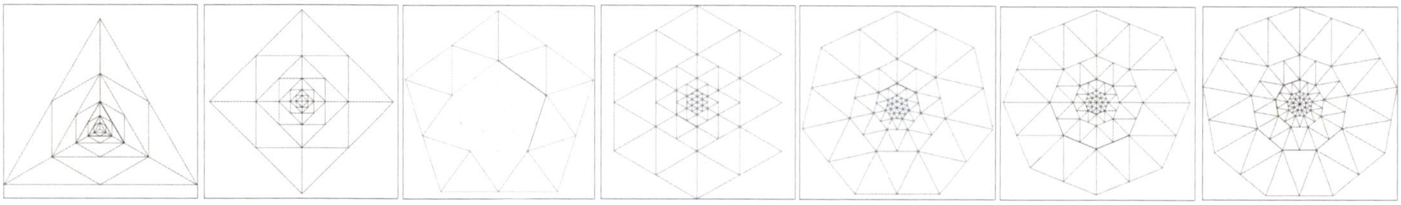

4.4. I invented fractal grids as a derivative of my polar, polygonal grids made for Color By Numbers Software. I created these manually and do not yet have automated software for this. These grids grow smaller as they converge on the center. The examples shown here are based on regular polygons from 3 - 9 sides. I exported Color by Numbers grids into Adobe Illustrator and used scaling to shrink the iterations. My primary interest is stained glass. I am only able to cut glass so small, so these are limited to only a few iterations. Unless they are created at a larger size.

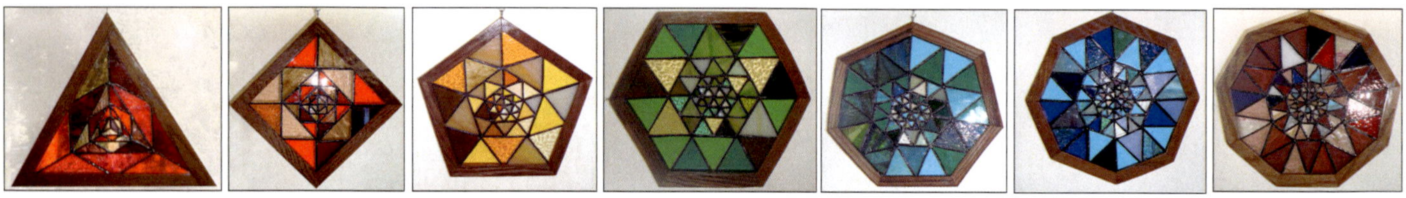

4.5. I enjoy giving them color themes, using dark and light variations in a more or less checkerboard fashion. These are colored like the chakras and represent the first 7 regular polygons. Stained Glass, 15" diameter, 2018.

I also invented another fractal grid variation. Similar, but based on different rules.

These fractal grids are developed by triangulating on the radial center point. Then I find the edge centers of those radial triangles and start connecting some existing points. This works with any number of radiations and creates a star motif in part of the design.

Imagine what else can be done with these concepts?

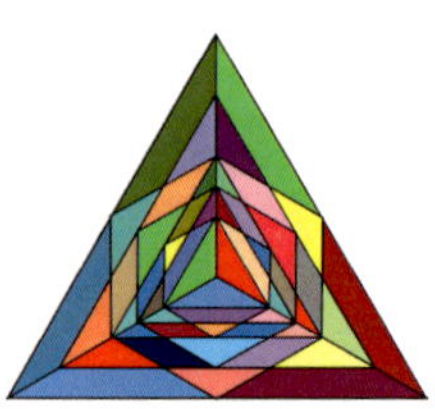

4.6a.

Adobe Illustrator file, 2020.

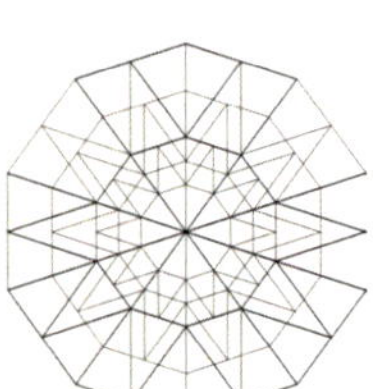

4.6b.

Adobe Illustrator file, 2020.

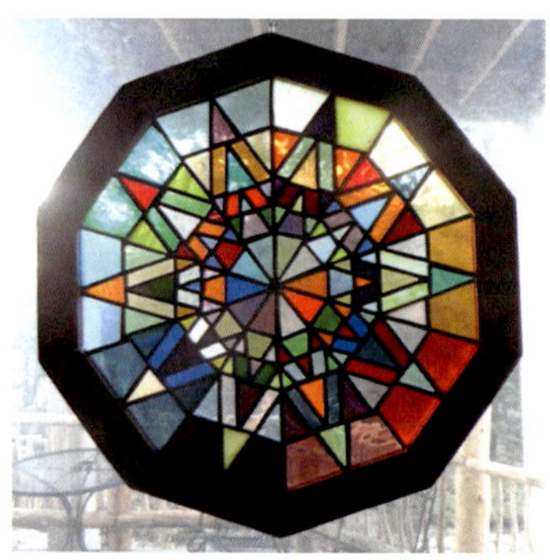

4.7a.

Stained glass, 16" diameter, 2020.

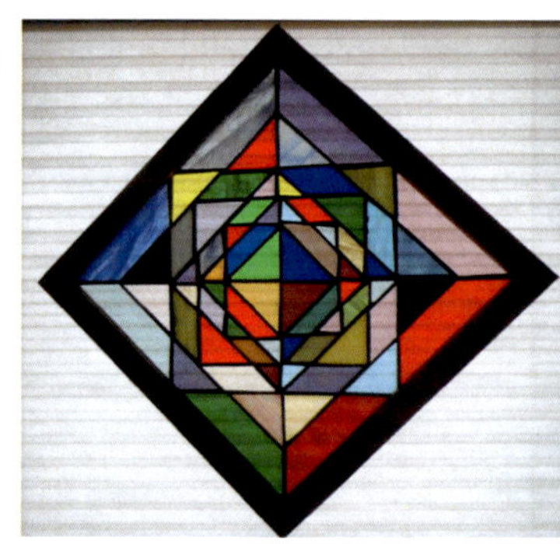

4.7b.

Stained glass, 16" x 16", 2020.

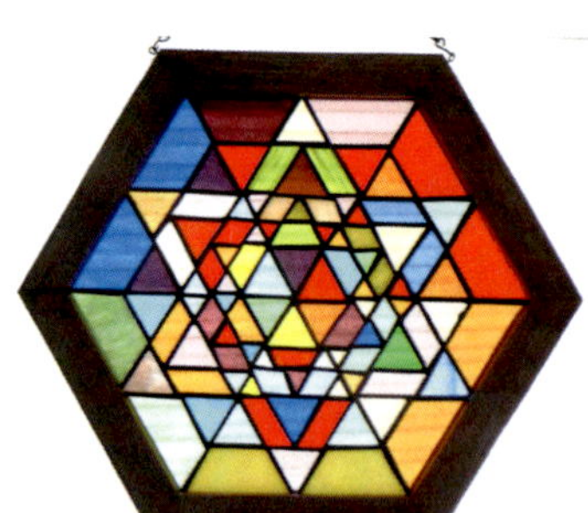

4.7c.

Stained glass, 16" diameter, 2020.

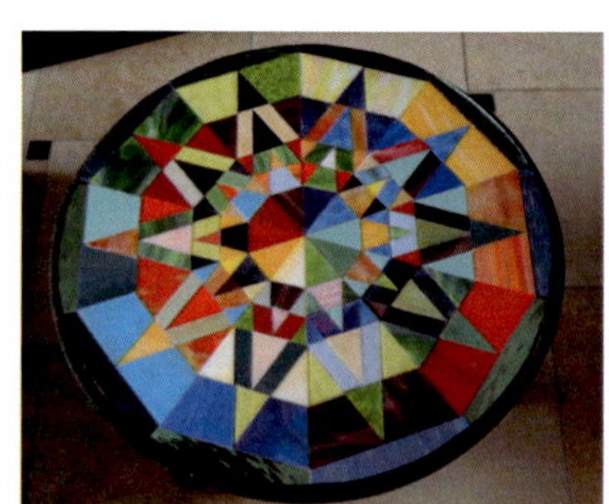

4.7d.

20" Glass mosaic table top, 30" diameter, 2020.

Computers opened lots of doors for exploring fractals. Since the 1970's many tools have been developed. Having access to a programmer was one of the biggest art benefits I got from collaborating with Jeff Yetter.

Since 1979 we have created a number of softwares for art creation on a number of computer platforms. I had a lot of ideas and Jeff was very skilled at programing. We focused on parametric graphics - a commonly used format with parameters to adjust the various aspects of the rendering we are creating.

In 1971 Scientific American release an article on Benoit Mandelbrot and the Mandelbrot Set and within 6 months Jeff made our own software with algorithmic adjustment parameters for tweaking a variety of aspects, especially "zooming in" where you explore a virtual infinity of self-similarity.

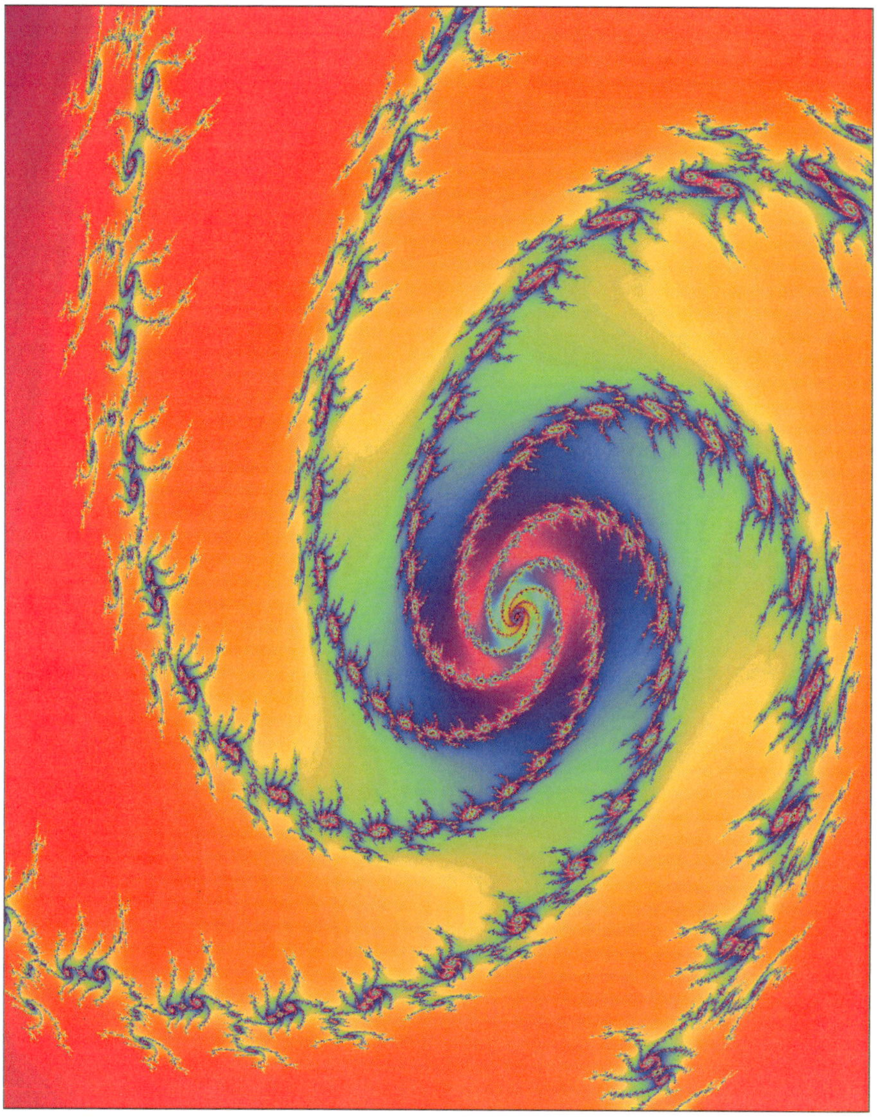

4.8.

A customized fractal created with our own formula similar to the Mandelbrot set. Digital, 1024 x 1280 pixels, 1980.

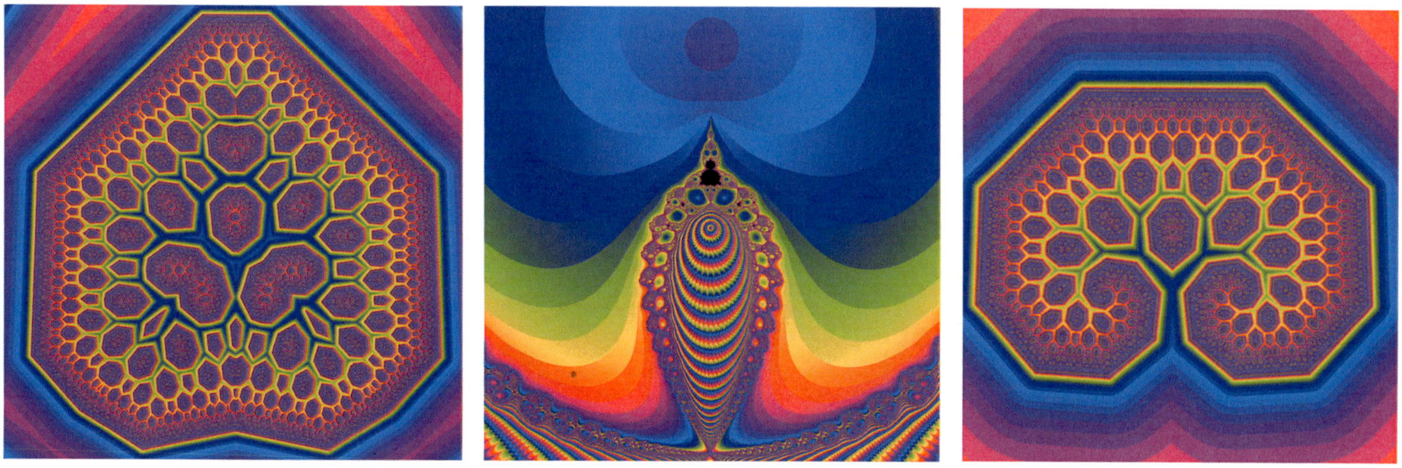

4.9. 3 more fractals, created with various software, digital, 3000 x 3000 pixels, 2009.

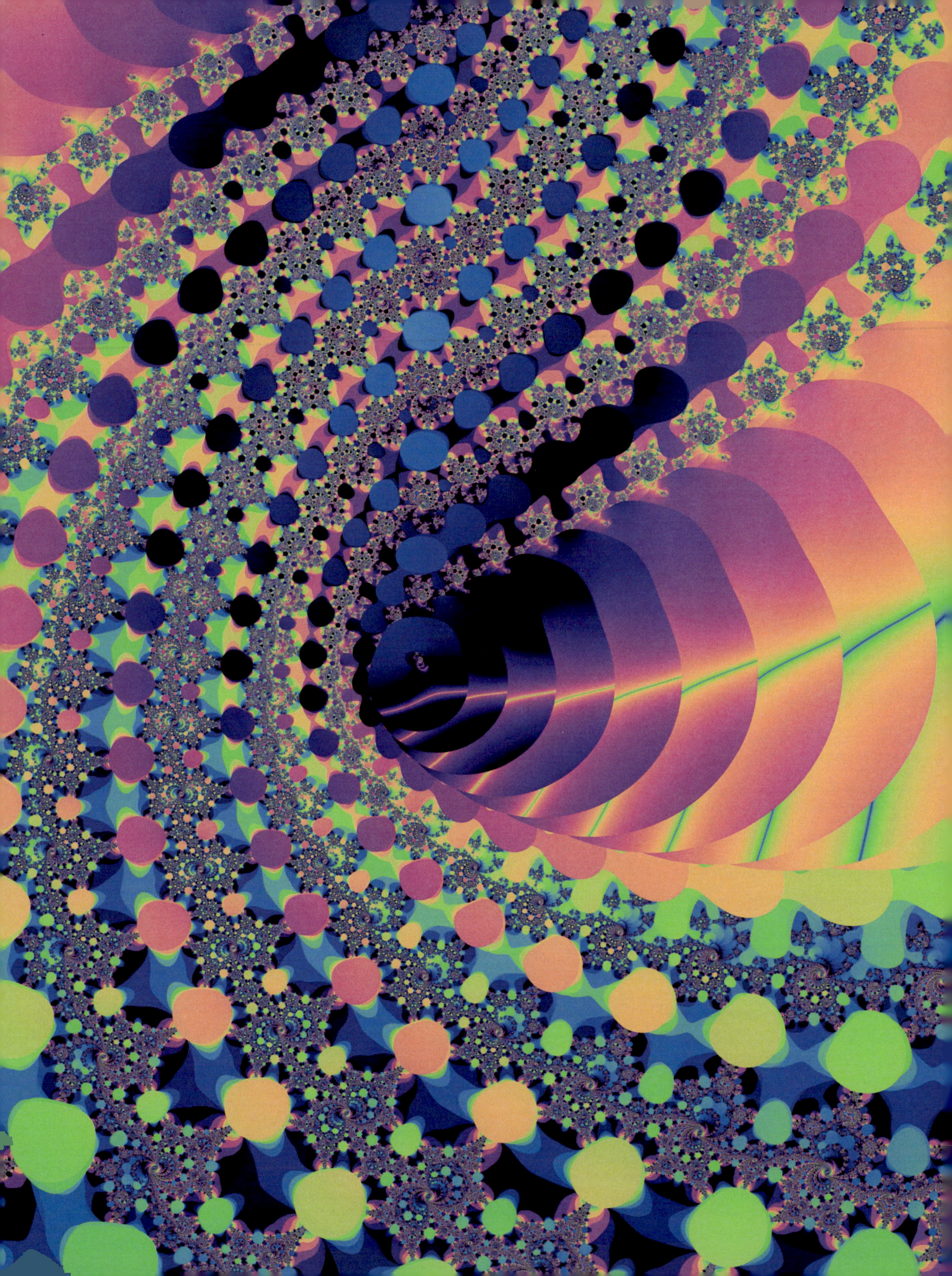

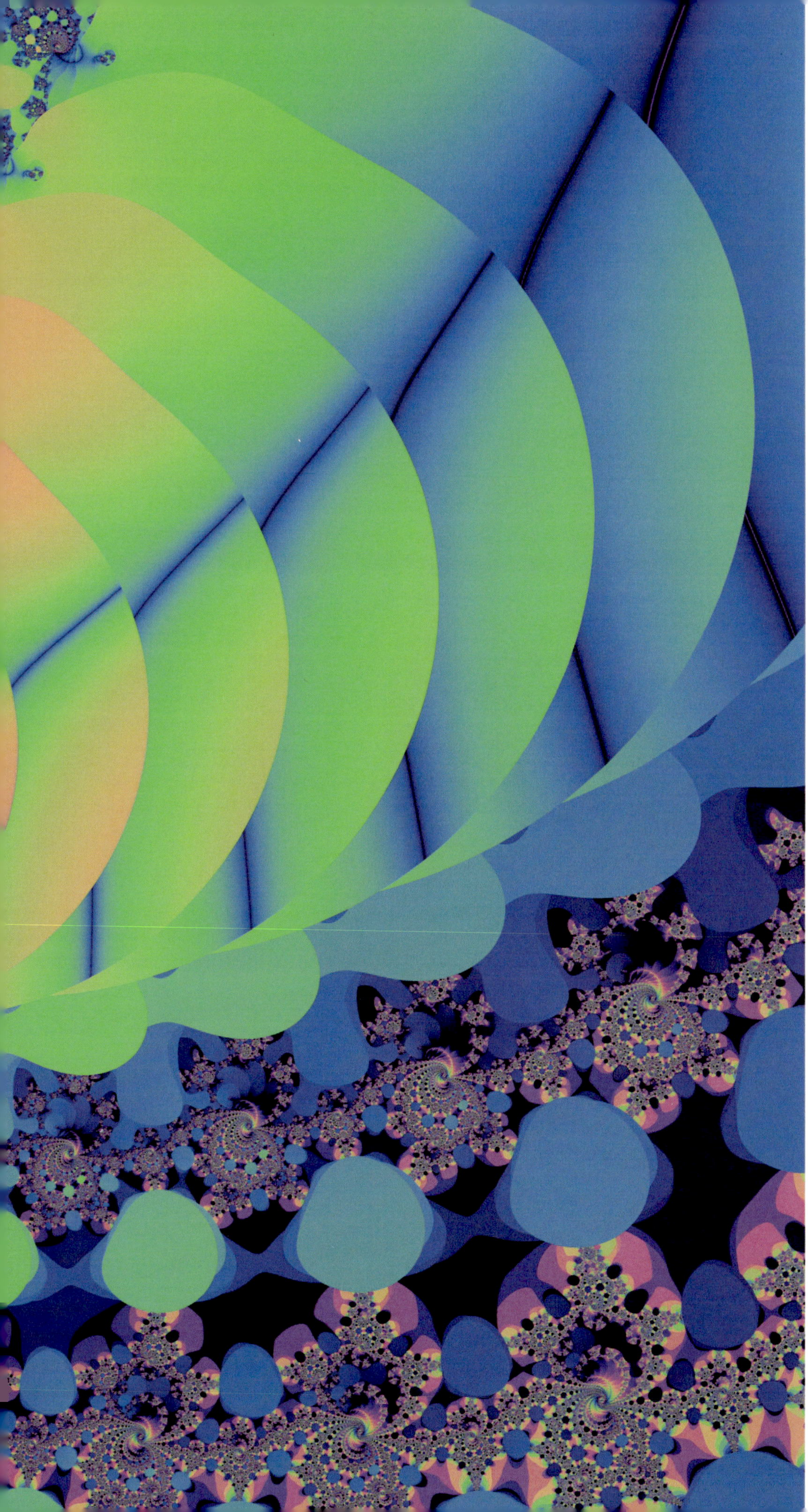

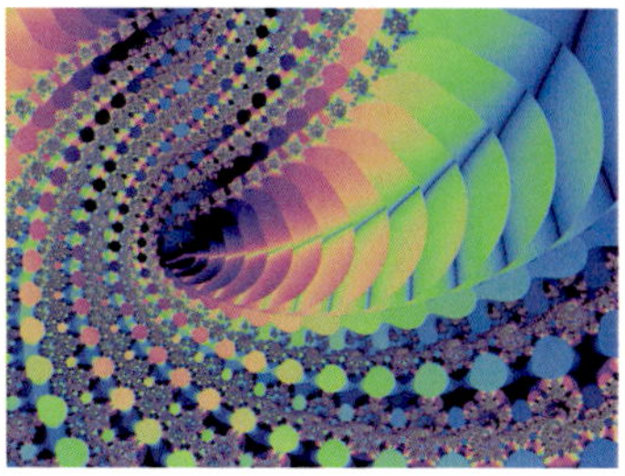

4.10.

Tunnel, Digital,
3000 x 2250 pixels,
2008.

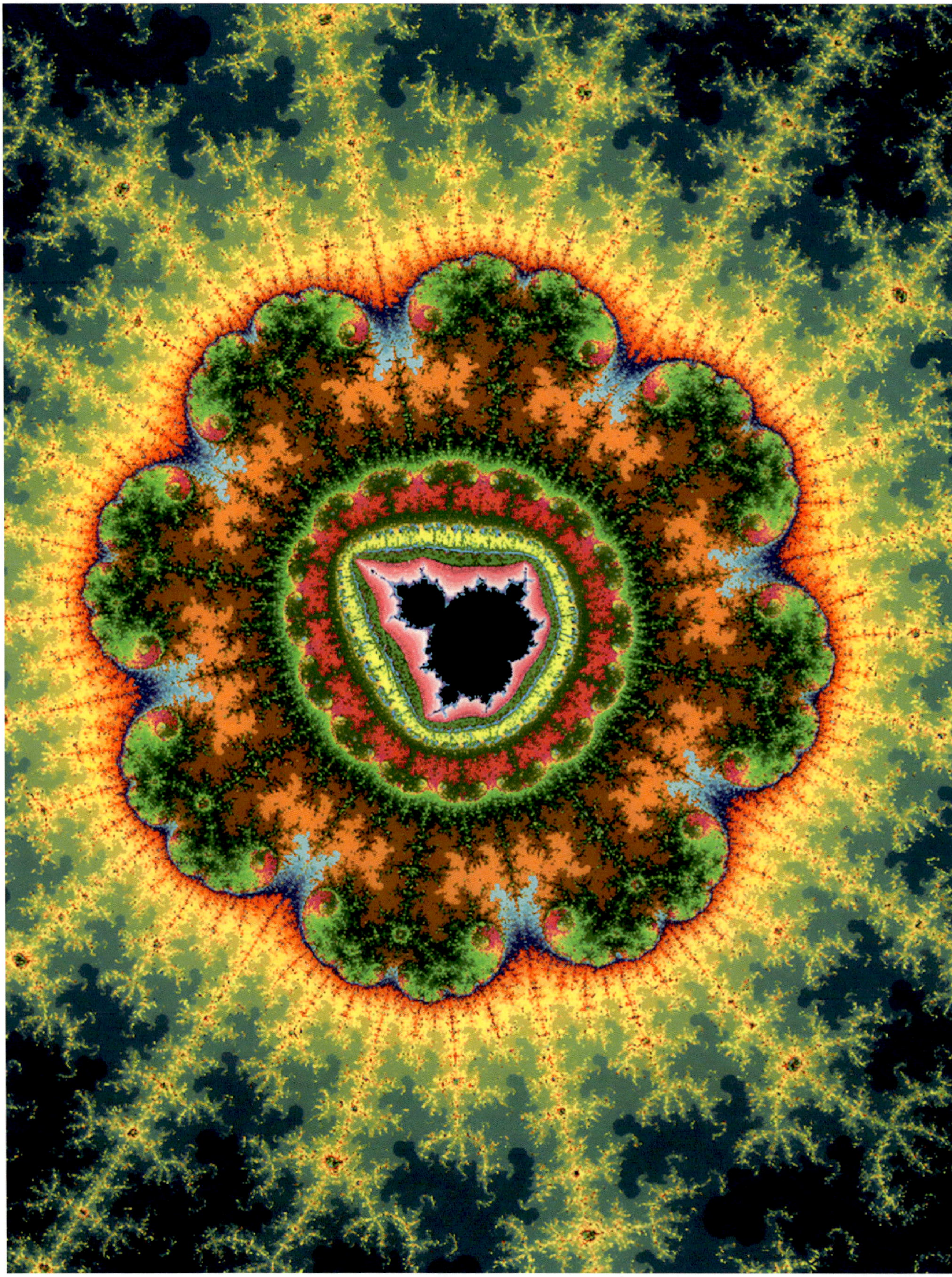

4.12. Mandala Flower, Digital, 800 x 600, Upscaled with AI, 1981

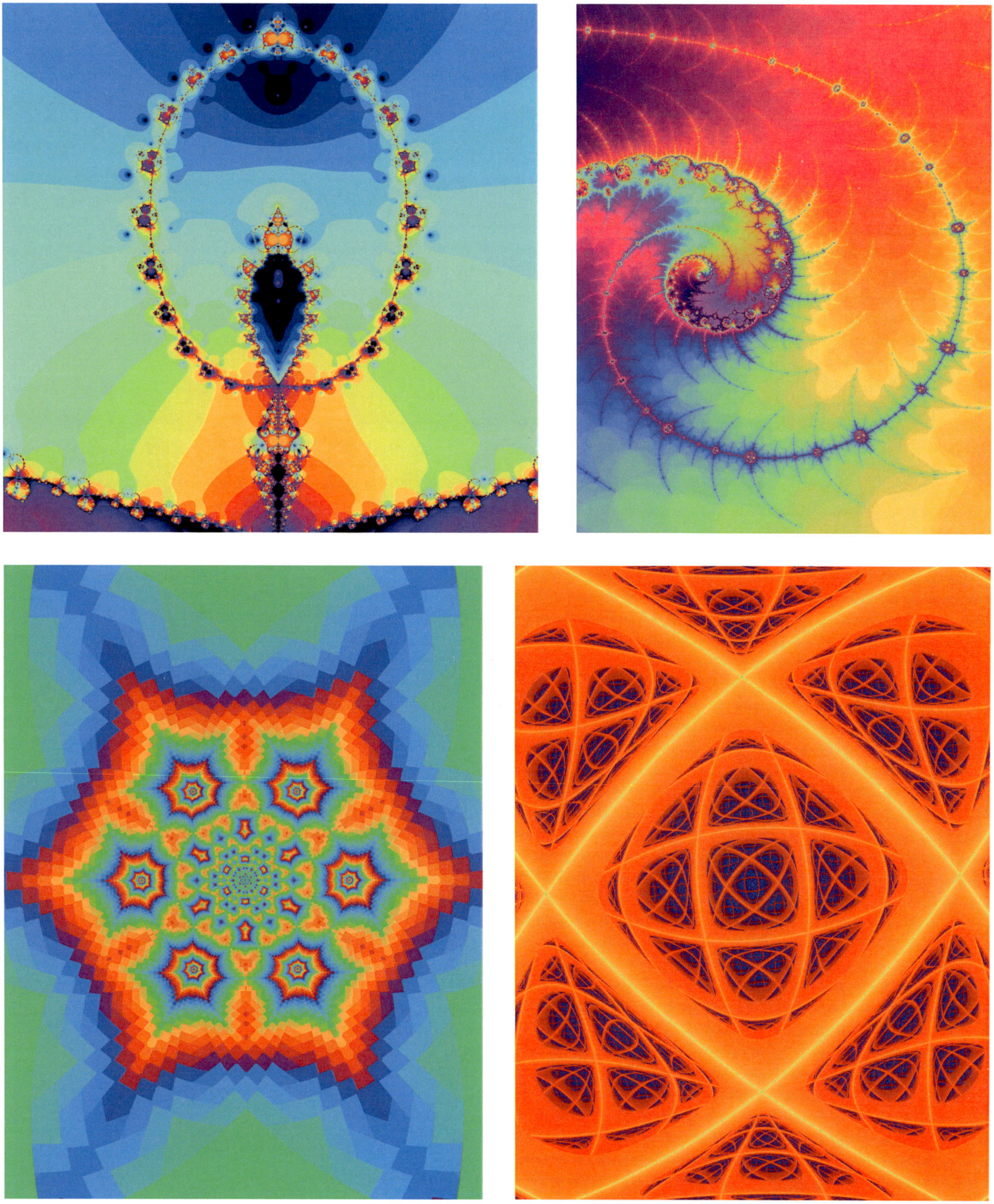

4.13.

Four examples of fractals generated during the 1980s, made with various software.

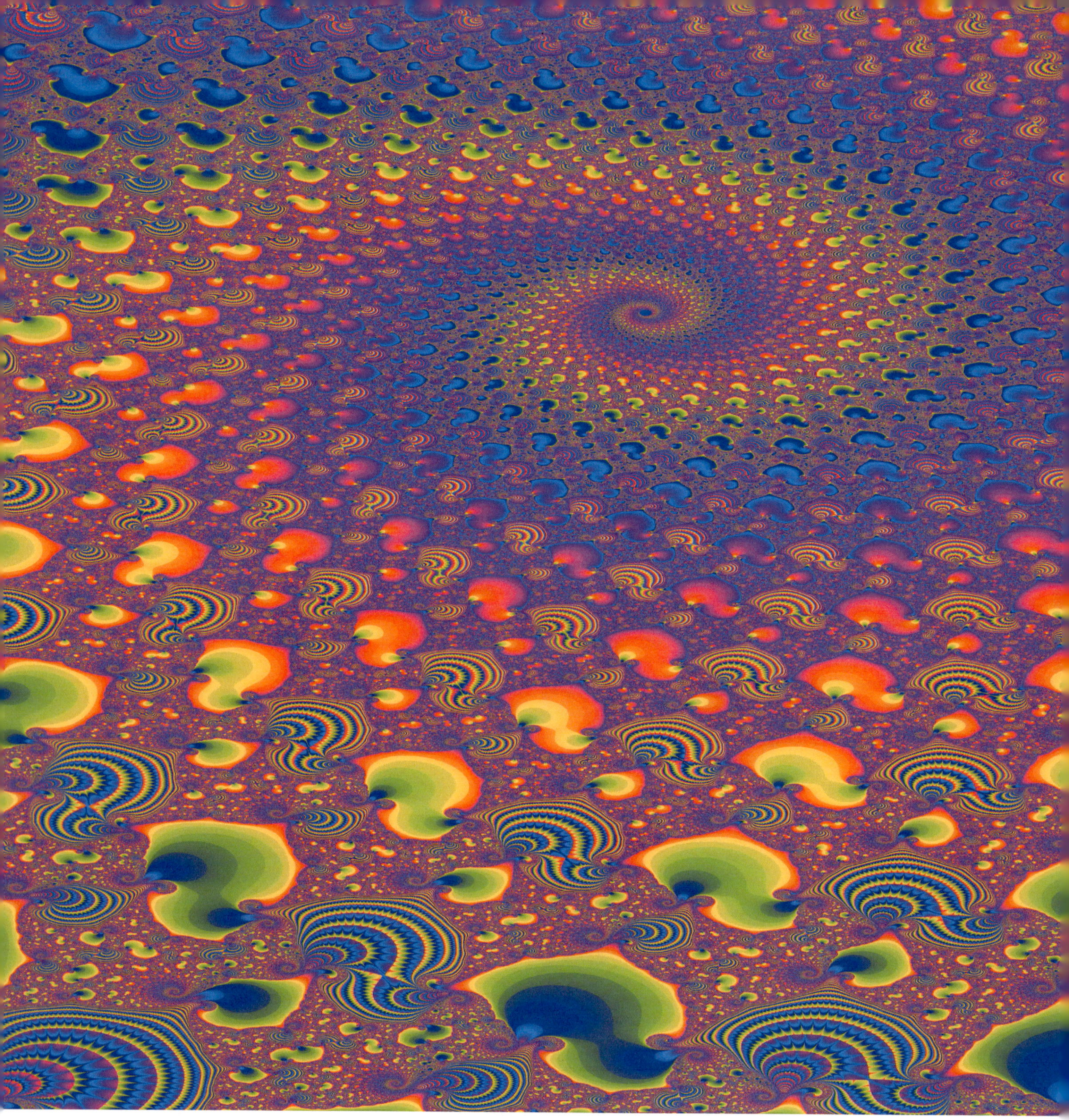

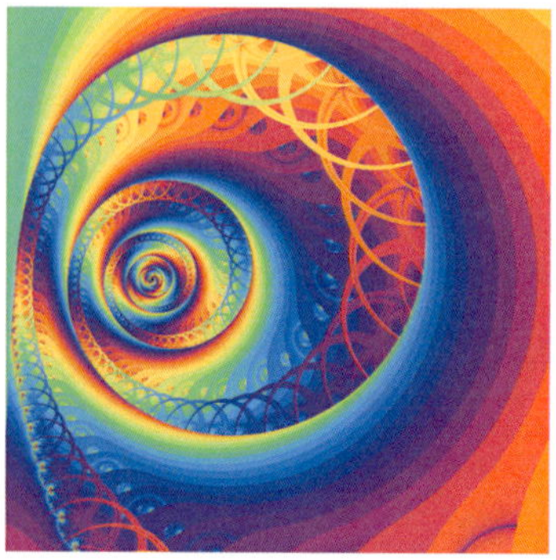

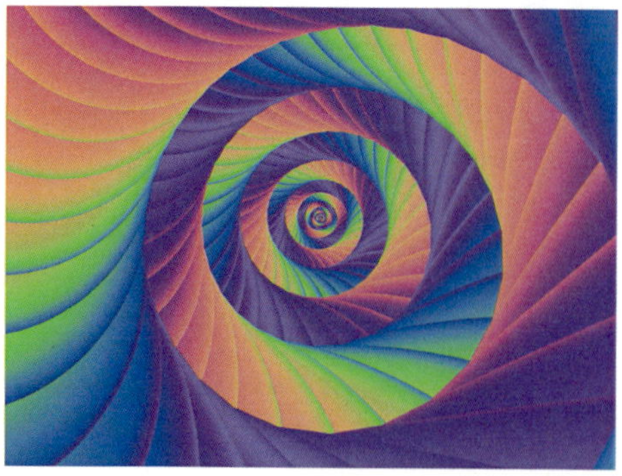

4.13.

Spiral Fractal, Digital, 3000 x 2250 pixels, 2018.

These 2D fractals have some potential to be presented in special ways by computer output.

I have printed some with metallic inks and have some interest in investing in an engraving device to print on wood, plastic, metal and glass.

They were used extensively for projection, mostly from slides I created, during the 1990s, at raves and other parties, displayed with cross fades.

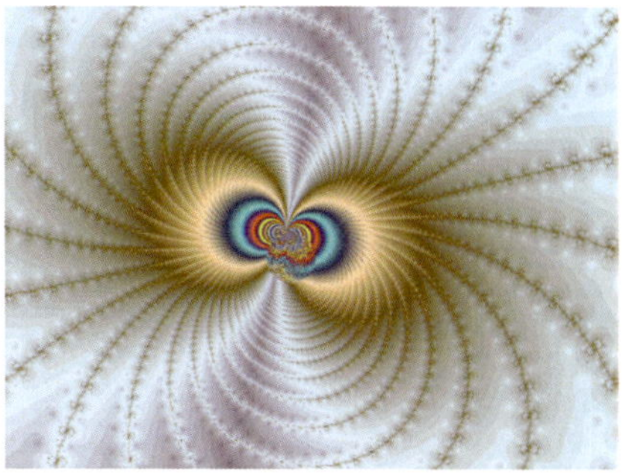

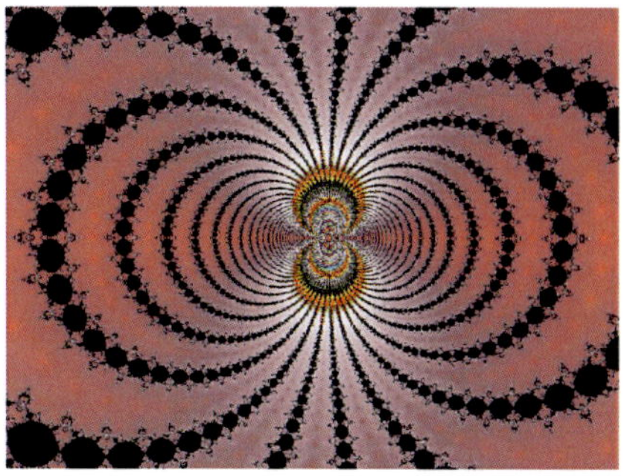

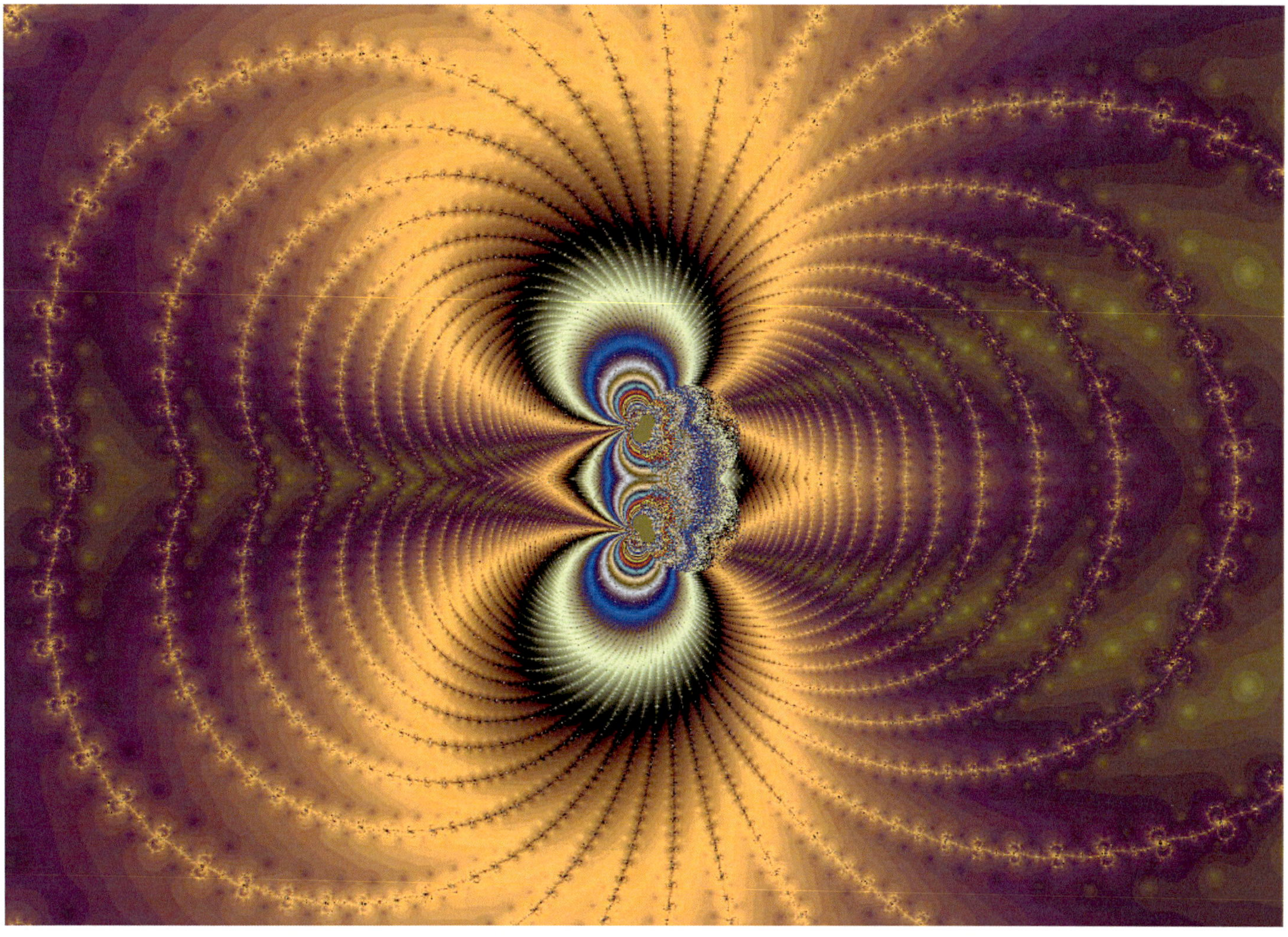

4.14. Moire fractals, Digital, 1024 x 768 pixels, 1990.

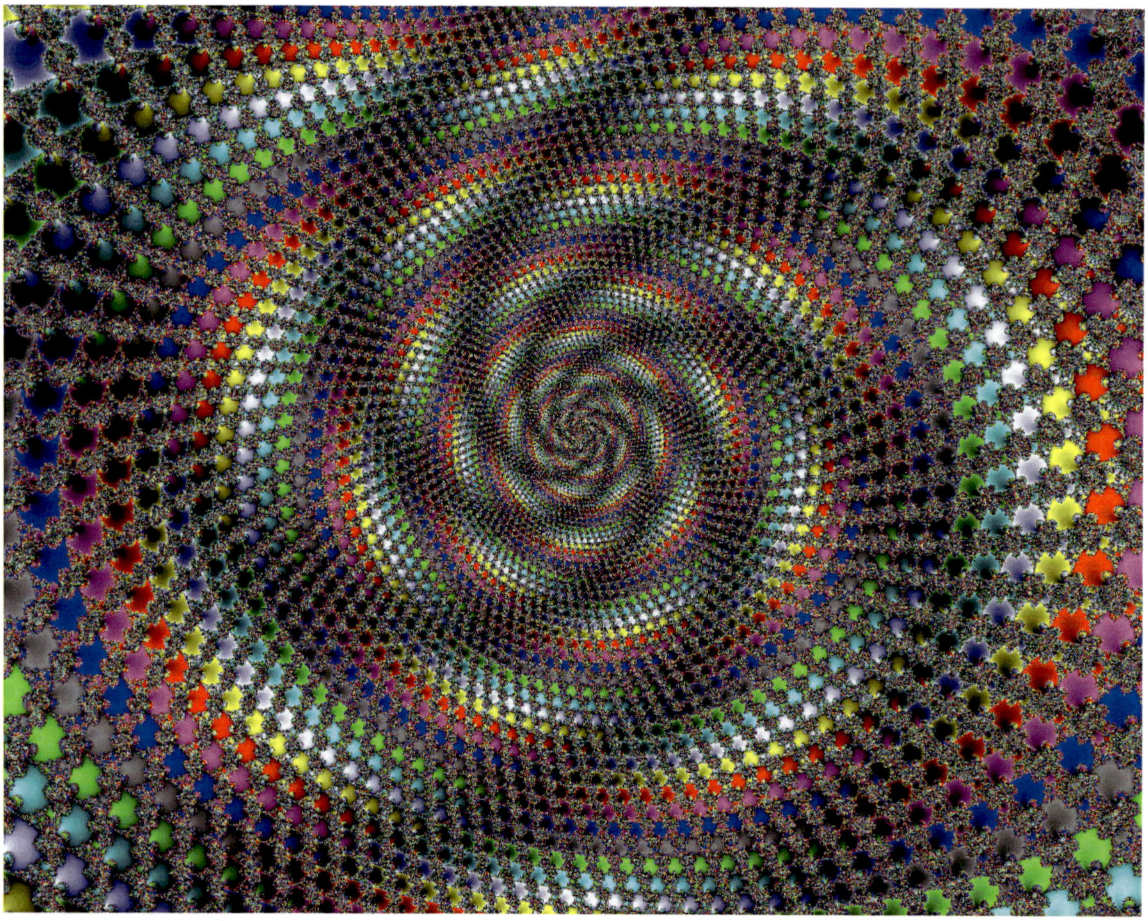

4.15.

Untitled, Digital,
1280 x 1024 pixels,
1984.

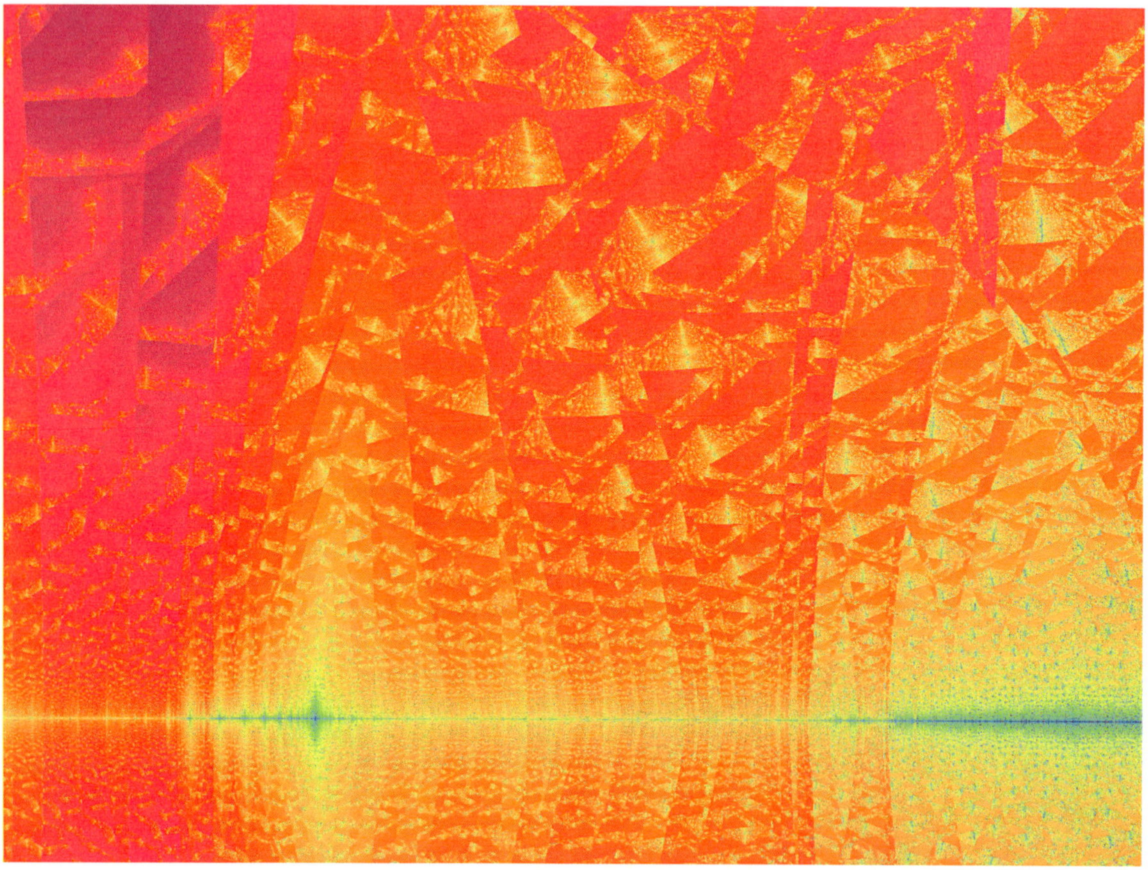

4.16.

Reflection, Digital,
1600 x 1200 pixels,
1985.

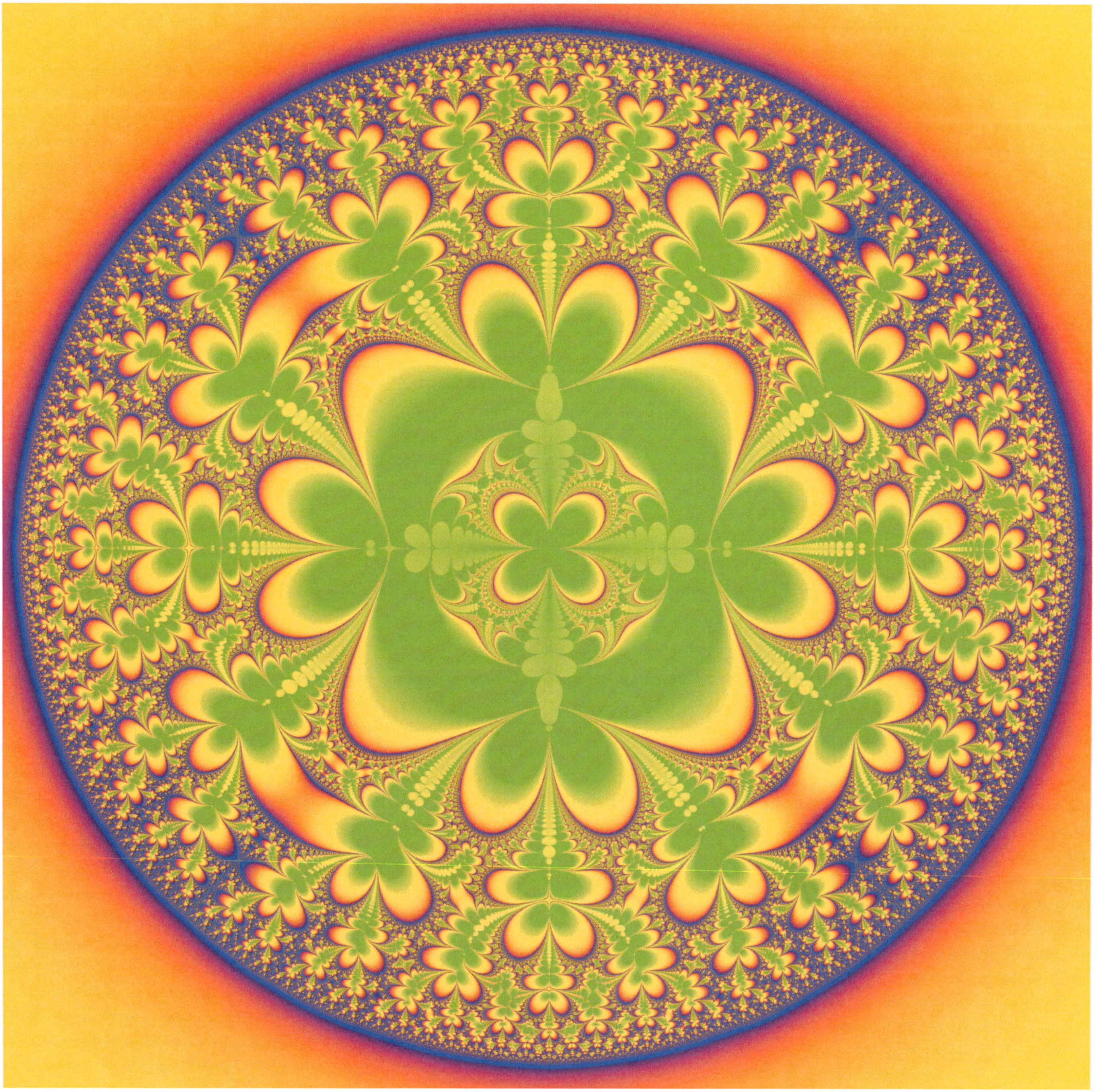

4.17. EscherBall, Digital, 3000 x 3000 pixels, 1994.

4.18.

Three additional untitled fractals, Digital, various resolutions, 1986.

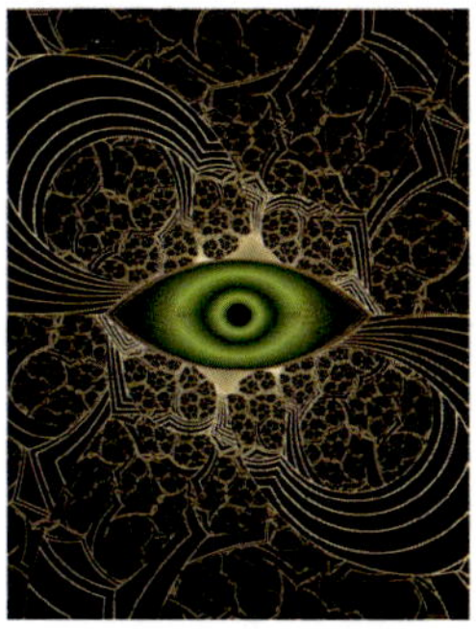

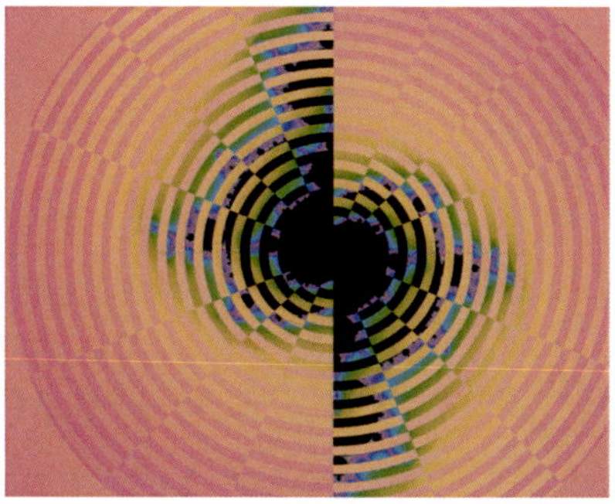

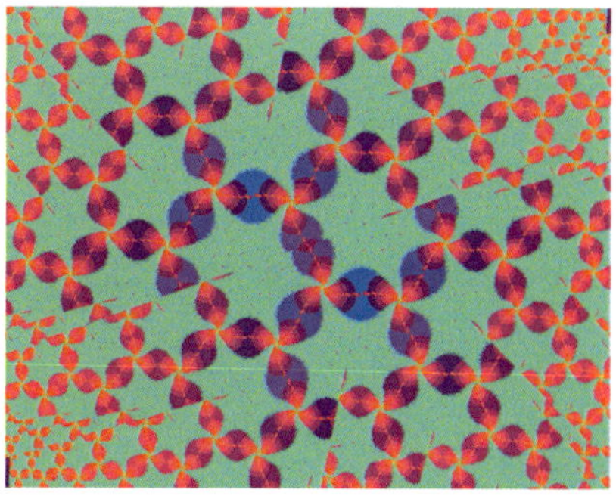

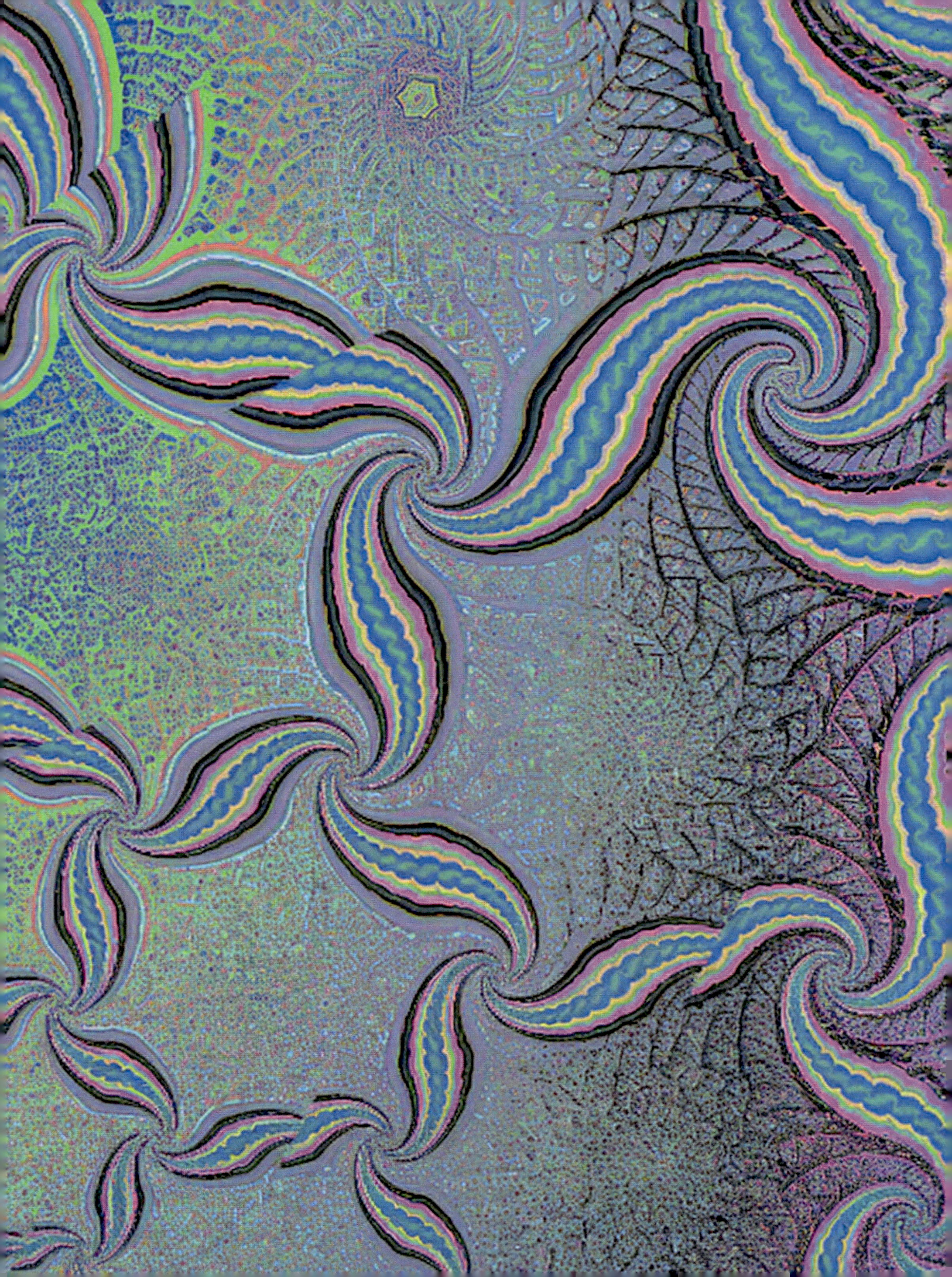

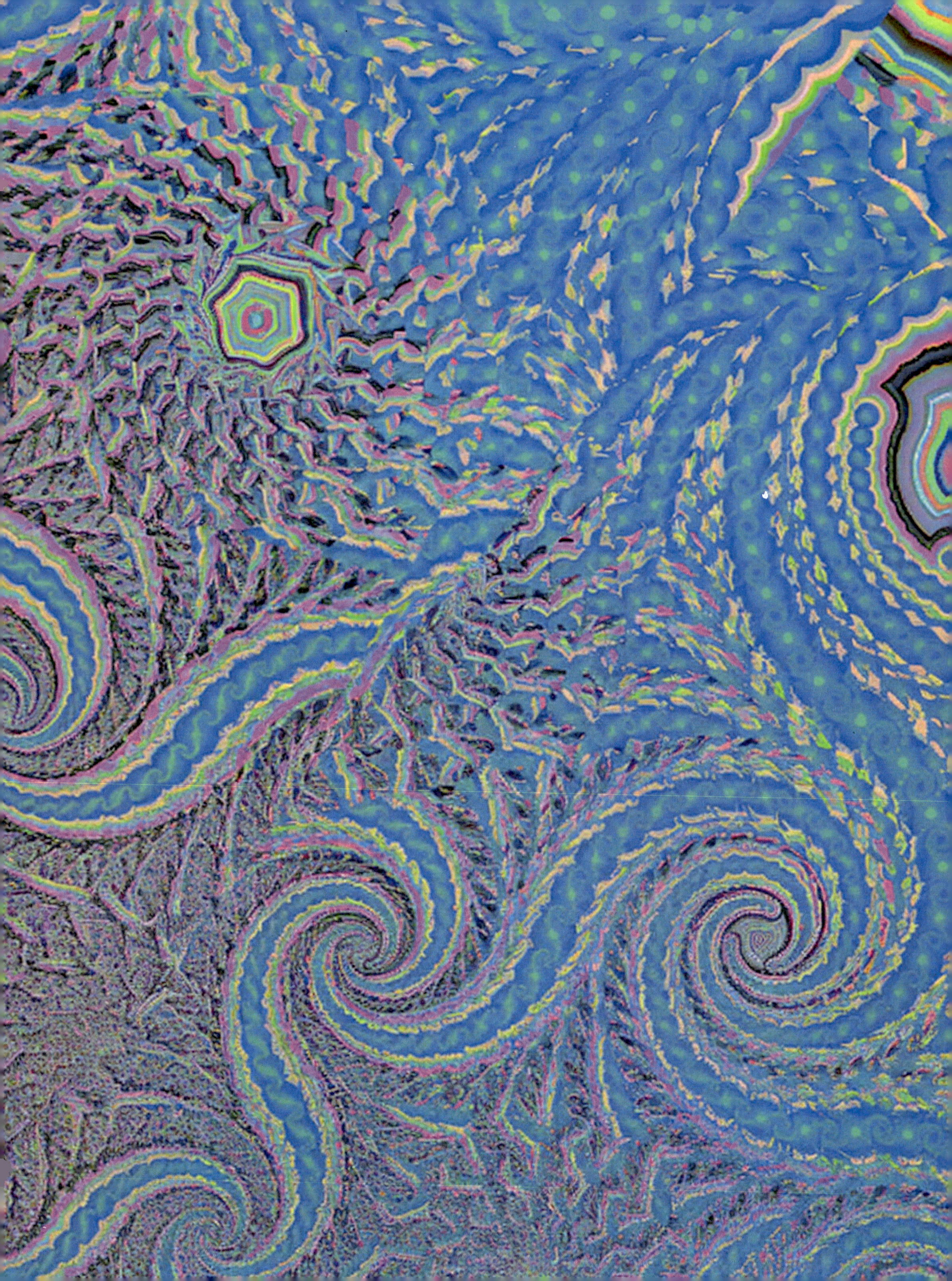

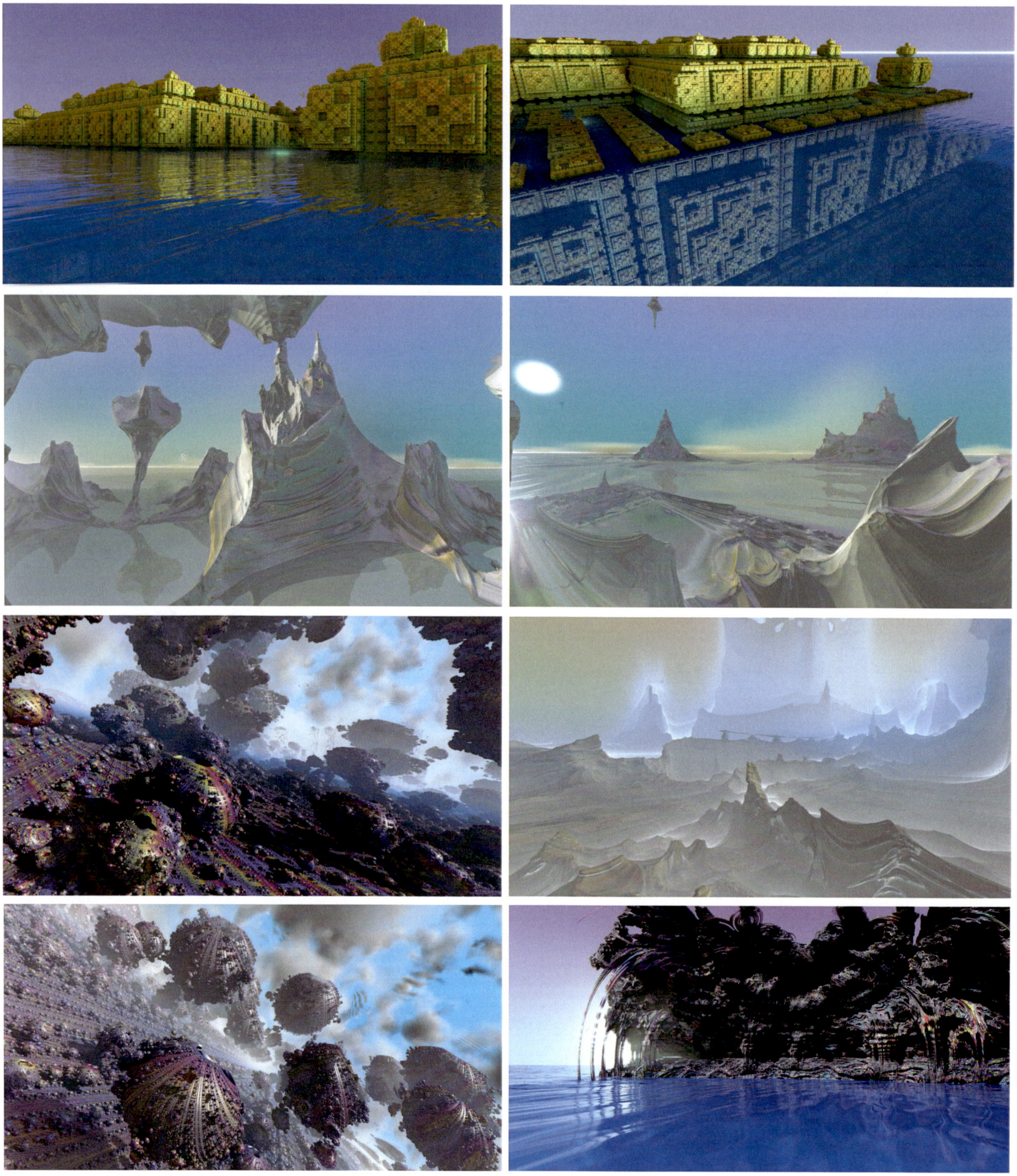

4.20.

Here are some synthetic landscapes made with Mandelburber 3D software. The software allows for creation of three-dimensional fractals, mixed with water, clouds, fog, glows and unique color mapping techniques. The software is distributed for free. These are taken from animations I have made. 3D fractals are quite an enhancement from 2D.

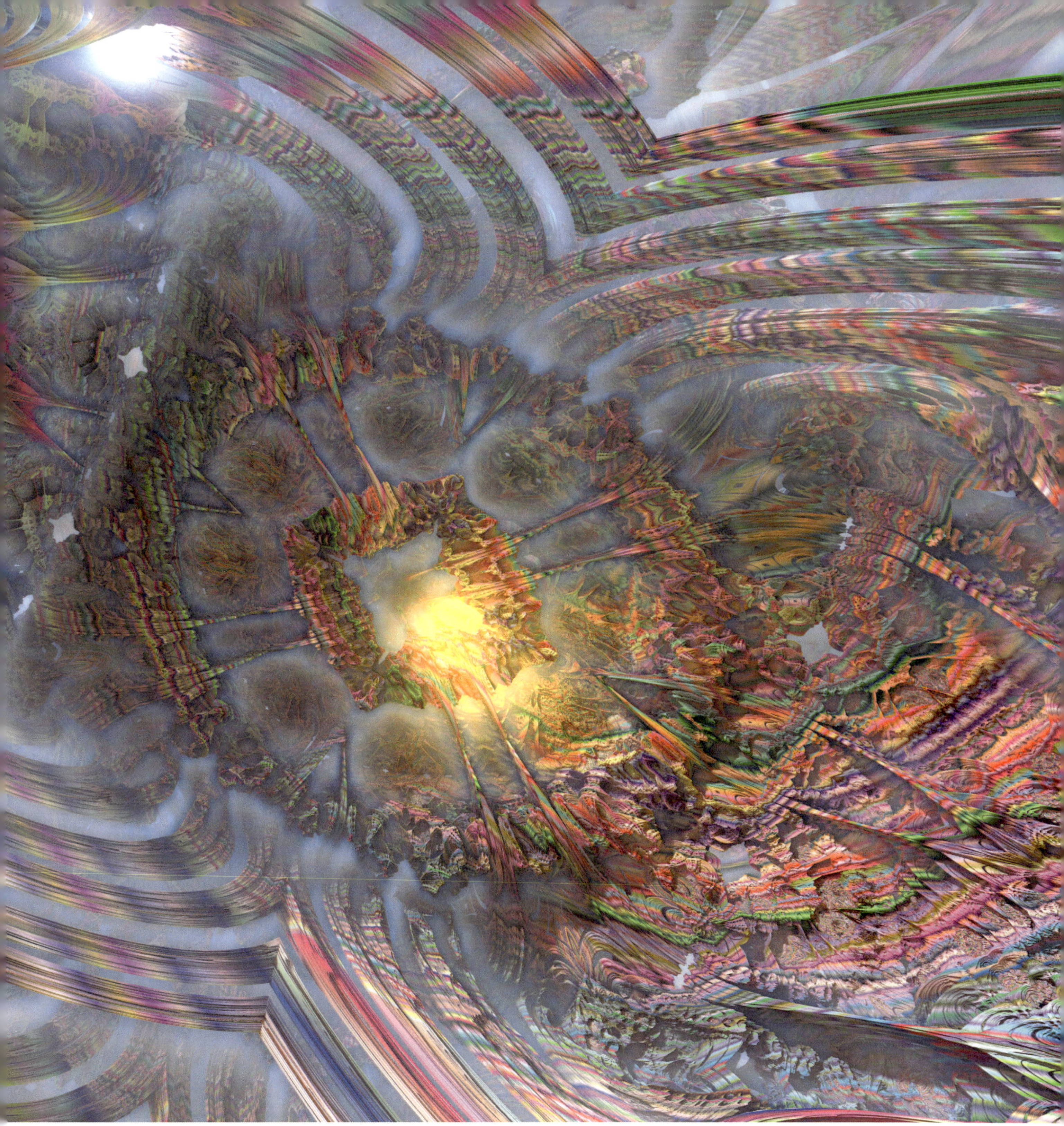

4.21.

An example of output from Mandelburber 3D.
Untitled, Digital, 4000 x 4000 pixels,
2018.

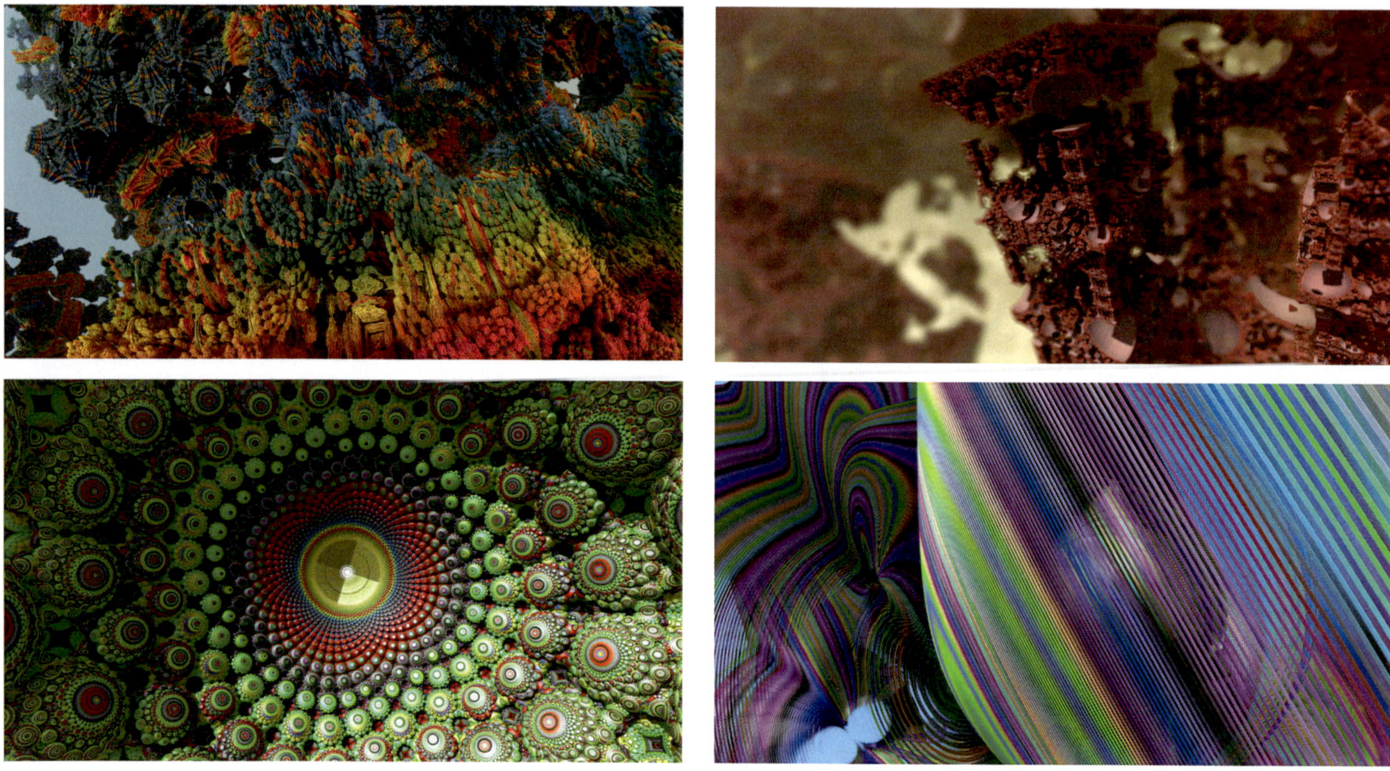

4.22.

More examples of output from Mandelburber 3D. Untitled fractals used in 4K animations, resolution 3840 x 2160 pixels, 2019.

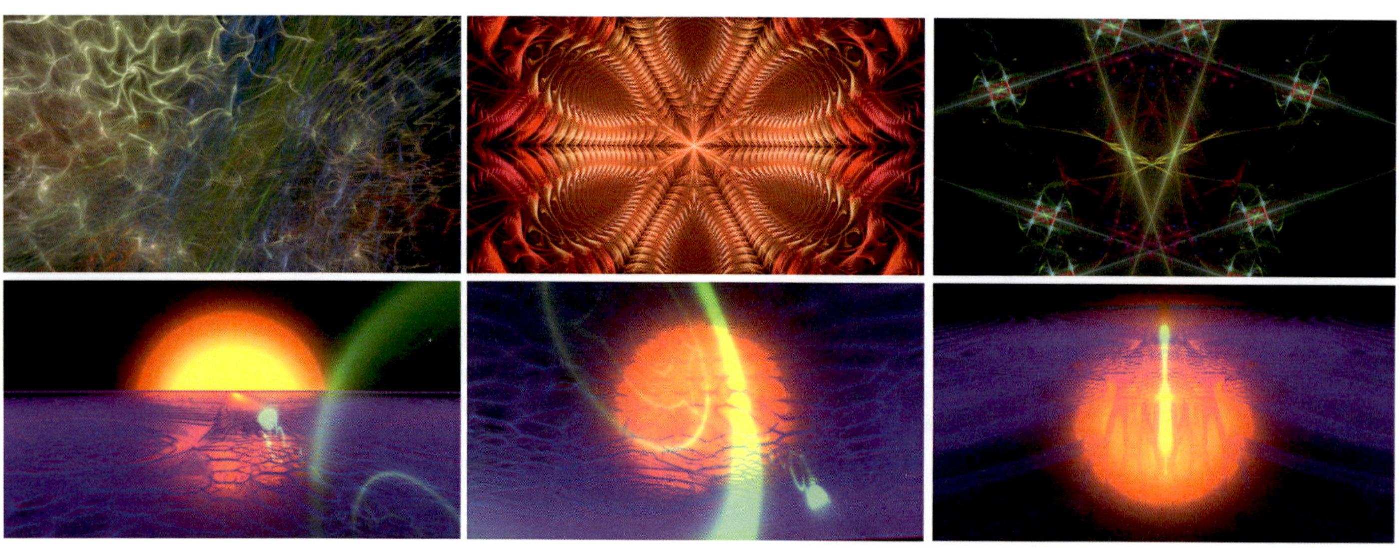

4.23.

Some examples created with another free software called J Wildfire. They seed these fractals with "flames"..

4.23a.

Opposite Page: Some examples created with another software called VUE. 3D fractals are implemented in landscape creation.

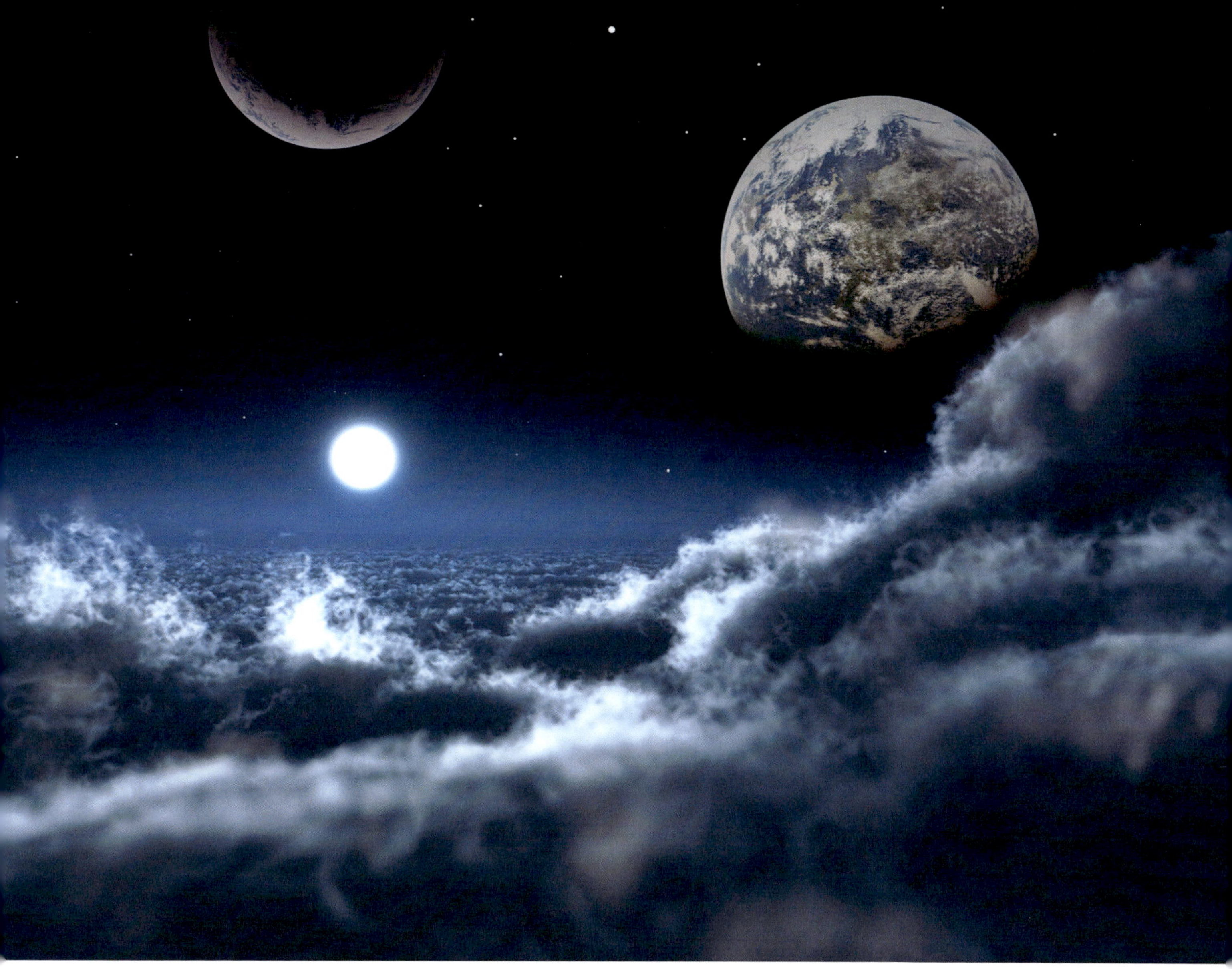

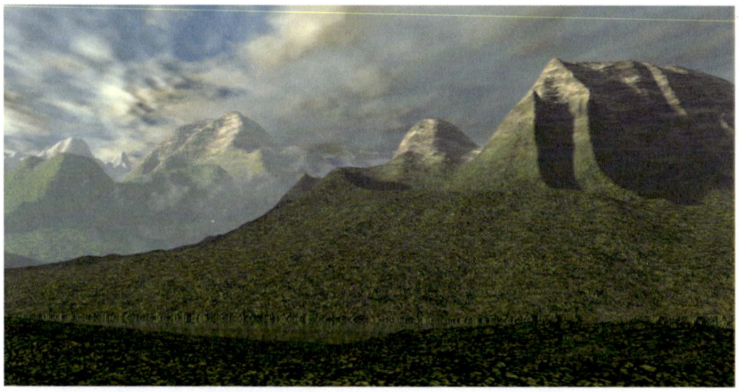

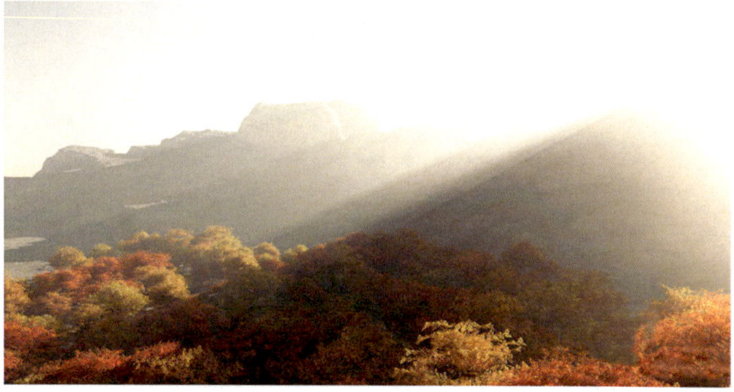

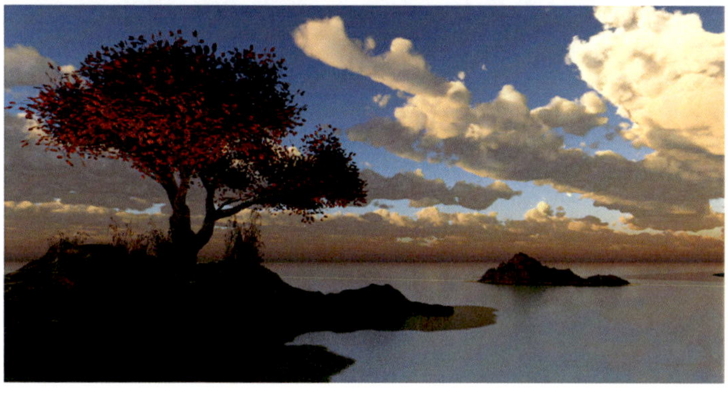

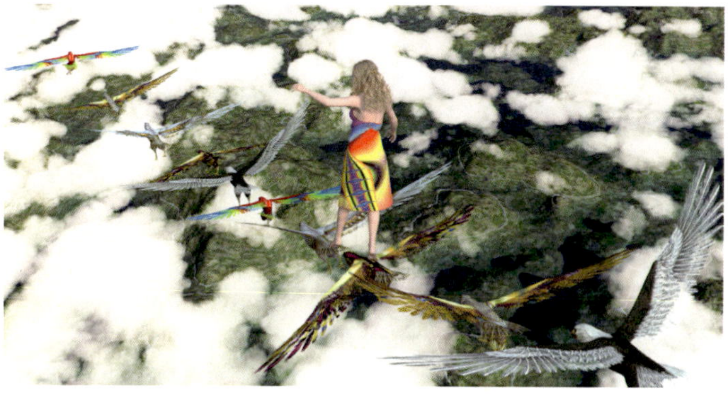

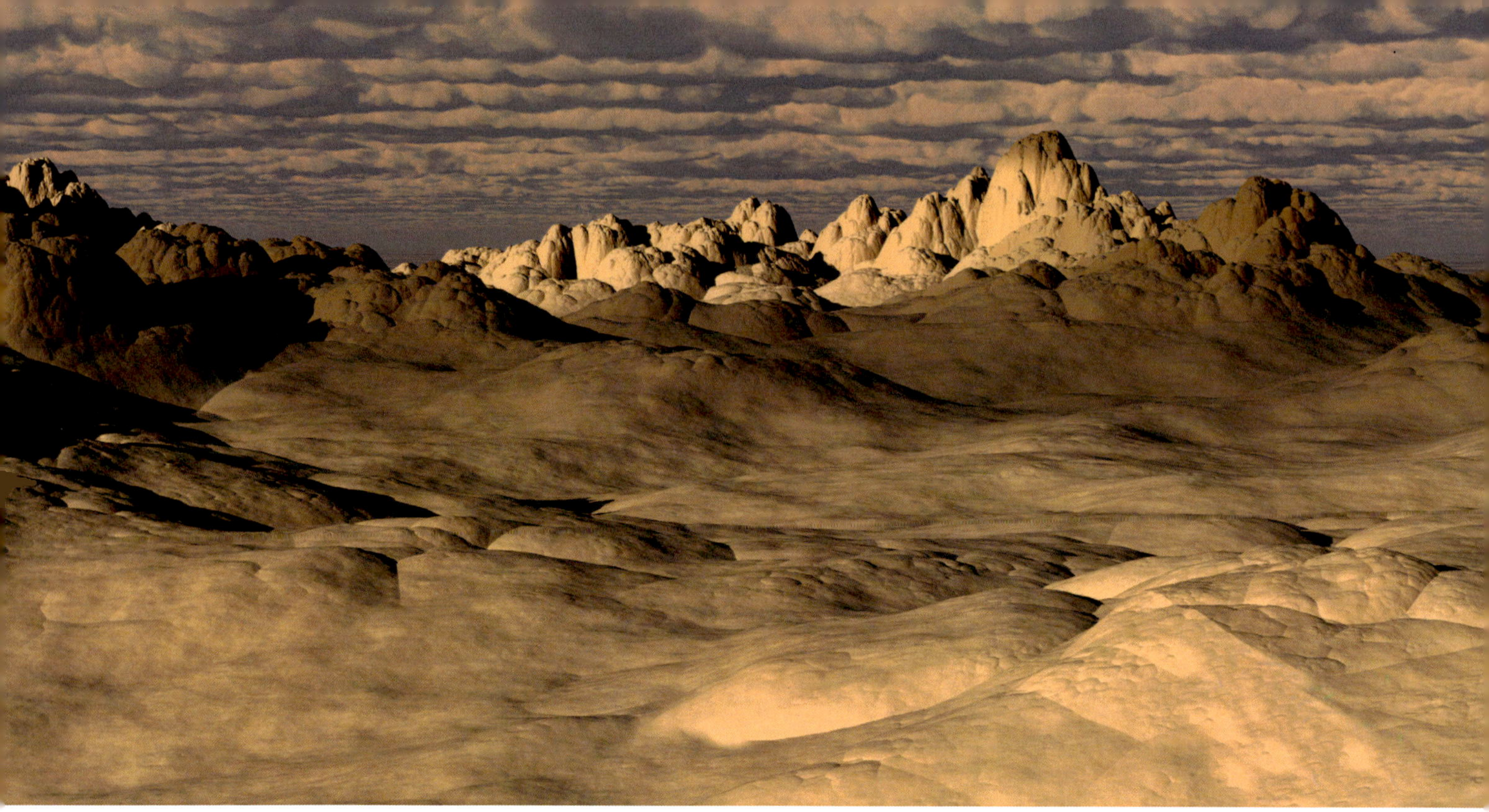

4.24. These more realistic 3D fractal images were generated in Vue software. This software expands on the theories of Benoit Mandelbrot, the "father" of fractals. The concepts and theories are explained in his book "The Fractal Geometry of Nature".

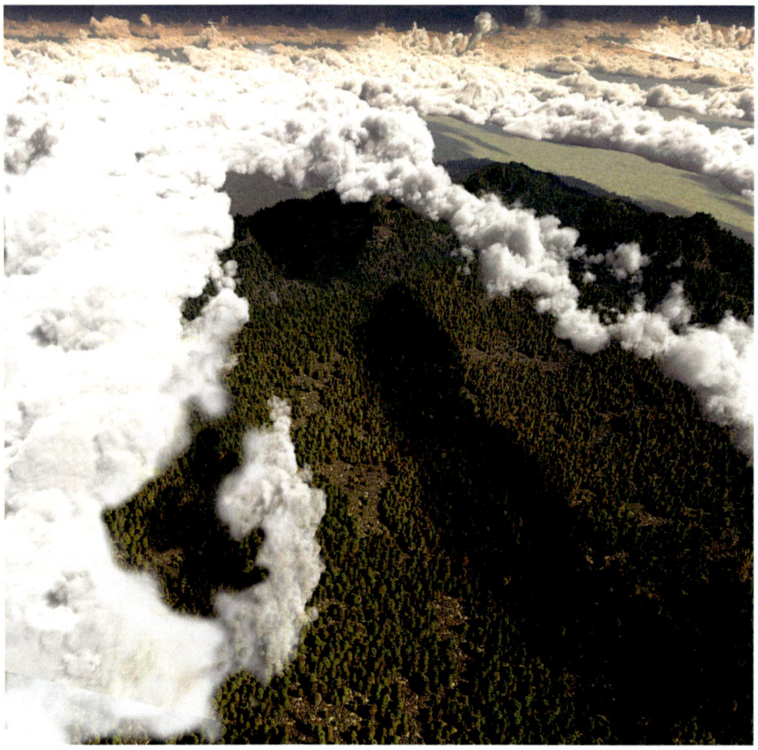

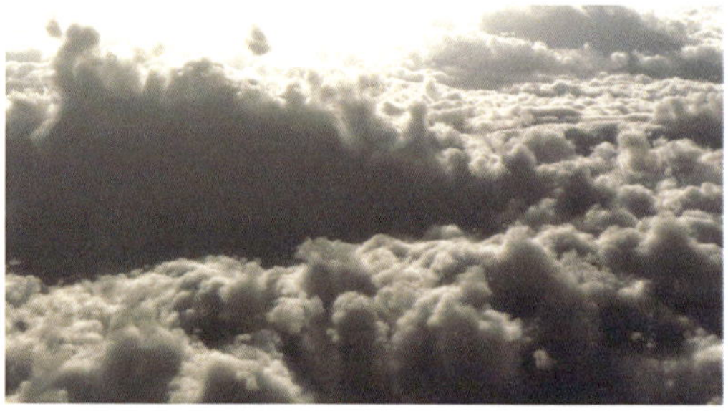

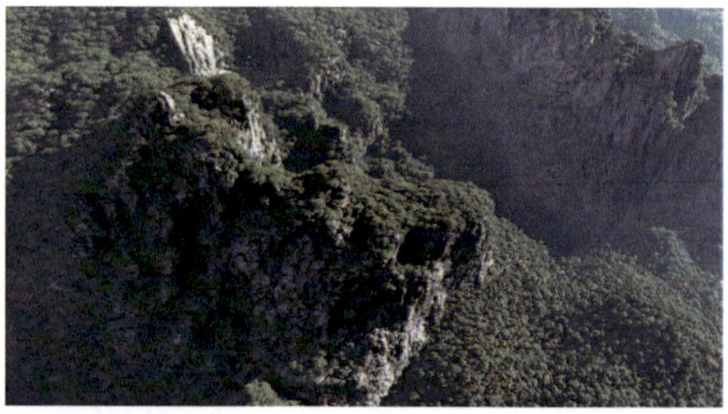

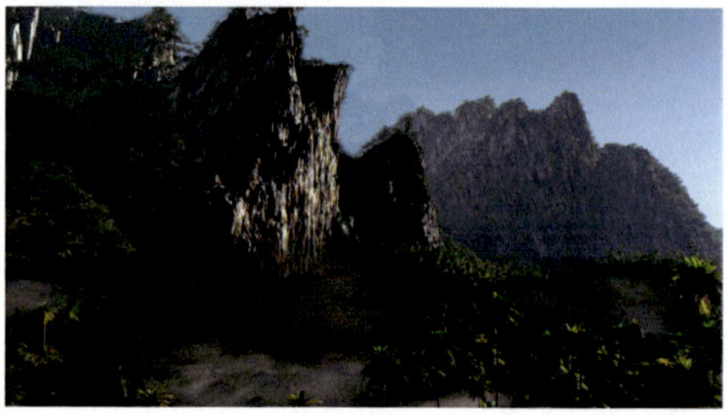

4.25.

Some additional examples created with Vue software.
All untitled 4K resolution, 2017.

ISOMETRIC PERSPECTIVE & OPTICAL ILLUSIONS

Optical Illusions are a lot of fun.

They are paradoxes and visual, mental calamities. There are many ways to fool the eye with color in context as Josef Albers demonstrated. in the early 20th century. Parallel lines that look bent and moires made by layers of grids or concentric circles create a visual playground for Op Artists. We can also devise figures that can be seen 2 ways (Dali), but hardly at the same time. Color can be used to enhance black and white checker-board-like images to vibrate. Victor Vasarely was a master at that. Look some of these artists up in a Google search sometime.

Your eye can connect missing lines across other shapes. Flat, isometric (non-perspective 3D) perspective can allow things from behind to cross to the front allowing 2D geometry to defy 3D. This was an area in which M.C. Escher was a master.

I have tried to incorporate many of these illusion concepts into my art.

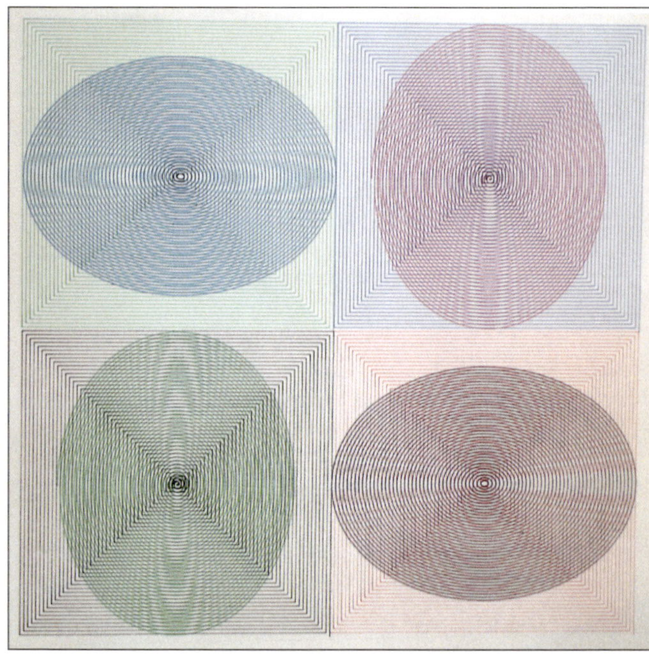

5.1. Overlaying grids for a moire effect.
Untitled, 11" x 11", Pen Plot, 1980.

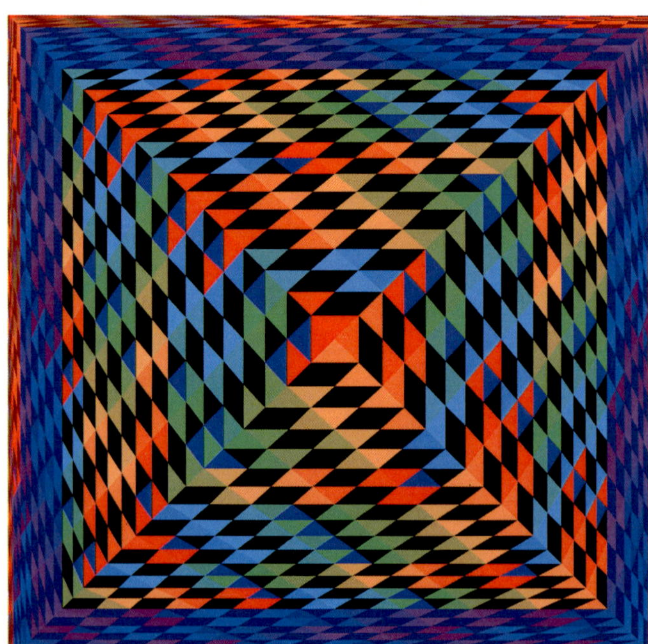

5.2. Illusion of a twist.
Untitled, Digital, 3229 x 3229 pixels, 2019.

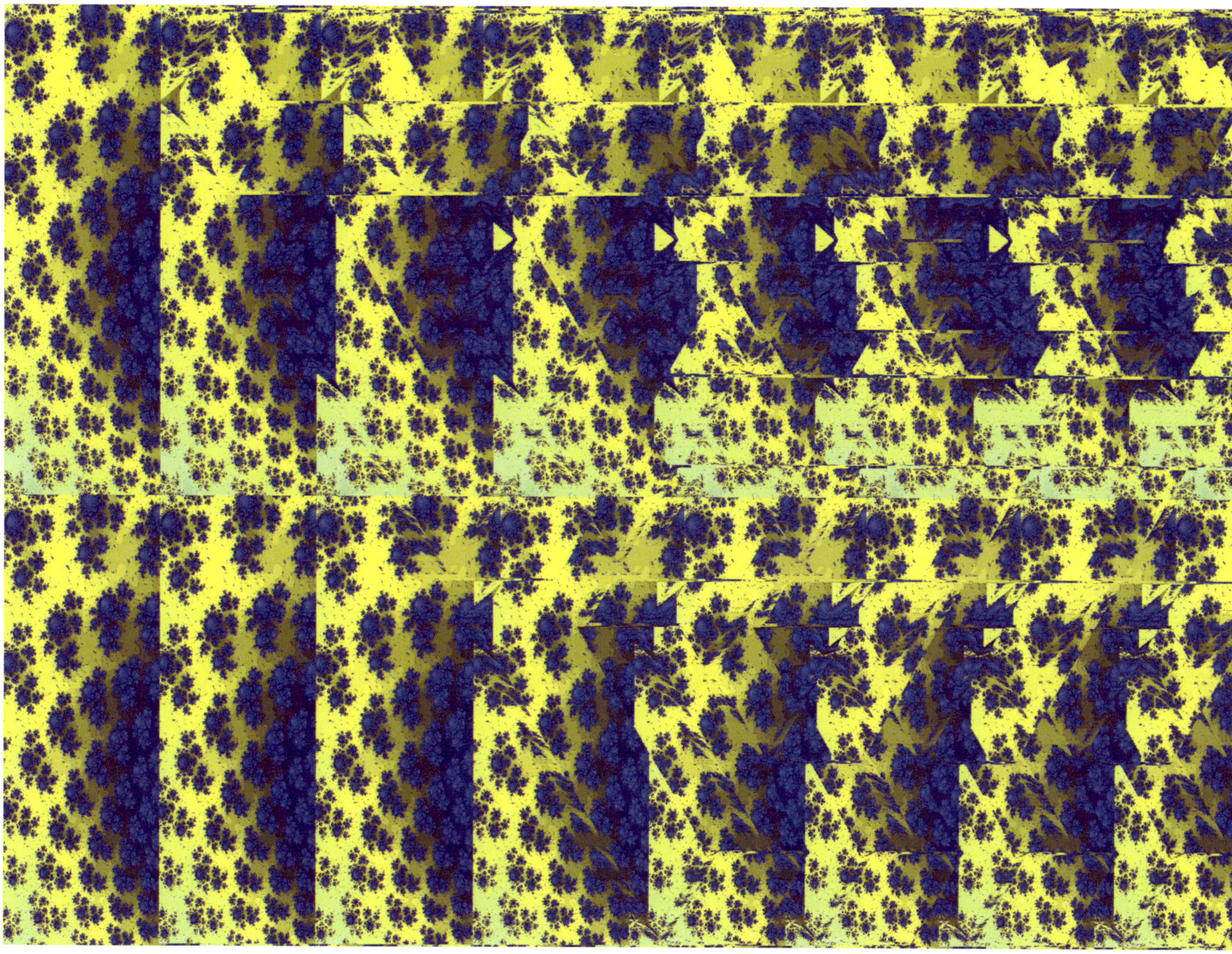

5.3.

Untitled Stereogram,
Digital, 6290 x 4800 pixels,
2021.

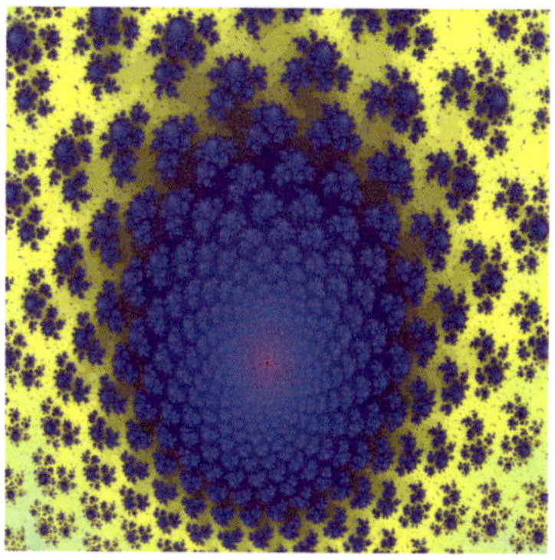

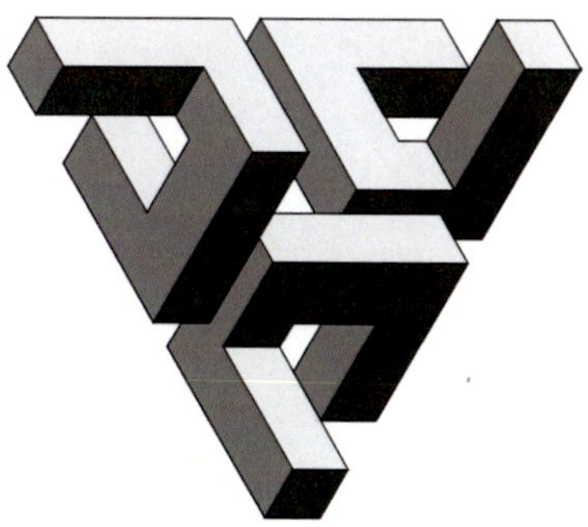

5.4. The two elements I created for entry into a stereogram software. One generates color and patterns, the other is a "depth scale" image in greyscale.

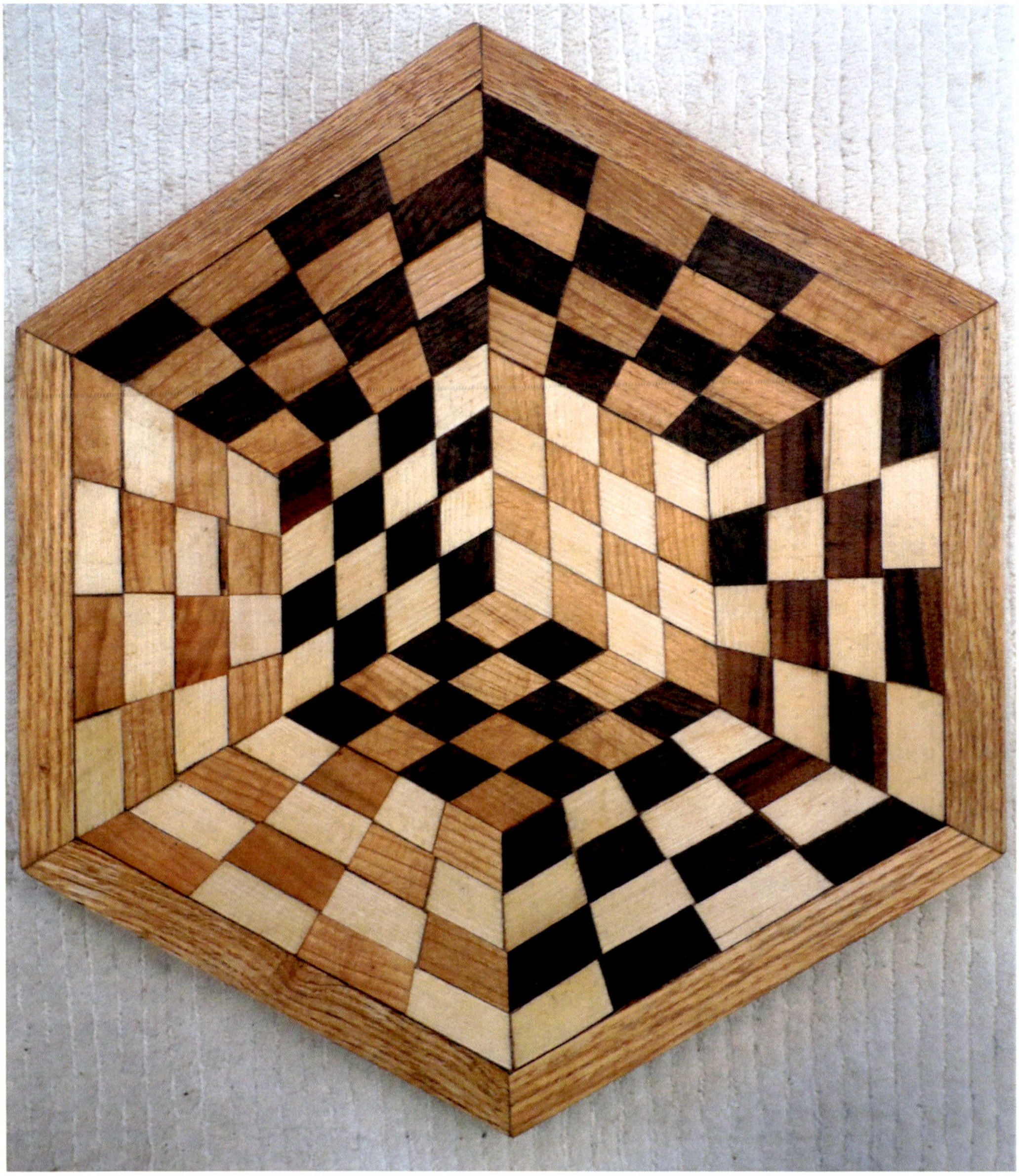

5.5. Three kinds of wood used to create an illusion of depth.
Untitled, 16" diameter. 2023.

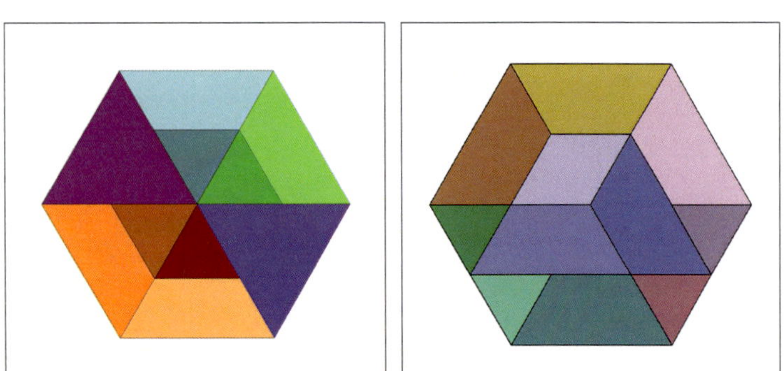

5.6.

Two designs created with Adobe Illustrator that have illusory features.

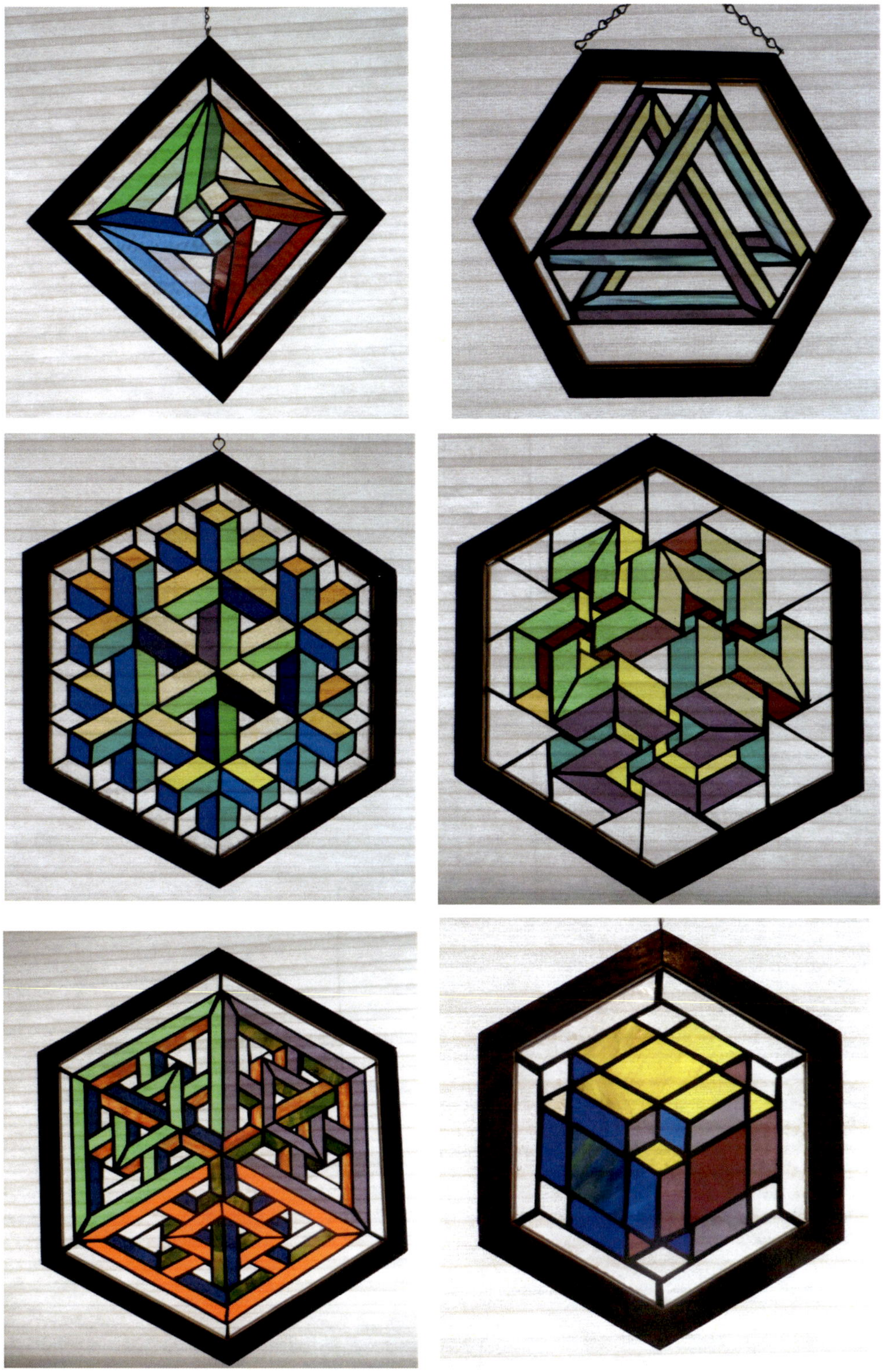

5.7.

Six Stained Glass pieces with Optical Illusion motifs. Sized Approx. 16" diameter, Created between 2017 and 2019.

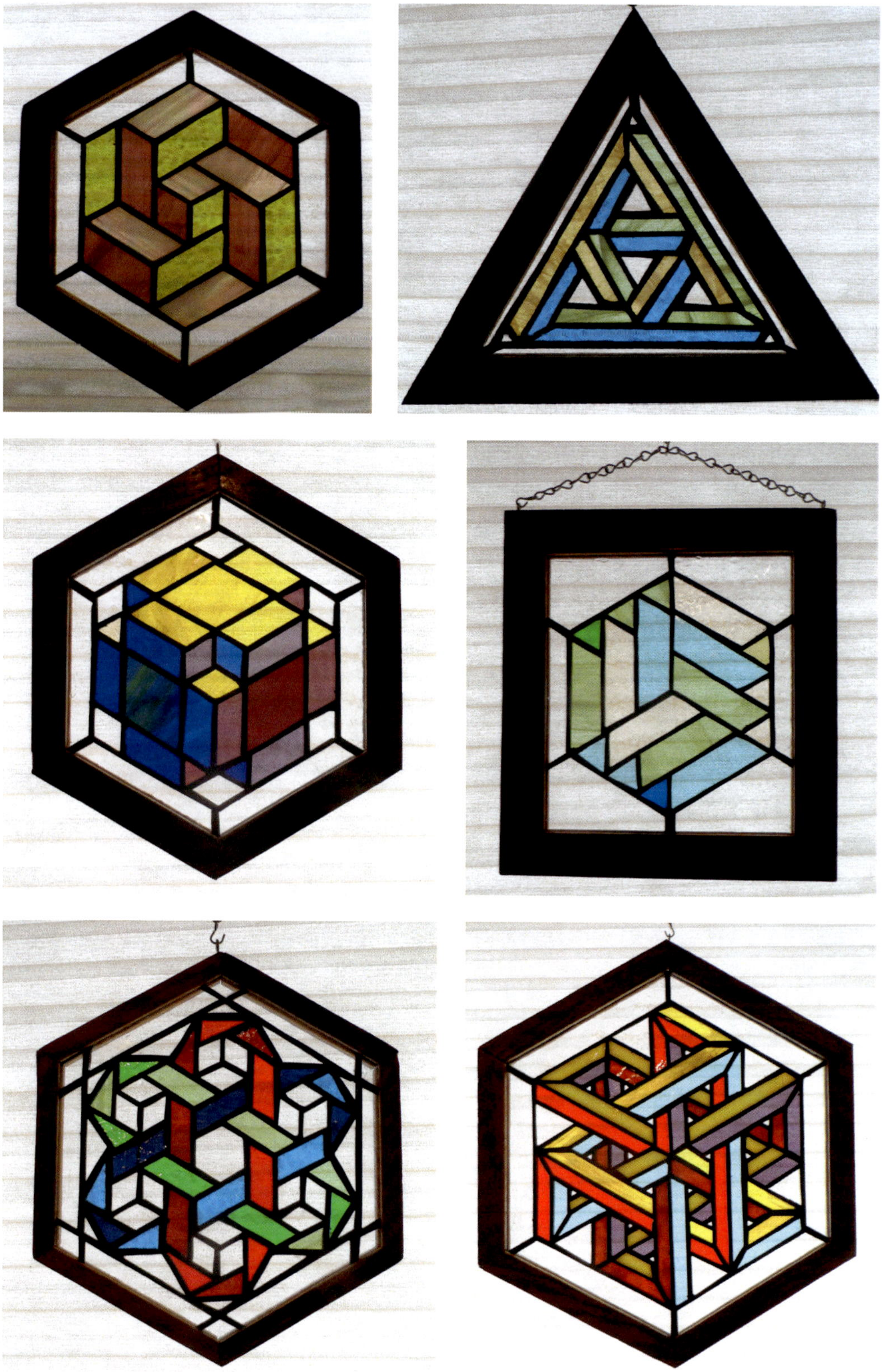

5.8.

Six more Stained Glass pieces with Optical Illusion motifs. Sized Approx. 12" diameter, Created between 2017 and 2019.

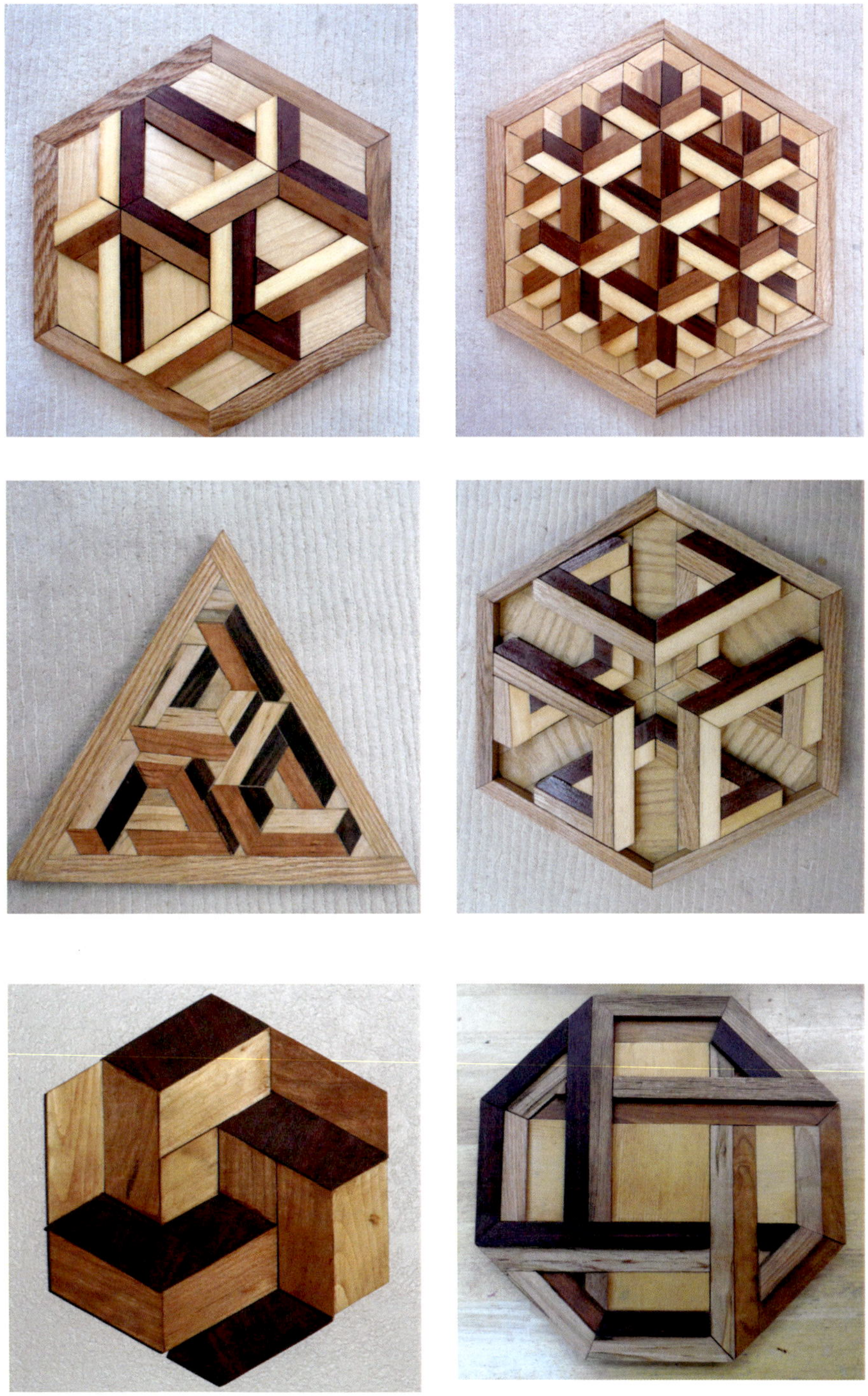

5.9.

Six more Optical Illusion motifs. Created as Wood Mosaics. Sized Approx. 12" diameter, Created between 2020 and 2022.

NEO-PLASTICISM

Neo-Plasticism was an art movement that was defined by Piet Mondrian and Theo Van Doesburg. I believe it was never fully explored. It included some odd, self-imposed limitations. The goal was harmony and coherence, with color and form as the driving forces. They never considered fractal principles.

Neo-plastic Art was invented as a purely abstract art form that carried no baggage from representing things in the world (non-representational art). It evolved from the De Stijl movement popularized by Theo Van Doesburg and is continued subconsciously in architectural design.

Proponents of De Stijl advocated pure abstraction and universality by a reduction to the essentials of form and color. They simplified visual compositions to vertical and horizontal, using only black, white and primary colors. The goal of Neo-Plasticism was harmonics and simple beauty within limitations. Non-objective art, free of "abstraction".

Here are some of Piet Mondrian's rules for Neo-Plasticism:
1. Only use rectangles and squares - commonly used square canvases.
2. Color restricted to Pure Red, Yellow, Blue, Black, White and Shades of Gray.
3. Vary line weight (usually black lines) as pleased.
4. Preference for asymmetry. Lots of white used.

These strict guidelines lead to works reliant on their compositional structure – works whose subjects were produced as "pure" and non-representational abstraction. These guidelines were very limiting yet have lead to an artistic language that has stood strong and influenced many throughout the years: as in fashion and typography design, product design as reinterpreted through the Bauhaus school, and architecture and visual art later in the 20th century.

Artists working in the template of Neo-Plasticism and De Stijl had just begun to experience success in the early 1940s when the emergence of Abstract Expressionism overpowered some of the achievements. Art went on to experienced Minimalism and other geometric

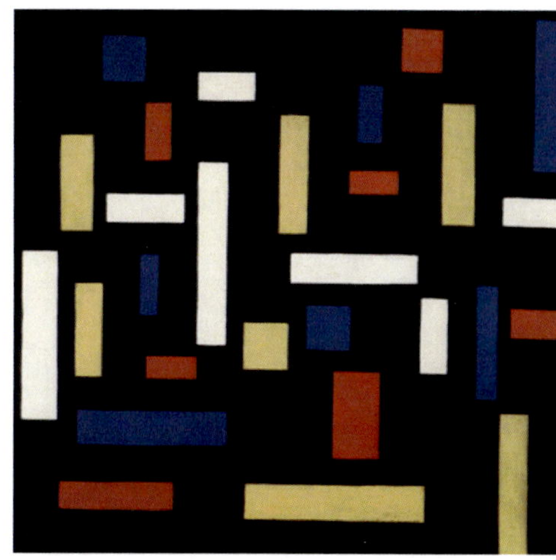

6.1. Theo Van Doesburg, Composition VII (The Three Graces), Oil on Canvas, 1917. Image from Wikipedia.

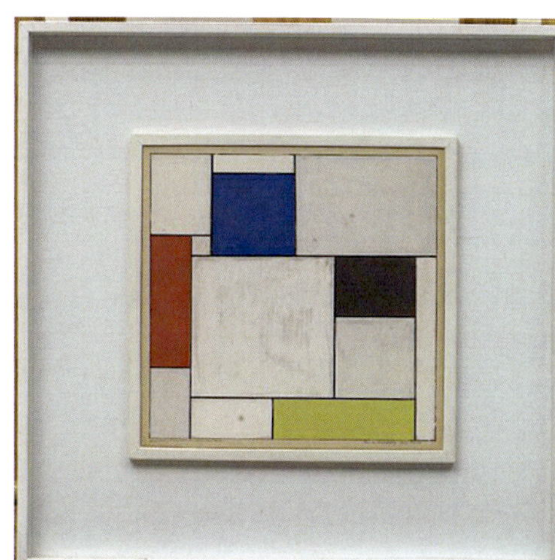

6.2. Theo Van Doesburg, Composition décentralisée, Gouache on board, 11 3/8 x 11 1/2 inches, 1924,

Solomon R. Guggenheim Museum, New York Bequest, Richard S. Zeisler, 2007. Image from Wikipedia.

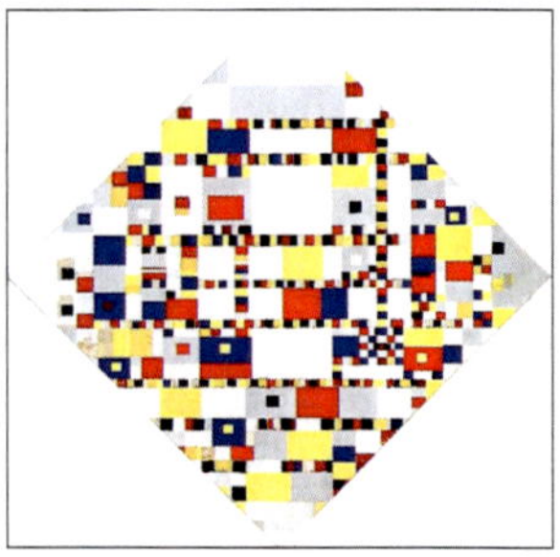

6.3.

Piet Mondrian, Victory Boogie Woogie, Oil on Canvas, (1942–1944), Kunstmuseum Den Haag. Image from Wikipedia.

movements. For the most part, Neo-Plasticism was short-lived and never fully explored by Mondrian and Van Doesburg.
Most of their successors broke their rules.
So I invented triangular Neo-Plasticism and Fractal Neo-Plasticism. Let's visit the "rules" for these. Why only rectangles? Triangles, especially equilateral, yield nice harmonic patterns within these rules as well.

Why did they use this weird list of colors? Saturation, Value and Transparency could be used to create a full spectrum of possibilities and still be within a restriction – 16 shades of RGB color, for instance. For some reason gray was on the short list for Neo-Plasticism, but hardly used by Mondrian. Rules could be orchestrated for those.

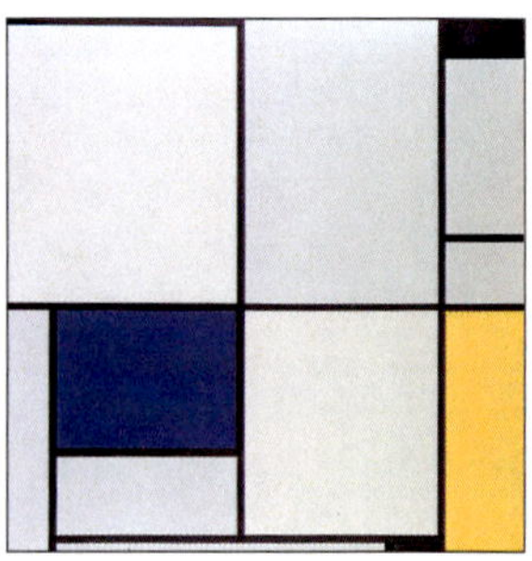

6.4.

Piet Mondrian, Tableau I, Oil on Canvas, 1921, Kunstmuseum Den Haag. Image from Wikipedia.

Neo-Plastic line weight follows no rhyme or reason, just like rectangular shape and placement.

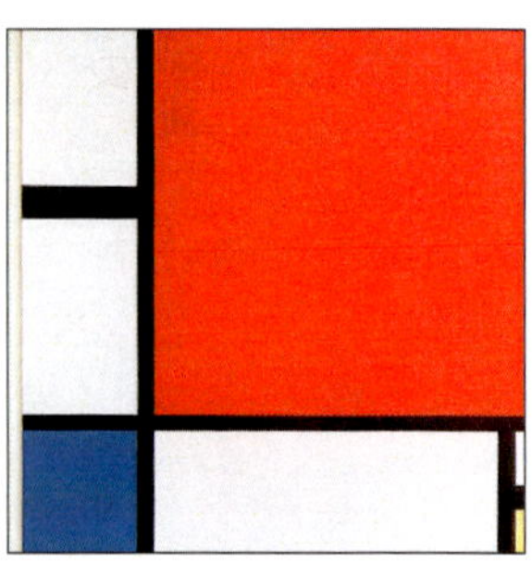

6.5.

Piet Mondrian, Composition II in Red, Blue, and Yellow, 1930, Kunsthaus Zürich. Image from Wikipedia.

A sort of space filling was applied in Neo-Plasticism – start big, subdivide, split to rectangles and fill the space.

This "space-filling" concept is related to fractals. A rectangular space can be filled with smaller rectangles of many sizes and shapes, down to a minute level if desired. This is how fractals perpetuate, to some degree. This concept can also be applied to triangles, hexagons and octagons with ease.

Hexagons and octagons have the additional benefit of accommodating triangles and rectangles respectively space is filled with this algorithm. It turns out that triangles can be ubiquitous to the number of sides in a container, allowing them to be used easily together with hexagons and octagons, or rectangles.

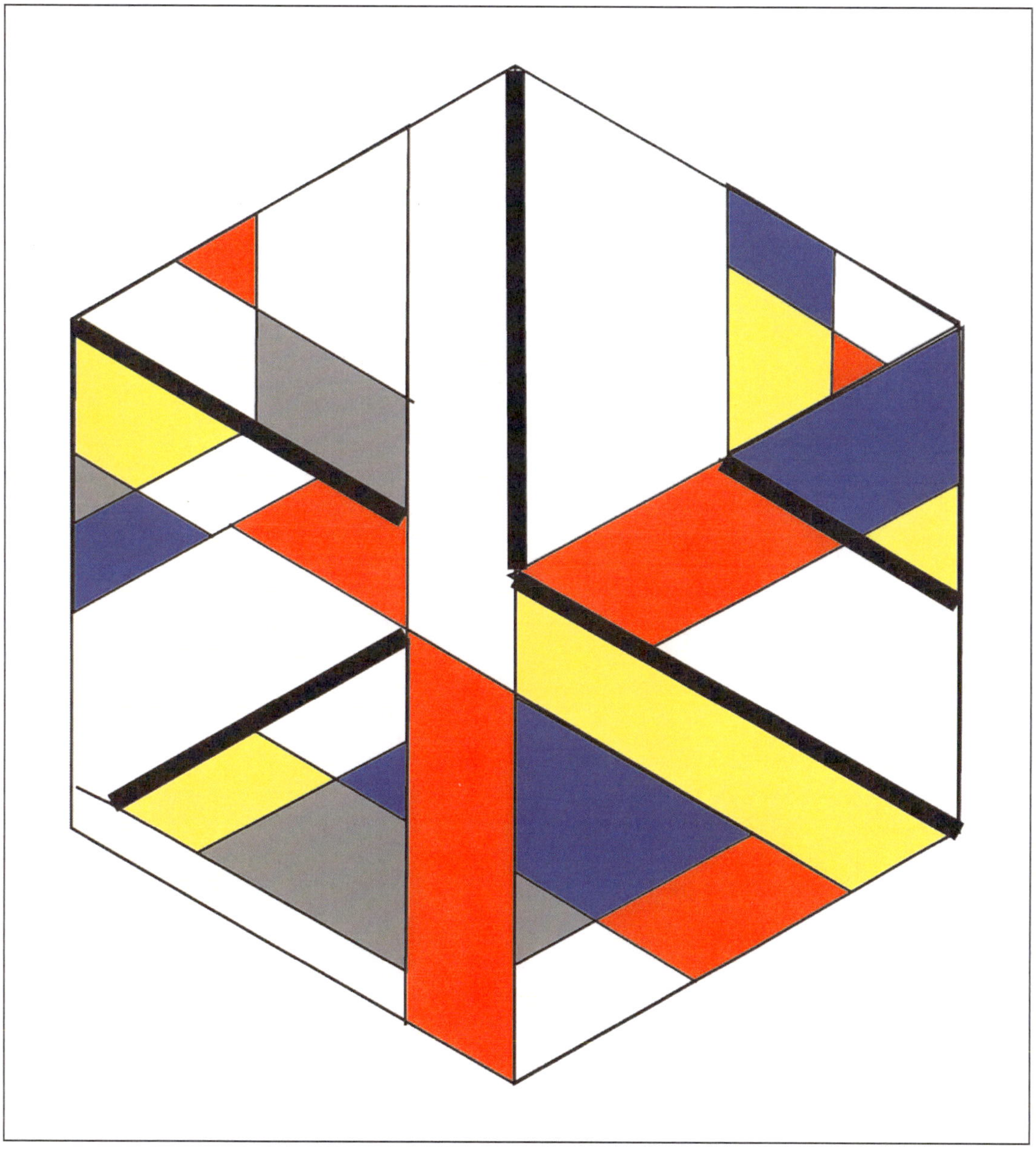

6.6.

An Adobe Illustrator design using Triangular Neo-Plasicism. A quick test.

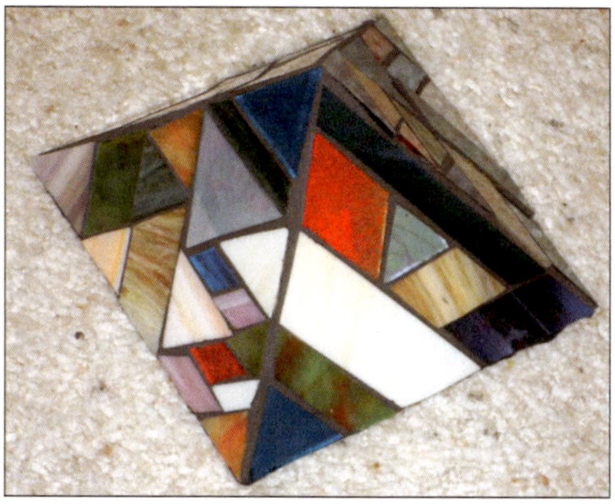

6.7a. Examples of Triangular Neo-Plasticism. Regular pyramid, Glass Mosaic, 12" tall, 2012.

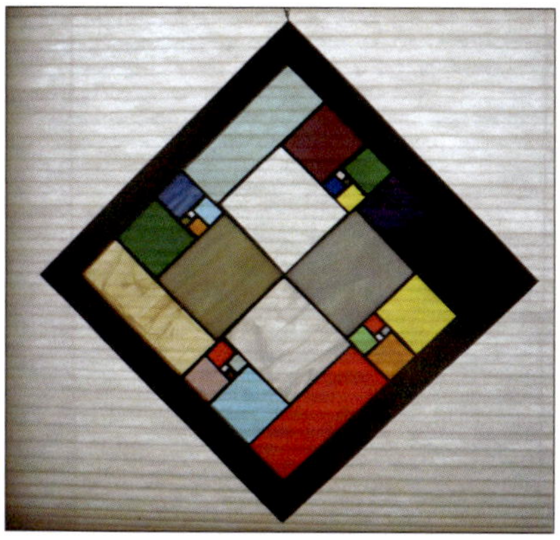

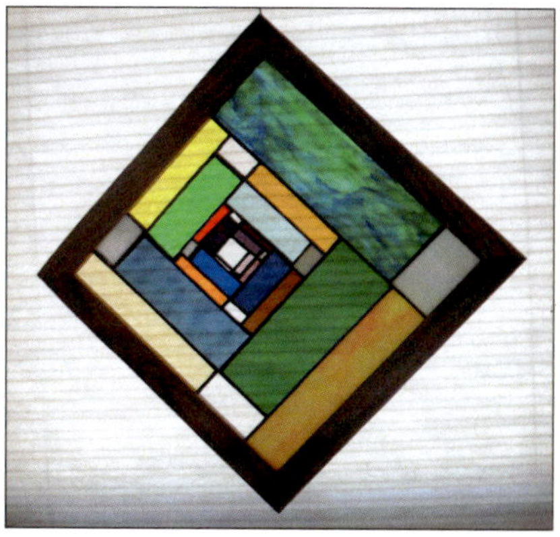

6.7a. Two Examples of Fractal Neo-Plasticism.
Stained Glass, 18" x 18", 2018.

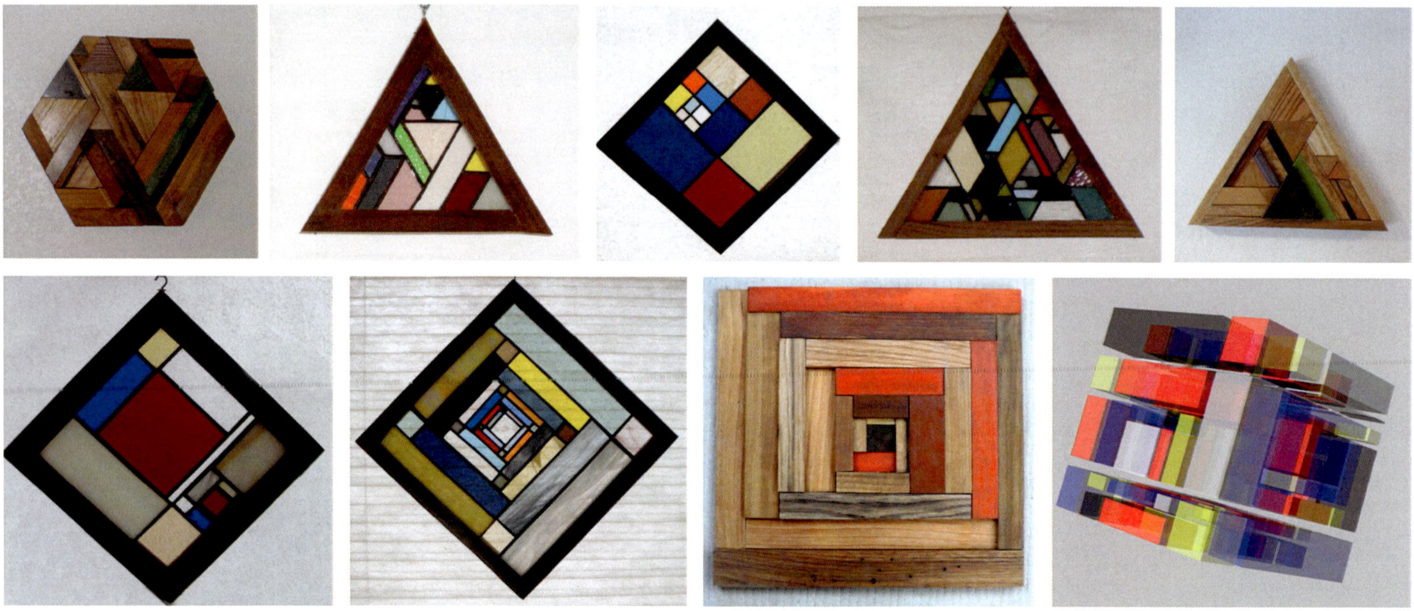

6.8. More examples of Triangular and Fractal Neo-Plasticism. Above are Stained Glass pieces, Glass Mosaic, Wood Relief and 3D Graphics of various sizes.

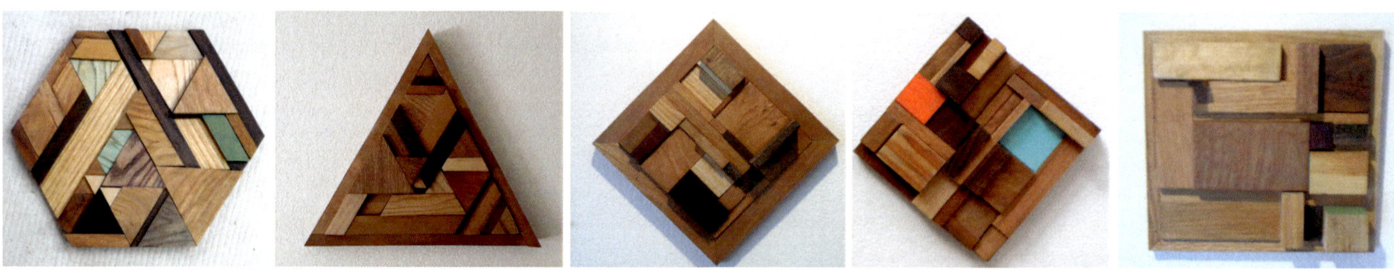

6.9. More examples that utilize space filling algorithms with Neo-Plasticism. These are Wood Mosaics, Approx. 8" diameter, from 2022.

Some interesting geometry can be created by halving the angles - for example using 45 degree isosceles triangles (or sliced squares) in conjunction with rectangles. These forms can be stretched along a 2D axis during the filling process. on the triangular and hexagonal forms this can be seen in the 4-sided forms inside the triangular and hexagonal containers (trapezoids and parallelograms). An example of this "stretching" is the olive green trapezoid in the triangular piece in the center below.

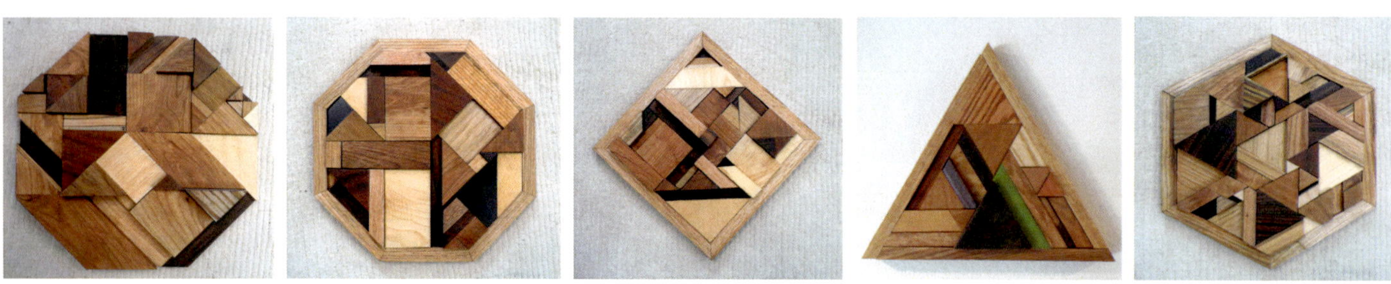

6.10. More examples that utilize a space filling algorithm.
Wood Mosaics, Approx. 9" diameter, from 2022.

A lot of modern (and current) architecture relies on Neo-Plastic concepts. So how could Fractal Neo-Plasticism be incorporated in architecture? The rectangle below was filled with fractal subdivisions. I show it vertically and horizontally.

This can easily be created with copy, paste and rotate in Adobe Illustrator or other software, ArtToyz Fractal Neo-Plasticism software included. Graph paper and a pencil might suffice.

Now imagine this design on the front of a building, delineating decks, windows, doors and material variations. Also imagine it as an influence or a seed for a floor plan. Now imagine interior details, such as shelf units and other decor to have a similar form. The windows could reflect this design from inside as well.

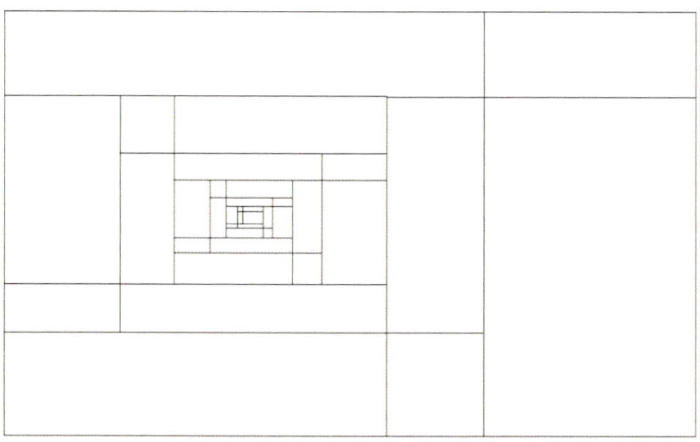

Instead of the current abstract grid design used in architecture (mostly random or utility level placement of forms), we would now have an integrated design with a fractal basis that could reflect functionality "towards infinity". This would allow visitors to explore the self-similar elements. Utilities could be made to fit the floor plan, or their placement could dictate the placement and size of certain repeated forms, delineating walls, floor treatment and stairs. All from a central design. Windows columns and materials could directly reflect these form relationships.

So, perhaps many forms of 3D design could benefit from a more holistic, fractal Neo-Plastic element. My opinion is that most modern architecture evolved from these Neo-Plastic concepts. And should continue to evolve.

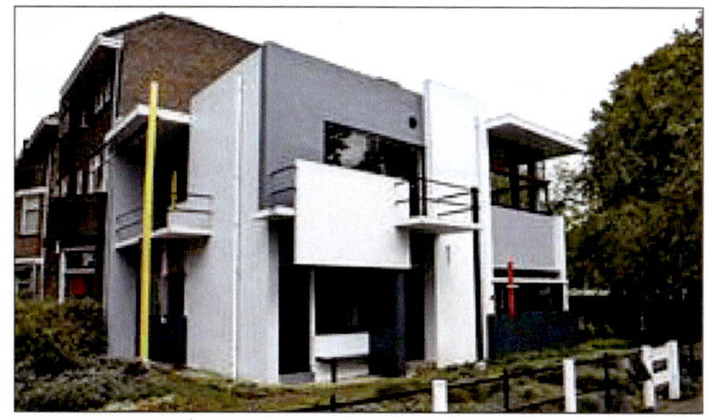

6.11. The Schroder House designed by Gerrit Rietveld in the Netherlands is one of the very few examples of early neo-plastic architecture. Current day design includes many Neo-Plastic elements.
Image from Wikipedia.

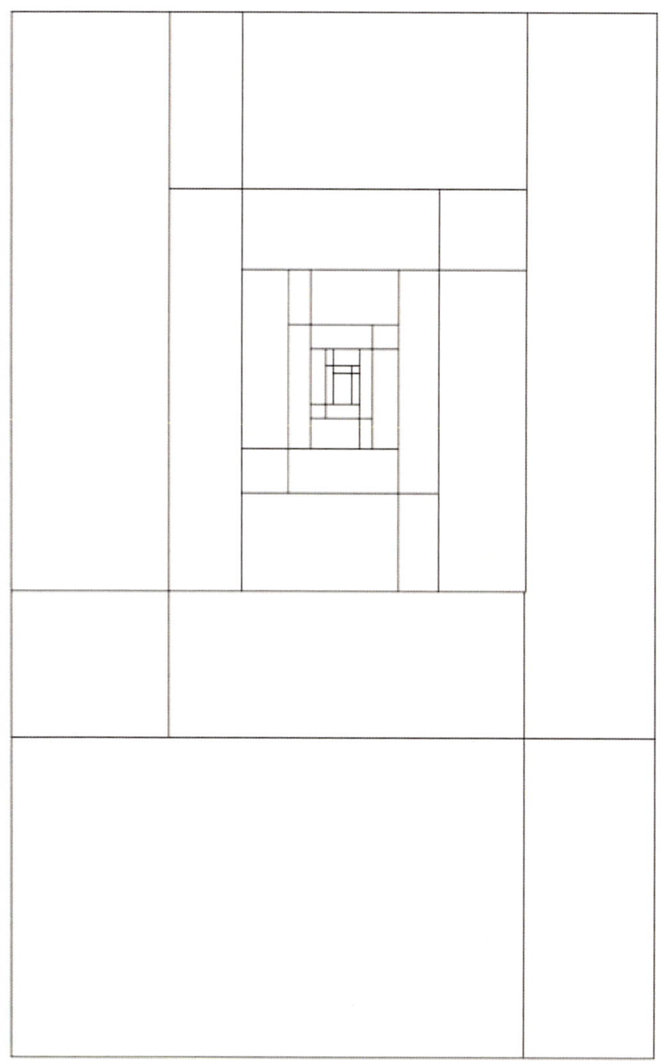

6.12. A rectangle can be filled with subdivisions that have fractal concepts applied.

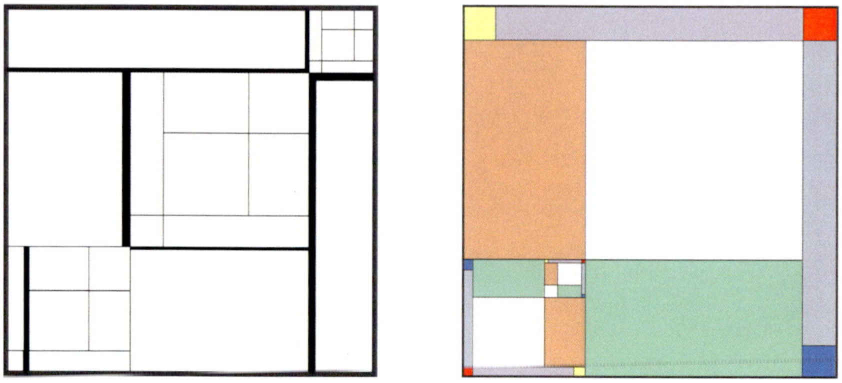

6.13.

Neo-Plastic Fractal Designs benefit from additional colors and line weight adjustment. Both design examples are output from my home made software for Fractal Neo-Plastic development. From 2016.

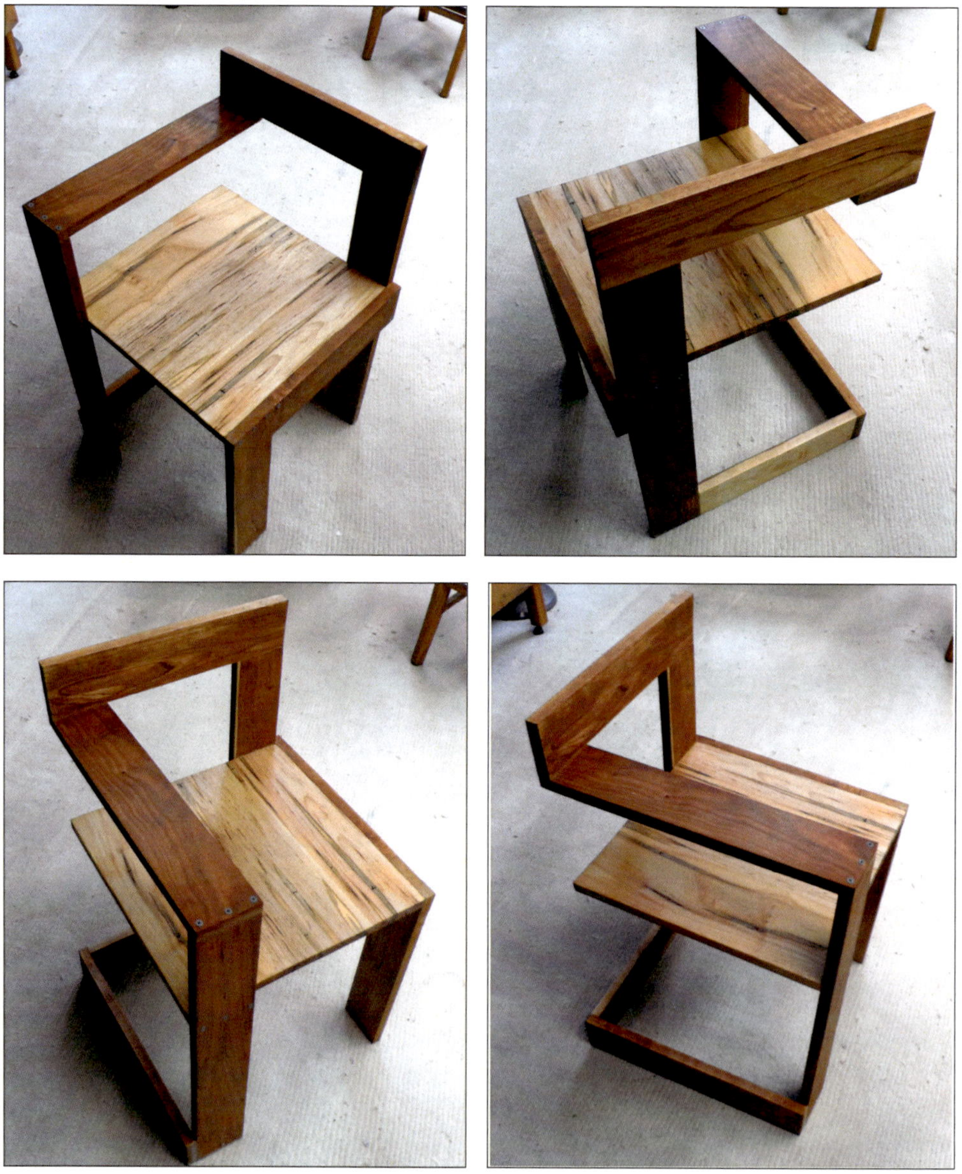

6.14. A chair I made.
Assorted Hardwoods,
Aprox. 24" x 24" x 36", 2013.

REALISM

An early art motif of mine was patterning integrated with the figure in various ways. My colored pencil drawings from the 1970s were inspired by Art Nouveau and Islamic patterning. These drawings are all in the 18" size range and are drawn on coquille paper. The grids truly were done with a ruler and a compass. Ouch!

Patterning fills the background and spills over into the clothing. This pattern exploration directly lead to the creation of Color by Numbers systems in the late '70s.

The reference photos were grabbed directly from magazines. Therefore, I consider them practice and I have never tried to sell them.

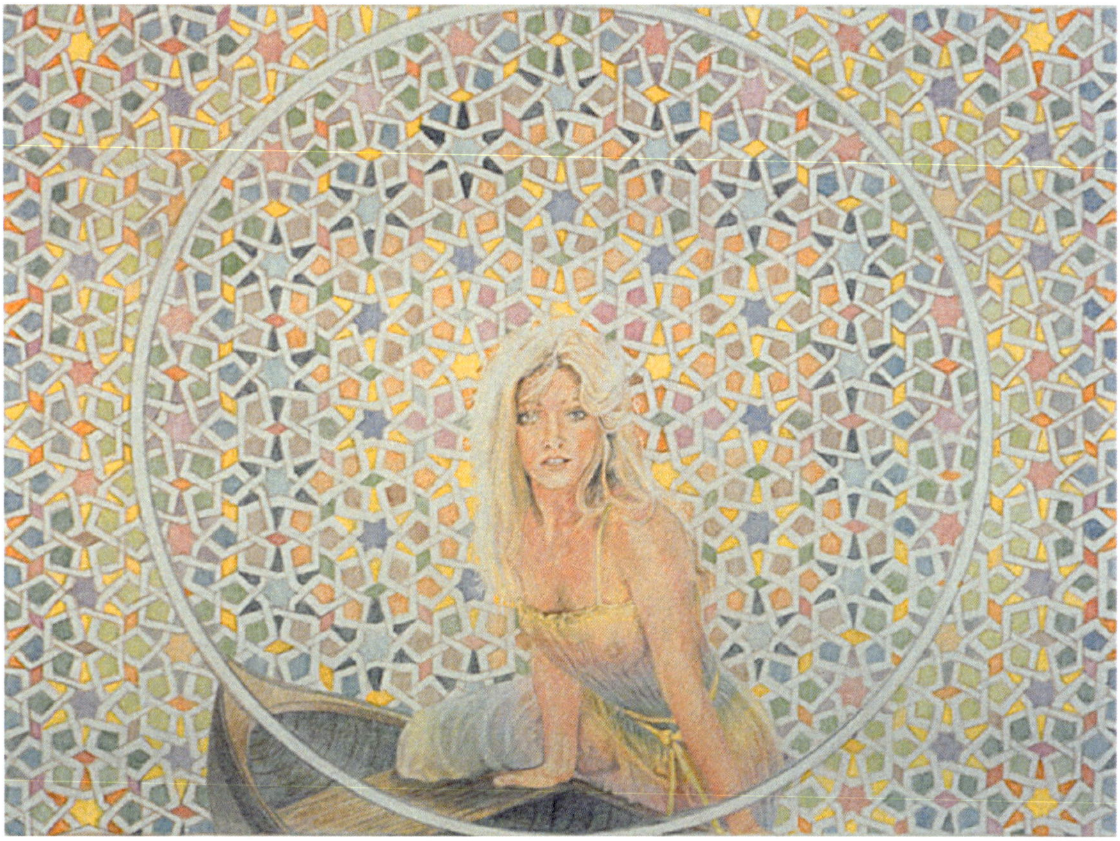

7.1.

Climbing into a Canoe, Colored Pencil on Paper, 18" x 24", 1976. Collection of Mick Dunn.

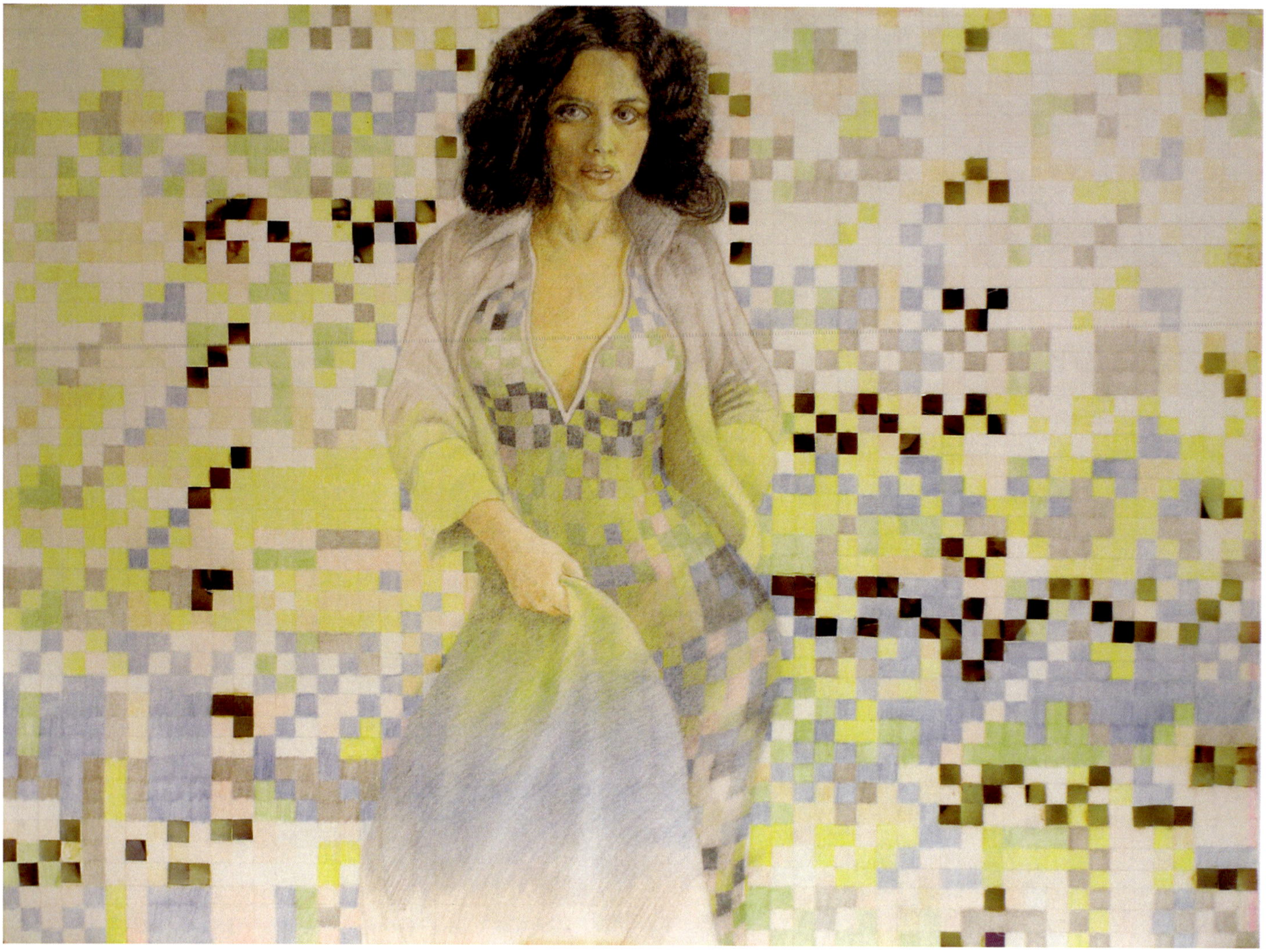

7.2.

Zero is the Real Picture, Colored Pencil and Collage on Paper,
18" x 24", 1978.

Pieces of the original photo are cut up and represent "zero" in a color by numbers pattern in the background.

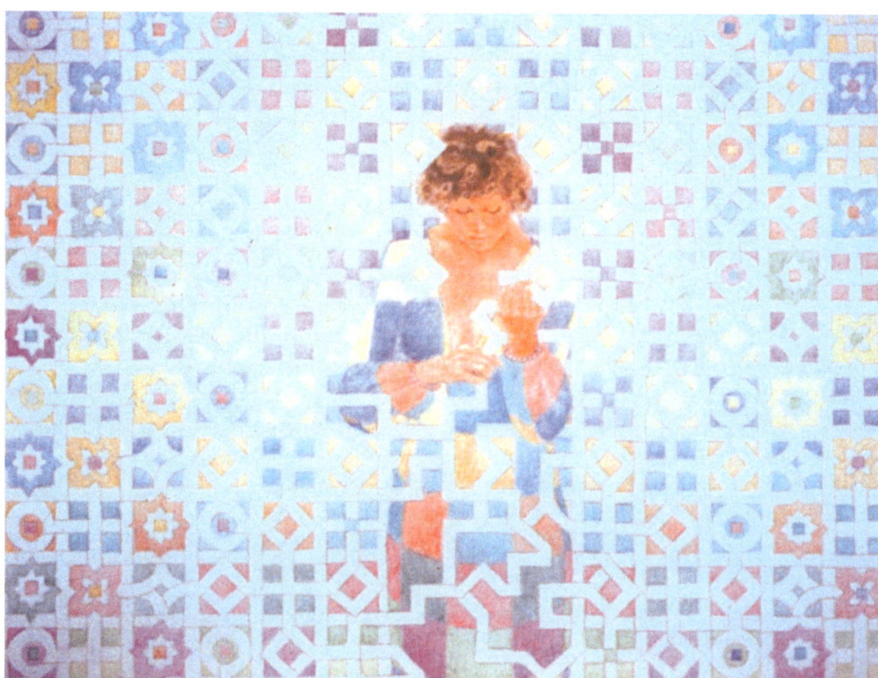

7.3.

Puzzle,
Colored Pencil on Paper,
18" x 24", 1977.

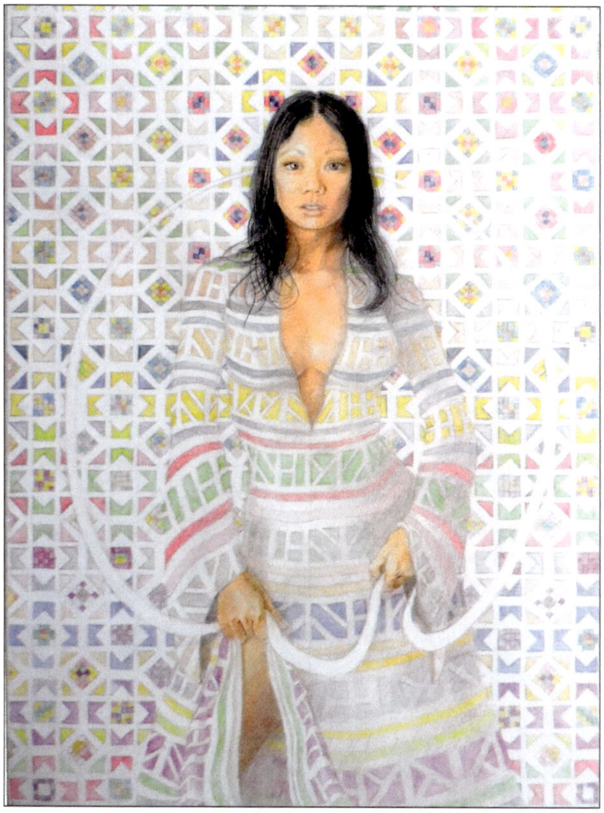

7.4. Asian Girl, Colored Pencil on Paper, 18" x 24", 1977.

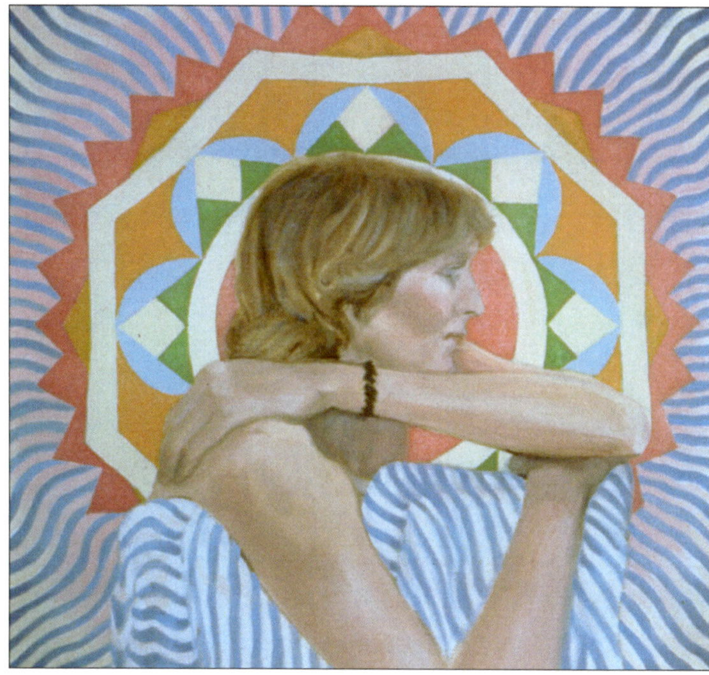

7.5. Jan, Oil on Canvas, 18" x 18", 1973.

I actually pride myself in my figure drawing abilities and practice them regularly. I can draw from life and can take that original "sketch" through to the finished work with as much detail as I care to add. At the right is a figure painting from life, done in art school, with, of course, some mandala geometry added. Visit the gallery sections under painting on my ArtToyz website to see more figurative work.

If you saw me, my bank account and the influential people I don't know, you would easily understand that I was not likely going to get a lot of models to pose for me. But, now here we are in the 21st century. Computer graphics has created a partial solution for my problem. Below are renderings from Daz 3D, one of my favorite new toys/tools. It's early versions were called Poser and the software was a bit crude (in the 1990's). However they have continued to develop it and have done a great job. Now I can even explore clothes designs - mostly with fractals and Color by Numbers.

In Daz, "Actors" can be posed manually or from saved poses. The developers have solved most of the problems with seams and image mapping to achieve some realism, as well as rigging for animation. And now the detail includes skin pores, veins and wrinkles.

This approach with digital figures is quite flexible. Using morphs and parametric adjustments the characters can be any weight, height, musculature, skin color, tattooed, aged, and pretty much anything you can imagine. You can purchase any age, sex or ethnicity, for a few bucks. And finally the hair is getting better.

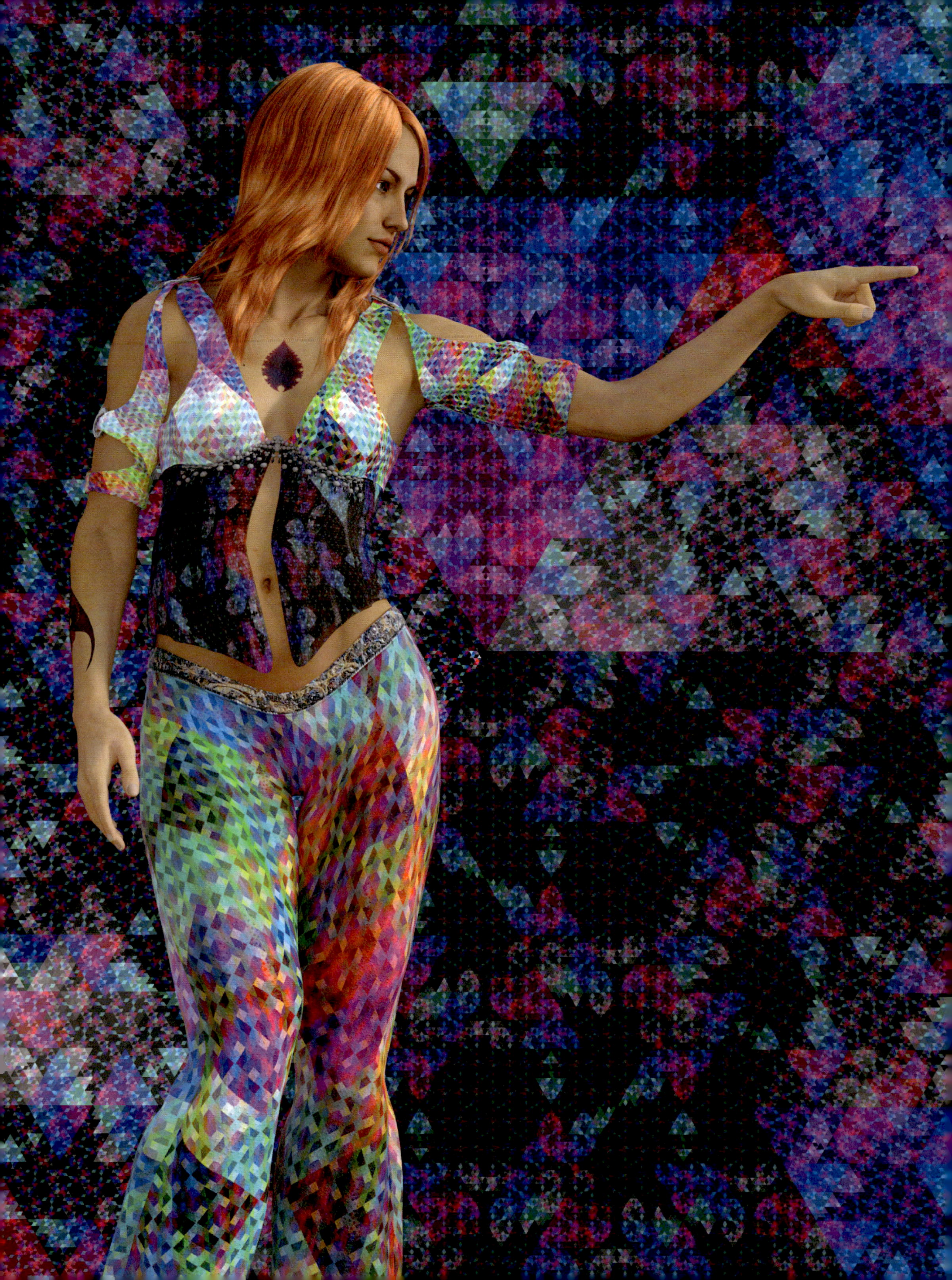

7.4. Point, digital.
2224 x 3943 pixels,
2019.

If you know Adobe PhotoShop, Gimp or After Effects it is easy to see how simple it is to composite these images. On the left over white is a .tif file rendering from Daz. Adding it on a layer over anything else is rather seamless. By the way, Daz is free software.

Here images are composited with 3D fractals and Color By Numbers designs.

You can easily see that the renderings can be re-purposed as well as the hair, clothing, poses and people. This program allows geometry from a variety of 3D programs and supports realistic renderers.

Daz also provides animals and other poseable creatures.

At this point with 3D graphics capabilities and some of the other computer tools available we can simulate, recreate, invent, animate and immerse ourselves in 3D worlds. Fractal landscapes, digital people and anything or any effect we can dream up.

And with AI generated images, the 21st century is only getting rolling.

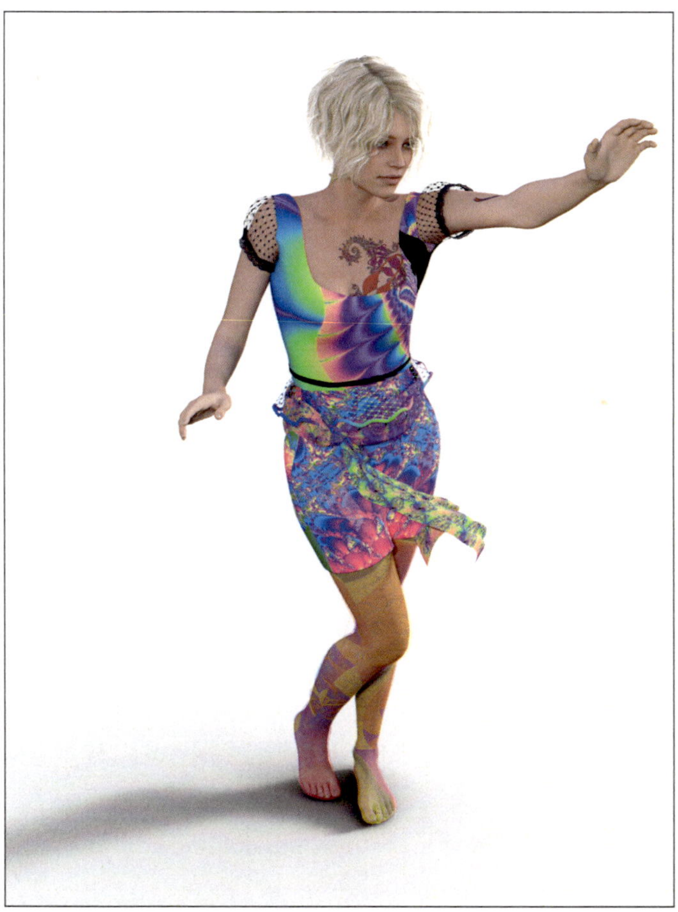

7.7.

Direct rendering from Daz, 3000 x 4096 pixels, 2019.

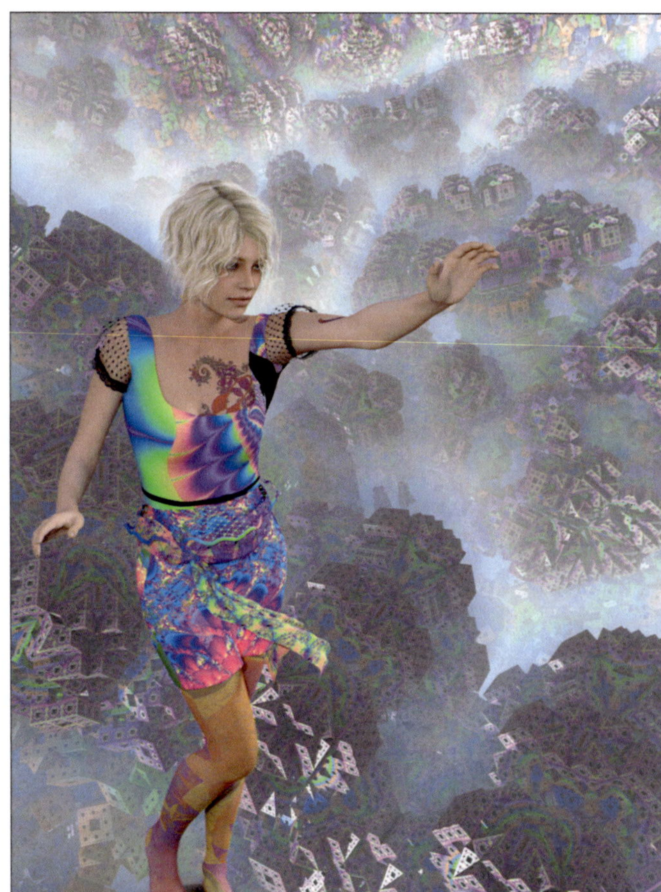

7.8.

Boxes (composited), 3000 x 4096 pixels, 2019.

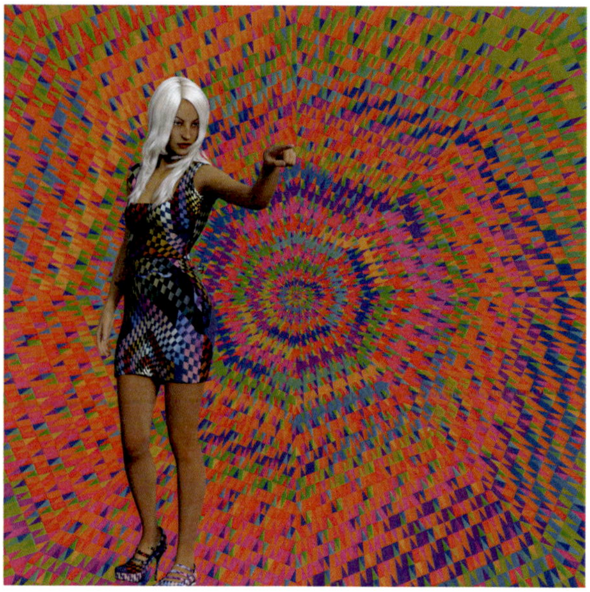

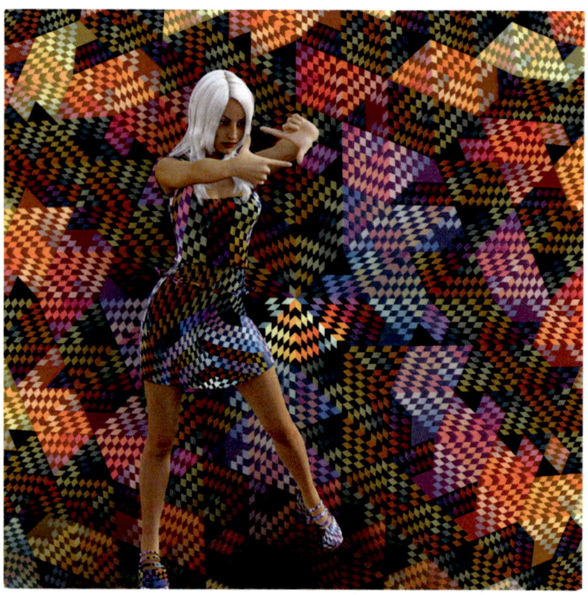

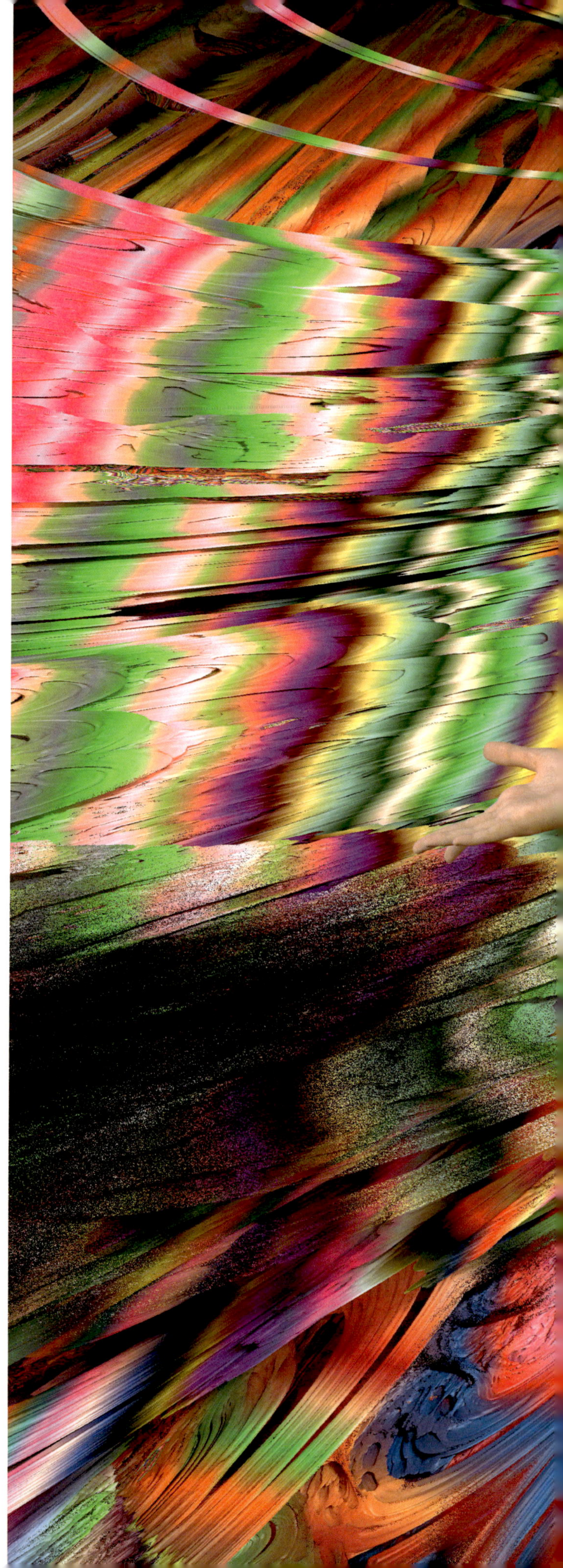

7.9.

2 pages of examples of Daz Figures composited with various Geometric Backgrounds, 2019

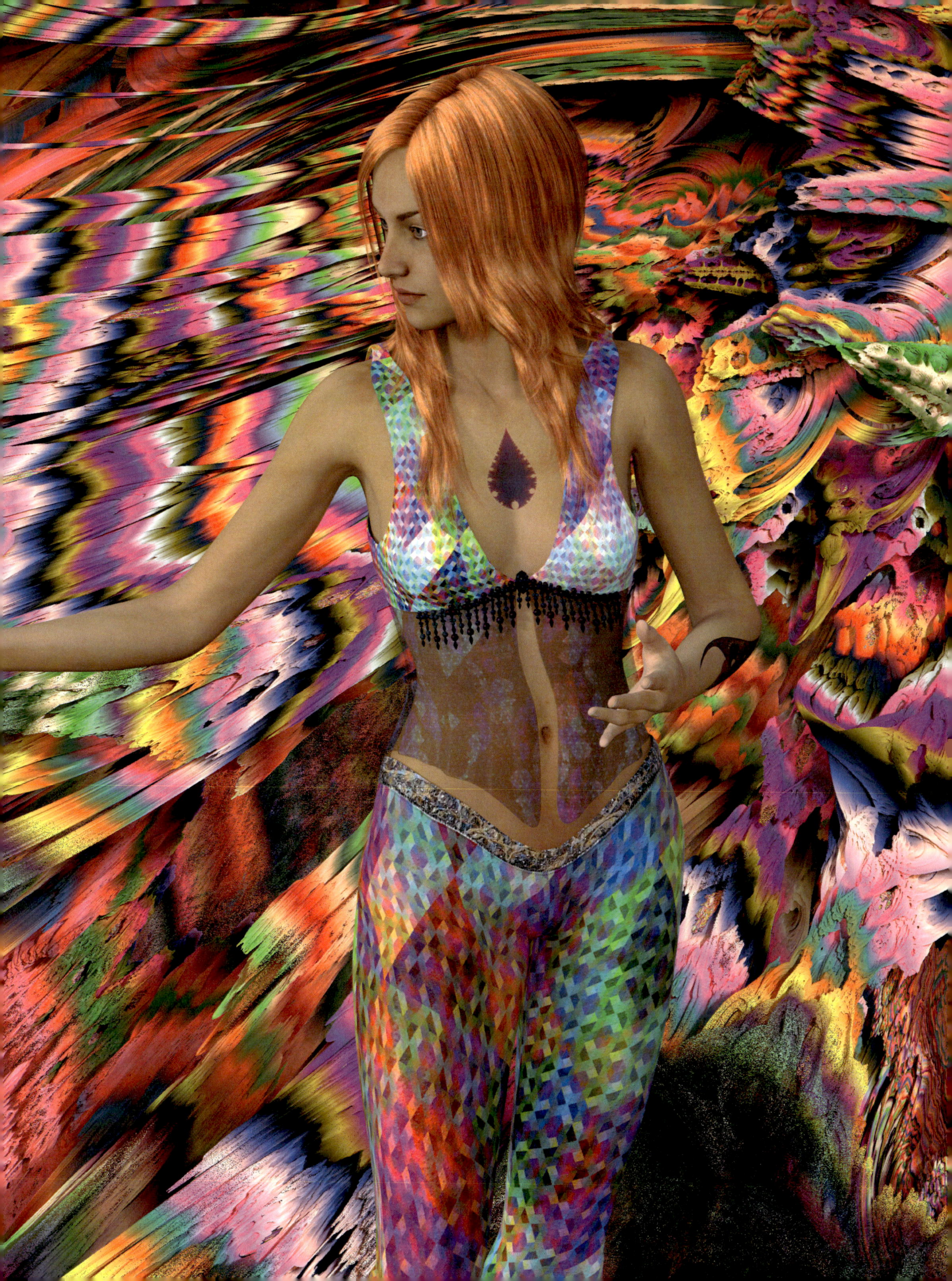

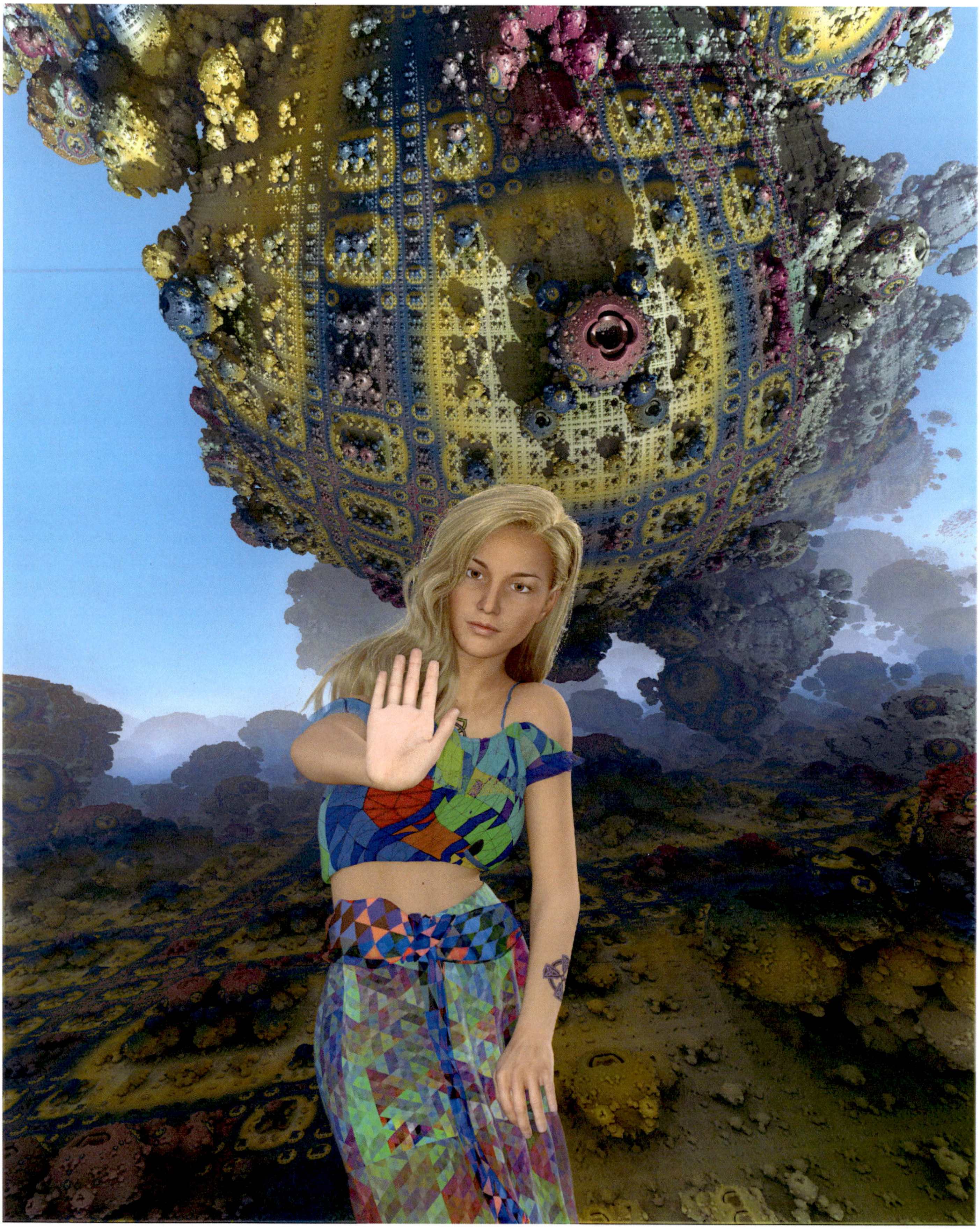

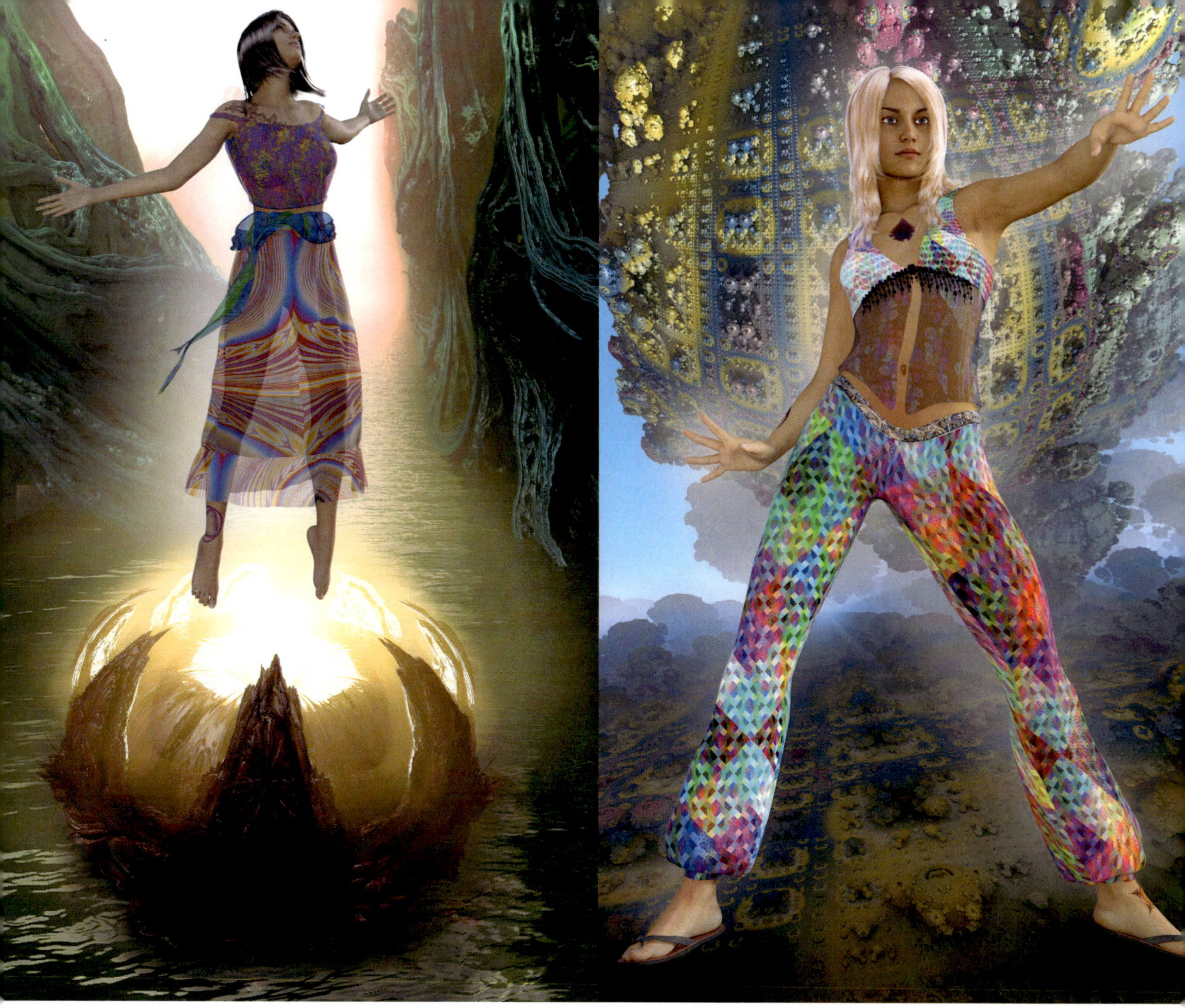

7.10. Two composites of Daz Figures with 3D fractals, 2018.

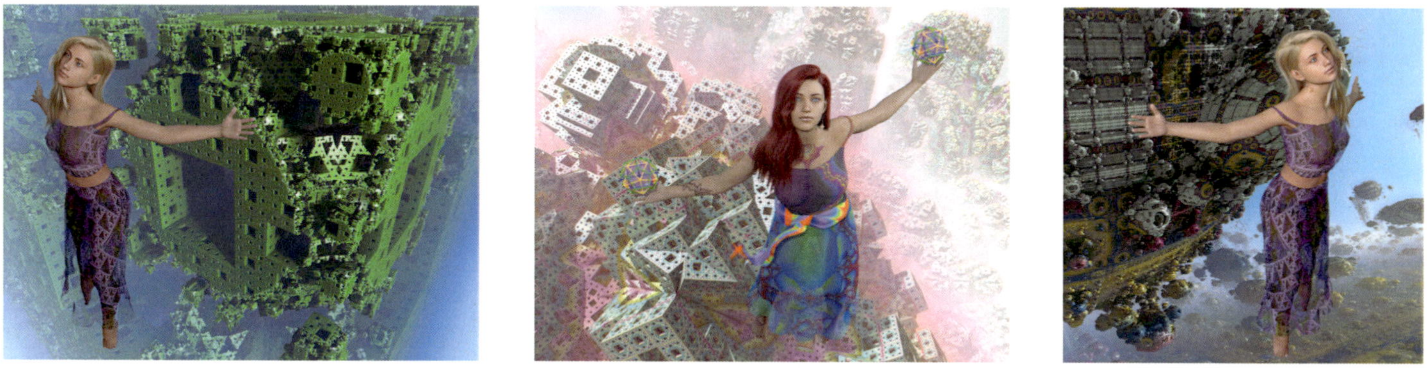

7.11 Some examples of digital figures, combined with various digital backgrounds. Mostly 4K renderings from 2018 and 2019.

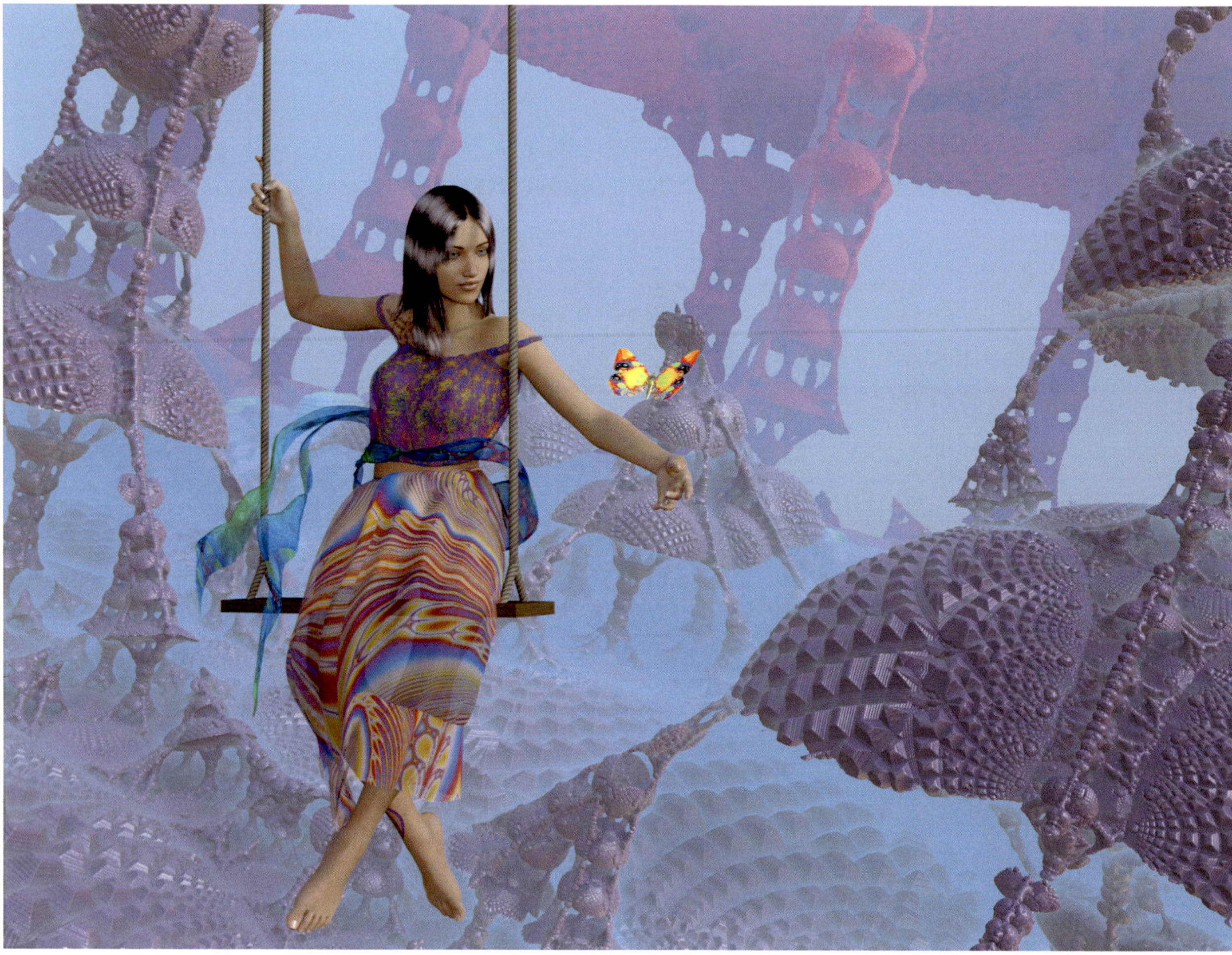

7.12. Alladin's Lost Playground, 3400 x 2550 Pixels, 2019.

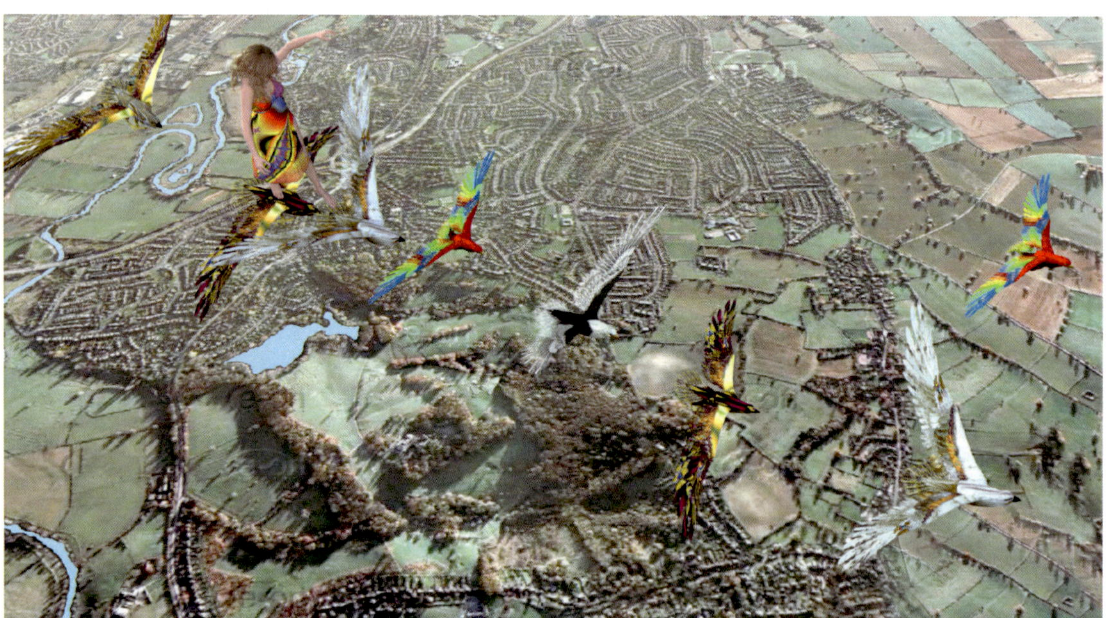

7.13.

Walking on Wings, 1920 x 1080 pixels, 2018.

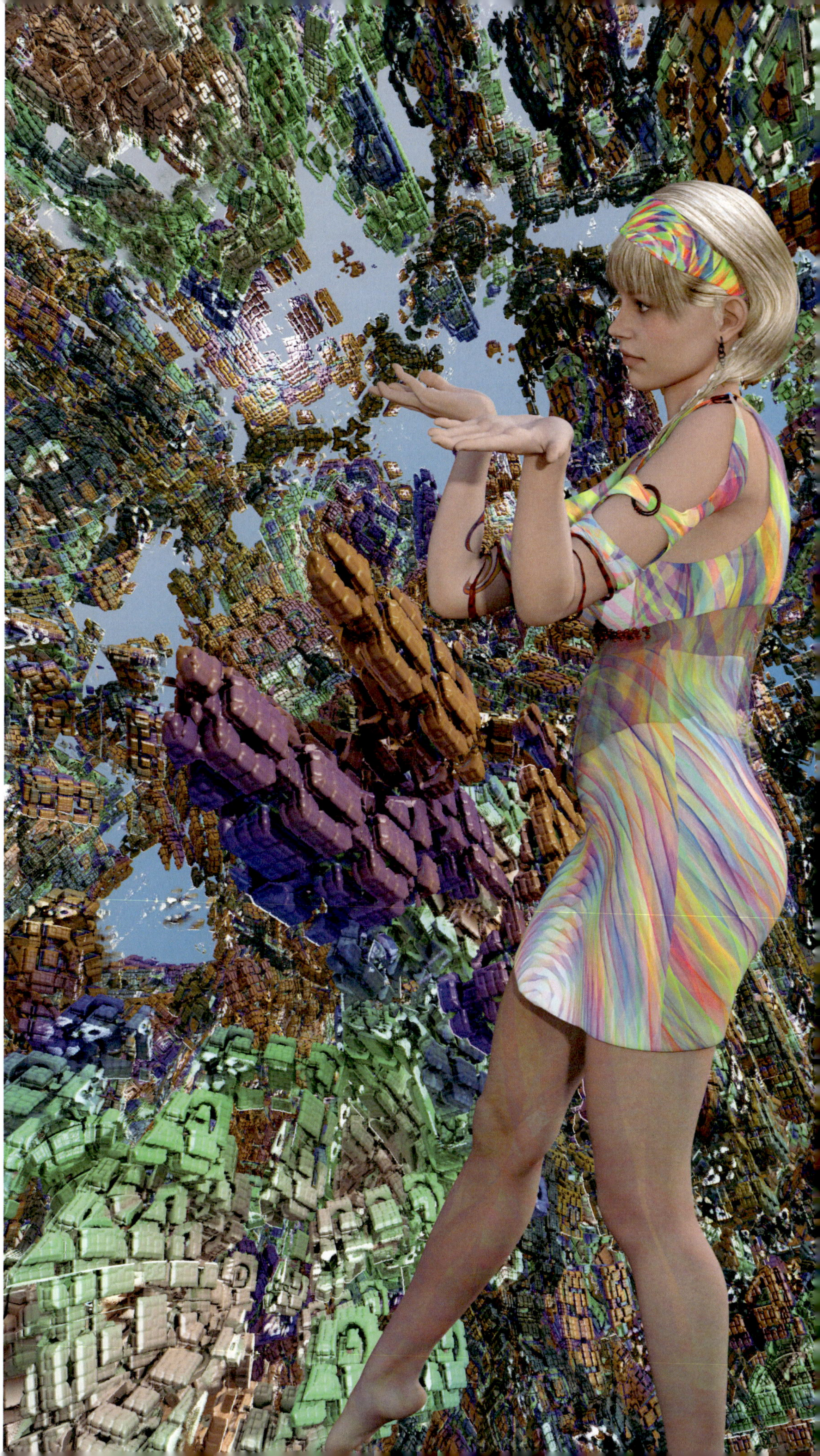

7.14.

Whatever, 2160 x 3840 pixels, 2020.

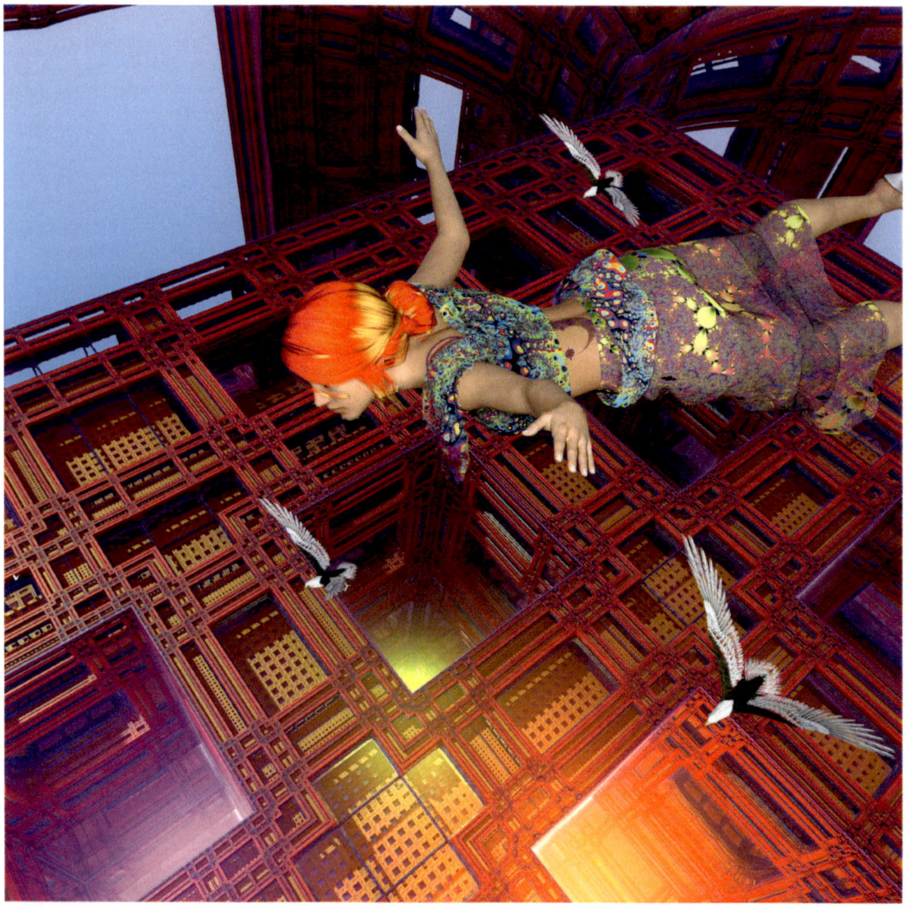

7.15.

Glow Floor, 3000 x 3000 pixels 2018.

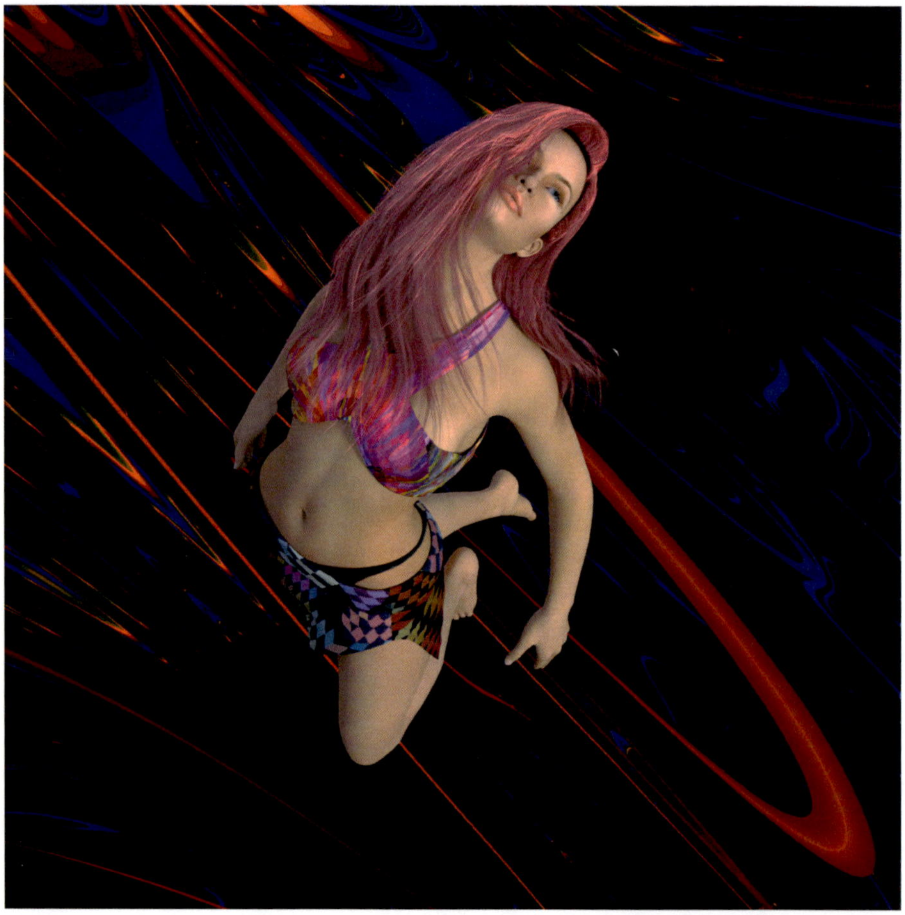

7.16.

Spinout, 3000 x 3000 pixels, 2018.

Realism leads to narrative art. It allows you to depict situations, expressions, and tell stories. And then of course there is surrealism.

Photo realistic surrealism was a life-long effort for Salvador Dali. He did an excellent job, but I wonder what he could have put together with tools like these.

I just got going myself.

Purists will hate this, perhaps feeling that generating these images with computers will yield inferior images. As sterile as they may seem, there is an incredible array of possibilities to post process these images. You can use effects to make them look like paintings, if that be the goal. I don't see any boundaries or limits, to where this will take us.

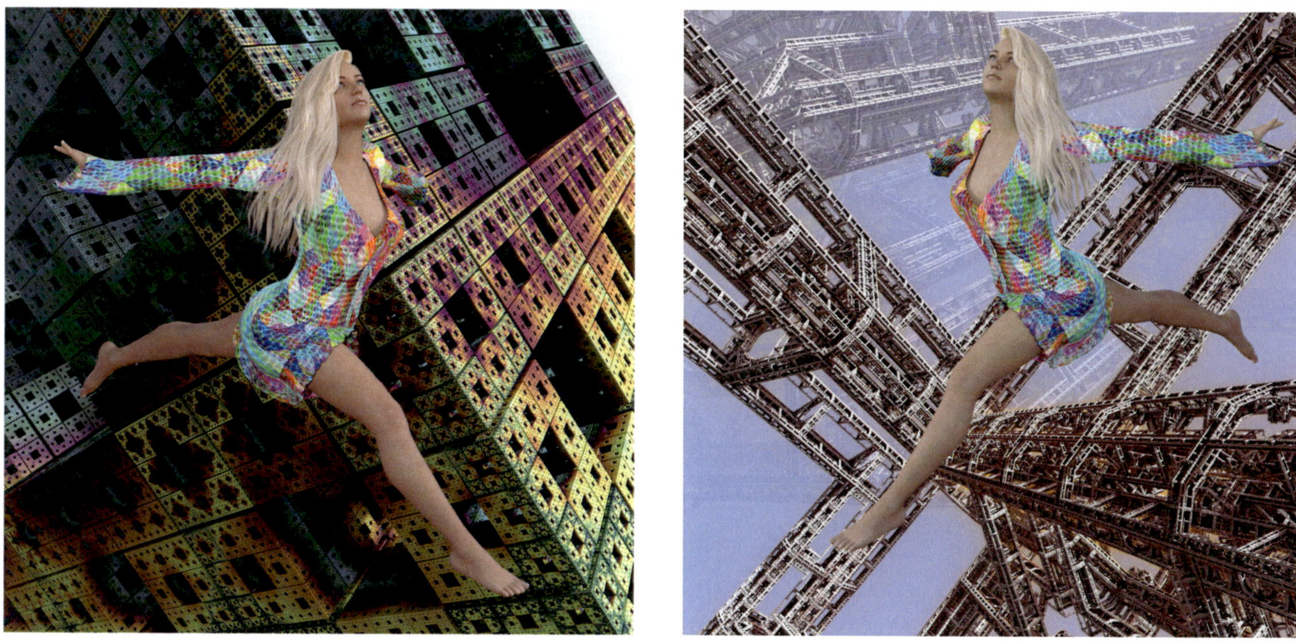

7.17. Leap Composites over 3D Fractals. 4096 x 4096 pixels, 2019.

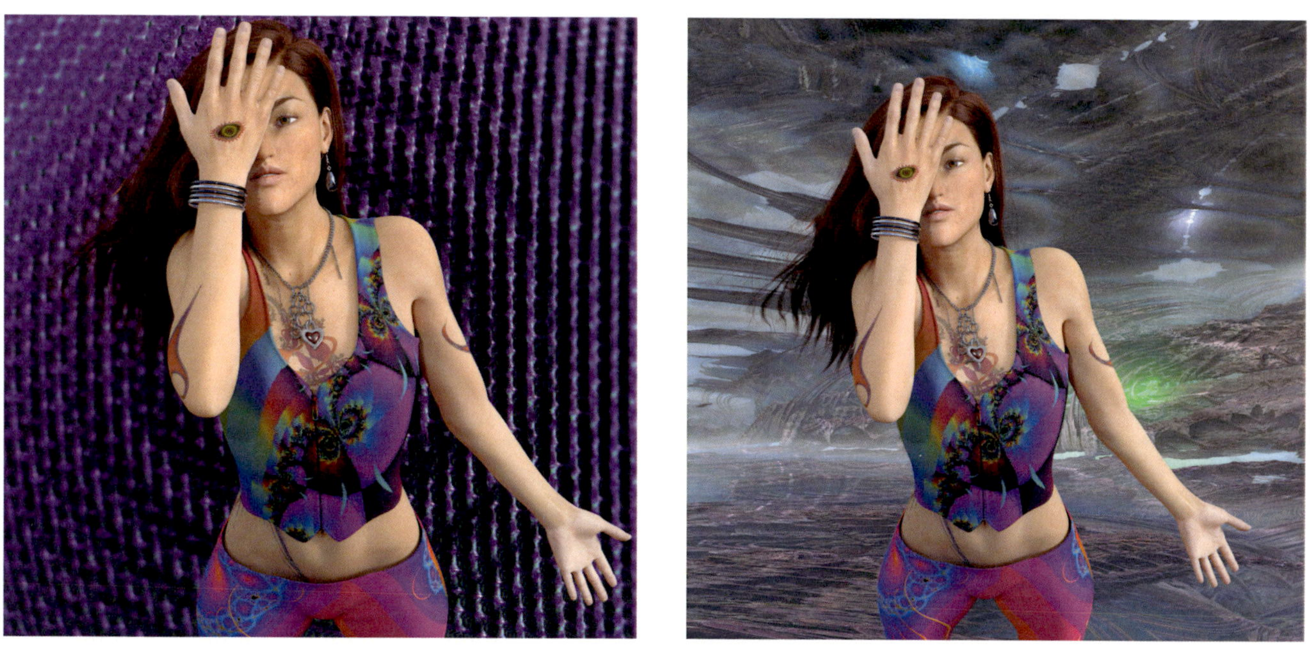

7.18. Hand to Eye Composites, 3000 x 3000 pixels 2021.

ANIMATION

As soon as I started making computer graphics I wanted to see the pictures move. The methods used to create many of these geometries, fractal and otherwise are "parametric", meaning you adjust parameters to get various end results. The software that ArtToyz Studios has come up with over the years has all been parametric. Adobe products are full of parameters, so are 3D Modeling, Rendering and Animation softwares and most fractal softwares. This is the way AI generated images are made. For me, the nice thing about all the parametric adjustments is that they commonly yield accurate controls for animation. As well they are commonly numeric, meaning they can be tied to Color By Numbers systems.

A lot of my animations are created with custom geometry that I adjust parametrically over time. I reference counting into the percent and numeric sliders for scale, rotation and any other appropriate factor I can dial in.

And then 3D lets me fly over, under, around, and through for a view.

That is the theme for my 3D fractal animations. Move around them while I morph and animate the parameters. I am looking for ways to hook this to music parameters as well.

As these pictures illustrate, this geometric approach turns out to be quite flexible to projection on various shapes of architecture.

Some doors have been opened to me because of this adaptability of geometry to various shapes and formats. Pink Floyd used round video projection. We now have much more powerful projection technology and TVs themselves are already super-sized. This will change entertainment venues and immersive experiences in the future. Like rooms with video walls, floors and ceilings.

A few years ago, computers weren't up to high res editing for the most part. Compression technology has evolved as well. So of course, I have to keep my computer beefed up and updated, with a lot of storage. I use PCs with added help from the video cards, mostly developed for gaming.

I have actually been involved in Game and Virtual Reality development since the 1990s, topics not covered here. Check for more on the Geometry for Art webpage in the future.

The flexibility of geometry to various shapes and sizes gives it an edge over temporal media with human images contained. People in pictures don't look good stretched and distorted, at least not to me. Combine this with control of color, mood and event-related subject matter and animation will be here forever. But for now I would like to see real time, interactive realism grow in technical capabilities.

I am sure I'll think of something else...

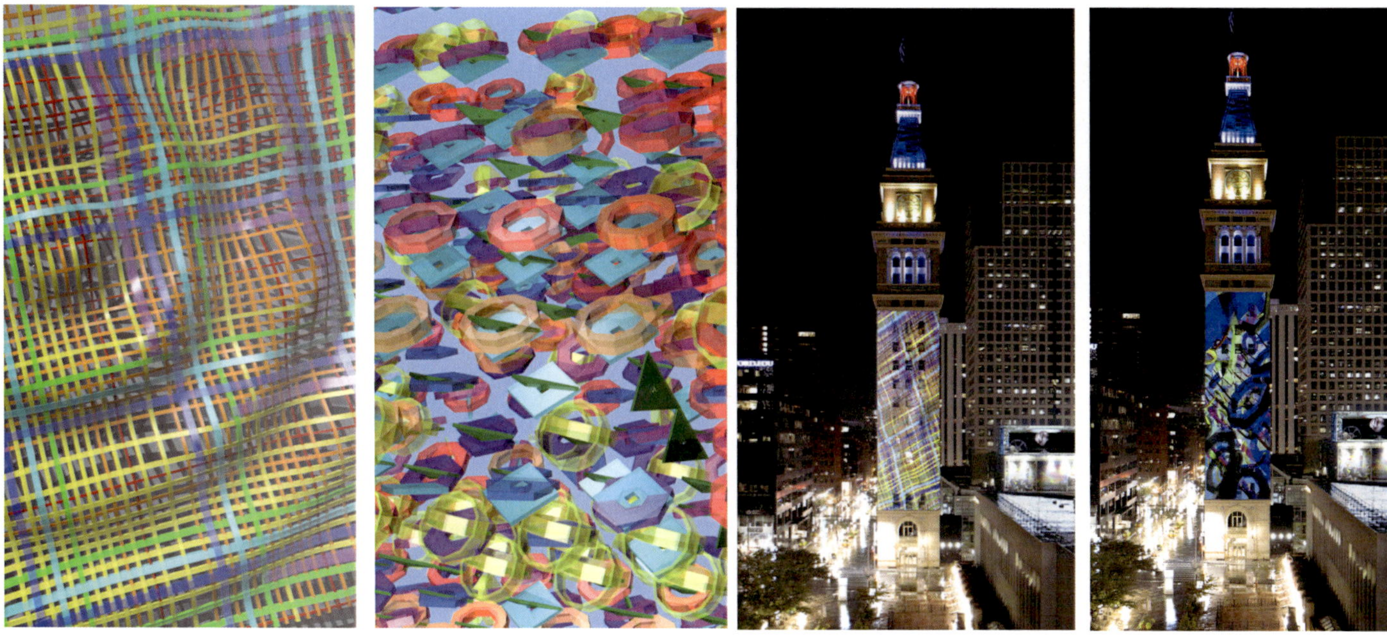

8.1. Some examples of geometric, Color By Numbers animation adapted to the thin vertical format of the D & F clock tower in Downtown Denver, 2020.

Photos courtesy of Night-Lights Denver. What fun to see animation that large!
Large means High Definition, so I try to make all of my content as high resolution as possible. I also save the rendered frames or an uncompressed master movie for re-purposing.

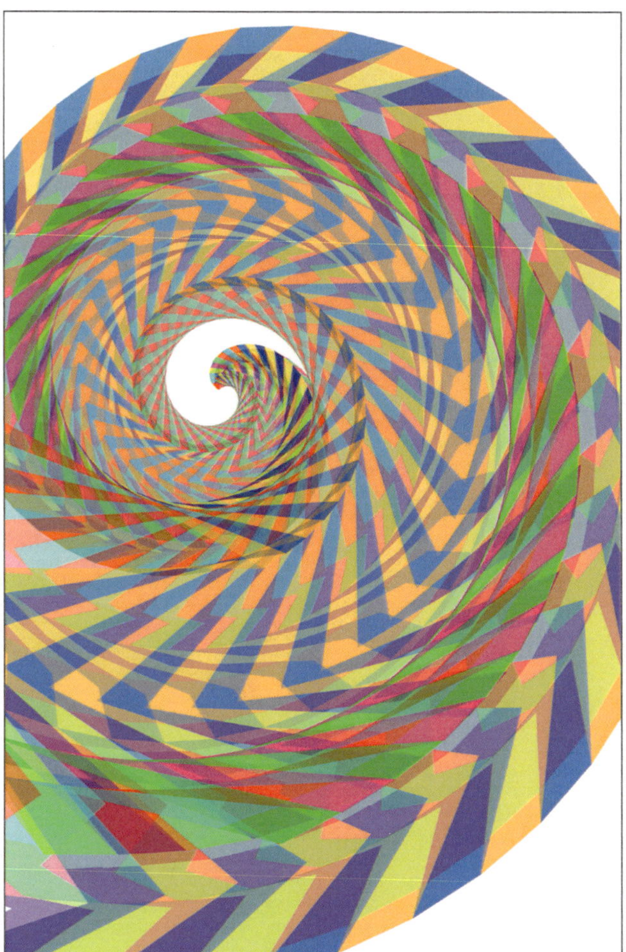

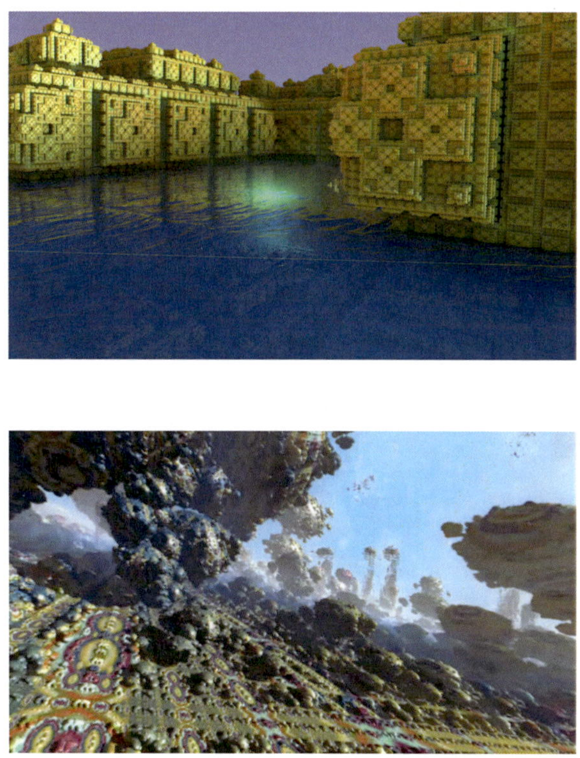

8.2.

Stills from animations used in public presentations. Scan the QR code to see some of these animations.

APPENDIX AND ADDITIONAL MATERIAL

Color By Numbers, Eschersketch and Fractal Neo-Plasticism are somewhat available for the PC. Collaboration and creative use of CBN are welcomed. Software is home-made, unrefined and with few instructions - sorry. My programmer is deceased. A webpage was set up for interactive links that are in the book.

Visit http://www.arttoyz.com. The website has software and images that are free of charge and of copyright restrictions. If anyone is interested in source code, I would love some help refining and continuing these softwares, perhaps getting some hand-held apps available. If you want to take these concepts as algorithms to more advanced levels, I would be delighted to be involved or offer code.

Steve Smith can be contacted via email at SteveSmith@ArtToyz.com.

Visit http://www.arttoyz.com. The website has software and images that are free of charge and of copyright restrictions.

The Platonic Solids. Which are which?

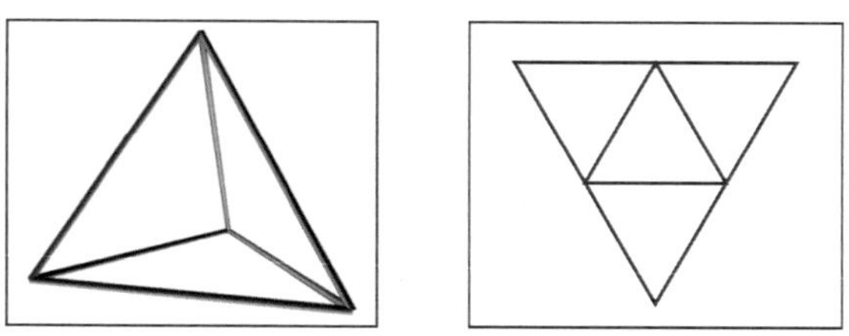

9.1. Tetrahedron, and tetrahedron flattened.

If you flatten a tetrahedron, you have 4 equilateral triangles (Our regular triangular grid).

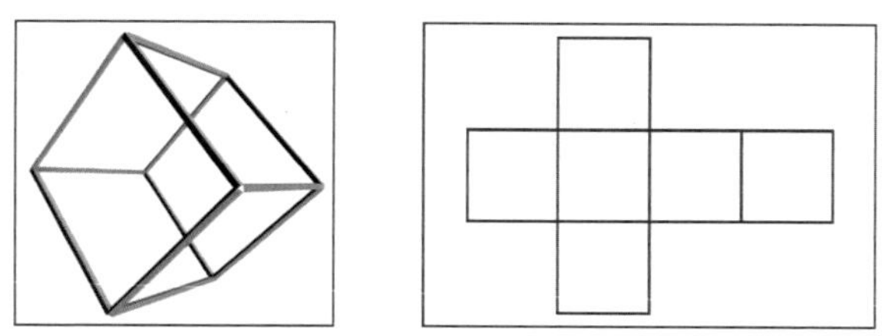

9.2. Cube, and cube flattened.

If you flatten a cube, you have 4 squares (Our regular rectangular grid.)

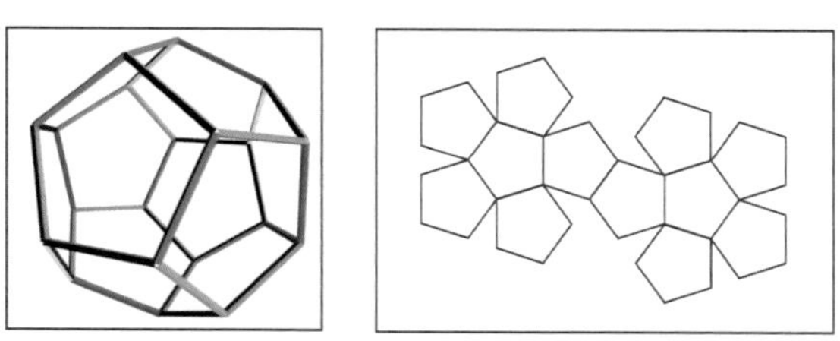

9.3. Dodecahedron, and dodecahedron flattened.

If you flatten a dodecahedron, you have ten regular pentagons and you can see why they don't tessellate.

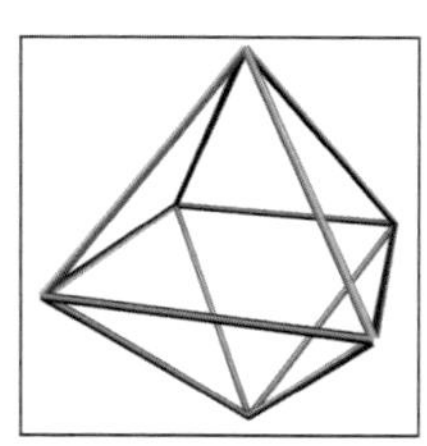

9.4.

Octahedron.

Octahedrons are made of 8 equilateral triangles.

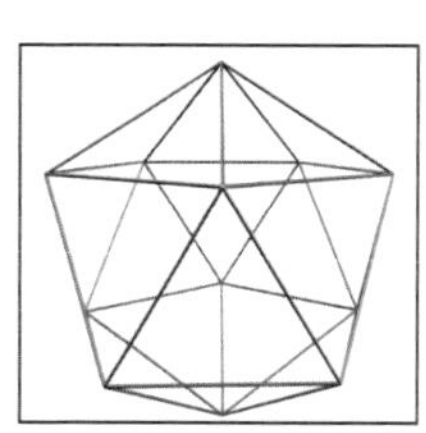

9.5.

Icosahedron.

Icosahedrons are made of 20 equilateral triangles. Both octahedrons and icosahedrons flatten out nicely to the regular triangular grid.

NOTES ON GENERATIVE ART AND AI ART

Art has no rules and needs no self imposed limitations. Craft is the area that limits art the most. Many artists don't even think of painting or sculpture as craft. Art is the motivation, the theme, the idea. Craft yields an execution of those concepts. And a machine can create some pretty sterile craft.

My art has often been created with computers. One of my delights is to fill in parameters and have the computer solve them into a design. This is generative art. Color By Numbers is based on this principal. Fractals are based on it. These systemic art forms have rules and limitations. I have used machines to craft precise renditions that would be impossible or quite difficult and time consuming by hand. I have also hand-crafted many geometric art pieces when I was capable of doing so.

In 2022, I was able to build my own computer environment for making AI generative art. I quickly fed in my trove of Color by Numbers, fractals and other art to train my own prompt-driven AI art. I also fed in my figure painting, mandalas and psychedelic creations.

As I have been creating art with parametric systems since the 1970's, this was a natural evolution (and a delightful one) for my art. AI art has taken my concepts to another level and involves a crafting of images and techniques that can be surprising and wonderful. AI is trained in aesthetics and does not copy existing art unless you ask it to. Its craft is to use design to compose and invent images in a high quality way. Some examples from 2023 are shown below.

My main interest is animation - a field that has been absorbed into the digital realm. Animation without computers is mostly historic. And digital AI animation easily encompasses the issues of copyrights, ownership and value of digital art. I am not interested in exploiting actors, music or scripts that I do not have permission to. AI animation is leading us to a more frame by frame surrealistic approach as we move into the future.

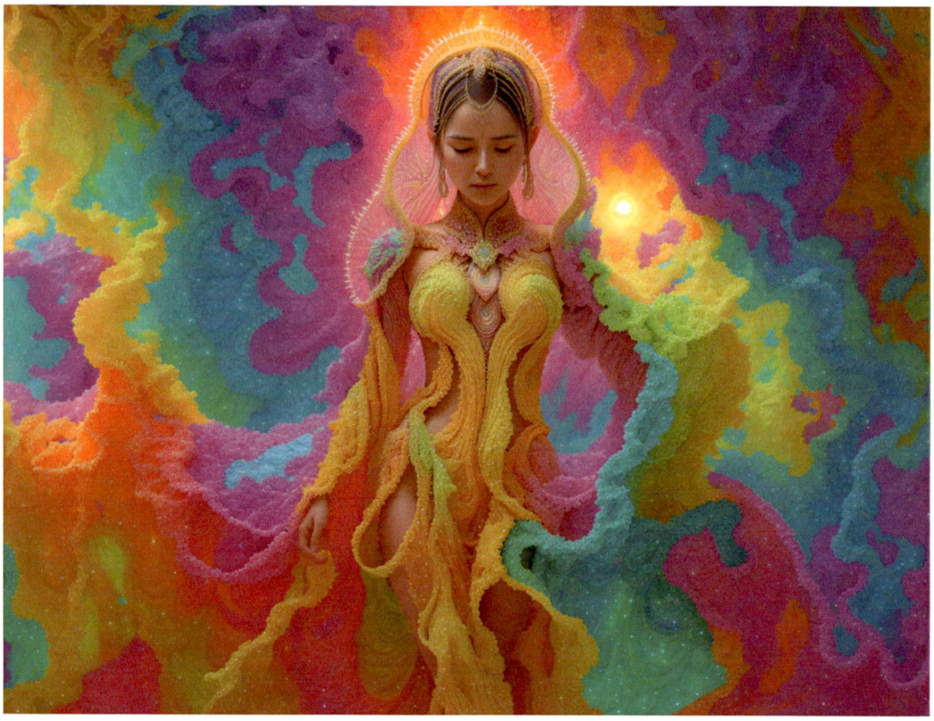

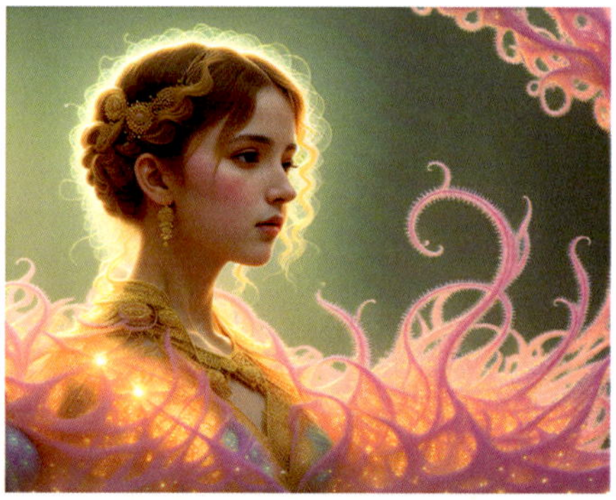

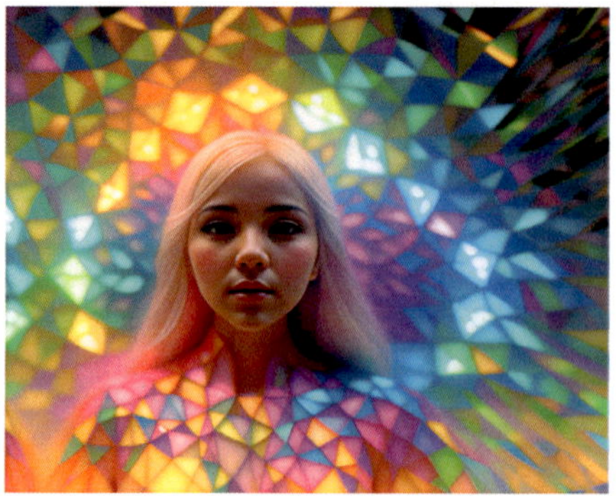

9.6a. Some examples of AI Generated Art I have created with Stable Diffusion trained by ArtToyz Studios in 2023.

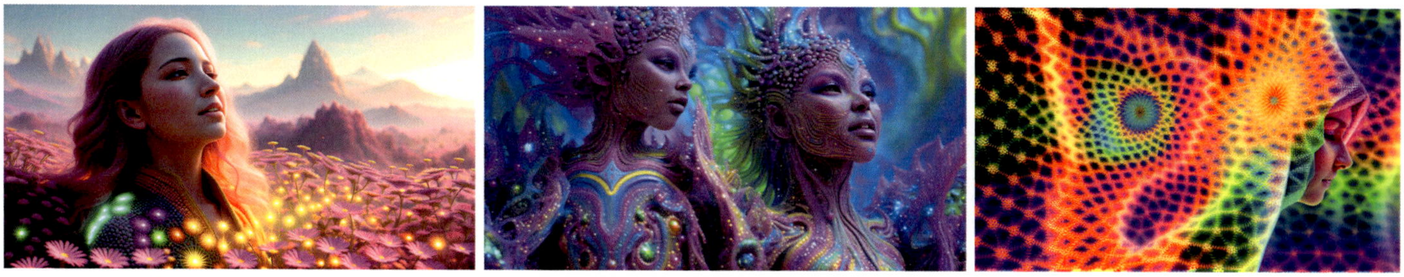

9.6b. Some examples of AI Generated Art I have created with Stable Diffusion, 2023.

Excerpt from Buckminster Fuller's notes on the exhibition "Projection – Anti Materialism". La Jolla Museum of Art, May 15 – July 5, 1970:

> *"More than 99.9 percent of all the physical and metaphysical events which are evolutionarily scheduled to effect the further regeneration of life aboard our spaceship earth transpire within the vast non-sensorial reaches of the electromagnetic spectrum. The main difference between our yesterdays and today is that man is now intellectually apprehending and usefully employing a large number of those 99.9 percent invisible energetic events. Humanity has therefore created for itself a new set of responsibilities requiring a ninety-nine fold step-up in its vision and comprehension. This calls for an intuitive revision of humanity's aesthetical criteria, philosophical orientation, conscious action, cooperation and initiative in accommodating evolution's inexorable drive to have mind comprehend and surmount every physical eventuality. Intuition and aesthetics automatedly trigger us into consciousness of the existence of opportunities to consider and selectively initiate alternative acts or position-taking regarding oncoming events, potential realizations or unprecedented breakthroughs in art, technology and other human productivity.*
>
> *Today's epochal aesthetic is almost exclusively involved with the invisible, intellectual integrity manifest by the explorers and formulators operating sensorially unreachable, yet vast, ranges of the electro, chemical and mathematical realms of the physical and metaphysical realities. Their invisible discoveries and developments will eventuate as sensible instruments, tools, machines and automation, in general."*

Thanks to Lucy R. Lippard from: "Six Years: the Dematerialization of the Art Object from 1966 to 1972 ...", University of California Press, Copyright 1973.

My art was influenced by a number of conceptual artists. Sol LeWitt, Buckminster Fuller, Andy Goldsworthy, Claes Oldenburg are a few. I saw computer generated art for the first time in the late 1970s, in printed books of course. Around that time, I met a technical specialist in computers – Jeff Yetter, and created software to visualize my ideas. Jeff never fully agreed, but I always felt this software itself was the materialization of the idea. The idea was to visualize geometry using computers and it worked. It was an automation of art, like printing and photography had been in the past. It was a big flop in the art world....

One of the ongoing criticisms of Digital Art is that it is too easy, and does not involve working with your hands – craft. Try to write a program or learn to use a software and you might feel differently. Computers need to be exploited by artists for prototyping, pre-visualizing, recording and proliferating art, if for no other reasons. But they can be powerful tools for creating Systemic and Generative Art. These art systems create individual works which cohere to a philosophy, method or other strict criteria (as software does). This has long been a part of art movements throughout art history. In fact the specific criteria or method usually defines the movement. Look at Neo-Plasticism and the art of Piet Mondrian for example.

Probably an extension of what Marcel Duchamp and Dada portrayed, the Conceptual Artists from the late '60s and '70's pushed the idea of what art could be into any direction they could think of. Some art went beyond non-objective, all the way to de-materialized. Google some of these artists for a flavor of what they did: Carl Andre, Jan Dibbets, Bruce

Nauman, Yoko Ono, Edward Ruscha, Richard Serra, Robert Smithson, Joseph Beuys, and John Baldessari. Remember the social and consciousness revolution that was expanding at this time in history (the 1960's).

Little did the Conceptual Artists of the late 20th Century know they were validating Digital Art. This truly paved an evolutionary path towards technology to come. Digital art's materialization is invisible bits and bytes.

Digital Art is the major new art movement of the 21st century I feel. I am sure there are numerous stylistic movements historians could mention, but do they outweigh the immensity and social necessity of Digital Art (easily including Digital Photography)?

De-materialized art is not that complicated to understand. Consider music as an art, it can be collected as material or digital "objects". I was thinking about how music has dematerialized over the last 100 years. (Not that it was ever truly an "object", just commercial packaging and playback gadgetry.)

I now have plenty of room on my shelves, still have all my music and only need more bytes from a memory disc to store it.

> *"People assume immediately, if a work is not visible, it is particularly conceptual. That is a very materialistic way of thinking if one has any thought and reverses it in itself. That is incredibly primitive because it is evidently the same thought only in reverse. Nothing has changed at all."*

Joseph Beuys, from a conversation with Ursula Meyer

(Thanks to Lucy R. Lippard - from "Six Years: the De-materialization of the Art Object from 1966 to 1972 ...", University of California Press, Copyright 1973)

NOTES ON NON-FUNGIBLE TOKENS OR NFT'S

As the art world progressed and the concepts of multiples from an original evolved, the concept of ownership and value of art evolved. (14th century to current times). Essentially this was driven by printmaking and then later on by photography (also printed).

In printmaking, which evolved earlier, the value was focused on an original vs. an edition. A monoprint (or 1 of 1) was more unique than an edition of prints. The earlier in the edition, the higher the value is, to an extent. This was largely based on the fact that the print quality decayed as the master plate was printed repeatedly. The works were also worth more if they were signed and numbered. Perhaps you have seen 10 of 100 or some such notation on a print. This is usually not a part of commercial, 4 color printing as those editions can be quite large. Commercial printing yields good quality throughout and signing 10,000 prints is a bit ridiculous.

As photography entered the scene it had trouble with being accepted in the art world and print editions opened this door. Photography adopted this edition, numbering and signing convention. Photos could degrade as the negatives were used more and more, though in a bit different of a way.

In the 1960's conceptual art paved the way for a "de-materialization" of artworks and the galleries and museums largely rejected it. (no objects=nothing to sell). I believe that conceptual art was paving the way for digital art. Enter the computer, software, digital printing methods and of course the internet. Conceptual art defined an artwork as a concept, an idea or instructions for executing the artwork without the personal touch or craftsmanship of the artist. It also allowed for ideas that were never turned into "art objects" to be considered art.

Wait 60 years for this evolution to be even close to viable for the art world. A lot of people think using software or creating artwork with algorithms is "easy" or "not art" because it lacks the craftsmanship and personal touch of the artist. Computers are just tools, like cameras or printing presses. All art involves craftsmanship, but hand-done craftsmanship should not be confused with Art. Art should not be reduced to craft, because ideas are important. A basket can be art or craft, but it's art is tied up in the concept of basket making. Digital art can be fast, but the aesthetic of an image is still the realm of the artist and in many cases the reproduction method is still digital. The end result of digital art is not an object, but a digital file. It is "printed" to a display screen with zero degradation from re-use.

Digital files can be displayed on monitors or projected. They can also be printed by a plethora of techniques, sizes and methods. They are currently being grabbed offline by anyone, for no cost, violating copyright laws that are only enforceable with lawsuits. The artist is forced to accept this or to "watermark" it so that it is not usable (or properly viewable) by the public. Copyright laws protect "media", which digital art is part of.

Enter the concept of the Non-Fungible Tokens (BTW, I hate the name) The Wiktionary defines fungible as: "able to be substituted for something of equal value or utility" . (Gold and Silver are fungible). Non-Fungible would imply not able to be substituted. With a suspicious connection to digital money (though not a requirement), NFTs can be sold to protect the copyrights of digital art. They can also be used to allow their owners to benefit from viral usage in the same way that royalties work. It seems to me that an NFT could allow full reproduction rights or be limited to a certain printing methodology and/or a certain size. They could allow an owner to print "x" copies, print unlimited copies or allow limited (or unlimited) digital usage, depending on how they are defined. This is a new concept and allows plenty of flexibility to be defined by the owner to various situations. The future use and access by the artist is another point of definition. The form of the "token" is a bit vague, but ultimately is a contract or a legal agreement when purchased. It could take the form of a physical object with the contract embedded, but would also include the digital file.

From My Master's Thesis, University of Colorado, Master of Fine Arts, 1982

"Color By Numbers" is a methodology for patterning regular geometric structures with counting.

Counting is a numeric fractal which iterates and scales to infinity.

Colors are mapped to numbers which create linear pattern sequences.

These sequences can be arranged on grids or in temporal arrangements to create audio and video.

Patterns are created through repetition and scaling as counting evolves and adds to itself.

Colors, patterns, images, audio or video bits can represent the digits of the numbers or can be mixed to represent complete integers.

If red represents 2 and blue represents 1, 21 could be represented by red following blue or by mixing red and blue in even quantities, yielding purple.

Patterns can be controlled by starting to count at a certain number or by arranging the linear stream of elements into unique structures.

You can count (colorize) in various number bases depending on how many various elements you would like to work with. Base 10 uses 10 colors, Base 2 uses 2.

Base 5 has 5 colors (elements) representing 0 1 2 3 4.

Though using a computer is more accurate, pleasing patterns can be created with colored pencils on graph paper or with grid-based media such as tile, weaving, hook rugs and needlepoint.

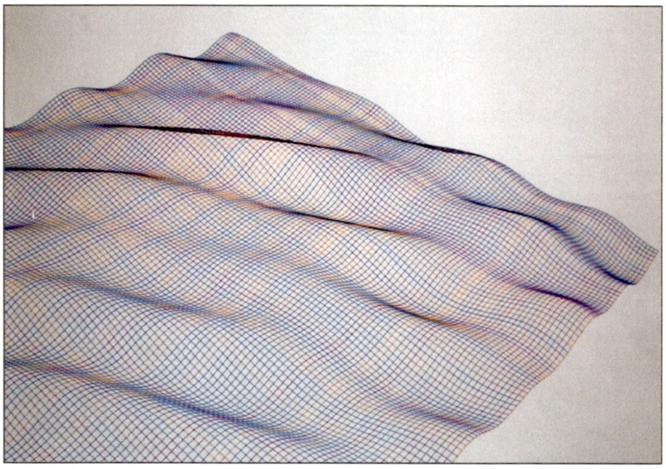

9.7. Pen plot from my Master's Thesis Show. University of Colorado, Boulder, 1982.

Following is a document created to explain the math and processes of creating tessellations in EscherSketch Software, created by ArtToyz Studios.

EscherSketch

Jeffry D. Yetter
Independent technologist

Steven M. Smith
Arttoyz Studios

ABSTRACT

Tessellation, also called mosaic is an art form that has been practiced for millennia. Examples of Roman mosaics have been uncovered dating back to the second century BC. Islamic art provides exquisite examples that cover floors, walls and ceilings. The Dutch artist M.C. Escher (1898-1972) was captivated at an early age by this art and he developed his own intriguing version of improbable tessellating creatures that are oriented in all directions and that fit together seamlessly like puzzle pieces. Escher's methodology is described in this paper along with a software drawing tool that assists artists and designers who aspire to create these images on their own, but with a level of automation that the master could only dream of.

Keywords: Tessellation, Escher, …
Index Terms:

1 INTRODUCTION

Tessellations are the basis of many familiar art forms. By definition, a tessellation is a covering of an infinite geometric plane without gaps or overlaps by congruent plane figures of one type or a few types. In practice artists are limited to finite planes and typically choose media such as ceramic tiles, stained glass or just hand sketches or paintings. Islamic art provides us exquisite examples of highly intricate and beautiful geometric designs. Many early civilizations have left behind enduring figures and scenes created by tessellating stone tiles secured with mortar.

EscherSketch, the application described herein is designed to assist artists, designers, students and enthusiasts in creating tessellations.

The twentieth century Dutch graphic artist M. C. Escher developed a style of tessellation using complex tile shapes depicting fantastic creatures that are oriented in many directions and that fit together seamlessly. These captivating images create a sense of wonder that compels the viewer to contemplate the origin of these seemingly incomprehensible tiles. Actually, there is a method to it. Eschersketch is further designed to teach this method and assist designers to create complex tessellating tiles on their own.

2 THEORY

The core structure of Eschersketch consists of two main panels. The first panel is a basic tile editor. The tile editor allows a user to create polygons of basic shapes representing tiles. Once created, a tile or a group of tiles can be colored, moved, copied, rotated, reflected (mirrored) or modified.

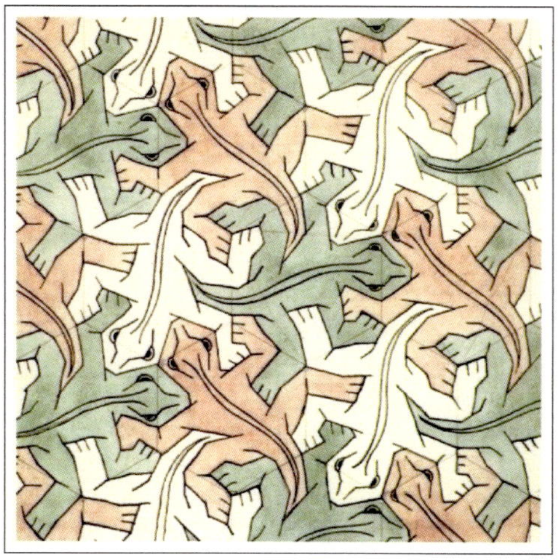

9.8. M.C Escher design of tessellating reptiles.

A key feature of the tile editor is a precise snap grid that facilitates a tight fitting result devoid of gaps or overlaps. Both rectangular (Cartesian) and hexagonal grids are supported. By definition the tessellation plane is infinite, but of course in practice the viewable (and editable) portion is limited by the size and resolution of the display, but expanded using a range of pan and zoom tools. The tile editor also includes facilities for creating high quality anti-aliased bitmap images for printing, or alternatively, vector files for interfacing to a variety of cutting or milling machinery.

The second panel is called the tile transformation editor (or just the transform editor). This panel provides the user with the ability to productively create complex tiles with potentially thousands of vertices that will fit together seamlessly with copies of themselves, perhaps after rotating or reflecting the copies. With a little practice and imagination, these tiles can be made to resemble objects or creatures, but completely abstract shapes can be equally interesting.

The fundamental capability of the transform editor is the ability to apply similar edits to multiple edges of a polygon simultaneously. By adding a vertex to one edge, a properly transformed vertex will automatically be added to a second specified edge in such a manner that the vertex pair will align perfectly in a subsequently assembled tessellation. There are five edge transformation types supported by the EscherSketch transform editor which will be described in detail. An essential capability of this panel is a full featured curve editor. The user is allowed to use a vertex as an anchor point and apply Bezier curves along adjoining segments. As before, a second properly transformed curve is automatically applied to a second specified edge. One final capability of the transformation editor is the ability to add rudimentary sketches to the tile to enhance its character and identity.

The user can return the tile back to the tile editor to check its form and fit, then back again to the transform editor for further work. When the transformation work is satisfactory, the tile editor capabilities are used to assemble the final tessellation.

3 COMPLEX TILE METHODOLOGY

At first glance it is hard to imagine how M.C. Escher and other artists were able to create those fantastic images of interlocking creatures going this way and that, but there is a method to it. At their core, these images are just tessellations. The trick is to generate these seemingly incomprehensible tiles with shapes that remind us of the creatures they become, and that go back together with no gaps or spaces.

The methods used to create tiles like this are rigorous from a mathematical standpoint, and overall not too hard to understand (after all they are visual). They stem from the three familiar symmetries inherent in some polygons, namely translational, rotational and reflective symmetry, and a fourth one that is less familiar called glide reflection symmetry.

These properties of polygons must have been abundantly familiar to Escher and others who created these captivating images, but the task is still daunting using traditional tools like pencils, tracing paper and compass points. To create these tessellations with extreme precision is even more arduous, and a testament to the patience and skill of those artists.

3.1 Basic Rules

Complex tessellating tiles must always start with a basic polygon which itself must tessellate.

EscherSketch restricts starting tiles to one of three types: triangles, quadrilaterals or "special" hexagons, those being hexagons with opposite edges that are both parallel and congruent. These specific polygon types always tessellate, and were used exclusively by Escher as his starting shapes. Furthermore, once established, the vertices of the starting shape must not be moved in order to ensure that the final complex tile will snap together seamlessly.

With these simple rules in mind (and enforced by EscherSketch) the user can move the polygon to the transformation editor and begin to apply edge transformations.

3.2 Transformation by Translation

The translation transform is the easiest to describe and visualize. It can be applied to any pair of edges of the starting polygon that are both parallel and congruent. To use this tool the user selects the translation tool and is prompted to pick a source edge, then the transform editor finds the appropriate destination edge (if it exists). The user can then create intermediate points along the source edge by picking a point and dragging it to a new location. The editor will then add a corresponding point on the destination edge that is translated in the plane by the distance and offset between the source and destination edge. Points can be removed with a right mouse click, and the corresponding point on the destination edge will be deleted as well. Any number of points can be added; no matter how complex the edges become the resulting tile will always tessellate exactly with a copy of the resulting tile that is translated by the same offset in the tessellation plane.

The user can at any time move to another edge to apply a different transformation, then return to the first edge to continue editing. Additionally the user can return the partially completed complex tile to the tile editor to check form and fit, and subsequently return to the transformation editor to resume modifications.

3.3 Transformation by Center Rotation

The center rotation tool is unique in that there are no restrictive rules regarding the edge to be edited. This is possible because the source and destination are both on the same edge. After the center rotation tool is selected the user is prompted to identify the edge to be edited. The transformation editor marks the center point of the identified edge with a new vertex. This vertex cannot be moved but rather delineates the edge into a source half and destination half. As in the translation tool, the user can pick and drag new points on the source half, then the editor will add corresponding points on the destination half that are rotated 180 degrees bout the center point. The resulting tile will always tessellate exactly with a copy of that tile that is rotated 180 degrees.

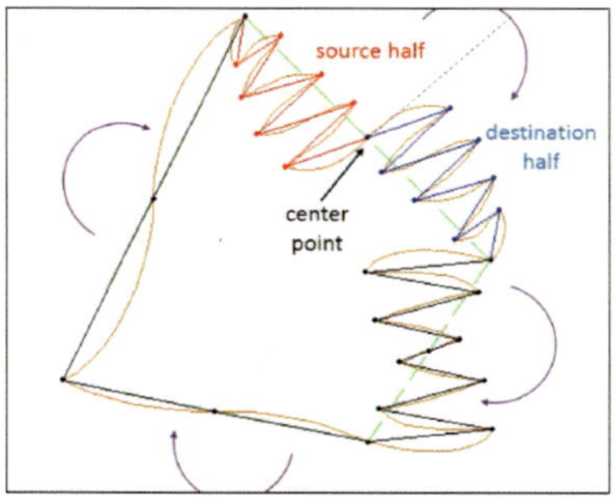

9.9. Transform editor view of a fish created from a scalene quadrilateral using four center rotation transformations.

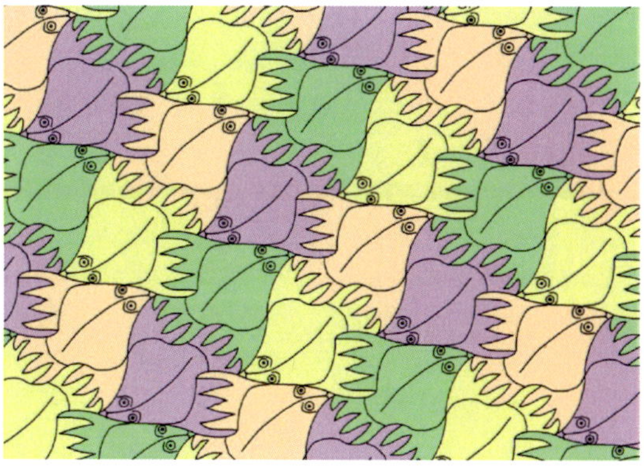

9.10. View of the fish in the tessellation plane.

3.4 Transformation by Vertex Rotation

Like translation, the vertex rotation transformation is applied to a pair of edges. In this case the edge pair must be congruent and share a common vertex. After selecting the vertex rotation tool the user is prompted to identify a source edge, and the editor choses the destination edge (if it exists). The editor then computes the angle between the source and destination edge. As before the user adds points along the source edge and the editor supplies corresponding points on the destination edge that are rotated about the common vertex by the angle between the source and destination edges. The resulting complex tile will always tessellate exactly with a copy of itself that is rotated (negatively) by the same angle and translated so that the endpoint vertices are stacked.

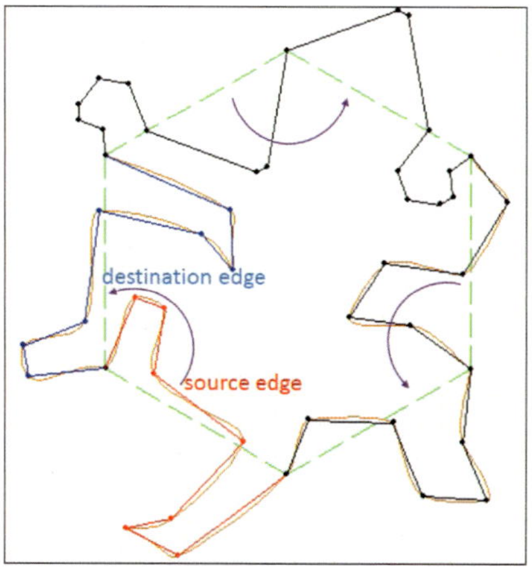

9.11. Transform editor view of a reptile created from a hexagon using three vertex rotation transformations.

3.5 Transformation by Glide Reflection

Glide reflective symmetry is a generalization of reflective symmetry and is defined in a plane as a reflection about a line combined with a translation along the line of reflection. The glide reflection edge transformation tool does precisely that. Like other transformation tools, a source and destination edge are required. In this case, the only requirement for the destination edge is that it be congruent to the source edge. The two edges need not be either parallel or adjacent, thus the user is prompted individually to identify the source and destination edges. The transformation applied is best described by the following series of steps:

1. A line of reflection is determined by the midpoints of the source and destination edges.

2. Each point placed on the source edge is reflected about the reflection line.

3. A corresponding point is placed on the destination edge that is the reflected point of step 2 translated by an offset equal to the distance between the two edge midpoints determined in step 1.

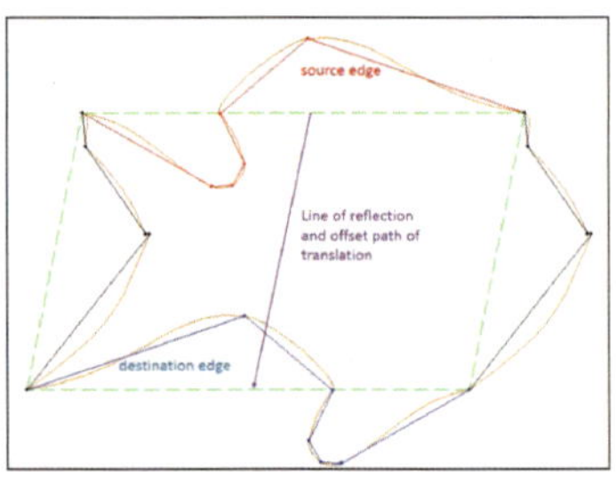

9.12. Transformation editor view of a fish created from a parallelogram using a glide reflection.

The resulting complex tile will always tessellate exactly with a copy of itself that has been reflected about the transformation line of reflection and translated by the transformation offset.

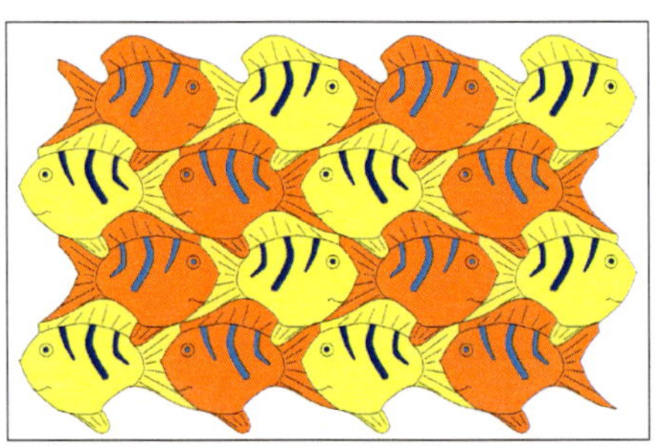

9.13. Transform editor view of a fish created from a rectangle.

3.6 The Reflection Tool

The reflection tool does not provide an edge transformation capability, but rather is a convenience for the creation of tiles with perfect reflective symmetry. To use this tool a user would complete transformations on all but one edge of the starting tile. By selecting the reflection tool the editor immediately creates a second half-tile by reflecting the transformed vertices and points about the remaining (unedited) edge. (It is the only tool in the transform editor that modifies the vertices of the starting tile). Due to its nature, the reflection tool must be the last tool applied to complete a transformed tile. In other words, no further edge transformations can be applied to a tile that has been reflected. For this reason the transform editor includes an unreflect tool.

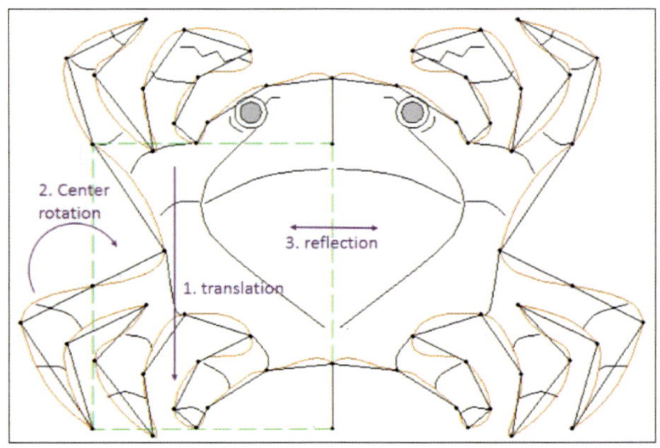

3.7 Curve Editing

The previous examples demonstrate that arbitrarily complex shapes can be applied to edges with enough patience and perseverance to add and move a large number of points. This process can be tedious and time consuming, and without extreme care can lead to curves that are jagged or otherwise misshapen. To simplify this process the transform editor provides a rich set of curve editing tools. Curve editors can be viewed as unapproachable for many users so every attempt has been made to enhance the usability and intuitive feel of the Eschersketch curve editor.

Curves can be applied to edges at any time that a transformation tool is active. A single button is used to enter and exit curve editing mode; the button is illuminated to indicate that the curve editor is active. Once activated, the mouse interpreter is conditioned to respond to mouse clicks in ways that are appropriate to curve editing. All curves generated are cubic Bezier curves.

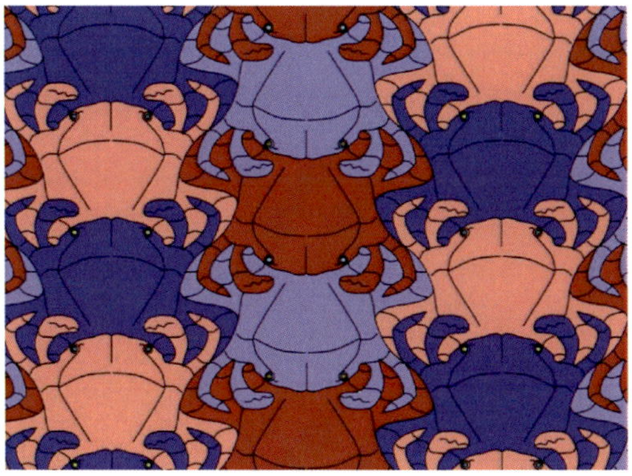

Any vertex can be used as an anchor point for a curve. (This includes the immovable vertices of the starting rectangle and center points of center rotated edges.) Some of the curve editor's capabilities and operations are described as follows:

• Clicking a line segment (between anchor points) enables that segment for curve editing. Control points on either edge of the segment become visible and moveable. (The tangent lines between the anchor points and control points are also visible.) If no previous curve exists, a default curve is established that ensures the smoothest possible tangent through the anchor points.*

• Clicking an anchor point enables curve editing on both adjacent segments. Control points on either side of the anchor point become visible and moveable. If no previous curve exists on either or both of the adjacent segments, default curves are established as before.

• Control points that are visible can be moved by clicking and dragging them. The effect of the movement on the resulting curve is displayed in real time.

• Anchor points can be moved by clicking and dragging them, and their associated control points move along with them by the same offset. The effect of the movement on the resulting curve is displayed in real time.

• By selecting a curved segment, a slider bar is enabled that allow adjustment of the number of intermediate points in the curve (up to 24), thus the accuracy (/ complexity) of each segment can be controlled independently.

• Curves can be deleted (returned to a straight line) by right clicking on a vertex or segment.

*Default curves are 10 point cubic Bezier curves. The position of the control points associated with a vertex are set on a line passing through that vertex and parallel to a line that connects the control points that precede and follow the defaulting vertex. In many cases this initialization produces a satisfactory result without the need to even move any control points.

3.8 The Sketch Editor

The final capability of the transform editor is a rudimentary sketch editor. This facility allows a user to add features to a tile, for example hair or scales or feathers to give the tile personality and character. The primitive drawing types include lines, polylines, polygons or regular polygons. Lines and polygon outlines can be drawn in black or alternatively in the inverse color (color negative) of the tile on which they are displayed. Polygons can be left empty (with transparent interiors) or filled with the inverse tile color. Stacked elements are drawn (in the tessellation plane) in the order in which they are entered. Elements drawn outside the tile will appear in the tessellation plane on top of neighboring tiles.

REFERENCES

[1] J. Allebach. Binary display of images when spot size exceeds step size. Applied Optics, 15:2513–2519, August 1980.
[2] E. Catmull. A tutorial on compensation tables. In Computer Graphics, volume 13, pages 1–7. ACM SIGGRAPH, 1979.
[3] Peter Litwinowicz and Lance Williams. Animating images with drawings. In Andrew Glassner, editor, Proceedings of SIGGRAPH '94 (Orlando, Florida, July 24–29, 1994), Computer Graphics Proceedings, Annual Conference Series, pages 409–412. ACM SIGGRAPH, ACM Press, July 1994

EsherSketch Documentation

Scan for access to documentation made to explain the math and processes of creating tessellations in Escher-Sketch Software, created by ArtToyz Studios.

Special Thanks to:

Heath Burr and Robert Voyvodic for Editing and Graphic Design. This version of Geometry for Art would not have happened without them.
Cindy Smith for hanging in there.
My sons and grandsons, who will inevitably deal with a pile of art.
Many friends who have stuck with me over the years, helping me share my art.
Corwin Bell, Randall Wilson, Randy Yeates, Rick Rydell, Andy McEwen, Kurt Smith, Mark Kaufman, David Moke, Sandeep Kulkarni, Theresa Crush-Warren, Brad Leistikow, Denise and Randy Byers, Carol Keymer, and a lot of my other friends and some former students.

Thank you.

My post-houmous mentors:
Jeff Yetter for all of his contributions as part of ArtToyz Studios.
Chris Thomas who instilled a love for 3D geometry and software in me.
Steve Lanning who piqued my interest in woodworking and stained glass.
Bob Gillespie who helped me get back to Italy.
Santino Santori who helped me work on impeccability.
Ray Albrecht who restored my passion for life and music.
Adobe, Autodesk, Daz, Mandelburber 3D and a host of others for making good art toys.

BIBLIOGRAPHY AND REFERENCE

Benoit B. Mandelbrot, "The Fractal Geometry of Nature" , W.H Freeman and Co., 1977.
James Gleick, "Chaos - Making a New Science", Penguin Publishing Group, 1987.
Michael Barnsley, "Fractals Everywhere", Academic Press, 1988.
M.C. Escher, "Escher on Escher", Harry N. Abrams, Inc., 1986.
Bruno Ernst, "The Magic Mirror of M.C. Escher", Amsterdam, 1976.
J.L. Locher et al, "The World of M.C. Escher", Harry N. Abrams, Inc., 1988.
Philip Rawson, "The Art of Tantra", New York Graphic Society, Ltd., 1973.
Jose and Miriam Arguelles, "Mandala", Shambala Publications, Inc., 1972.
Drunvalo Melchizedek, "The Ancient Secret of the Flower of Life Vols. 1 and 2", Light Technology Publishing, 2000.
John Michell and Allan Brown, "How the World is Made - The Story of Creation according to Sacred Geometry", Inner Traditions, 2012.
David Wade, "Pattern in Islamic Art", The Overlook Press, 1976.
Laqueline B. Thurston and Ronald G. Carraher, "Optical Illusions and the Visual Arts", Van Nostrand Reinhold Company, 1966.
Dale Seymour and Jill Btitton, "Introduction to Tessellations", Dale Seymour Publications, 1989.
The Metropolitan Museum of Art, "Islamic Art and Geometric Design Activities for Learning", The Metropolitan Museum of Art, 2004.

A stack of these books on my shelf.
I realized they were all written during my adult lifetime, except for the Optical Illusion book, I was 12 years old in 1966. The most recent is in 2012. I was 58.
The bulk of them were written in the 1970's and 80s.

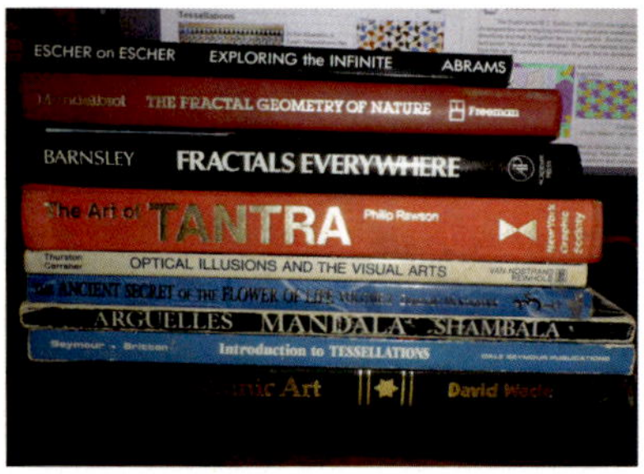

www.ingramcontent.com/pod-product-compliance
Lightning Source LLC
LaVergne TN
LVRC080247220926
848482LV00042B/346

* 9 7 9 8 9 8 9 0 8 2 0 0 1 *